MACHO ROW

MACHO ROW

THE 1993 PHILLIES AND BASEBALL'S UNWRITTEN CODE

WILLIAM C. KASHATUS

University of Nebraska Press ▪ Lincoln & London

Portions of chapter 2 originally appeared in William C. Kashatus,
Almost a Dynasty: The Rise and Fall of the 1980 Phillies.
Printed with permission of the University of Pennsylvania Press,
© 2008.

Library of Congress Cataloging-in-Publication Data
Names: Kashatus, William C., 1959– author.
Title: Macho row: the 1993 Phillies and baseball's unwritten code /
William C. Kashatus.
Description: Lincoln: University of Nebraska Press, [2017]
| Includes bibliographical references and index.
Identifiers: LCCN 2016034808 (print)
LCCN 2016035750 (ebook)
ISBN 9780803290860 (cloth: alk. paper)
ISBN 9781496214089 (paper: alk. paper)
ISBN 9781496200235 (epub)
ISBN 9781496200242 (mobi)
ISBN 9781496200259 (pdf)
Subjects: LCSH: Philadelphia Phillies (Baseball team)—History.
Classification: LCC GV875.P45 K274 2017 (print) | LCC GV875.P45
(ebook) | DDC 796.357/640974811—dc23
LC record available at https://lccn.loc.gov/2016034808

Set in Whitman by Rachel Gould.

For Chris Baumann, a Phillies fan for better and (mostly) worse

CONTENTS

ILLUSTRATIONS

ACKNOWLEDGMENTS

This book is dedicated to Chris Baumann, my nephew, a good friend, and a passionate Phillies fan since 1993. That was the year Chris fell in love with baseball. Despite my own miserable experience with the Fightins, I encouraged Chris's early addiction. I left my summer job as a ranger at Independence National Historical Park a week early so I could coach at one of the Phillies' summer baseball camps for kids and he could attend it. Every day for a week that August, Chris and I "played baseball" together. The highlight of the camp was a trip to Veterans Stadium, where we enjoyed a tour, met with infielder Mariano Duncan, and practiced on the Astroturf field. By summer's end, my nephew was a Phillies fan for life, joining the ranks of the most pathetic creatures on earth. At a time when I had lost interest in baseball and the Phillies, Chris rekindled my love for both. For those gifts, and for helping me coach my son's American Legion and tournament teams, I will always be grateful to him.

Special thanks is due to all the individuals who agreed to be interviewed for his book, including Larry Andersen, Mike Arbuckle, Steve Bazarnic, Larry Bowa, Mark Carfagno, Carol Daulton, Darren Daulton, David Daulton Sr., Mike Dobson, Lenny Dykstra, Jim Eisenreich, Frank Fitzpatrick, Jim Fregosi, Bill Giles, Tommy Greene, Paul Hagen, Ron Hill, Dave Hollins, Pete Incaviglia, Danny

Jackson, John Kruk, Larry Kruk, Lena Kruk, Roger Mason, Mickey Morandini, Johnny Podres, Jack Reynolds, Curt Schilling, Dan Stephenson, Lee Thomas, John Vukovich, and Mitch Williams.

Although I provided Daulton, Kruk, and Williams with copies of the manuscript, they declined to comment on it. I tried to contact Dykstra, Hollins, and Incaviglia for the same purpose, but they did not return my emails or phone calls. Thus, I am especially grateful to Billy Beane, John Burkhart, Paul Hagen, and Curt Schilling, who read various parts of the manuscript and offered constructive criticism. Beane and Hagen also wrote endorsements. I am also grateful to Janet Fries of the law firm of Drinker, Biddle & Reath, who vetted the manuscript for any potential legal issues; Al Tielemans of *Sports Illustrated,* whose riveting photographs adorn the cover and interior of the book and who also wrote an endorsement; Rob Dougherty of Baseball Info Solutions and Julian McCracken for their assistance with sabermetrics; John Horne of the National Baseball Hall of Fame for providing other images; and Rob Taylor, Courtney Ochsner, and Joeth Zucco of the University of Nebraska Press for their guidance and counsel in improving the book. Any mistakes that remain are mine alone.

Finally, a special thanks is owed to my family. My parents, Balbina and William, encouraged my early love of baseball and gave me their unconditional support in my decision to become a writer. My sons, Tim, Peter, and Ben, have tolerated those twin passions all their lives and still seem to care about me. Someday they will hopefully understand, like their mother, Jackie. Words cannot adequately describe the love and respect I have for her.

INTRODUCTION

On Saturday evening, October 23, 1993, the Philadelphia Phillies were fighting for their baseball lives. Down three games to two in the World Series against the defending champion Toronto Blue Jays, the Phillies were clinging to a precarious 6–5 lead in Game Six.

Until now the Phillies had ridden the wave of a Cinderella season. The roguish band of veterans, rookies, and castoffs defied the experts by going from worst to first in the National League's (NL) Eastern Division. Somehow they defeated the Atlanta Braves, the most feared team in baseball, in the National League Championship Series (NLCS).[1] Now the Fightin' Phils had taken the heavily favored Blue Jays to a sixth game in a world championship Series that they, if nobody else, believed was theirs to win.

It was the bottom of the ninth inning at Toronto's SkyDome, and Mitch Williams, the Phils' erratic closer, took the mound, determined to preserve the one-run lead and force a seventh and deciding game. Williams, nicknamed "Wild Thing" because his unpredictable pitching unnerved his teammates, recorded a club record forty-three saves that year. But after sixty-five regular-season appearances and six more in the postseason, his arm was hanging by a thread. Worse, Williams was coming off a devastating blown save (SV) in Game Four, a dreadful performance that elicited death threats from some deranged Phillies fans.[2] Still, Phillies manager

Jim Fregosi refused to deviate from his routine, sending his closer out to pitch the ninth. Thus, the Phillies were pinning their hopes for a seventh game on Williams's tired left arm.

True to form, Wild Thing walked Toronto's lead-off hitter, Rickey Henderson, on four straight balls. Pitching coach Johnny Podres called time and ambled out to the mound. He suggested that Williams pitch from the slide step because the quicker delivery would prevent Henderson from stealing second base. First baseman John Kruk, a slovenly throwback from the hills of West Virginia, also trotted to the mound to offer his teammate some encouragement. "There's no fuckin' way we're losing this game!" snarled the burly Kruk. "Get them motherfuckers out!"[3]

Inspired by the support, Williams retired Devon White on a deep fly ball to left, but then served up a base hit to Jays designated hitter (DH) Paul Molitor. With runners on first and second and one out, Toronto's dangerous cleanup hitter, Joe Carter, stepped to the plate. Tension filled the Phillies' dugout.

Wild Thing, who once pitched for the American League's (AL) Texas Rangers, had faced Carter on four previous occasions, and the power hitter lost every single one of those battles, going 0 for 4. It looked as if Williams would prevail once again when he worked the count to 2-2. Carter chased a slider for the second strike and was guessing that Williams would throw another one. Behind the plate, catcher Darren "Dutch" Daulton was thinking the same thing and called for the slider. But Wild Thing shook him off. He wanted to throw a fastball up and away in the zone, figuring he could get Carter to chase it for a strike out or, at worst, force him to hit a lazy fly ball to the outfield. The catcher reluctantly agreed.

The stage was set. Wild Thing toed the rubber, looked in for the sign, and threw his fastball. He had the right idea but the wrong execution. Instead of throwing the heater up and away, he delivered the 2-2 pitch down and in. The slide step had altered his ability to locate the pitch. Carter, a natural low-ball hitter, drilled the delivery over the left-field fence to clinch the game and the World Series for Toronto.[4] Williams didn't bother to turn around; he knew the ball was gone the second he released it.

Lenny Dykstra, the Phils' impish center fielder, was stunned. "It was a weird feeling watching that ball go out," he told a group of reporters in the visitors' clubhouse afterward. "I can't describe it. I really thought this was meant to be our year."[5]

To his credit, Williams didn't run and hide from the wave upon wave of sportswriters who surrounded his locker after the game. Nor did he alibi or apologize. "Ain't nobody walking this earth that feels worse than I do," he said. "There are no excuses. I just didn't get the job done. I threw a fastball down and in. It was a bad pitch. I'll have to deal with it. But don't expect me to curl up and hide because I gave up a home run in a World Series."[6] He went on like that until well after midnight. Finally, pitcher Terry Mulholland walked over and grabbed him by the hand. "C'mon, Mitch, season's over," he said and led Williams into a trainer's room that was off-limits to the media.[7]

The Phillies' joyride had come to an inglorious end.

To be sure, no one expected the Philadelphia Phillies to go from worst to first in 1993. Contending was more than wishful thinking for the faithful. Appearing in the Fall Classic? Downright delusional. Yet the '93 Phillies made believers of their fans, the sportswriters, and the city of Philadelphia itself. The team was embraced not only because they won a pennant but because of the *way* they won it. They were "lovable" in a blue-collar way, much like the St. Louis Cardinals' famed "Gashouse Gang," who captured the 1934 World Series, or the more colorful Oakland A's, who fought and feuded their way to three straight world championships between 1972 and 1974. Pitchers threw inside, hitters glared at opposing hurlers, and runners crashed second base to break up double plays. The players performed with pain and reckless abandon, wore their emotions on their sleeves, and could care less about their personal appearances. In Philadelphia parlance, the '93 Phillies had "attytood," and for good reason. Most of the players were throwbacks from other organizations who had given up on them.

Only five of the twenty-five-man roster came through the Phillies' farm system: Kim Batiste, Darren Daulton, Ricky Jordan, Mickey Morandini, and Kevin Stocker. All the other players were signed as free agents (Larry Andersen, Mariano Duncan, Jim Eisenreich, Tommy Greene, Pete Incaviglia, and Milt Thompson), acquired in trades (Wes Chamberlain, Lenny Dykstra, Danny Jackson, John Kruk, Tony Longmire, Roger Mason, Terry Mulholland, Ben Rivera, Curt Schilling, Bobby Thigpen, David West, and Mitch Williams), or drafted from other teams (Dave Hollins and Todd Pratt).[8] Collectively, they were also among the least expensive teams money could buy, with an average salary of $916,383.[9]

Profane, arrogant, unkempt, and determined to overachieve, these Phillies had something to prove to the baseball world. No one wanted them. Except Lee Thomas, the Phillies' general manager (GM), who assembled the team, and Jim Fregosi, the individual who managed them on the playing field. "I like 'em," insisted Fregosi. "They play hard. They work hard. They police their own. That's what makes a good team."[10] If nothing else, those attributes make for good team chemistry, which was instrumental to the Phillies' success. But special chemistry wasn't the only reason they won.

The 1993 Phillies won because they played *smart* baseball. On the mound their pitchers knew how to set up hitters and get them out because they carefully studied the opposing lineup. Infielders and outfielders understood the responsibilities of their respective positions, the best defensive strategies in a given situation, and executed them well. At the plate Phillies' hitters were patient. If they saw that the pitcher was having difficulty locating, they'd make him throw strikes. Nor did they try to do too much in a single at bat. They knew the value of getting on base and that a walk was just as good as a hit. What made it all work was the fact that Fregosi knew his team. He never made wholesale changes to a lineup that had finished in last place the previous season. Instead, he kept the lineup intact, made effective use of platoons, and managed all of the players according to their capabilities.

The '93 Phillies also won because they played by *the Code*, baseball parlance for the unwritten rules of the game. The Code governs all aspects of baseball, from hitting, pitching, and base running to dealing with management, umpires, and the media. Designed to preserve the moral fabric of the game, the Code contains rules for individual and team behavior in common situations, punishments for ignoring the rules, and the understanding that those rules must never be discussed outside the clubhouse. In short, the Code is about respect—respect for the team, respect for teammates, and, above all, respect for the game itself.[11] By the 1990s these idiosyncratic rules had become passé in Major League Baseball (MLB). Free agency had ushered in an era of multimillion-dollar athletes who placed personal success above the team. Most refused to risk injury by retaliating for another team's infringement of the Code. After all, the injury might prove to be career ending, costing them millions in income. Nothing—not even the game itself—was worth that for the high-priced athletes who placed money above anything else. The '93 Phillies were a refreshing change to that selfish attitude. They restored the significance of the Code and made it an integral part of their success. They were an "old school" *team* in every sense of the word. There were no superstars. Players seemed to check their egos at the clubhouse door and protected each other when a teammate was disrespected by an opponent, the media, or management.

Six players, in particular, reflected the club's colorful but gruff personality: Darren Daulton, Lenny Dykstra, John Kruk, Mitch Williams, Dave Hollins, and Pete Incaviglia. They lockered together at the far corner of the Phillies' fraternity-like clubhouse in a cozy but cluttered section called "the Ghetto," or at least that's how the players referred to it. The beat writers, compelled to be politically correct, dubbed the area "Macho Row."[12] Together, the six veterans gave the '93 Phillies a hard-core edge. They could be cantankerous, profane, and brutally candid, flaunting their image as outcasts and underdogs. Masters of the one-liner and no-holds-barred zingers, the veterans of Macho Row could make life miserable for a rookie until he proved himself. Few, if any, teammates dared to cross them.

At the same time, Daulton, Dykstra, Kruk, Williams, Hollins, and Incaviglia could be disarmingly funny, fiercely loyal, and remarkably insightful in their knowledge of the game. They endeared themselves to the fans, especially the clock punchers who wore their passion on their sleeves. And they embraced a blue-collar approach to the game. But the stars of Macho Row were cautious with the Philadelphia beat writers and self-styled "analysts" of sports-talk radio known for their intrusiveness and arrogance. Only Darren Daulton, who'd been with the organization for more than a decade, had earned their begrudging respect. As a result, Daulton was the only player willing to protect his teammates from the media. While the savvy catcher met with the press in front of his locker, the other members of Macho Row often retreated to the trainer's room. Afterward, Daulton would join them to talk baseball into the early-morning hours. As the season progressed they opened their inner sanctum to other teammates until nearly everyone spent some time in the trainer's room after games. It became a ritual, a way of cultivating team loyalty among a diverse group of personalities.

"We accepted people for who they were," explained Kruk, who loved the clubhouse so much he actually spent many nights sleeping over between games. "On most teams, you'd have the black guys in one corner or the Latin guys hanging out with each other and nobody would mix. Not with this team. We talked baseball, we busted on each other and we all went out together—blacks, Latinos and whites."[13]

Darren Daulton presided over Macho Row from a secondhand lounge chair crammed inside his locker stall. Daulton, affectionately known to fans as "Dutch" and to teammates as "Bubba," was a hard-edged catcher admired for overcoming a career-threatening knee injury to become a three-time All-Star. He was also the longest-tenured Phillie, the only homegrown regular, and the team's uncontested leader. Daulton signed with the Phils in 1980 as a 170-pound catcher after being drafted in the twenty-fifth round out of Arkansas City High School in Kansas. Promoted to the Majors in 1983, the promising backstop suffered repeated injuries, postponing his rise to stardom for six years. Never did the setbacks alter his "take no prisoners" approach to the game, though.

Daulton was both physically and mentally tough, a "man's man." His chiseled physique and movie-star good looks made him the envy of male fans and an object of desire for females. When he spoke, teammates, coaches, and the manager listened. Most of the time, however, he chose to do his talking behind the plate or up at bat. In '93 Dutch hit 24 homers and drove in 105 runs and was the National League's starting catcher in the All-Star Game. Behind the plate he got the very most out of a makeshift pitching staff and threw out 33 percent of the runners who attempted to steal on him.[14] For Daulton, the Code was more than the unwritten rules of the game; it was a way of life.

Lenny Dykstra, a feisty lead-off hitter and center fielder, was the team's most prominent castoff. Unwanted in New York, Dykstra was traded by the Mets to Philadelphia, where he found a home. A native of Southern California, he favored words like *dude* and *bro*, played with reckless abandon, indulged in high-stakes (and high-loss) gambling, and took pride in the fact that he never read a book because it would ruin his batting eye. Dykstra, appropriately nicknamed "Nails," endeared himself to the city's blue-collar fans with his arrogance, tobacco chewing, and scrappy play.[15] He was the type opposing teams and fans love to hate, a throwback to an earlier era when ballplayers played hard and partied even harder. On the road Dykstra would chide the opponent, "We're going to take your money and fuck your women."[16] Win or lose, he allegedly made good on the threat.

Like Daulton, Dykstra's career had been riddled with injury, though he had already begun to take measures to eliminate the problem by the time he arrived in Philadelphia in 1989. He was a gym rat who in the off-season could be found in the weight room pumping away feverishly to add muscle. He also took "vitamins" to build body mass, suggesting that they were nutritional supplements. In 1993 Dykstra reported to spring training thirty pounds over his normal 165-pound weight. It wasn't fat—it was muscle— thanks to performance-enhancing anabolic steroids.[17] PEDs not only improved Dykstra's recovery time from injury, but also increased his power hitting and speed on the base paths. The results were impressive, almost earning him the National League's Most Valuable Player (MVP) Award that year. In addition to batting .305, Nails led the league in runs (143), hits (194), and at bats (637).[18] He was the catalyst in the Phillies' batting order, the player who got the offense started.

At a time when Major League Baseball had no policy prohibiting the use of PEDS, Dykstra was free to use whatever edge the drugs provided. Even if baseball had had an established policy against steroids, Nails would have ignored it. "Cheating," he once admitted, "is okay if that's what it takes to win."[19] And Lenny Dykstra played to win. To be sure, Dykstra's use of PEDS was a violation of the Code because many players considered it a form of cheating even before Major League Baseball outlawed the practice. Nevertheless, there were players who were already juicing, like José Canseco and Mark McGwire of the Oakland A's, Ken Caminiti of the San Diego Padres, and others who were highly suspect, like Pete Incaviglia, Dave Hollins, and Daulton of the Phillies.[20] At the same time, Dykstra's steroid use was protected by the Code that prohibited his teammates from speaking about anything that was said or done in the clubhouse.[21]

First baseman John Kruk was a kindred spirit of Dykstra's and the most slovenly looking player on the team. With his ample belly, shaggy hair, and fondness for beer, he looked more like a weekend softball player than an athlete. Kruk actually took pride in that fact, correcting a female fan who once berated him for being out of shape. "I ain't an athlete, lady," he replied. "I'm a ballplayer."[22] Despite the denial and his portly appearance, Kruk was a remarkable athlete and a consistent .300 hitter, which made him the hero of many slovenly fans.

A third-round pick of the San Diego Padres in the June 1981 draft, Kruk earned a starting job in the Padres' outfield in 1987 when he hit .313 with 20 home runs (HR) and 91 runs batted in (RBI). The following season was a nightmare, as his batting average plummeted to .241.[23] Once, owner Joan Kroc tried to shout some encouragement to him from her field box after he struck out. Without looking Kruk snapped, "Go fuck yourself!"[24] Thus, it was no surprise when the Padres, in June 1989, shipped the irreverent outfielder to Philadelphia, where he felt right at home.

Born on the West Virginia panhandle, Kruk flattered himself a "hillbilly" and exploited that self-deprecating image with the media. "In the minors, one of my managers said I reminded him of an

Alabama truck driver," he once told Paul Hagen, a beat writer for the *Philadelphia Daily News*. "That followed me to the big leagues where I became a dumb hillbilly. Well, I live in the hills. But I don't think I'm that dumb. I'm getting dumber every year, but I don't think I've reached stupidity yet."[25] A natural comedian, Kruk captured the national spotlight in '93 when he appeared on *Late Night with David Letterman*. When asked later about the appearance, he said, "I drove two hours for five minutes on the show; that kind of sucked."[26] It was all an act.

Kruk was arguably the smartest player on the '93 Phils, and he used his baseball acumen to compensate for what he lacked in natural ability. He hit third in the lineup not only because he was the best hitter on the team, but because he somehow also managed to get his chubby body on base, advance runners, and drive them home. In 1993 Kruk hit .316 with 85 RBI and an on-base percentage (OBP) of .430, the highest of any regular on the team. He also made his third straight All-Star Game appearance that season, this time as the National League's starting first baseman.[27] Like Daulton, Kruk considered the Code a way of life, and he would give the shirt off his back to any of his teammates, especially if it would help the Phillies win.

Mitch Williams, the team's closer, was known for his proclivity for pitching into trouble before getting out of it. Signed by the San Diego Padres in 1982, Williams made it to the Majors in 1986 with the Texas Rangers. But Texas soon tired of his nerve-racking tendency to walk the bases loaded before striking out the side and shipped him to the Chicago Cubs.

Williams looked as if his career was over in 1991 when the hapless Phillies traded for him. If nothing else, Wild Thing was entertaining, as his unorthodox delivery sent his body flying sideways through the air, a sight made even scarier by his long, unruly hair. In fact, Kruk once observed that Williams "pitched like his hair was on fire."[28] To his credit Williams never allowed his critics to get the best of him. Instead, he kept his job in proper perspective. "You need two things to be a closer: no mind and a short memory," he explained. "I'm a genius when it comes to the 'no mind' stuff," he added.[29]

There was no denying his success with the Phillies, though. In his three seasons in the City of Brotherly Love, Williams appeared in 207 games, including 7 in the postseason, compiling a total of 105 saves. In 1993 alone he set a new club record 43 saves, including 13 straight between July 18 and August 24. His 3.34 earned run average (ERA) in 65 appearances was good enough to propel the Phillies into the postseason that year.[30]

Wild Thing was also a clubhouse prankster who assaulted the star of a game with a shaving-cream pie in the face and challenged fellow reliever Larry Andersen to belching contests. He could also be extremely generous to others. During an off day, for example, Williams flew Andersen, pitcher Danny Jackson, and play-by-play announcer Harry Kalas out to Reno, Nevada, for a good time and paid for the entire trip.[31] On another occasion he purchased expensive ostrich boots for the entire bullpen staff to express his gratitude to them.[32] Nor did he forget the clubhouse staff. Wild Thing *always* left money (at least twenty dollars, but often fifty or a hundred) in the back pocket of his game pants, telling Pete Cera, who did the laundry, that if he found the bills, "they're yours to keep." Whenever Cera tried to return the money, telling him it was "too much," the closer refused, insisting that "it's only paper."[33]

But Williams could be downright nasty when a save opportunity presented itself. No opponent was spared—veteran or rookie, journeyman or future Hall of Famer. Wild Thing would just as soon deck a batter with a high, hard, inside fastball than get beaten in the series of one-on-one battles that took place between hitter and closer in what was usually the final inning of play. Williams's motto was "No Fear," a core principle of the Code, which he embraced whenever he stepped onto the mound.

Third baseman Dave Hollins was the most intense member of Macho Row. Teammates claimed he had an alter ego named "Mikey," who reflected his game face. In other words, *Dave* Hollins was a hustling third baseman and an enthusiastic player loved and admired by his teammates. But once he stepped into the clubhouse or onto the playing field, he became *Mikey*, a foul-mouthed, hotheaded son of a bitch who played the game with reckless abandon and brooded about how much better he should have performed after it. "If you had twenty-five guys on the team like Hollins," said Larry Bowa, the Phils' third base coach, "they would have all killed each other by the third week of the season."

An All-State quarterback at Orchard Park High School, near Buffalo, New York, Hollins began his professional career with the San Diego Padres. But in December 1989 when the team left Hollins off their roster, the Phillies swiped the switch-hitting infielder in the Rule Five draft. The move paid off big time. In 1992, his first full year in the Majors, Hollins hit .270 and was second in the National League with 104 runs and tied for fourth with 27 home runs and seventh with 93 RBI.

In '93 the six-foot-one, two-hundred-pound third baseman enjoyed another productive season. Named to the NL All-Star team, Hollins finished the regular season with a .273 batting average, 18 home runs, 30 doubles, and 104 RBI. When Hollins wasn't hitting so well, he was still determined to get on base, even if it meant taking a walk or getting plunked by a pitch. Once on base there was nobody better going from first to third or breaking up a double play. Nicknamed "Headly" for his disproportionately large skull, Hollins was arguably the most hard-nosed player on the team. He took the game so seriously that the other members of Macho Row made him the enforcer of the Code for the rest of the team.[34]

Finally, there was Pete Incaviglia, a burly outfielder who added to the often bawdy clubhouse with his witty one-liners and supplied some right-handed power to an overloaded left-handed lineup. At Oklahoma State Incaviglia's power hitting led the Cowboys to the College World Series for three straight seasons between 1982 and 1985. One of the greatest power hitters in National Collegiate Athletic Association (NCAA) Division I history, "Inky" hit a total of 100 home runs for a career slugging percentage (SLG) of .915 over his three-year collegiate baseball career. He was selected in the first round of the 1985 amateur draft by the Montreal Expos but was traded later the same year to the Texas Rangers.

Having never played a single game in the Minor Leagues, Incaviglia made his Major League debut on April 8, 1986, and went on to hit 30 home runs, a new Rangers club record, and 88 RBI. It was a standard he was unable to match in subsequent years, as his home run total steadily dropped with Texas. Traded to the Detroit Tigers in 1991, Incaviglia became a part-time player, hitting just 11 homers and 38 RBI in ninety-seven games. He posted similar numbers the next year after he was traded to the Houston Astros. It looked like his career was over, until the Phillies signed him as a free agent after the '92 season. Inky resurrected his career in 1993, batting a career-best .274 with 24 homers and 89 RBI. His blue-collar approach to the game endeared Incaviglia to teammates and fans. Along with Hollins, Inky was dubbed an enforcer for Macho Row.[35]

Darren "Dutch" Daulton, Lenny "Nails" Dykstra, John "Krukker" Kruk, Mitch "Wild Thing" Williams, Dave "Mikey" Hollins, and Pete "Inky" Incaviglia—the motley sextet of Macho Row—lived by and enforced the Code. But they also made the game fun for each other, their teammates, and the fans. The 1993 Phillies were made for Philadelphia. The swaggering, trash-talking band of outcasts went from worst to first in a year when there were absolutely no expectations to succeed. Like their fans, those Phillies were diehards who lived in the same black-and-white world of heroes and bums. We embraced them because they showed their humanness—warts and all—and we admired them because they were throwbacks to the days when baseball was played for little more than the love of the game. Rooting for those wild, wacky, woefully wonderful Phillies was, for many of us, like cheering for ourselves.

Macho Row explores the 1993 Philadelphia Phillies and their remarkable season, which fell just short of a World Series title. The book goes beyond the existing accounts of the team by focusing on the six members of Macho Row.[36] It also examines the Phillies' pennant-winning season in the context of baseball's unwritten code of ethics and the beginnings of steroid use at the Major League level. The book does *not* pretend to be a comprehensive study of either subject. Readers interested in the Code or baseball's steroids era can find many other books that are more suitable.[37] Instead, *Macho Row* offers a fresh examination of a team whose approach to the game was both historic and futuristic. Not only were the players throwbacks to an earlier era that emphasized team accountability, but they also anticipated changes on the horizon, specifically the so-called Moneyball system of player evaluation and the power explosion created by anabolic steroids.

Like the old-time players, the 1993 Phillies played hard and partied hard. That kind of lifestyle took an unforgiving toll. Cancer, alcoholism, drug abuse, bankruptcy, and jail time were among the reality checks for some of the key members of the team after their playing careers ended.

Ultimately, *Macho Row* is a story of winning and losing, success and failure, and the emotional highs and lows that accompany it. Uproariously funny and profoundly tragic, this is a very *human* story about baseball stars, their dreams, and the fragility of fame as well as of life itself.

MACHO ROW

FIG. 1. Darren Daulton, the longest-tenured Phillie on the 1993 team, was the hard-edged catcher who presided over Macho Row. Photo by Al Tielemans.

ONE
Dutch

On March 15, 1987, Darren Daulton was rehabbing from a left-knee injury in the weight room at the Phillies' spring-training camp in Clearwater, Florida. Nine months earlier Mike Heath of the St. Louis Cardinals barreled him over at home plate, bringing Dutch's season to an inglorious end. Three separate surgeries on the injured knee followed before the end of the year. But after three months of intensive rehabilitation, Daulton still couldn't fully extend the knee without excruciating pain.[1]

Shortly after completing the rigorous workout, Dutch learned that team president Bill Giles had signed free-agent catcher Lance Parrish to a one-million-dollar contract. The news struck like a lightning bolt. In short order disbelief morphed into frustration, then anger, and finally rage.[2] Daulton felt deceived. He had already paid his dues.

Drafted out of Arkansas City (Kansas) High School by the Phillies in the twenty-fifth round in 1980, the six-foot-two catcher had spent the better part of five seasons in the Minors. When he was finally promoted to the Majors in 1985, Daulton rode the bench, first as an understudy to Bo Diaz and, later, Ozzie Virgil. Not once did he complain—about bouncing between Philadelphia and the farm system, about the sparse playing time he received in the Majors, or even about the near-career-ending injury he sustained from the home-plate collision in 1986. But now Diaz and Virgil were gone, traded to other organizations. Daulton was next in line to become the Phillies' starting catcher, and he was justifiably upset when Giles signed Parrish, a perennial All-Star.[3]

Daulton confronted the team president later that day, demanding to know "what the hell was going on." Dutch liked Giles as a person, and his affection for him would become so great that, by 1993, he would address the Phillies' president as "Uncle Bill." The feelings were mutual. Giles prided himself in being a father figure to the young catcher. Known for a strong desire to make others happy, Giles assumed the role of a Dutch uncle for many of the team's younger players. But the Phillies' president also knew how to take the "hard love" approach when necessary. He anticipated a confrontation with Daulton and was fully prepared.

"I just heard some pretty upsetting news, Mr. Giles," began the young catcher, cutting to the chase. "Is it true that you signed Lance Parrish?"

When Giles acknowledged that he had made the deal, Daulton braced himself for what he had to say next. He was a quiet, reserved person by nature. "Speeches" never came easily for him, so he had to choose his words carefully. Giles was, after all, his boss and deserved his respect.[4] But Dutch also felt compelled to defend himself. It was a lesson his mother had taught him as a youngster. "If you've got a problem with another person," she'd say, "you go to him and straighten it out. Don't ever go behind his back. That person might not like it, but they'll respect you for it."[5] Now it was time to put the lesson to use.

"Since 1980, I've given everything to this organization," said Daulton, looking the team president straight in the eye. "Before last season I was told to be patient; that my time would come. Well, last season my time came."[6]

Giles was impressed. He had never seen this side of the young catcher. But he still defended his decision to sign Parrish, explaining that the Phillies' performance "had declined" since they "won their last pennant in 1983, and the star players were aging." "If I can sign a top-notch catcher who can also hit for power, I think we can legitimately compete for one more division title before we rebuild."[7]

Daulton took exception to the suggestion that he couldn't hit for power. "Before I got hurt in June, I caught forty-nine games, and I hit eight homers and knocked in twenty-one runs," he argued. "Only Schmitty [Mike Schmidt] had more at the time. If I hadn't destroyed my knee, I would've had at least twenty homers and sixty-some RBI. And that was hitting in the bottom of the order. If I'd hit higher, I'd've had even more!"[8]

Giles hesitated. He realized that Daulton had shown promise as a power hitter the previous season and that his slugging helped the team jump from the .500 mark in May to third place in June before he tore up his knee. But the Phillies' president also felt that Dutch was still a year away from starting full-time and that Parrish was an established cleanup hitter, who would immediately improve the team's offense.

"Look Dutch, I know you're disappointed," Giles conceded. "But I'm getting a lot of pressure from the older veterans to sign Parrish. They want to win now, and time is running out for them. Schmidt's at the top of the list. Just think how much he would benefit with Parrish hitting behind him. He'd see a lot more fastballs, and that means a lot more RBI for us."[9]

Deep down, Daulton couldn't disagree with the logic. Parrish, who helped the Detroit Tigers win a world championship in 1984, was one of the most dominant catchers in the American League. He was a six-time All-Star who had won five Silver Slugger Awards and two Gold Gloves. Parrish was also an intimidating power hitter, averaging twenty-eight home runs and ninety-two RBI per year during his last five years in Detroit.[10] By comparison, Dutch, in parts of three seasons with the Phillies, never batted higher than .225 and hit a total of just twelve homers and thirty-two RBI. Nor had he proved himself behind the plate. The twenty-five-year-old Kansan was much better known for his movie-star good looks and chiseled physique, which resembled that of a Greek god.[11] He still had pride, though.

"Don't give up on me," Daulton told Giles before walking away. "I'll be an All-Star one day, too."[12]

It would've been foolish to bet against him.

Born on January 3, 1962, in Arkansas City, Kansas, Darren Arthur Daulton was destined to be a Major League catcher. Raised by a family of strong German stock, Daulton learned mental and physical toughness, the will to achieve whatever goals he set for himself, and the leadership skills that made others around him better. Mental and physical toughness was cultivated by his older brother, Dave Jr. "Darren and [Dave] Junior got into it all the time," recalled Dave Daulton Sr., their father. "Junior was two years older and had to work pretty hard at school and sports, but those things came naturally for Darren. So they were bitter rivals growing up."

One night Junior got so mad at his younger brother that he jumped into his '65 Mustang and chased him around the local Little League field. The two brothers caused such a commotion that the neighbors called the police. When they were hauled down to the station, their father had to bail them out. At six foot seven, 260 pounds, Dave Sr. was an intimidating figure. "They were pretty scared when I showed up," he said. "They didn't mess with me. I was big on accountability. They knew what was coming. I lifted Junior's [car] keys and grounded both of them for two weeks."[13] On another occasion Darren, who was physically smaller than his brother, instigated a fight. Then he ran inside the house, locked the door, and stuck his face up against the window to taunt his older brother. "It was the dumbest thing I ever did," recalled Darren years later. "Junior punched me in the face. He just put his fist right through that window."[14] Not until Darren left home to pursue a career in professional baseball did the two brothers end their rivalry. Since then they've been close friends.

"Darren was pretty ornery when he was a kid," said his father. "But he was also compassionate," added his mother, Carol.

I taught both of my sons to respect other people and never be critical of anyone until you've walked in their shoes. I remember when Darren was in middle school. We had a little boy across the street who was always getting into trouble. His parents were divorced. He had no friends, and he just wanted someone to pay attention to him. I told Darren that he should be nice to the boy because he was hurting. Whenever the kids picked on that boy in school, Darren would go up to the bullies and tell them to stop. It took a lot of compassion and courage to do something like that at his age, and I know that that little boy looked up to Darren because of it.[15]

"Compassion," "courage," and "sympathy"—three qualities that Carol Daulton instilled in her sons and would later inform the leadership Darren demonstrated as a Major League catcher. "My mother taught me those things," he said in a 2013 interview. "She always took the underdog's side, no matter how unpopular it was. That taught me the importance of putting myself in another person's position, the importance of listening to someone else's side of a story." But it was his father, Dave Sr., who gave Darren his work ethic and explained how to apply the sympathy his mother taught him on a baseball diamond. "My dad tossed me a catcher's mitt when I was six and told me, 'That's your position,'" he recalled. "Even in winter, we'd clear snow in the driveway to play catch. My dad worked with me year-round, insisting that I had to put in the time if I wanted to be good at it, that catching comes first. He also told me that handling pitchers is a big part of catching and that I needed to know how to call a game, how to get the most out of my pitching staff. A catcher needs to know his staff inside out. And that lesson registered loud and clear."[16]

Daulton's will to succeed, however, was learned in three different sports. Although he was a natural athlete, Darren possessed a fierce competitiveness and a unique ability to prevail in any athletic endeavor. He was also ambidextrous and exceptionally coordinated, attributes that allowed the youngster to excel in wrestling and football, as well as in baseball. At age ten Darren weighed just sixty pounds, but he was such an aggressive wrestler that he earned the respect of teammates and opponents alike. His youth coaches were so impressed they voted him into the Ark City Takedown Club's Hall of Fame. Daulton was also known to put the team first, something that enhanced his capacity to lead others. As a sopho-more at Arkansas City High School, he was only five foot nine and 140 pounds, but he slipped his weight up or down into whatever class the team needed to compete successfully. Not only did Dar-ren earn two varsity letters in wrestling, but he also received All-State honors in his senior year.[17]

In football Daulton starred at cornerback for the Arkansas City Bulldogs in both his junior and his senior years. "Darren was out-standing defensively because he was such a tough kid and a real hard hitter," recalled Ron Hill, the Bulldogs' head football coach from 1977 to 1980. "Of the thirty interceptions our team had in 1978, Darren, as a junior, had one-third of them." One of those inter-ceptions came in the state championship game. The Bulldogs were clinging to a two-point lead late in the fourth quarter when Daulton intercepted a pass. It should have clinched the state title for Arkan-sas City, but the Bulldog offense turned the ball over on the next set of downs and lost the game in the final seconds on a field goal. In 1979, Daulton's senior year, he quarterbacked the Bulldogs to a perfect 12-0 record and led the team to a 19–7 victory against Lib-eral High School in the state championship game. "Darren was by nature a running quarterback," said Hill. "We didn't throw the ball much. Instead, we played a Wing T formation and divided up the carries among our backs. We also ran a pitch-sweep, and Darren, as the QB, would lead the blocking. He was one of the very few quar-terbacks in the state who could block backside because he was so tough. That offense worked so well that in 1979 we were ranked one of the top teams in the nation, averaging forty-seven points a game."[18]

Despite his small size, Hill believes that Daulton could have played Division I football. "Darren would have been a good defen-sive back at that level," he said. "What he might've lacked in speed, he made up for in aggressiveness and intelligence. But I knew that Darren never had any intention of playing college football. Base-ball *always* came first with him."[19] Hill came to appreciate that fact in August 1978. That summer Daulton's American Legion base-ball team won their region and was competing for the state title. While the team was in Hayes, Kansas, where the state tournament was being played, Hill notified the rising juniors that they had better return to Arkansas City for preseason practice, or they would lose their starting positions that season. Four of the five kids who played both baseball and football did as they were told. But when Daulton learned of the ultimatum, he said, "Bullshit! I'm staying here. Baseball's more important!"[20]

To be sure, Daulton's love affair with baseball began at age six when his eight-year-old brother began playing Little League. Their father, a former pitcher and catcher, coached the team. He allowed Darren to play in games until the other parents began to complain that he was too young to be eligible. Despite Darren's pleas his father complied with the league's rules and benched his younger son. But he continued to coach Darren through Babe Ruth League. American Legion and tournament baseball followed. One season Darren caught for a Chandler Bat team that went undefeated with a perfect 41-0 record.[21] At Arkansas City High School he was the starting varsity catcher his sophomore, junior, and senior years. "Darren was a five-tool player who could field, run, throw, hit, and hit for power," said Mike West, who was the head baseball coach at the school. "In addition, he was a left-handed-hitting catcher. So he was truly exceptional, and I think he knew early on just how good he was." Although the game came naturally to Daulton, West said that he also worked hard to become better and that his desire and drive made the team better.

"Once, in a game against our rival, Winfield High School, our starting pitcher was trying to do too much, and he was getting hit pretty bad," recalled West. "I asked the umpire for time to go talk with him. When I reached the mound, Darren was already there, chewing him out. He knew all our pitchers, how to handle them, and he was always spot-on.

"Darren made people step up. He always gave his very best whenever he stepped on to the field, and he wouldn't tolerate anything less from his teammates. To find someone that young with that kind of passion, selflessness, work ethic, and integrity was truly exceptional."

Baseball was the driving force in Daulton's young life. Although he had the potential to play the game at the Division I level, Darren wanted to play in the Majors and to get there as soon as possible. Pro scouts began coming around in his junior year, but their numbers swelled in his senior year. Many high school athletes would let all the attention go to their head; not Daulton. "Darren was a very polite and intelligent young man," said West. "He had a certain swagger, but his parents made sure he stayed grounded."[22]

Mike Dobson, who taught world history at Arkansas City High School, remembers Daulton as a "solid B student who could've easily been an A student." "He just didn't apply himself because school wasn't as important to him as baseball," recalled Dobson. "I knew he was a good kid who could make something of himself if he went to college." One day Dobson tried to convince Daulton that a college education would take him much further in life than baseball.

"Darren, what are you going to do with yourself after high school?" asked the history teacher.

"I'm going to play Major League Baseball," he replied.

Dobson had anticipated the response and persisted. "Darren, when I was your age I told everyone that I was going to play professional football. But that never happened. So, let me ask you again, 'What are you going to do with your life?'"

The teen looked his teacher straight in the eye and said, "I'm going to play Major League Baseball."

"Okay," said Dobson, determined to give his student a reality check. "What are you going to do when baseball doesn't work out?"

For the third and final time, Daulton replied, "I'm going to play Major League Baseball."

There was nothing discourteous about the exchange. Darren was always respectful to his teachers. But he was adamant that his future was in professional baseball, and no one was going to convince him otherwise. "I look back on that conversation now, and I realize how foolish I was to ever question him," said Dobson in a recent interview. "Darren knew what he wanted, went after it, and achieved it."[23]

That fact didn't register with Carol Daulton until June 1980. Until then she had been hoping that her son would accept a baseball scholarship to the University of Kansas or to the University of Arkansas. But she realized that Don Williams and Dave Burroughs, scouts for the Philadelphia Phillies, had been following him closely since March. After the Phillies drafted him in June, Carol, Dave, and Darren met the two scouts at a Wichita hotel, where he signed his first professional baseball contract. It was one of the saddest days of her life. "On the car ride home, I began to cry," she recalled. "When Darren asked what was wrong, I told him how upset I was because I really wanted him to get a college education. After I said that, he and his dad looked at me like I had four heads. At that point I knew Darren's future was in baseball."[24]

To be sure, Daulton's signing didn't attract much attention in June 1980. The Phillies and their fans were in the midst of a season that would culminate in the organization's first world championship. Besides, the 170-pound Arkansas City native was one of only four catchers selected in the draft by Philadelphia that summer, and the least promising. Henry Powell of Pine Forest High School in Pensacola, Florida, was the Phils' first-round pick. Doug Maggio of Shaler High School in Pittsburgh was selected in the second round and Jerome Kovar of Southern Methodist University in the tenth. The Phillies picked Daulton in the twenty-fifth round (the 628th overall selection).[25] It was hardly an auspicious beginning. But Dutch would prove to be the most successful of them all.

Daulton began his professional career in the Pioneer League at Helena, Montana, where he hit .200 in 37 games with 1 home run and 10 RBI. During the next five years he would make a slow but steady rise from Class A ball at Spartanburg, South Carolina, of the South Atlantic League (.230, 3 HR, 29 RBI) and Peninsula, Virginia, of the Carolina League (.241, 11 HR, 44 RBI) to Double A at Reading, Pennsylvania, of the Eastern League (.262, 19 HR, 83 RBI), and to Triple A at Portland, Oregon, of the Pacific Coast League (.297, 9 HR, 48 RBI).[26] Bill Dancy, who managed Daulton at Reading, called him a "good defensive catcher, who runs well," and a "left-handed hitter with power, who has a good eye at the plate."[27]

Dutch spent parts of the 1983, '85, '86, and '87 seasons with the Phillies but was used sparingly. Between those four seasons, he played in a total of 140 games, batting .209, with 13 doubles, 1 tri-

FIG. 2. Daulton, shown here in 1985, was drafted by
the Phillies in 1980, but repeated injury kept him from
becoming the team's regular catcher until 1989. National
Baseball Hall of Fame Library, Cooperstown, New York.

ple, 15 home runs, and 45 RBI.[28] "Daulton's not much of a ballplayer,
but he's a great guy to be seen with in the hotel lobby," quipped
Richie Ashburn, the former Phillies outfielder turned broadcaster,
referring to the catcher's handsomeness.[29] Despite his mediocre
performance, Dutch's experience exposed him to the daily routine
of a Major Leaguer and taught him how to prepare himself, both
physically and mentally, for the demands of the game at that level.

Daulton learned the most from future Hall of Famers "Lefty" Steve Carlton and Mike Schmidt. "Lefty was definitely a great role model," said Daulton.

By the time I came up to the Phillies he was near the end of his career, but he was in better physical condition than guys my age. He was an expert in martial arts, which gave him unbelievable strength and flexibility and the power to concentrate on the mound. Lefty showed me how to prepare myself, how to stay in top physical shape. He also taught me about good food and wine by taking me and some of the younger guys out to nice restaurants when we were on the road. Lefty always told us how important it was to live life to the fullest because a Major League career is so short.

Carlton also had a rowdy side. One night after a game against the San Francisco Giants, Carlton took Daulton and a few of the other young players out to dinner at a nice restaurant in a small Bay Area town. It happened to be the mayor's birthday, and the restaurant presented him with a huge cake that was cut into slices and shared with the patrons. "We had already polished off a few bottles of wine and were feeling pretty good," recalled Daulton. "When Lefty got his piece of cake, he started a food fight. Let me tell you, he just tore the place apart. It finally ended when he head-butted the mayor's wife. We're lucky we weren't thrown in jail that night."

Mike Schmidt had a more staid personality. He cared about his image too much to participate in such sophomoric behavior. But Schmidt also took his role as a mentor to the younger players very seriously. "Schmitty taught me that you have to work at this game to survive in it," said Daulton.

The fans and the media always thought the game came easy to him. But let me tell you, he spent a lot of time in the [batting] cages working on his swing. Schmitty also reinvented himself as a hitter. He wasn't just a slugger at the end of his career. He also hit for a pretty high average, which is why he was able to win that third MVP in 1986. Schmitty also cared about the younger guys. He was always there to encourage us, to share his knowledge, anything he could do to help us out. I tried to emulate that kind of leadership later in my career when I saw younger guys coming up.[30]

But in March 1987 when Bill Giles signed Lance Parrish, it seemed like Daulton would never enjoy the luxury of having a long-term career with the Phillies, let alone realize his ultimate goal of becoming a dominant big-league catcher. But Giles was desperate for one more chance to win a world championship, so desperate he made the deal at the risk of alienating himself from the other owners.

Two years earlier the owners reached an unwritten agreement not to compete against each other for free agents and to reduce significantly the length of contracts they would offer. The agreement was allegedly a response to Commissioner Peter Ueberroth's demand that the owners exercise more fiscal responsibility as well as greater discipline and discretion in free-agent negotiations in order to prevent the financial ruin of the sport. In meetings with the owners, Ueberroth repeatedly invoked the term *fiscal responsibility*, which was code for short-term contracts, no free agents, and owner conformity.[31] The action, however, was in direct violation of Major League Baseball's Collective Bargaining Agreement, which prohibited collusion among the owners.[32] Giles believed that collusive behavior was wrong. But he had to weigh his loyalty to the other owners and the commissioner against his obligation to Phillies fans and his ownership partners to improve the team. It was an extremely difficult decision for a man whose father, former National League president Warren Giles, had always taught him to do the right thing. The elder Giles came from a time when baseball ownership was more of a noble calling than a means to gain wealth. As a result, Bill acted cautiously in making a legitimate effort to sign Parrish.

Adopting a "get-along-to-go-along approach," the fifty-two-year-old Phillies president asked the owners' player relations committee (PRC) for permission. Barry Rona, one of the owners' lawyers and an authority on the arbitration process, gave him the green light. "You're free to do what you want," Rona told Giles. "No other club can tell you what to do, but I suggest that you pay no more than a $700,000 base salary, with performance incentives on top." To be certain, Giles contacted Lou Hoynes, another one of the owners' lawyers. Hoynes was even more encouraging. "Sign Parrish," he said. "It's good for the Phillies and it's good for baseball. There's got to be *somebody* signing a free agent."[33]

The deadline for a free agent to sign with his original club was January 8, 1987. If Parrish didn't reach an agreement with the Tigers by that date, Detroit could not sign him until the following May. Giles, hoping to avoid charges of stealing another club's star player, waited until late January to meet with Parrish and his agent, Tom Reich. At the meeting the Phillies' president explained the best he could do was a one-year $1 million contract. "That's more than the PRC wants me to offer," Giles admitted. "You have to understand that I'm catching tremendous heat from all over. Some clubs are even saying that they won't trade with the Phillies anymore if we sign you." Parrish and Reich were clearly disappointed in the offer. Considering the Phillies' pay structure at the time, they wanted a salary somewhere between the $1.3 million that Von Hayes was earning and Mike Schmidt's $2.1 million salary. To make his offer more palatable, Giles offered to supplement Parrish's salary with promotional and endorsement work and promised to do better the following year once he had played in Philadelphia.[34] Parrish agreed to entertain the offer.

The two sides met again in mid-February and appeared to be close to an agreement on a one-year $1 million contract. But when Giles insisted that Parrish waive all rights to future litigation, the negotiations broke down. Reich refused to agree to such a clause. The implication was that Giles had buckled under pressure from the PRC, which took its orders from Ueberroth. But Giles insisted otherwise. "We wanted Parrish to sign a contract that would hold the Phillies harmless, but not baseball," he said. "The origin of the idea came from Phillies attorney Bill Webb. I don't recall being pressured by the commissioner's office or the Players Relations Committee."

Not until mid-March did the parties reach a compromise. The contract stipulated that Parrish would not sue the Phillies but would not prevent the players' union from taking appropriate legal action.

The language satisfied both the Phillies and the players' association, which had already filed a grievance over the manner in which Parrish had been treated as a free agent. Parrish, on the other hand, reportedly retained the right to sue baseball officials or clubs other than the Phillies over alleged collusion. According to the terms of the one-year contract, Parrish would earn $1 million, plus $200,000 if he remained injury free from a chronic back problem. The contract also included incentives for making the All-Star team and for winning the league's Most Valuable Player Award. Although Giles got his man, the Phillies were slapped with a $750,000 fine by the commissioner's office for signing Parrish against Ueberroth's and the other owners' wishes.[35]

Giles hoped that Parrish would push the team over the top. It never happened. In 1987 the Phillies came within six and a half games of first place in mid-August but finished the season in fourth place. Mike Schmidt, the franchise player, enjoyed his last productive year, hitting .293 with 35 home runs and 113 RBI. Von Hayes (.277, 21 HR, 84 RBI), Glenn Wilson (.264, 14 HR, 54 RBI), and Parrish (.245, 17 HR, 67 RBI) did not produce the numbers or power hitting they were expected to deliver. Nor was the pitching very solid. Aside from reliever Steve Bedrosian (5-3, 2.83 ERA, 40 SV), who won the Cy Young Award, the most consistent hurler was Shane Rawley (17-11, 123 K, 4.39 ERA). Bruce Ruffin (11–14, 93 K, 4.35 ERA) put up some respectable numbers, but would never again win more than six games in a season with the Phillies and was traded four years later.

Daulton played in only fifty-three games in 1987, splitting the backup catching duties with John Russell. In 129 at bats Dutch hit just .194, the lowest in his professional career, with 3 home runs and 13 RBI.[36] But he learned a lot from watching Parrish. Dutch carefully studied the way he called a game against some of the league's toughest hitters, how he handled the various personalities on the pitching staff, and how he kept himself in good physical condition during the season. The two catchers would often lift weights together and sometimes wrestle each other on the clubhouse floor. "Both Daulton and Parrish were big men," recalled Dan

Stephenson, the Phillies' videographer. "Dutch was six foot two and weighed about 190 at that time, and Parrish was six foot three and about 220 pounds. But Darren had been an All-State wrestler in high school, so he could actually pin Lance in under a minute. That shows you just how quick and strong he was, because Parrish outweighed him by 30 pounds. So I guess you could say, Darren taught him a thing or two himself."[37]

In 1988 the Phillies dropped to sixth place. The team played poorly from the start, and Schmidt's performance was partly to blame. He was hitting .214 by the beginning of June, with just 5 homers and 23 RBI. His play at third base was just as dismal, having committed 16 errors by mid-July.[38] Parrish was in and out of the lineup with a chronic back problem, which meant that Schmidt no longer enjoyed any protection in the batting order. Daulton wasn't much help, either. In 144 at bats that season, he hit .208, with just 1 homer and 12 RBI. Then, after an especially bad performance, Dutch, out of sheer frustration, punched a clubhouse wall and broke his hand, putting an end to yet another miserable season.[39]

"I was a bad ballplayer, and I knew it," Daulton admitted years later.

> I had lost my mobility after the knee injury, and there were things I just couldn't do anymore. I was trying to come back after a complete reconstruction of my left knee, and there was a lot of pain that affected my hitting as well as my running. After every season I had to have more surgery just to clean the thing out. The fans didn't understand, and they booed me. You want to explain it to them, to tell them about the pain. But that's not the way it works in Philly.
>
> Deep down, I always thought I could be a better player, but I had reached a point where I didn't know if that would happen. I just about accepted that there was nothing else.[40]

Then Daulton's luck began to change. On June 21 Bill Giles announced the hiring of Lee Thomas, director of player development for the St. Louis Cardinals, as the Phillies' new general manager. Thomas made immediate changes. Before the end of the '88 season, manager Lee Elia was fired and replaced by Cardinals coach

Nick Leyva the following season. Farm director Jim Baumer was also gone, replaced by Lance Nichols, who had served in a similar capacity in St. Louis. Thomas also replaced unproductive veterans like Parrish (.215, 15 HR, 60 RBI) with younger prospects and began revamping the Minor League and scouting systems.[41] No one was safe, not even established stars like Juan Samuel, who was once being groomed to replace Schmidt as the franchise player. Samuel was asked to change positions from second base to center field to make room for another former Cardinal, Tommy Herr. Thomas hoped to improve attendance with Herr, who grew up in nearby Lancaster County, which had a considerable fan base. But Herr only played second base. Thomas believed that Samuel, one of the top second basemen in the National League, could make an easy transition to center field because of his speed. Von Hayes was the organization's other untouchable star before Thomas was hired. Within three years both Samuel and Hayes were gone, traded to other organizations.[42]

By the spring of 1989 the Phillies were well into the rebuilding process. As the team continued to lose, Schmidt received the lion's share of blame, both from the fans and from the local media. After a solid April, when he hit 5 home runs and 18 RBI, the veteran third baseman went into a monthlong tailspin. His fielding deteriorated, and there was very little consistency in his performance at the plate. At the end of May, Schmidt was hitting a dismal .203, with just 1 homer for the month. With the Phillies languishing in last place, the future Hall of Famer, on Sunday, May 28, decided to retire. Schmidt's announcement marked the end of the organization's longest period of sustained success.[43]

For twenty-seven-year-old Darren Daulton, however, it was a new beginning. Dutch was healthy and getting his first real opportunity to start as the Phillies' regular catcher. Success was just around the corner.

TWO
Gang of Six

Bill Giles's hiring of Lee Thomas as the Phillies' general manger was a tacit admission that he had failed to realize his dream. Giles had always wanted to run his own Major League Baseball team. Specifically, he wanted to be in charge of player personnel. Giles longed to cultivate a homegrown core of players and to negotiate the deals for talented veterans of other clubs. Of course, his ultimate dream was to build a baseball dynasty, a perennial contender that could win two or more world championships. For most owners such visions of grandeur remain little more than a dream. But Giles was different. He had the bloodlines to realize his dream.

Bill's father, Warren Giles, served as the president and general manager of the Cincinnati Reds for more than a decade before becoming president of the National League. As a youngster Bill adored his father and watched in awe as he engineered the deals to improve the Reds' fortunes from a cellar dweller in 1937 to pennant winners in 1939 and finally world champions in 1940.[1] Bill yearned to do the same with the Phillies after he became part-owner and team president in the winter of 1982. In fact, Giles was so confident that he could achieve his dream that on the day he took over, he predicted that the Phillies were going to be the "Team of the Decade" in the 1980s.[2] Within two years he began to deliver on the prediction.

The 1983 Phillies won the National League East Division title with a record of 90-72, a six-game margin over the second-place Pittsburgh Pirates. They went on to defeat the Los Angeles Dodgers, three games to one, in the National League Championship Series, before losing the World Series to the Baltimore Orioles, four games to one. The team was led by the power hitting of perennial All-Star third baseman Mike Schmidt and the pitching of Cy Young Award winner John Denny. Other members included holdovers from the 1980 world championship team, including first baseman Pete Rose, center fielder Garry Maddox, and pitchers Steve Carlton, Larry Christensen, and Dick Ruthven. Giles, always looking for a promotional gimmick, reunited Rose with his former Cincinnati teammates Joe Morgan and Tony Perez. Since the average age of the regulars was thirty-six, the Phils were dubbed the "Wheeze Kids." It was a fitting nickname in a year that the organization was celebrating its centennial anniversary.[3]

Giles was off to a great start. With some savvy trades, a farm system still considered among the best in baseball, and a little luck, the new president might go even further than his father and create a championship dynasty. It appeared as if Bill Giles's entire career had been building to this singular moment when he actually had the power to control his destiny. Rarely do dreamers receive such an opportunity.

William Yale Giles was born on September 7, 1934, at Rochester, New York. His mother died when he was eight years old, so he was raised by his father, who, as president and general manger of the Reds, spent most of his time at Cincinnati's Crosley Field. While the elder Giles took a very active role in his only child's upbringing, he refused to be a doting father or a disciplinarian. Nor did he force baseball on him. What was important to Warren Giles was that his son knew the value of hard work, how to make his own decisions in life, and how to be the best at whatever career he pursued. Naturally, Bill decided to follow his father's example.[4]

By age fifteen Bill knew that he "wasn't talented enough to play past high school" and that he "wanted to be the general manager of a Major League team before the age of forty."[5] He pursued the dream with an exceptional passion. At nineteen he volunteered to become general manager of a financially troubled independent-league team in Morristown, Tennessee. Although the league folded soon after, Giles's efforts were recognized by Gabe Paul, president of the Reds. After three years in the air force, Giles returned to baseball as general manager of the Reds' farm club in Nashville. Once again Paul was impressed by the young man's work ethic and asked Giles to go with him when Major League Baseball expanded to Houston in 1962. Giles jumped at the offer. Shortly after Paul was installed as president of the Houston Colt .45s, he appointed Giles as the team's traveling secretary and publicity director.

Within five years Giles earned an exceptional reputation for promotions and was elevated to vice president. After the Astrodome opened in 1965, Houston built an amusement park called "Astroworld," and Giles was appointed marketing director for the entire complex. Using his creative genius, the young VP introduced a range of promotions, including rodeos, motorcycle races, polo matches, bloodless bull fights, and three of Muhammad Ali's boxing matches. Despite his success Bill did not want to be locked into a career as a promoter and felt that his dream of being a baseball executive was slipping away.[6]

Phillies president Bob Carpenter was familiar with Giles's exceptional reputation and realized that with the move to a new multipurpose stadium, the organization would have to be much more aggressive in marketing if the team wanted to expand their fan base. In September 1969 Carpenter offered Giles the newly created position of "vice president of marketing operations" with the understanding that, in time, his responsibilities would include running the team itself. He jumped at the opportunity.[7]

Within the next decade Giles would transform Philadelphia baseball from a tired old game to cutting-edge entertainment. He targeted families by creating a circus-like atmosphere at Veterans Stadium. There were fascinating pregame programs, including rock concerts, air force jet flyovers, cash scrambles, cow-milking contests, parachute jumps, ostrich races, and tightrope walks. There were also memorable giveaways, including bats, baseballs, plas-

FIG. 3. Bill Giles, part-owner and president of the Phillies,
had a genius for promoting the team, but lacked the baseball
savvy of his father, National League president Warren Giles.
Bad trades, poor draft choices, and questionable decision
making resulted in the demise of the Phillies from their
glory years of 1976–83. Photo by Al Tielemans.

tic batting helmets, and warm-up jackets. The most unique—and
entertaining—innovation was the Phillie Phanatic, a seven-foot,
three-hundred-pound furry green creature with a huge round belly
and a large circular beak. Inside the beak was a curled red tongue
that shot out whenever he disagreed with an umpire's call or wanted
to capture the attention of a fan. The Phanatic entertained crowds
during all eighty-one home games. He began with a twenty-minute
pregame performance, cajoling opposing players and dancing with
fans atop the Phillies' dugout. A similar display followed the bottom of the fifth inning, and after the seventh inning he would lead
the crowd in singing "Take Me Out to the Ball Game." During the
contest the Phanatic roamed the stands, visiting fans, giving "happy
birthday" wishes, and stealing a kiss from attractive young women.[8]

Gang of Six

Giles also lured fans to the game by hiring Harry Kalas, the play-by-play radio announcer for the Houston Astros. Beginning in 1971 Kalas teamed up with Richie Ashburn, the former Phillies center fielder and Hall of Famer, and By Saam, the longtime Philadelphia baseball broadcaster. Together the trio brought the game into the living rooms, backyards, and summer homes of fans throughout eastern Pennsylvania, southern New Jersey, and Delaware. Over the next three decades Kalas's silky-smooth voice would generate a large listening audience as he popularized such catchphrases as "Outta here" and "Watch that baby."[9] Giles's promotional expertise was instrumental in turning the Phillies organization into one of the Major Leagues' most lucrative franchises.

On the field the Phillies were enjoying the most successful period in team history. Perennial losers for nearly a century, the franchise reversed its fortunes between 1976 and 1983. During the eight-year span the Phillies captured five National League Eastern Division titles, two pennants, and the organization's first world championship. Those teams were among the very best in Major League Baseball, highlighted by a talented homegrown core of Mike Schmidt, Larry Bowa, Bob Boone, and Greg Luzinski. Veteran players acquired through trades and free agency provided the experience and inspiration for the youngsters to become perennial contenders. Pitching ace Steve Carlton came from the St. Louis Cardinals, closer Tug McGraw from the New York Mets, center fielder Garry Maddox from the San Francisco Giants, right fielder Bake McBride from the St. Louis Cardinals, second baseman Manny Trillo from the Chicago Cubs, and first baseman Pete Rose from the Cincinnati Reds. After the disappointment of losing three straight National League Championship Series in 1976, '77, and '78, the Phils won it all in 1980, defeating the Houston Astros in the NLCS and, later, the Kansas City Royals in the World Series.[10]

During this same period Giles ingratiated himself with the Carpenters. He cemented his position as Carpenter's successor in 1979, when he secured the finances necessary from cable television to sign free agent Pete Rose to an $800,000 contract, the highest in baseball at the time. Rose provided the experience, leadership, and enthusiasm to put the Phillies over the top to win the first and only world championship in franchise history to that point in time.[11] At the end of the strike-abbreviated 1981 season, Ruly Carpenter, who succeeded his father as president and owner, sold the club to a group headed by Giles for $30 million. Family-owned and -operated teams throughout baseball were becoming obsolete, yielding to a new corporate ownership tied more to business interests than to a love of the game.[12]

After the sale Giles didn't have to answer to anybody. The contractual agreement between him and the other owners stipulated that he had complete authority for the day-to-day operation of the club and, hence, its success on the playing field.[13] "I had complete authority with only two caveats," admitted the new team president. "First, the owners didn't care if they made any money, but they certainly didn't want to borrow or lose any. The other, related, caveat was that I was limited as to the amount of money I could spend on any given player or any large TV or concession deal without asking for their permission."[14] Unlike Ruly Carpenter, whose inclusion of front-office members in the decision-making process resulted in the Phillies' longest period of sustained success, Giles's desire to call the shots led to the decline of the organization. Poor decisions were made from the start.

In his desire to squeeze another pennant out of the 1980 world champions, Giles mortgaged the future. On January 27, 1982, the Phillies traded shortstop Larry Bowa and Minor League prospect Ryne Sandberg to the Chicago Cubs. Sandberg was a "throw-in" in the deal for Cubs shortstop Iván DeJesús. In Chicago Bowa mentored Sandberg, who became a perennial All-Star second baseman and, later, a Hall of Famer. DeJesús, on the other hand, proved a reliable middle infielder for the Phillies for three seasons but never hit more than .257.[15] Other poor trades followed.

At the end of the 1982 season, the Phils made a controversial "five-for-one" deal with the Cleveland Indians that brought Von Hayes to Philadelphia. In return the Indians received second baseman Manny Trillo, shortstop Julio Franco, outfielder George Vukovich, pitcher Jay Baller, and catcher Jerry Willard. While Hayes spent nine seasons with the Phillies, he never lived up to his billing as "the next Ted Williams." His best season came in 1986, when he batted .305 with 19 homers, 98 RBI, 24 stolen bases, and a league-leading 107 runs scored. Hayes never came close to those numbers again. Conversely, Franco became a power-hitting shortstop and three-time All-Star with the Texas Rangers.[16] While Paul Owens held the title of Phillies general manager, Giles authorized the ill-fated trades and is believed to have engineered them as well.[17]

When Owens resigned as general manager to manage the team in 1983, Giles, along with five other members of the front office, took over the baseball operation. Infamously known as "the Gang of Six," the new brain trust consisted of Giles, Owens, farm director Jim Baumer, and special assistants Hugh Alexander and Ray Shore. The "sixth" member of the group was supposedly a bottle of Jack Daniels, the preferred beverage and one, apparently, that often swayed their better judgment when making deals.[18] Over the next four years, the "Gang" presided over the decline of what was once a first-rate baseball organization. Although Owens was still a highly visible member of the front office, he was muted by the other members, and Giles exercised veto power over all acquisitions. Despite the considerable years of baseball experience among the group's members, it was almost comical to watch them operate at the winter meetings. "Some teams make trades only as a last resort while others are more willing but try to hide their intentions," explained beat writer Peter Pascarelli of the *Philadelphia Inquirer*. "Then there are the Phillies who unleash their front office point men like so many sharks in a feeding frenzy. They make no effort to hide whom they are talking to and what they're looking for, talking loudly about their intentions with an almost hyperactive openness and flair."[19]

The Gang's worst trades came in the spring of 1984. On March 24 they sent relief pitcher Willie Hernández to the Detroit Tigers for outfielder Glenn Wilson and catcher John Wockenfuss. While Wockenfuss hit a respectable .267 as a part-time catcher in two seasons for Philadelphia, Wilson was a solid player, hitting .265 with 49 home runs and 271 RBI during his four years with the Phillies.

Selected to the National League All-Star Team in 1985, Wilson's rifle-like arm made him the leader in assists among NL outfielders for three straight seasons, 1985, '86, and '87. But Hernández fared much better in Detroit. The former Phillies setup man became a closer and led the Tigers to the 1984 world championship. Not only was Hernández voted the American League's Cy Young Award winner, but he was also named the Most Valuable Player.[20] Then on March 26 the Gang of Six traded outfielders Gary Matthews, the MVP of the 1983 National League Championship Series, and Bob Dernier to the Chicago Cubs for pitcher Bill Campbell. Campbell pitched just one year for the Phillies, posting a 6-5 record and a 3.43 earned run average in fifty-seven appearances. But Matthews and Dernier played instrumental roles in leading the Cubs to the National League Eastern Division championship.[21]

Subsequent deals were not as controversial, though they failed to achieve the Gang's intention of securing quality pitching at a cost-effective price. For example, an April 20, 1985, trade sent Al Holland, the closer for the 1983 pennant-winning team, to the Pittsburgh Pirates for reliever Kent Tekulve. Both Holland and Tekulve were on the verge of becoming "ten-and-five" players (that is, ten years' experience in the Majors and five years with the same team) who would enjoy a no-trade clause in contracts. To avoid arbitration the Phillies and the Pirates swapped the two pitchers.[22] Similar trades sent catcher Bo Diaz to the Cincinnati Reds for pitcher Fred Toliver, and John Denny, the 1983 Cy Young Award winner, to the Reds for outfielder Gary Redus and pitcher Tom Hume.[23] While Tekulve gave the Phillies some stability in the bullpen for four years (24 wins, 196 K, 3.05 ERA), Toliver (1-7, 4.67 ERA, 1 SV in 26 games over three seasons), Hume (5–5, 3.98 ERA, 4 SV, in 86 games over two seasons), and Redus (.247 in 90 games during one season) became part of a long list of forgettable acquisitions the Gang of Six made in the mid- to late 1980s.[24] More frustrating was the organization's inability to develop homegrown talent, especially quality pitching.

The Phillies' Minor Leagues had not yielded an All-Star-caliber pitcher since Chris Short in 1966 or a bona fide ace since Robin Roberts in 1948. Although the inability to cultivate pitching talent dates to the Carpenters' ownership of the club, the Gang of Six not only failed to recognize the potential of the young pitchers in their system, but also traded away some remarkable talent. Mike Jackson, for example, compiled a 3-10 record with one save and a 4.11 ERA in the 64 appearances he made during his two-year career with the Phillies. He was traded along with Glenn Wilson in December 1987 for outfielder Phil Bradley, another forgettable player. Jackson would go on to become a closer for several pennant contenders, including the 1997 American League champion Cleveland Indians.[25] Similarly, Dave Stewart appeared in only 12 games for the Phillies in 1985–86 with a 0-0 record and a 6.48 ERA. Released by the Phillies on May 9, 1986, he would go on to become the ace of the Oakland A's, perennial contenders who captured a world championship in 1989. He would join the Toronto Blue Jays in 1993 and help that club to another world championship, this one against the Phillies.[26] What made matters worse was that the Gang of Six abandoned a rich Latin American market, scouts were not replaced when they left the organization, and poor decisions were routinely made in the June amateur draft. Thus, the farm system, once the crown jewel of the organization, was routinely ranked near the bottom by publications like *Baseball America*.[27]

Not surprisingly, the Gang of Six, in general, and Giles, in particular, were excoriated in the local press. Perhaps the harshest critic was Bill Conlin of the *Philadelphia Daily News*, who considered Giles an "elitist at heart," someone who "never understood what drove Phillies fans." "The fans in this city have an insane loyalty to the team," explained Conlin in a 2009 interview.

> But that loyalty is mitigated by a sense of frustrated entitlement. They've waited and waited for years to have a world championship, and only once, in 1980, did the Phillies come through for them. As a result, Phillies fans feel entitled to boo, to be critical of management on sports-talk radio. And Giles never understood that because he surrounded himself with other country clubbers who tell him what a great job he's doing. The fact is Giles can't take criticism. When I began attacking his farm system, he told the *Daily News*

that I was full of shit and that his farm system was ranked as one of the best in baseball. So the *Daily News* assigned four other writers to investigate the Phillies' Minor Leagues, and they found out that I hadn't been critical enough.[28]

Giles, in a 2005 interview, admitted that his organization had "overrated the farm system," and "we weren't getting the best draft picks." As a result, the Phillies "didn't have many good young ballplayers in the late 1980s." But Giles was quick to add that the poor draft picks were due to the fact that "we were drafting way down the list" because the Phillies "had won so much during the period 1976 to 1983." At the same time, he insisted that he was always sensitive to the local fan base. "I'm probably too much of a fan myself," he admitted. "People know that I'm passionate and that I live and die with the team, just as any dedicated fan does. I also think the fans liked me when I was president of the club. True, some of the local sportswriters and sports-talk radio criticized the things I did, but that's part of the game. Besides, I really believe those people are a small minority of our fan base."[29]

To be sure, Bill Giles was not part of the blue-collar culture of his team's fan base. As president and part-owner of the Phillies, his income bracket distanced him from the majority of fans, making it impossible for him to relate to them. Conlin's assertion that Giles "surrounded himself with other country clubbers who told him what a great job he's doing" had much validity. The Phillies were always an "old buddy" organization with a fierce loyalty among the members of the front office. It began with the Carpenters, heirs to the DuPont fortune, who cultivated strong ties to the power brokers of both Philadelphia and Wilmington, Delaware. Members of the front office attended and later sent their sons to private schools like Tower Hill, Penn Charter, and the Episcopal Academy before matriculating to the Ivy League, usually the University of Pennsylvania. There they learned the financial realities of running a corporation and later eagerly applied the lessons to their boyhood passion of baseball. They also brought with them a fraternity-like culture that operated on certain rules: never allow the press to control the team's decision making, build a winning team but not at a significant financial loss, never admit a mistake in public, and, above all, cover for the other members when a mistake is made. Giles and the Gang of Six continued to operate on those same rules.

The front office became complacent, resting on the laurels of the Carpenter regime. Certain individuals, like Hugh Alexander and Ray Shore, were allowed to operate with great independence, often to the detriment of the club. Others, like Paul Owens, who had experienced success and had a clear vision for the future, were stifled. As the veterans of the 1980 world champions were dealt away or retired, the complacency filtered down to the players, and, as a result, the team languished. "Complacency" in any business is a death knell, and in baseball the consequences cannot be hidden as easily from the public. The Phillies no longer "expected" to win when they took the field; they "hoped" they could win with as little effort as possible. In the process the team and its owners held Philadelphia's die-hard baseball fans "hostage" to their mediocrity. As the 1980s unfolded the fans became increasingly bitter, feeling as if they no longer mattered. By the end of the decade they boycotted the Phillies, leaving an ocean of empty seats behind.

But any suggestion that Giles was insensitive to the feelings of Phillies fans is false. If anything, he cared too much about fan sentiment and the players they adopted as heroes. Giles had tremendous difficulty releasing members of the 1980 world championship team. In 1983, when the Gang of Six pressured him to part with Tug McGraw, he refused to do so. Two years later, when McGraw's contract expired, Giles delayed the decision to retain him, hoping that the colorful reliever would be picked up by another team in the reentry draft. When that didn't happen, he offered to keep Tug in the organization in another capacity, suggesting a position on the broadcast team or the public relations department.[30] Giles was, at heart, a passionate fan himself. No event illustrated that fact more than the decision to release future Hall of Famer Steve Carlton in 1986. For Giles, the decision was emotionally devastating, as if he were losing a member of his own family. When he made the announcement at a June 25, 1986, press conference, he had tremendous difficulty keeping his feelings in check.[31] The following evening, before the Phillies played the St. Louis Cardinals at the Vet, highlights of Carlton's remarkable career beamed across the large scoreboard in right center field. Giles, watching from his 400-level executive suite, wept convulsively.[32] In fact, Carlton admitted that his release was "tougher on Bill than it was on me."[33] Nor was Giles insensitive to the needs of the larger Philadelphia community.

Recognizing the important relationship between the Phillies and their fans, Giles, in 1982, established a Community Relations Department in order to reach out to many charities in southeastern Pennsylvania, southern New Jersey, and Delaware. The new department created a variety of programs to support such concerns as cystic fibrosis, ALS (amyotrophic lateral sclerosis, or Lou Gehrig's disease), Children's Hospital of the University of Pennsylvania, Handicapped Boy Scouts, Gaudenzia Drug and Alcohol Rehabilitation House, the Philadelphia Child Guidance Clinic, and the No Greater Love organization, which benefits the children of American soldiers killed while serving their country. In the first year of operation, the Phillies raised more than $50,000. That amount grew to more than $250,000 in 1985 and continued to increase throughout Giles's tenure as team president.[34] Although poor decision making might have haunted him, the Phillies' president did demonstrate a well-intentioned commitment to the fans of the Delaware Valley region.

Despite their best intentions, Giles and the Gang of Six were unable to sign veteran players who could help or foster young talent to jump-start the franchise. As the Phillies continued to flounder, the fans became increasingly disenchanted. The decision to relinquish his role as general manager indicated just how desperate Giles was to win back the approval of the fan base. But even that proved to be a disaster.

On October 28, 1987, Giles hired Woody Woodward, president of baseball operations for the New York Yankees, to be the team's new general manager. But the relationship quickly soured. Eight months later Woodward was fired, and veteran scout Ray Shore became interim general manager.[35] Giles explained that Woodward was "let go" because he "alienated the Minor League staff as well as some of the front office's longtime employees, who felt he was secretive and autocratic."[36] Still in need of a general manager, the Phillies' president, in June 1988, turned to Lee Thomas.

Thomas proved to be the right man for rebuilding the organization. He had a keen eye for unappreciated talent and a riverboat gambler's instinct when dealing with other general managers. Some of the feistiness was acquired over the course of a fifteen-year playing career. Nicknamed "Mad Dog" for his ferocious style of play, the burly outfielder–first baseman bounced between six teams during that period. Thomas's best seasons came with the California Angeles in 1961 and 1962 when he slugged 50 homers and batted .285 and .290, respectively. After his playing career ended, Mad Dog spent another eighteen years in the St. Louis Cardinals organization. He began as a Minor League coach and worked his way up the ladder: Minor League manager, bullpen coach with the parent club, assistant in sales and promotions, traveling secretary, and finally director of player development. Having served for seven years in the latter position, he was well prepared for the challenge that he faced in Philadelphia.[37]

Only time would tell if he could succeed.

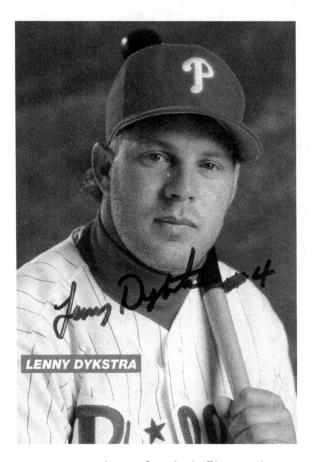

FIG. 4. Lenny Dykstra, a feisty lead-off hitter and center fielder, was the catalyst of the Phillies' offense. In 1993 Dykstra hit .305 and led the National League in runs, hits, and at-bats. Fourteen years later he was identified as a PED user in the Mitchell Report on steroid use in Major League Baseball. Photo by Al Tielemans.

THREE
Nails

Lee Thomas faced a daunting task when he arrived in Philadelphia. The Phillies were in sharp decline. To reduce the budget Giles had abandoned a talent-rich Latin American market and failed to replace scouting positions when old-timers left the organization. Years of poor decision making left the Phillies with a roster rife with declining stars, unproductive veterans, and fill-ins, and the farm system was in shambles. "It was a difficult situation," Thomas recalled years later. "But the biggest challenge was that I didn't have much of a budget to work with, only $29 or $30 million, which was way down."[1]

The new general manager began rebuilding the team immediately after the 1988 season ended. The deal making was ruthless and continued steadily for the next four years until Thomas secured the talent he believed he needed to capture a pennant. Catcher Lance Parrish was jettisoned to the California Angels to make room for Daulton behind the plate. Chris James was dealt to the San Diego Padres for outfielder John Kruk and infielder Randy Ready. Thomas pilfered pitchers Terry Mulholland and Dennis Cook and third baseman Charlie Hayes from the San Francisco Giants for Steve Bedrosian. Outfielder Dale Murphy and pitcher Tommy Greene were pried from the Atlanta Braves for Jeff Parrett and two Minor Leaguers. The new general manager acquired Curt Schilling from the Houston Astros for Jason Grimsley and snatched reliever Mitch Williams from the Chicago Cubs for Chuck McElroy and Bob Scanlon. But Thomas's biggest coup came on June 18, 1989, when he coaxed the New York Mets to trade outfielder Lenny Dykstra and relief pitcher Roger McDowell for Juan Samuel.[2]

"I loved Dykstra when I was with St. Louis," said Thomas. "I liked his confidence. I liked the aggressive way he played the game, and I especially liked the way he got on base. I really believed that to be successful, the Phillies needed a lead-off hitter like Lenny to set the table for the rest of the order. If we could do that, then we had an opportunity to score a lot of runs because a guy like that sparks the offense. If I had Dykstra, all I needed was another hitter and some good starting pitching. But Lenny was the key."[3]

Thomas was correct about Dykstra's competitive drive. Nothing intimidated him. He had nerves of steel and played the game with an intensity that burned white-hot, earning him the nickname "Nails."[4] What's more, Lenny was at his very best in high-pressure situations when the camera lights were on. He was, in baseball parlance, a "red-light player." In 1986 Dykstra was instrumental in the Mets' bid to win their first World Series title in seventeen years. In Game Three of the NLCS against the Houston Astros, Nails came off the bench to hit a two-run homer, giving New York a 6–5 come-from-behind victory. Dykstra was called on again in Game Six. With the Mets down 3–0 in the ninth, Lenny came to the plate and ripped a triple to jump-start the offense. He later scored the first of New York's three runs that inning to tie the game. The Mets prevailed in extra innings, 7–6, to clinch the pennant.

Nails was just as critical to the Mets' success in the World Series against the Boston Red Sox. After dropping the first two games at New York's Shea Stadium, the Mets faced a *must*-win situation in Game Three at Boston's Fenway Park. Dykstra, having earned the start, led off with a solo homer off Red Sox pitcher Dennis "Oil Can" Boyd to give the Mets a quick 1–0 lead. New York scored three more times in the first, increasing their lead to 4–0. Before the game ended, Dykstra collected four hits in five at-bats with an RBI and two runs scored in the 7–1 New York whitewashing.

Nails struck again the following night in Game Four. With the Mets holding a 3–0 lead in the seventh, he hit a two-run homer off Boston reliever Steve Crawford to ensure the 6–2 victory and even the Series at two games apiece. After New York's infamous win in Game Six, when Mookie Wilson's slow roller squeezed between the legs of Red Sox first baseman Bill Buckner to spark an improbable come-from-behind victory, the Mets went on to win the World Series in the decisive Game Seven.[5]

Dykstra's postseason heroics endeared him to the Mets' front office, which increased his salary from $92,500 to $202,500. The fans also adored Lenny. His book *Nails: The Inside Story of an Amazin' Season*, published in March 1987, was even more popular than manager Davey Johnson's account of the '86 campaign.[6] In fact, everyone seemed to love Lenny except Johnson, who believed that Dykstra was not an everyday player. "The way Johnson saw it, Lenny, who was a lefty hitter, was only going to play center field against right-handed pitchers, and Mookie [Wilson] was going to play center against left-handers," recalled Mets catcher Gary Carter in a 2005 interview. "Davey didn't think Nails could be an everyday player because he was little and he had a crouched-down type of [batting] stance that made him vulnerable to left-handed pitching. In my opinion, Lenny may not have been an everyday player in '86, but when called upon, he came through. He was very instrumental in us winning the championship."[7]

Despite his ability to perform in the clutch, Dykstra continued to platoon center field with Wilson in 1987. By midseason Nails began to complain. "I'm rusting away on the bench," he told Michael Martinez of the *New York Times*. "Someone needs to be traded soon, and I don't want to be the one. I want to play in New York, and I stress the word, *play*."[8] Dykstra was an ornery individual. If things didn't go his way, he would impose his will on others to turn the situation to his advantage. It had always been that way.

Born on February 10, 1963, in Santa Ana, California, Leonard Kyle Leswick was the second of three sons of Terry and Marilyn Leswick. After Terry walked out on the family, Marilyn took a job at the Pacific Telephone Company, where she met Dennis Dykstra, a divorced father of three girls. When the couple married, Lenny and his brothers moved to Dykstra's house in Garden Grove, a working-class suburb of Anaheim. Dennis adopted all three boys and proved to be a more devoted father than their own. He spent countless hours with them playing football and baseball, attending their games, and providing encouragement. Dennis became not only a strong father figure for Lenny, but also the driving force in his life. The youngster also cared very deeply for his mother; two brothers, Brian and Kevin; and three stepsisters, Johna, Danna, and Brenda. In fact, he was so protective of his stepsisters that he chose the boys he felt they should date.[9]

Lenny, a short, scrappy kid, was also the chief mischief maker in the family, and he often enlisted his siblings to help him carry out pranks. As a teenager he stole fire extinguishers from local gas stations and then persuaded Danna to drive him to Disneyland. There, he sprayed unassuming tourists from the passenger side of her Mustang. Sometimes Lenny coaxed his brothers to sneak into nearby Anaheim Stadium on the afternoons of Angels games. "It was heaven," recalled Brian Dykstra, his older brother. "We'd dive after balls, pretending we were real Angels. Then the ushers would kick us out. But for 15 minutes it was a living dream."[10] After he turned sixteen and learned how to drive, Lenny stalked his favorite player, Angels second baseman Rod Carew. Waiting outside of Anaheim Stadium in his Volkswagen Beetle, the gutsy adolescent followed Carew home, despite the fact that the Angels star had reported him to local police. Dykstra continued to stalk Carew for nearly two years until the police came to his home and threatened to arrest him if he didn't stop. Still, Lenny never stopped idolizing Carew, going so far as to adopt the second baseman's habit of chewing tobacco during games.[11]

Dykstra was never interested in school. But he knew how to make a buck there. Pretending that he had no lunch money, the shrewd teen would roam the hallways asking other students for a quarter so he could buy something to eat. Sometimes he collected as much as ten dollars in a single day, preying on the sympathies of others.[12] School also provided an outlet for his pent-up energy.

At five foot eight and 120 pounds, Lenny was smaller than most athletes at Garden Grove High School, but he still played tailback in football and shooting guard in basketball. It was baseball, however, where he excelled.

Watching his parents work forty hours a week and earning "barely enough money to raise their family," Lenny promised himself at an early age to channel his love for baseball and the "sixth sense" he had for the game into a successful Major League career. "I did everything in my power to never worry about money when I got older," he insists. "By the time I was in high school, baseball was my life. When I had to make a decision about something, I'd always ask myself, 'Is this going to help me become a better baseball player?' If the answer was no, even if it sounded like something fun to do, I had the discipline to stick with my game plan."[13]

Dykstra was the first freshman ever to play varsity baseball under head coach Dan Drake. By sophomore year he was the best player on the team and by senior year the best high school player in Orange County, boasting a .550 batting average.[14] "Lenny had the best instincts I've ever seen," recalled Drake. "I've never had another athlete or seen another athlete do what he did in all the years I coached. No one—black or white—could run the bases as well. If Lenny got to third, you knew he was going to score, somehow, some way." On the base paths, Dykstra pressured opposing pitchers, forcing them to make errant pickoff throws. On defense he made headfirst diving catches and had a rifle for an arm. He was a workaholic, too. Lenny routinely stayed after practice until dark to take extra batting. Then he went to the local batting cages to hit for another two hours.[15] In fact, Dykstra was so obsessed with baseball that in his senior year, he dumped his girlfriend before the start of the season. "I'm sorry," he told her. "We're done. It's time for baseball. Nothing is going to stand in my way—not even a chick!"[16]

There was no question in Lenny's mind that he was going to play Major League Baseball. "I knew early on that I was going to play in the Majors," he said in a 2001 interview. "That's why I dedicated myself to the game in high school. I did anything I needed to get an edge. I practiced and played every chance I got. I learned everything I could—how to be selective at the plate, how to read pitchers. I even read books about the game so I could improve, and I don't like to read!"[17] The only question was how Dykstra was going to overcome his small size.

Although Lenny had grown to five foot ten and boosted his weight to 150 pounds by the time he graduated from high school, no Major League organization was interested in him because of his small size. "He was always underestimated," said his older brother, Brian. "People didn't take Lenny seriously because he didn't look all that imposing. That pissed him off in a major way. He always felt he had to prove himself."[18] Still, Dykstra believed that his hometown Angels would select him in the first round of the June 1981 amateur draft. It didn't happen. Not until the thirteenth round did the lowly New York Mets take a chance, selecting Lenny with the 315th overall pick. The Mets offered him a $25,000 bonus, which was good money for a player who was selected that low. Insulted, Dykstra refused to sign. New York then raised the offer to $27,500, but Lenny still rejected it. The Mets countered with a $30,000 offer, but the answer remained no. "I'm the best fucking player in the draft," he told Mets scout Roger Jongwaard. "I should be paid like it." To be sure, Dykstra had a fallback plan—he had already signed a letter of intent to play for Arizona State. But he really wanted to go pro. Thus, when the Mets made a final offer of $35,000, Lenny agreed to sign until he was told that he would start in the Rookie League, where most draftees play their first season.[19] "If you don't send me to A-ball," he told Mets scouting director Joe McIlvaine, "I'm not signing. I'm too good for the Rookie League." McIlvaine wanted Dykstra so much that he granted the demand and sent him to the Mets' low-A club in Shelby, North Carolina.[20]

Dykstra played in Shelby for two seasons before being promoted to the Lynchburg Mets. "He was the hardest-playing athlete I'd ever seen," said a Minor League teammate who requested anonymity. "But he was also very disrespectful, and he didn't give a shit if he had to run you over to gain an edge. It was all about Lenny, Lenny, Lenny." The teammate also claimed that Dykstra corked his bats, had an insatiable appetite for sex, and spent his bonus money on a white Porsche 911 that he drove as recklessly as he played. There were also early signs of a gambling addiction. Marlin McPhail, a teammate at Lynchburg, recalled that Dykstra was bad at poker and even worse at golf, but he never turned down a bet. "I used to kick his ass up and down the golf course, but Lenny refused to play without betting," said McPhail. "There was no reason for him to bet me because he couldn't possibly win. But he needed to have a stake on everything."[21] Dykstra couldn't help himself. The reckless abandon that made him so successful on the playing field also defined his behavior off it. The self-destructive pattern got only worse when he reached the Major Leagues, where he felt even more entitled to indulge in decadent behavior.

Dykstra's career took off in 1983 at Lynchburg, where he batted .358 with 8 home runs and 81 RBI and a record-setting 105 stolen bases.[22] Voted the Carolina League's Most Valuable Player, Lenny's success captured the attention of Mets manager Davey Johnson, who invited him to big-league spring training the following season. There was speculation within the organization that Dykstra would replace Mookie Wilson in center field and that Billy Beane, a bonus baby, was being groomed to replace aging slugger George Foster in left. Darryl Strawberry, the 1983 National League Rookie of the Year, had already established himself as a fixture in right field. Dykstra and Beane, who were roommates, were also a study in contrasts. As their first-round pick in the 1980 draft, the Mets projected Beane as a star. Admitted to Stanford University before signing with the Mets, the outfield prospect was extraordinarily talented. He was an intelligent, naturally gifted athlete with a lean but muscular physique. Dykstra, on the other hand, was a low draft pick with a small body type and limited intelligence. But Lenny was superior in terms of confidence, which in his case bordered on arrogance. Dykstra was afraid of nothing.

Prior to a 1984 spring-training game against Philadelphia, the two roommates were seated in the Mets' dugout, watching Phillies ace Steve Carlton warm up.

"So who's that big dumbass out there on the hill?" Lenny asked

Beane, demonstrating a complete ignorance of Carlton, already a four-time Cy Young Award winner.

Astonished by the question, Beane replied, "Lenny, you're kidding me, right? That's Steve Carlton. He's probably the greatest left-hander in the history of the game!"

"Oh, yeah, I knew that," said Dykstra in a cocky attempt to hide his ignorance.

A few minutes later, Nails chirped up, "So what's he got?"

Dumbfounded, Beane responded, "Lenny, come on! *Steve C-a-r-l-t-o-n.* He's got heat and maybe the nastiest slider ever!"

Dykstra sat there for a while longer, thinking about it. "Shit!" he finally said. "I'll stick 'em!"

Delivering on the boast, Dykstra slapped a single to right center in his first at bat against the future Hall of Famer.

Unlike Beane, an intelligent student of the game who thought too much for his own good, Dykstra didn't permit his mind to interfere with his confidence. "Lenny was perfectly designed, emotionally, to play the game," recalled Beane, who went on to become a very successful general manager with the Oakland A's. "He was able to forget any failure in an instant and draw strength from every success. He had no concept of failure. And he had no idea of where he was. Sometimes Lenny would come back to the room and find me reading a book. He'd look at me and say, 'Dude, you shouldn't be doing that. That shit'll ruin your eyes.' Lenny's attitude was: 'I'm not going to do anything that'll interfere with getting to the big leagues, including learning.'"[23] That kind of arrogance would make him a very successful Major League player.

Dykstra made his Major League debut on May 3, 1985, when Mookie Wilson, the Mets' regular center fielder, was placed on the disabled list. The twenty-two-year-old rookie's fearless style of play and hard-nosed personality seemed to energize the Mets. In eighty-three games Lenny, hitting lead-off, collected 60 hits and 30 walks and scored 40 runs. He also fielded his position at a .994 clip. The team surged to 98 wins that season and nearly captured the National League's Eastern Division title. The '86 season was even better. Dykstra took over center field and the lead-off spot after Wilson suffered a severe eye injury. In 147 games he hit .295, with 127 hits, 58 walks, and 77 runs scored and recorded an on-base percentage of .377. The impressive numbers allowed him to finish among the top-twenty candidates for the National League's MVP Award.[24] Mets fans loved Dykstra and soon nicknamed him "Nails" for his scrappy, balls-to-the-wall approach to the game. Lenny basked in all the attention.

New York seemed to be the perfect city for a player with a huge appetite for success and for the fast life. What's more, the 1986 Mets were a star-studded team with a reputation for arrogance. Their prodigious power hitting, acrobatic defense, and white-hot pitching allowed them to punish opposing teams and smile while they were doing it. Strutting their way to a franchise record 108 wins, the Amazins clinched the National League East title in mid-September, distancing the second-place Phillies by twenty-one and a half games. Opponents considered them "boorish," "insufferable," and "a bunch of assholes." Not surprisingly, the '86 Mets were involved in four bench-clearing brawls, full-bore mob scenes, complete with blood and torn uniforms.

While the Mets played hard, they partied even harder. Drugs, sex, and groupies abounded. Led by Danny Heep, Jesse Orosco, and Doug Sisk, the Mets left a wide trail of wreckage in their wake. The three veterans nicknamed themselves the "Scum Bunch" and made it their mission to corrupt the younger players. They were extremely successful, too. The drug use that would become public later was not addressed at the time, though it was obvious to the sportswriters who covered the team. Alcohol was more rampant. The Mets kept a refrigerator stocked with beer in their clubhouse at Shea. After games players stayed late into the night, emptying it. As long as they won, however, all was forgiven by manager Davey Johnson, who made light of the frat-like behavior.[25]

Dykstra learned from his experience with the Mets, and he learned well. Sisk and Orosco made him a regular member of the Scum Bunch's back-of-the-plane beer-fueled poker games and encouraged his boorish behavior. Once, while preparing to play golf at the prestigious Nassau Country Club in Glen Cove, New

Fig. 5. Unwanted by the New York Mets, Dykstra was
traded to Philadelphia in 1989. Nicknamed "Nails" for his
scrappy play, he quickly endeared himself to Philadelphia's
blue-collar fans. National Baseball Hall of Fame Library,
Cooperstown, New York.

York, he walked past a group of Catholic priests in the clubhouse,
lifted his leg, and farted. "He fit in as well as anyone," said Sisk.
"Lenny was gritty and disgusting. So were we."[26] But Dykstra's fortunes began to change in 1987. Off the field he would lose nearly
$80,000 in high-stakes poker over the next two years.[27] On the
field his batting average dipped 10 points from the previous season, to .285.[28]

Determined to get bigger and stronger for the '88 campaign, he told sportswriter Joe Durso of the *New York Times*, "It's a strong man's game and I want to be stronger."[29] At five foot ten and 160 pounds, Dykstra was a slap hitter with very little power. Instead, he pumped out line-drive base hits or advanced the runner with a hard ground ball. He was better known for his speed: reaching base by beating out a slow grounder or a well-placed bunt, stealing bases, and making the diving catch in center field. He had to work extremely hard to get the most from his limited talent. Lenny believed that adding 20 to 30 more pounds during the off-season would help him improve his game by increasing his strength, durability, and power. It was his initial foray into a small but growing steroids culture within professional baseball.

There was nothing new about the use of performance-enhancing drugs in sports.[30] During the early 1950s, Soviet weight lifters, aided by testosterone supplements, routinely distanced their American opponents at the Olympic Games. Suspicious of their success and not wanting to be left behind, U.S. coach John Ziegler unearthed their secret. Shortly after, Ziegler and a team of chemists produced an anabolic steroid, now known as Dianabol, for the U.S. weight lifters.[31] Bodybuilders also began to use PEDS, known as "molecule-17 steroids" in medical circles, to gain a competitive advantage.[32] Over the next decade several deaths and allegations of drug use led the International Olympic Committee, in 1967, to establish a Medical Commission that banned the use of drugs and other performance-enhancing substances. Small-scale testing was introduced at the 1968 Mexico Olympics, followed by full-scale testing at the next Games, at Munich in 1972. Although anabolic steroid use was banned three years later, blood doping and the use of more sophisticated compounds continued for the next few decades due to the lack of a reliable test and the ability of East German, Russian, and American athletes to avoid detection through the development of new compounds.[33] Nor were Olympic athletes the only ones juicing.[34]

PED use dates to the late 1960s in the National Football League. Lyle Alzado, a former defensive lineman for the Raiders, exposed doping among NFL players in a July 8, 1991, *Sports Illustrated* article, contending that "a number of players on a number of [NFL] teams were heavy users" during the late 1960s and 1970s.[35] Former NFL player and coach Jim Haslett confirmed Alzado's contention in 2005, stating that "half of the players in the league used some type of steroid" in the 1980s.[36]

Motivated by the lure of big money, the record books, or simply hoping to remain in the game, pro baseball players also began using PEDs in the mid-1980s. In his tell-all book, *Juiced* (2005), José Canseco insists that he "single-handedly changed baseball by introducing anabolic steroids into the game" in 1985.[37] Doping was rare among ballplayers at the time, so Canseco was a guinea pig for the PEDs that were just beginning to infiltrate the black market. What he discovered was that anabolic steroids augmented the quickness essential to his swing as well as to stealing bases. Steroids also built muscle mass, giving Canseco unprecedented power, and improved his recovery time, enabling him to heal faster from injury or muscle fatigue.[38] As a result, Canseco, who began his career with the Oakland A's in 1986, was voted the American League's Rookie of the Year for his 33 homers and 117 RBI. Two years later he was the league's Most Valuable Player, hitting 42 homers and stealing 40 bases, a very rare combination of speed and power among Major League players at the time. The A's power hitter was also injury free during those three years. Essentially, anabolic steroids had allowed Canseco not only to survive the 162-game grind of a Major League season, but to pad his personal statistics and his bank account while increasing his national media exposure.[39]

Together with Mark McGwire, Canseco formed Oakland's "Bash Brothers" and led the A's to a world championship in 1989. By that time Canseco had experimented with anabolic steroids and human growth hormone (HGH) so extensively that he was known as "the Chemist" among ballplayers and trainers throughout the league. Canseco claims that he shared his knowledge with fellow players like McGwire and later, after being traded to the Texas Rangers in 1992, Rafael Palmeiro, Juan González, and Ivan Rodriguez.[40]

By the mid-1990s steroid use was common in Major League Baseball. If players, trainers, coaches, or even managers saw other players doping, they kept their mouths shut. While they might have been ethically opposed to the practice, they respected the Code and its emphasis on clubhouse confidentiality. It hardly mattered that the U.S. Congress, in 1990, passed the Anabolic Steroid Control Act, making the substance illegal, or that baseball commissioner Fay Vincent specifically prohibited the drug's use in a 1991 memo.[41] MLB's disregard for those measures was so blatant that there was even a "secret" conventional wisdom about which drugs to use in order to achieve a specific body type. Those players who sought a bulky body were likely using Deca-Durabolin or Nandrolone. Others, who sought more muscle definition, used Winstrol.[42] At the same time, there was a silent majority of players who remained clean and were tired of having their achievements undermined by the impression that steroids, rather than sweat equity, were the assumed reason for their success. But they, too, refused to speak out publicly because of their allegiance to the unwritten rule "What's done in the clubhouse stays in the clubhouse."[43]

Like Canseco, Lenny Dykstra also flattered himself a "pioneer" when it came to steroid use in Major League Baseball.[44] In March 1988 he arrived at the Mets' Port Lucie training camp thirty pounds heavier than his normal playing weight. He credited the increased muscle mass to "really good vitamins," a veiled reference to steroids.[45] Kirk Radomski, a Mets clubhouse attendant, was astonished by his physical size. Radomski, who supplied players with nutritional supplements and, later, steroids and human growth hormone, would, in 2005, become the key informer for a federal investigation on steroid use in Major League Baseball.[46] "Lenny looked like Popeye [the cartoon character] with muscles bulging from his arms and legs," recalled the clubhouse attendant. "I took one look at him and I knew what he was doing. But I also knew he was doing it all wrong. He looked puffy, which I knew was both muscle and water."

"I'm on the juice," admitted Dykstra. "I want to add some power."

"You mean you want to hit more homers?" Radomski asked.

"Nah, hitting 30 homers and batting .210 isn't going to help me," he replied. "But 20 dingers and .290 could get me a good contract."

"So, what are you taking?"

"I don't know," said Dykstra, shaking his head. "A friend gave me the stuff and showed me how to cycle."

Radomski knew that Dykstra was making a common mistake. "Oh, c'mon Nails," he snapped in disbelief. "How the fuck can you put shit in your body without knowing what it is? You can't do that, it's crazy! There's lots of ways to take this stuff, but you can't just throw anything into your body. Some of it shouldn't be mixed together."

Dykstra just smiled and walked away.[47]

Dykstra tells a different story. He insists that when he was with the Mets, he "never took a single steroid." Nails claims that he began doping after the 1989 season when Phillies general manager Lee Thomas told him that he was going to give him the opportunity to "prove he could be an everyday centerfielder in 1990." Dykstra, realizing that he "wasn't physically constructed to withstand the rigors of a grueling 162-game season," turned to steroids.

While at home in Jackson, Mississippi, during the off-season, he read about Ben Johnson, the Canadian sprinter who was able to win the 100-meter dash in the Olympics because doping had increased his speed and strength. Lenny quickly convinced himself that steroids would allow him to "gain the weight, maintain it, and stay strong so [he] could perform at the level [he] was capable of performing."

Choosing a local physician from the Yellow Pages, Dykstra explained to the doctor that the upcoming season was going to "determine whether [he] was going to be a millionaire, or whether [he'd] have to get a real job." After the doctor wrote him a prescription for Deca-Durabolin, Nails went to the local pharmacy and purchased the steroid. After Dykstra returned to the doctor's office, the physician showed him how to inject the drug and explained how to achieve the best results: inject every day for a six-week cycle and then off for two weeks.[48]

Regardless of when Dykstra began doping or how he did it, his understanding of steroids and the cycling process was primitive at best. Most first-time users operate on a basic understanding that steroids accelerate muscle growth by increasing testosterone levels in the body and provide the energy necessary to engage in strenuous—and constant—training, especially weight lifting. What they don't understand is that all steroids are not the same in terms of composition and effect. In fact, there are three different types of steroids—anabolic, androgenic, and cortico steroids—and each one has a different effect on the body as well as a range of side effects. Anabolic steroids, for example, promote the processing of protein cells that build muscle. Androgenic steroids, on the other hand, enhance masculine characteristics, such as the growth of the vocal chords and body hair. Finally, cortico steroids are an anti-inflammatory substance used for the treatment of allergies, asthma, eczema, and kidney diseases. All three types of steroids can be used for medical treatments, but anabolic and androgenic steroids are also used for nonmedical purposes, mostly by athletes and body builders. Anabolic steroids are by far the most abused of all other types of steroids because they enhance muscle mass, strength, and physical appearance as well as increase virility. Research shows that athletes and body builders who are in their twenties are lured to these types of drugs. In addition, there are more than one hundred types of anabolic-androgenic steroids that are used by athletes. Some are injected, others taken orally, and still others are stacked, or taken simultaneously.[49] If the user is not properly educated, he can do serious damage to his mental or physical health, or both. The negative side effects can include severe mood swings, rage, depression, suicidal tendencies, tendon and ligament tears, kidney and liver damage, impotence, heart disease, and cancer.[50]

When Dykstra began his steroid use, he did not have a clear understanding of the effects, the side effects, or the cycling process that regulates the practice. Instead, he was so desperate to become a power hitter that he wanted quick results and was willing to do anything to achieve that goal. While Nails succeeded in gaining the muscle mass he desired, it proved to be a short-term gain. When the dog days of August arrived, he lost the muscle mass because it was partially due to water retention. "I knew exactly what was going to happen to Lenny as the season progressed," said Radomski. "I'd seen it with weightlifters in the gym. The steroids he was taking was just water and his body wasn't going to be able to hold it. I even told him, 'When it gets hot in July and August, you're going to shrink like a son of a bitch.'"[51]

When the 1988 season began Dykstra was driving balls into the gaps and hitting for power. The soft singles and bloopers he once hit were now hard line drives. But the impressive results came more from the tremendous confidence that accompanied steroid use rather than the drug itself. Essentially, Nails wanted to believe that juicing was going to improve his power, so it did. In the heat of late July and early August, however, Lenny's weight dropped considerably, just as Radomski predicted.[52] In fact, he lost almost all thirty pounds he had gained in the off-season, which sapped his strength and stamina. As a result, he struggled during the second half of the season.

Manager Davey Johnson lost patience with the prickly center fielder. In September Johnson benched him and made Mookie Wilson the regular center fielder and lead-off hitter.[53] At season's end Dykstra's power numbers (8 HR, 33 RBI) weren't much different from those of past seasons, and his batting average slipped even further, to .270.[54] But Nails redeemed himself in the NLCS against the Los Angeles Dodgers.

After starting the first four games of the NLCS, Wilson was hitting a dismal .154. Needing more production from the top of the order, Johnson started Dykstra for the final three games. He responded by hitting .429, with three doubles and a home run. True to form, Nails predicted that he would hit the homer prior to Game Five at Shea. "Dude, I'm going deep today," he told Tom Romano, another Mets clubhouse attendant. "I'm going yard." When Romano chuckled, Dykstra became more insistent: "You don't understand—the red light is on. I'm a big-game fucking player." Two hours later his prediction came true. With two outs and two runners on base in the third inning, Lenny stepped to the plate and slammed Tim Belcher's second pitch into the right-field stands for a three-run homer.[55] Unfortunately for the Mets, the Dodgers prevailed in the seventh and deciding game to clinch the pennant.

During the off-season Mets general manager Frank Cashen rewarded Dykstra with a $575,000 salary for 1989, which represented a $270,000 raise. At the same time, Cashen picked up a $1 million option on Wilson's contract, signaling Johnson's intention to continue the platoon for a fourth straight season.[56] Nails had had enough.

Throughout the winter and early spring he lobbied to be traded. When the 1989 season began, Lenny pressed even harder. "I have to be an everyday player," he told Mike Francesa, WFAN's Sportstalk Radio host. "I told them if you don't give me a chance to play every day, then trade me. I'm here to play baseball, not sit on a bench." Cashen saw that the center-field platoon was having an adverse effect on Lenny. His base stealing and run production were down throughout April and May. The Mets' general manager tried to accommodate him by attempting various trade possibilities with several clubs, including the Atlanta Braves, Boston Red Sox, and San Diego Padres. But the negotiations eventually broke down.

Finally, on Father's Day, June 18, 1989, Cashen summoned Dykstra to his office and informed him that he and reliever Roger McDowell had been traded to the Phillies for Juan Samuel. While Johnson was ecstatic about the deal, Mets fans were highly critical, believing that Dykstra was one of the few players who defined the heart and soul of the team.[57] There were also those in Philadelphia who weren't happy with the trade.

Samuel had been a fan favorite. More affectionately known as "Sammy," the homegrown second baseman electrified the Phillies with his blazing speed, quick bat, and incandescent smile. He was the first player in MLB history to reach double figures in doubles, triples, home runs, and stolen bases in each of his first four seasons, making him the best offensive second baseman in Phillies history during those years. In 1984 Samuel led the National League in triples with 19, and his 72 stolen bases were the most by a Phillies player in the twentieth century. In 1987, before he reached the age of twenty-seven, Sammy hit 28 home runs, 100 RBI, and a league-leading 15 triples. He also stole 35 bases that season.[58]

"I wouldn't have made the trade," admitted Bill Giles. "I loved

Samuel. When Lee told me he was going to trade Sammy for Dykstra, I didn't like it. I didn't want to trade homegrown talent. I also had questions about whether Dykstra could be an everyday player. But Lee seemed to feel that Samuel was on the downside of his career and that Dykstra still hadn't realized his full potential. So I didn't stand in his way. Besides, I hired Lee to be the GM and to do what he thought was best for the organization, so he made the deal."[59]

For as much as Dykstra lobbied for the trade, his performance in Philadelphia did not improve. While the Phillies made him their everyday center fielder, he hit just .222 in his 352 at bats. It was by far his worst season in the Majors.[60] Thomas attributed the poor performance to impending fatherhood, since Lenny's wife, Terri, was pregnant with their first child.[61] But Phils second baseman Tommy Herr told Howard Eskin, a WIP Sports Radio host, that Dykstra had quit on the season and liked the nightlife too much. There was even some speculation that Nails hated playing for a losing team and that he was demanding to be traded again, this time to a winning organization. Trade rumors mentioned Dykstra's hometown California Angels as a potential suitor. The Phillies were even reported to have offered him back to the Mets, who promptly rejected the deal.[62] But Thomas adamantly denied the rumors in a 2011 interview. "There was no way I would've traded Lenny," he insisted. "He was our key guy. There was no way we were going to get that one big free agent to turn the club around. But with Lenny we had a guy who could play center field, hit, get on base, and steal bases. And to win you have to have a good lead-off hitter like that."[63]

Thomas ensured his investment by raising Dykstra's salary to $700,000 for the 1990 season.[64] Over the next four years Nails would become one of the most popular players in Phillies history.

FOUR
Boo Birds

To say that Phillies fans were "frustrated" with the inability of Bill Giles and the Gang of Six to put a winning team on the field would be a gross understatement. Being a fan during those miserable years was to experience Dante's *Inferno*, and perhaps that would have been an improvement. Once they had devoured the ecstasy of winning the 1980 World Series, the fans seemed to believe that they were entitled to watch the hometown team contend for the title on an annual basis. Anything less was an abject failure. Certainly, these were unreasonable expectations. A more forgiving fan base would have simply been grateful for the team's successes of the mid- to late 1970s and early 1980s, considering the century of losing that preceded it. But not in Philadelphia, where losing is taken personally and where the faithful have suffered more than any other MLB fan base.

The Phillies elevated losing to an art form. No other Major League franchise compiled more losses (more than 10,600) or experienced as many last-place finishes (twenty-eight).[1] No other club has lost twenty-three consecutive games, but the hapless Phils managed to do that in 1961.[2] No other team has blown a pennant with a six-and-a-half-game lead and just twelve left to play in the regular season. But the 1964 Phillies somehow managed to do that by dropping ten straight and finishing in a tie for second place.[3] It remains the most devastating collapse in the history of Philadelphia sports. Even after the Phils captured their first World Series title in 1980, the '64 swoon continued to haunt the city.[4] Failure became so ingrained that Phillies fans continue to embrace the belief that if anything bad can happen, it will.

Perhaps Joe Queenan, a native Philadelphia sports junkie, expressed the collective—and historic—frustration best. "Rooting for the Phillies," he wrote, "is the Vale of Tears, the Stations of the Cross, the Crown of Thorns, the Bataan Death March, and the Babylonian Captivity all rolled into one."[5] Disgusted with the misfortunes of his boyhood Phillies, Queenan relocated to New York City, where he adopted the regal New York Yankees, winners of twenty-seven World Series titles.

Despite all the foiled heroism, however, the Phillies still retain a devoted following. The silent majority possesses a good understanding of the game, acts respectfully at the ballpark, and tends to suffer in private when the Phillies lose. Their fidelity is unconditional because the team reminds them of their youth, their family, and even their love for the city itself. The fans also appreciate the exceptionally talented players in the team's exasperating history— Grover Alexander, Chuck Klein, Richie Ashburn, Robin Roberts, Jim Bunning, Steve Carlton, and Mike Schmidt. They realize how rarely a Hall of Famer surfaces in the city's sports culture and how fortunate they are to witness such gifted careers. Although the silent majority of fans are disappointed when the Phillies go down to defeat, they refuse to lose sleep over it. They know that baseball is only a game and that winning as well as losing must be kept in perspective. But the defining spirit of Philadelphia's baseball fandom— for better, but mostly worse—can be found in a vocal minority of clock punchers and blue collars known as the "Boo Birds."

The Boo Birds go to the ballpark to seek refuge from the disappointments of their own lives. It's a place where they can drown their sorrows in beer and express their passion by cheering, but mostly booing, the players. They rely on the Phillies to provide an imaginary escape from a rotten job, a lousy marriage, or ungrateful children. If the team fails—as it so often does—the Boo Birds become vindictive. Sitting up in the cheap seats, the cantankerous bunch rains down their venom on the hometown players. They are like pigeons that build nests under the rafters and crap on unsuspecting victims. If the game is out of reach, the Boo Bird blasts his boom box simply to annoy others. Popular selections include country music, rock, rap, or, depending upon the season, a play-by-play broadcast of an Eagles, Flyers, or Sixers game. Occasionally, a Boo Bird becomes so unruly that he provokes a donnybrook in the stands. According to Queenan, "He's the kind of fan who dreams about beating someone senseless and getting away with it."[6]

At the same time, the Boo Birds can be extremely grateful when the Phillies are successful. "Winning" is the balm to their pent-up hostility. Put a winning team on the field, and the Phillies can do no wrong. Boo Birds will be effusive in their praise of the players and the organization itself. They will happily lend their hand to a winning effort by heckling the umpire who makes a bad call in a close game. Pelting the star player of an opposing team with beer, batteries, and even giveaway items is also popular. Boo Birds will spend exorbitant sums on team merchandise, tailgate parties, tickets, and even road trips to New York, Washington, and Pittsburgh to cheer on the Phillies when they're winning. If they meet one of the hometown heroes in a bar, he gets a free beer. If in a restaurant, the player will get a free meal. All the Boo Bird asks in return is a few minutes of time to chat and an autograph or perhaps a photo op. In other words, the Boo Bird can show his love as passionately as he can spew his venom for the hometown team.

Truth be told, the Boo Bird is to be pitied. He's either a disillusioned idealist, who truly believes the Phillies have the potential to contend each and every season and pelts the team with a hailstorm of boos if it doesn't, or a fool, who's delusional enough to think that if handed a bat, glove, and uniform he could perform much better than the current roster of players. What he really thinks is that he would play harder, show more emotion, and get his uniform dirty. It's why the Boo Bird has never been able to identify with the Phillies' supremely gifted ballplayers like Mike Schmidt. Instead, he idolizes the scrappers like Pete Rose or Lenny Dykstra, who have to scratch and claw for everything they earn. It's as if he's looking in the mirror at a reflection of himself, or actually the self he wants to see.

Essentially, the Boo Bird lives on the edge. He desperately clings to the hope that the Phillies will win but is never able to rid himself completely of the gnawing feeling that they will crash and burn. This relentless insecurity is so acute that it causes even the most religiously devout Boo Birds to have an ambivalent relationship with God. Because he believes so strongly that the Almighty regularly controls the outcome of a baseball game, the Boo Bird blames God for wielding a negative impact on the Phillies.[7] While such pain would be enough to drive a normal fan to atheism, the Boo Bird gets a perverse pleasure from the masochism and always returns to the ballpark for more.

The silent majority and the Boo Birds dominated the Phillies' fan base until the glory era of 1976 to 1983. During and immediately following that period, another type of fan emerged—the "front-runner." These are fair-weather fans. The front-runner disassociates himself from the Phillies when they are losing for fear that he might become branded a "loser." Instead, the front-runner transfers his allegiance to a perennial winner like the New York Yankees. Some even have the audacity to support the New York Mets, the Phillies' most despised rival. Front-runners are also frauds. They flatter themselves "baseball connoisseurs" who know the game better than the Boo Birds or the silent majority and often try to impress each other with their superficial knowledge. Many front-runners have the disposable income to indulge themselves at the expense of the true believers. For example, when the Phillies are winning, the front-runner buys himself a reproduction jersey and a season-ticket plan so he can socialize in the stands with like-minded souls. In so doing, he deprives the loyal lower-income-earning fans the better seats.

What's worse, the front-runner buys up as many tickets as possible when the Phillies reach the postseason. Not only does the hoarding allow the front office to inflate the prices, but it limits the opportunity for the true believers to attend any playoff or World Series games. In blue-collar parlance, the front-runner is an "asshole."[8] With fans like that, the Boo Birds become an attractive alternative. If nothing else, they care passionately about the fortunes of the team, win or lose.

When John Kruk arrived in Philadelphia in June 1989, he was given a crash course in Phillies fandom. In his fifth game with the last-place Phils, Kruk, playing left field, made a costly mental error. The Phillies were playing the Pittsburgh Pirates at Veterans Stadium and held a rare 3–0 lead going into the fourth inning. Barry Bonds homered to lead off the top of the fourth. José Lind followed with a single. Andy Van Slyke grounded out. Lind went to second on the play, advanced to third on a wild pitch, and scored on a Bobby Bonilla double. The Pirates had cut the Phils' lead to one run, 3–2.

With Bonilla on second and one out, R. J. Reynolds stepped to the plate and hit a lazy fly ball to left field. Kruk made the catch for the second out of the inning. Believing that the side had been retired, however, he put his head down and began jogging in to the infield. Bonilla tagged up and scored the tying run all the way from second on the sacrifice fly.

All hell broke loose in the stands. The Boo Birds lashed out at their new left fielder with expletives that he himself had never heard before. And that's saying something for an individual who was born and raised in the backwoods of West Virginia.

"I got booed pretty bad," recalled Kruk. "When the media asked me about it after the game, I told them the truth: 'I just had a brain fart.'" In fact, he thought the mental gaffe was "about the lowest he could go."

"I'd had a bad year the season before in San Diego and I was having a real horseshit year when I got traded to Philadelphia," he explained. "I was hitting just .180. I remember saying to myself, 'If you're hitting .180 you'd better be damn intelligent. You'd better move all the runners and make all the plays. And you'd damn sure better remember how many outs there are.'"[9]

Third base coach Larry Bowa realized that Kruk was pressing. Bowa had managed him in San Diego the previous two years and knew that the pudgy outfielder had a tremendous respect for the game and the way he played it. He also knew how demanding the blue-collar fans can be, having alternately earned their love and their wrath during his playing days with the Phillies. If Kruk could win over the fans and the few like-minded teammates who also respected the game and played hard, Bowa believed that he could be a positive influence in the clubhouse. His team-first mentality and self-deprecating sense of humor would be a refreshing change to the listless team. "Guys pouted all the time," Bowa remembered. "They didn't care if we won or lost as long as they got a couple of hits. It wasn't a good place to play back then. We really needed to change the attitude, and Kruk played a huge role in that."[10]

"Just be yourself," Bowa told him. "Have fun. We've got a bunch of deadasses here, but don't let them bring you down. Play your game and don't worry about the rest of the bullshit that goes on here."[11] Kruk followed the advice. "I decided right then that if I was going to be released by the Phillies, I would enjoy the hell out of my last season, because I might never get a chance to play ball again," he explained. "I just said to hell with it. And I started to hit."[12] Kruk batted .331 that season and never stopped. In fact, he was the best natural hitter on the Phillies during his six-year tenure in Philadelphia.[13]

Kruk also gravitated to teammates who shared his respect for the game and had a strong desire to win like Dykstra, who lockered next to him. "When I was playing against him, I thought he was the biggest asshole in the world," said Kruk in a 2001 interview. "In San Diego, we thought he was such a prick that we told our pitchers to drill him every time he came to bat. But I think to be a great lead-off hitter, you have to be that way. And when we were playing together in Philly, Lenny was the perfect asshole to lead off for us. There wasn't a better guy to play with."[14]

Daulton became another close friend, though the Krukker initially denied it. "He was another guy I didn't like when I played against him," said the West Virginia native. "I thought he was just a pretty boy. Something about him rubbed me the wrong way. Even when I was first traded to the Phillies, we didn't hang together. He was too pretty. I thought, 'Fuck him, let him do his own thing.' I figured he didn't like me, either." But as they got to know each other better, the two teammates became the "closest friends." It was an "Odd Couple thing," according to Kruk. "After a while I realized that Darren's as much of a dirtball as Lenny and me," he explained. "He just looks better. Underneath, though, he's the same—a derelict who talks shit. Those are beautiful compliments, by the way. Outside our domain, people have a hard time understanding that. It's like calling Lenny a little asshole; he is, but he's a good little asshole."[15]

Although manager Nick Leyva appreciated the talent as well as the humor of the trio, he did not always appreciate their profane vocabulary. Leyva had never played or managed in the big leagues before he came to Philadelphia. His entire Major League experience consisted of the five years he coached for the St. Louis Cardinals. As a result, the new skipper did not truly understand the importance big leaguers attach to a vulgar camaraderie. When he was hired, Leyva was asked by the local sportswriters how difficult the transition would be to managing in the Majors when his only managerial experience had been at the Minor League level. Insisting that he would be just as tough as he was as a Minor Leaguer manager, Leyva maintained that he "wouldn't be intimidated by the big salaries of the team's star players" and that he would "demand hustle from everyone." "I'm dealing with grown men," he added. "I'm not a babysitter. As long as the players give one-hundred percent and don't embarrass me or the organization, we'll be all right."[16] The strategy sounded convincing, but it was difficult to employ on a team where most of the players failed to hustle and spent more time pouting. Even the more talented ones who did hustle, like Dykstra, Kruk, and Daulton, grated on Leyva when they didn't meet his wholesome expectations of big-league behavior.

During spring training in 1990, Leyva asked Dykstra and Kruk to watch their language when the fans were in close proximity, especially youngsters. It was a reasonable request, considering that the faithful flocked to the team's Clearwater, Florida, training complex every spring and that the virtually unobstructed fields made the players very accessible to them. While Nails and Krukker might have had the best intentions, it was impossible for them—as well as for most of their teammates—to curb their foul language, especially on the playing field. At one point, the players' use of profanity became so intolerable that Leyva asked Lee Thomas to address the issue. If nothing else, Leyva enjoyed the strong support of the Phillies' general manager. He was also confident that the problem would be corrected if the players knew the directive was coming from the front office.

One sun-drenched morning before practice, Thomas gathered the

Fig. 6. General manager Lee Thomas, who arrived in
Philadelphia in 1988, traded for other teams' castoffs because
the Phillies' budget wouldn't allow him to sign a major free-
agent pitcher or power hitter. Photo by Al Tielemans.

players in the clubhouse and lectured them on their responsibilities
as role models for the youngsters who came to watch them perform.

"What the fuck is wrong with you guys?!" he began in a mock
attempt at anger. "Don't you know that you can't use foul language
around here? How the fuck would you like it if your fuckin' kid
was hanging around these fuckin' fields wanting a fuckin' autograph or something?"

Boo Birds

Working himself into a bogus rage, Thomas continued the rant, living up to his "Mad Dog" nickname with each and every expletive.

"You fuckin' guys are supposed to be fuckin' role models and you use that kind of fuckin' language? You should be fuckin' ashamed of yourselves!"

The meeting lasted just three minutes, ending when Thomas threw up his arms in fake exasperation and stormed out of the clubhouse, screaming one last "Fuck!" for good measure.

When it was over Roger McDowell counted twenty-three *fucks*, an impressive display of vulgar showmanship. It was clear to the players that Thomas was supporting his manager's wishes, but that he was also more attuned to their feelings than the choirboy image that was being foisted upon them.[17]

To be sure, Thomas and Leyva had reasonable expectations for the 1990 Phillies. They expected the team to be competitive, they expected to win more often than the previous season when the Phils went 67-95, and they expected the Phillies to avoid the cellar. Secretly, they even allowed themselves on occasion to expect that the Phils might contend for the National League East title.[18] The wishful thinking didn't seem so far-fetched when the team got off to their best start since 1981, winning nineteen of their first thirty-four games. The Phillies were battling for second place until June, when they went into a tailspin. That month the team won just eleven of twenty-eight games and went into the All-Star Break with a 39-41 record.[19]

As the season progressed injuries to key players and a fading pitching staff took their toll. Leyva's inexperience also seemed to catch up with him. Prior to his arrival in Philadelphia, he had no big-league playing or managerial experience. Saddled with players who failed to hustle and tended to pout when things didn't go smoothly, Leyva was not always certain how to handle the clubhouse. On the field he occasionally second-guessed himself and the move would backfire, earning him the wrath of the Boo Birds and the press. At season's end the Phils were in fourth place with a record of 77-85.[20] But there were also some positive developments.

The highlight of the season came on August 15 when Terry Mulholland, acquired the previous year from San Francisco, threw a no-hitter against his former team at the Vet. "I planned ahead more than usual," said Mulholland after the game. "I was running pitch sequences through my mind, and I'm usually not that detailed or focused in my thinking during a game." Until the seventh inning, he was hurling a perfect game. But third baseman Charlie Hayes was credited with a throwing error that allowed Rick Parker to reach first base. The next batter, Dave Anderson, grounded into a double play, erasing the miscue. But Mulholland lost his bid for the perfecto. The decisive moment came with two outs in the ninth inning when Giant catcher Gary Carter, a dangerous power hitter, stepped to the plate. After working a 1-2 count, Mulholland suddenly became nervous, realizing that he could make history with the next pitch. He stepped off the mound to regain composure. Carter fouled off the next pitch and then smashed a hard line drive down the third base line. Hayes redeemed himself with a diving catch to secure the 6–0 no-hit victory.[21]

Mulholland joined an elite group of Phillies pitchers with the achievement. Only six other no-hitters had been thrown before in franchise history, the last coming in June 1971, when Rick Wise accomplished the feat against the Reds at Cincinnati's Riverfront Stadium. "One game does not make a career," Terry told the press after he was informed of the rarity of the feat. "I have to keep pitching, and develop more confidence. But the no-hitter gives me something to work from, a reference point to always keep in my mind."[22]

At season's end Mulholland had a 9-10 record, 75 K, and a 3.34 ERA and was a key contributor to a revamped pitching staff that performed remarkably well at various periods during the season. Pat Combs, the only returning starter from the previous year, enjoyed his best season in the Majors, recording a 10-10 record with 108 K and a 4.07 ERA. Ken Howell (8-7, 70 K, 4.64), José DeJesús (7-8, 87 K, 3.74 ERA), and Bruce Ruffin (6-13, 79 K, 5.38 ERA) rounded out the starting rotation.[23] The pitching staff also appeared to have a promising future with the early-season acquisition of Tommy Greene.

Signed as a first-round draft pick by Atlanta in 1985, Greene struggled in the Minors. By 1990 he was buried in the Braves' farm system because of the club's talent-rich pitching at the Major League level. When the Phillies scouted Greene, they saw that he was a hard worker who fielded his position well and believed that he could help the team in its rebuilding process. On August 3, 1990, Thomas stole the six-foot-five, 225-pound pitcher from Atlanta along with aging star outfielder Dale Murphy for Jeff Parrett and two Minor Leaguers. "All I want to do is go out and give the Phillies a chance to win when I pitch," said Greene when he arrived in Philadelphia. "I know I can't win all the time and that some nights I'm going to struggle. But I will always try my best not to let my teammates down." Greene would prove to be one of Philadelphia's most effective starting pitchers over the next four years.[24]

Darren Daulton handled the young pitching staff exceptionally well, spending countless hours learning how to motivate each one. Dutch was also an important part of the Phillies' offense. After the All-Star Break, he hit .303 with 10 home runs and 41 RBI. Daulton's performance convinced Thomas that he deserved a new three-year $6.75 million contract.[25] After all the injuries and all the years of hard work, the catcher's fortunes appeared to be changing, as he was doing just as well off the playing field, too.

The previous year Dutch married Lynne Austin, a striking 5'6½" blonde-haired beauty. Austin, a former *Playboy* Playmate, was also the original "Hooters Girl," the first waitress hired by the Florida restaurant chain. In spring training there was a huge Hooters advertisement plastered on the center-field fence at Clearwater's Jack Russell Stadium that featured Austin's eye-catching 35-24-35 likeness. Dutch, who was exceptionally handsome himself, just smiled at the sight and went about his business. Within the next year the attractive couple would have a baby boy, and life would become even sweeter for the Phillies' catcher.[26]

The Phillies' offense also showed flashes of brilliance. The addition of Dale Murphy gave the Phils a two-time National League Most Valuable Player and one of the most experienced power hitters in the Majors. A seven-time All-Star, Murphy had more than 370 career home runs and had hit 20 or more home runs eleven times in an illustrious fifteen-year tenure with Atlanta. But the Braves had not contended for a pennant since 1984, and their All-Star outfielder

FIG. 7. The Hooters billboard at Jack Russell Stadium in Clearwater, Florida, where the Phillies held spring training, featured Lynne Austin, the leading spokesperson for the restaurant chain. Some players made lewd comments about her likeness until she married Darren Daulton in 1989. Daulton is pictured at left with Lenny Dykstra. Photo by Al Tielemans.

was in the twilight of his career.[27] Entrenched in the NL West basement, Atlanta traded Murphy to the Phillies in August with the hope that he would reach the playoffs one more time before he retired. The change of scenery seemed to revive "Murph," as he was known to teammates. In September he went on a thirteen-game hitting streak, batting .396 during the two-week period. In fifty-seven games, Murphy, a spot starter, hit .266, with 7 home runs and 27 RBI.[28]

Although he was quiet by nature, Murphy, a devout Mormon who played hard and possessed a tremendous respect for the game, provided the younger Phillies with a wonderful example.[29] At the same time, "the Murph" had a sharp tongue and could put a teammate in his place if he wasn't hustling. "If one of our pitchers wasn't doing his job, I might just call him a fuckin' pussy," explained John Kruk, who had great respect for the former Brave. "But Murph would deliver the same point without cursing, and it hurt worse because you really had to stop and think about what he'd said. If somebody calls you a fuckin' pussy, you know what he means. There ain't much to think about. But when Murph said something you'd start thinking about what you should have done and you'd really feel bad because he was the last guy in the world you'd want to let down."[30]

On another occasion Kruk tried coax Murphy into using the team's most popular profanity, "fuck." True to his faith, the Mormon outfielder refused. Kruk wouldn't take no for an answer and continued to egg him on. Finally, Murph snapped. "Krukky," he barked, "if you say it again, I'm going to bop you!" Stunned by the threat, the rest of the team sat in stone-cold silence, waiting to see if Kruk would accept the challenge. Of course, he had too much respect for Murphy to press the issue.[31]

Along with his hillbilly humor, Kruk continued his impressive clutch hitting with a .291 average. He also shifted from the outfield to first base to spare his aching knees from the constant pressure of running down fly balls on the unforgiving Astroturf. Kruk, who also added a few pounds to his already pudgy body, appreciated the change. "I get to talk to the pitcher, the base runners, our second baseman, the umpires, anybody who's around," he noted. "And I feel like I'm in the game the whole time. When I was in the outfield and had a bad at bat, I went back out there and worked on my stance. At first base, I have too much on my mind to think about hitting. What the heck, all I have to do is catch a ground ball and decide whether to take it myself or toss it to the pitcher," he added.[32]

Right fielder Von Hayes (.261, 17 HR, 73 RBI) and third baseman Charlie Hayes (.258, 10 HR, 57 RBI) also provided some solid power. What's more, rookie outfielder Wes Chamberlain, acquired from Pittsburgh when the Pirates mistakenly left him on waivers, demonstrated enormous potential at the plate, where he hit .283 in eighteen games.[33] Lenny Dykstra, however, had the best season of them all.

In 1990 Nails not only made his first All-Star Game appearance, but also lived up to his own billing as "the best lead-off hitter in baseball." He batted .325, walked 89 times, scored 106 runs, knocked in 60 more, and led the National League with 192 hits and an on-base percentage of .418.[34] But Dykstra's remarkable stats were not achieved simply by rigorous training alone. Steroids fueled his success, and he would rely heavily on the drug in the future.

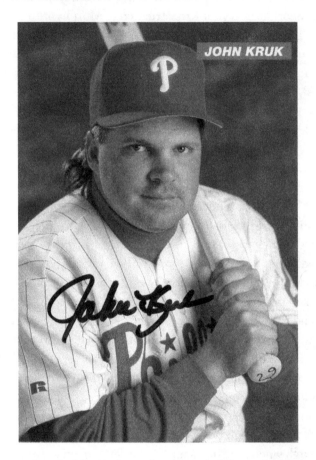

FIG. 8. John Kruk was the most colorful member of
Macho Row. Although he flattered himself a "hillbilly" and
exploited the self-deprecating image with the media, Kruk
was arguably the smartest player on the Phillies as well as
its most natural hitter. Photo by Al Tielemans.

FIVE

Krukker

In the early-morning hours of Monday, May 6, 1991, Lenny Dykstra and Darren Daulton were returning home from John Kruk's bachelor's party in suburban Philadelphia. Dykstra, driving intoxicated, lost control of his brand-new red Mercedes and crashed the sports car into a tree.[1] The $92,000 automobile was totaled. Neither player was wearing a safety belt and narrowly escaped death. They were lucky.

Dykstra broke his collarbone and cheekbone and fractured three ribs, one puncturing a lung. Daulton, who was riding shotgun, sustained a badly bruised chest, a broken eye socket, and a scratched cornea. For Dutch, the accident served as a wake-up call. "It's like God pulled my number out of his hat and said, 'Nah, let him live some more,'" he remarked a few days later. "You know, baseball used to be everything to me. Now I think more about my wife and son."[2]

Daulton was back behind the plate two weeks later, but he wasn't the same player. Struggling with double vision, he had difficulty seeing the ball, and his batting average plummeted to .196. Once, an opposing base runner took off for second, and Dutch shot out of his crouch, ready to throw him out, until he saw two second basemen and two shortstops. Trying to halt his throw, Dutch spiked the ball ten feet in front of the plate.[3] Catcalls and jeers rained down on him. The Boo Birds continued to spew their venom at him every home game. The most shameless episode of their boorish behavior occurred on "Family Day," when Daulton's wife, Lynne, and their thirteen-month-old son, Zach, were booed during their introduction before a father-son Wiffle-ball game. The painful incident reduced Lynne to tears and rightfully angered Dutch. "There was no need for that," said the catcher, still bitter at the memory. "If the fans want to boo, do it to me, but leave my family alone."[4]

When his playing didn't improve, Daulton realized that he had tried to come back too soon. Begrudgingly, he agreed to return to the disabled list, missing a total of sixty-three games.[5] He wasn't the only one struggling with the effects of the car accident, either.

Despite his gruff exterior and a colorful sense of humor, John Kruk, known more affectionately as "the Krukker," was a sensitive individual who initially blamed himself for the crash. Had they not attended his bachelor's party, he believed, Daulton and Dykstra would have been spared injury. Jamie, his fiancée, eventually convinced John that he had no control over what had happened, but it still took him a while for the guilt to subside. "The thing that hurt the most was I couldn't get through to them," said Kruk.

> When I heard about the accident I immediately called the hospital, but the doctors and nurses wouldn't put me through so I left messages.
>
> The next day, [the Phillies] flew to San Diego and I left messages for them to phone the hotel. But there were so many calls coming through for me, we couldn't connect. It was one of the most upsetting times I've ever had in baseball. I was so emotionally upset I didn't care to play. I didn't care if we won or lost. I just wanted to find out how my friends were. When I finally heard from them, and they both said they were going to be fine, I started worrying about what they thought of me, if they thought the accident was my fault because it happened after my party.[6]

They didn't. But his anxiety over the episode underscored Krukker's love for the two teammates.

The near deaths of his teammates reminded Kruk just how fragile life can be and that win or lose, baseball is just a game. There are more important things in life, like family and friends. Deep down he knew those things. He had learned them from his parents growing up in West Virginia. Deep down John Martin Kruk was just a small-town boy with a strong set of values and a genuine compassion for the underdog.

Born on February 9, 1961, at Charleston, West Virginia, John was the youngest of four sons born to Frank and Sarah "Lena" Kruk. Frank had been a star basketball player at Charleston High School in the early 1940s, once scoring ninety-nine points in a game. After graduation he joined the army and served in World War II before returning to Charleston, where he got a job at Anchor Glass & Container Company, a bottle manufacturer. Nicknamed "Moe," Frank married his high school sweetheart, Lena Aleshire, in 1950, and they began a family.[7]

In 1962 Anchor Glass transferred Moe to their main plant at Bergen County, New Jersey, where the family would spend the next decade. "Those were hard years for our family," said Lena in a recent interview. "Moe was always working, so I did the best I could with our boys. It was a big difference from West Virginia. But we were fortunate because we lived in a nice neighborhood, and the boys went to a nice school."[8]

Growing up outside New York City, the Kruk brothers—Joe, Tommy, Larry, and John—played all sports with the neighborhood kids, but John favored stickball and basketball. The only missing link in his young life was his father. "I hardly ever saw my dad," he said. "I was at that age where I was starting to play ball and I wanted to be around him, but he was never there because he had to work double shifts. He'd get home at six o'clock in the morning, sleep until ten, and then he'd go out and referee a high school football game on a Saturday afternoon. Then he'd go right back to work."[9] Moe's absence was difficult for his youngest son, who was a "very sensitive kid," according to Lena.[10] Fortunately, Moe's job responsibilities would become less demanding after 1971, when the family returned to West Virginia.

Settling in the small town of Keyser, the Kruks were able to live on a more comfortable budget than they had in expensive suburban

New York. That meant Moe no longer had to work additional shifts and could spend time coaching his boys or watching them play. "My dad was the kind of father every kid would want," said Larry Kruk, one of John's older brothers. "Dad coached all our teams in the youth and [recreational] leagues, and I honestly can't remember losing a single one of them. He probably knew more than the coaches we had in school, but back in those days you had to be a teacher if you wanted to coach school ball."[11] Larry, who was just a year older than John, played on all the same teams with his younger brother, and Moe coached them. But that was not always an advantage. "The only thing I didn't like was that dad wanted me to play shortstop," recalled John, who was age ten at the time. "Larry was our regular shortstop, so when he went in to pitch, Dad put me at short. It allowed him to limit the number of changes he made at different positions when he switched pitchers. But I kept making errors at short."

Moe tried to convince his youngest son that he could play the position. "There's nothing to it," he said. "All you have to do is catch the ball and throw it to first."

But John continued to make errors, which is not unusual for a left-handed infielder at that position. Frustrated and angry, he threw down his glove and told his father, "That's it! I'm not playing shortstop ever again. Put me somewhere else!"

Moe didn't tolerate the insolence. "If you don't want to play where I tell you, then go the hell home," he snapped. "I don't want you on this team. If you don't play shortstop, you ain't playing."

"After that, I was more than happy to go to shortstop," recalled Kruk, years later. "That situation with my father taught me to respect my coaches. It was a pretty useful lesson, because when I got to the pros I was not a high draft pick, so I knew that if I pissed off the manager I might never play again. If they tell you something, you damn well better do it."[12]

The Kruk brothers were among the best young athletes in Keyser during the 1970s. The family home sat on three and a half acres of land on the outskirts of town and was a popular destination for local kids. Moe had a pool built in the large backyard and constructed a backstop and a goal post so his sons could play football and baseball whenever their friends visited. "In the summer, the only rule we had was that you couldn't go swimming until we played baseball," said Larry. "Most of the time we had enough kids to play nine-on-nine, too."[13] The three Rotruck brothers, who lived next door, were regulars in those games. Like the Kruk boys, the Rotrucks were extremely competitive, and all of them were sore losers. "There were a lot of fights," admitted Rick Rotruck, "and the one thing for certain was that Johnny was involved. No matter the fight, it was always Johnny versus somebody."[14]

In addition to a hot temper, John was known for his exceptional hitting ability. "When he got to the Majors, folks said that Johnny was a natural hitter, but he really did work at it," said Larry Kruk. "Our mom had a garden in right field, and we weren't allowed to go in there. Johnny, being left-handed, taught himself to hit to left because he knew Mom would tan his hide if he pulled the ball into her garden. I once told Mom that if she had put that garden in left field, she'd have had three sons playing in the Majors instead of just the one."[15]

At Keyser High School Kruk excelled in basketball. The only reason he played baseball was to stay in shape for the hoops season. In addition, the baseball program wasn't well organized. "We just went out after school, loosened up and played," he said. "We didn't take batting practice or anything. When the game was over, we went home."[16] Thanks to Moe, John developed into a good, solid shortstop and pitcher. Larry was the team's catcher, and Rick Rotruck played second base. "Johnny might've been a left-handed shortstop, but he never dropped anything, and he could run, too," said Rotruck.[17]

After graduating in 1979, Kruk, just five foot ten and 150 pounds, went to Potomac State University, a two-year satellite of the University of West Virginia located in Keyser. Potomac competed in Region 20 of the National Junior College Athletic Association, which included fifteen schools in the West Virginia, Maryland, and Pennsylvania region. "I was at Potomac for one reason, to play basketball," Kruk admitted. But he quickly realized that he had no future in the sport because, as he put it, "I was too short. Too slow. Too white."[18] Instead, John switched to baseball. Jack Reynolds, the coach, recalled that he was "one tool short of being a five-tool player." "Johnny had an average arm, but he could do everything else—run, field, hit, and hit with power," he added.

Because Potomac already had one of the region's best shortstops, Kruk was converted to the outfield. "He worked his tail off to learn that position," said Reynolds. "We taught him how to get to the ball quick and release it quick, and by midseason he looked real good out there." But it was Kruk's hitting that made a stronger impression.

"Johnny was the best pure hitter I'd ever seen at this level," said Reynolds, who batted the youngster third in his lineup, the spot reserved for a team's best hitter. Kruk immediately rose to meet the challenge. On Potomac's spring trip to Florida, they played a double-header against the St. Louis Cardinals' B team. The Cards started a Triple-A pitcher in both games, with Kruk going five-for-six in the two games, hitting four doubles in the gap to left-center. "It was like those pitchers knew what was coming, but they just couldn't stop him," recalled Reynolds. "When we got back home for the regular season, Johnny went on a tear. Our ballpark had a big ol' hill in left field. It was about 240 feet down the line. Johnny could hit opposite field so well that he just peppered that hill with line drives all season long. I think he finished with a .410 average that year."

Pro scouts flocked to Potomac to watch Kruk hit. Originally, they were attracted by Jeff Reynolds, a teammate, who was the top power hitter in the region. He would later sign with the New York Yankees and enjoy an impressive Minor League career, earning Most Valuable Player Awards at the Single- and Double-A levels. But Kruk quickly captured the attention of the scouts with his remarkable hitting. "Once we had sixteen pro scouts show up at a game just to watch Johnny hit," recalled his coach. "Johnny turned quite a few heads that day. I think that's when the Padres put him on their radar. Of course, they were the team who later drafted him."

Unfortunately, the 1980 season did not end well for Kruk or the team. After posting a 19-4 record, Potomac State was one victory away from securing a bid to the Junior College World Series. "We were down in Baltimore, playing in the Region 20 tournament," recalled Jack Reynolds. "We had one more game to play, and if we won, we would go to the College World Series in Grand Junction. The day before our last game, I got a call from Potomac saying that I have to bring the boys back because they don't have the money to send us to Colorado if we win the tournament. Well, try going to those nineteen young men and telling them that they can't go to the College World Series when that was a lifelong dream for most of them." The team decided to forfeit their last game and returned to Keyser. Jack Reynolds was so angry, he resigned, and Potomac dropped the baseball program. "I wasn't as upset about my situation as I was for our players, especially Johnny," recalled Reynolds, who would mend his differences with the university and restart the baseball program in 1991. "Here was a young man who loved baseball to his core. Not only did he have the talent to go far, but he had all the intangibles: great concentration, a great work ethic, and the desire to make it to the top. And all I could do for him is get him a scholarship to a rival school."[19]

Transferring to Allegheny Community College in Cumberland, Maryland, Kruk continued his development. "John was a serious threat on the base paths back then, and he played center field for us," recalled head coach Steve Bazarnic, the winningest active junior college baseball coach in the country, with nearly fourteen hundred career victories. "By the time he came here, he was a five-tool player who could hit for average, hit for power, field, throw, and steal bases." Allegheny boasted one of the best junior college baseball programs in the East, too. In the 1980s the school was allowed to compete in the fall season against such Division I programs as Penn State, West Virginia, and George Mason. Kruk's bat was right in the middle of Allegheny's success against those teams as well as in the twenty-five victories the Trojans recorded in the spring. "What made John such a special player," added Bazarnic, "was that aside from all his natural ability, he loved the game, worked hard, and was extremely coachable."[20]

Kruk's big break came in the summer of 1981. Hank Zacharias, a scout for the San Diego Padres, discovered him playing for New

Market in the Shenandoah Valley League. Impressed by Kruk's hitting, he convinced the Padres to select the West Virginian in the June 1981 amateur draft.[21]

Kruk began his professional career with Walla Walla of the Northwest Rookie League. In sixty-three games he hit .242, with just 1 home run, 13 RBI, and 7 stolen bases, but played a flawless center field, with a 1.000 fielding percentage. The following year in high-A ball at Reno of the California League, the West Virginian improved his batting average by 69 percentage points to .311, with 11 homers and 92 RBI, while also stealing 17 bases and fielding his position at a .972 clip. He also suffered a knee injury while sliding into second base to break up a double play. Forced to wear a knee brace for two weeks, Kruk put on more weight. When he reinjured the same knee the following season at Double-A Beaumont of the Texas League, Kruk's stolen-base numbers (13) began to decline, while his production at the plate increased (.341, 41 doubles, 9 triples, 10 HR, 88 RBI). By the time Kruk reached Triple-A Las Vegas of the Pacific Coast League, he weighed more than 200 pounds, which was 25 pounds above normal for someone who was five foot ten. Afterward, he would fight a continuous "battle of the bulge," since San Diego's front office expected him to weigh no more than 190 pounds. Still, Kruk continued to hit. In two full seasons at Las Vegas, he hit .340 and averaged 130 hits, 27 doubles, and 58 RBI per season.[22]

Promoted to the Padres in 1986, Kruk hit .309 as a part-time player. His breakout year came in 1987, when he hit .313 with 20 home runs and 91 RBI and stole 18 bases.[23] Krukker credits Larry Bowa, then Padres manager, for his success. When first baseman Steve Garvey, who was finishing up his career, got injured, Bowa, despite the wishes of the front office, made Kruk his everyday first baseman. "I liked playing for Bowa," Kruk admitted. "I knew if I screwed up, he was going to call me in and yell at me.

"Bowa thought I had potential, and he wanted me to live up to it. I just wasn't quite smart enough at the time to realize it. Instead, I was in his office getting yelled at so much, someone even put a sign with my name on it over the door. He was such a pain in the ass, but we never lost respect for each other."[24] Kruk also made

FIG. 9. Kruk, shown here in 1986, was a third-round pick of
the San Diego Padres. But his irreverent sense of humor and
pudgy physique were not appreciated there, and he was traded
to Philadelphia in 1989. National Baseball Hall of
Fame Library, Cooperstown, New York.

the record books that season. On April 13, 1987, he, Tony Gwynn, and Marvell Wynne—all left-handers—became the first players in Major League history to open a game with three consecutive solo home runs in a 13–6 win over the San Francisco Giants.[25] The West Virginia outfielder made the news for another, less admirable, reason later that year.

In October 1987 John rented a house in San Diego with Roy

Plummer, a high school friend, and Jay Hafer, an acquaintance of Plummer's. The three men socialized and partied together, with Plummer almost always picking up the check. Unknown to Kruk, who moved out in November to play winter ball in Mexico, Plummer was funding the group's lifestyle by moonlighting as an armed robber, with Hafer serving as his getaway driver. The Federal Bureau of Investigation informed Kruk of his roommates' criminal activities during spring training in February 1988. According to the FBI, Plummer believed that John had turned him in to the police. The ongoing stress of a potential reprisal affected Krukker's playing performance that season, as his batting average slipped to .241, a dramatic 72 percentage point drop from the previous season. Kruk lived in fear until Plummer was apprehended on September 19, 1988.[26] But the damage was done.

Kruk started out the 1989 campaign poorly, hitting just .184 in 76 at bats. Together with Kruk's mediocre performance of the previous season, the Padres became convinced that he had no future in the organization. Bowa was no longer manager, having been replaced the previous season by Jack McKeon, who also served as the club's general manager. Since Kruk and "Trader Jack" McKeon did not get along, the outfielder became expendable. On June 2, 1989, Kruk was dealt to the Phillies with infielder Randy Ready for outfielder Chris James.[27] "I was glad to get out," he admitted later. "I thought management treated us like kids. I didn't like that they didn't let us have a beer in the clubhouse. I didn't like the way I was being used. I didn't like McKeon, but the one thing he did for me was to trade me. He gave me the opportunity to go to Philadelphia, and I'll always appreciate that."[28]

Reunited with Bowa, who had signed on as Philadelphia's third base coach, Kruk became the Phillies' starting left fielder. He began to hit and never stopped, recording batting averages of .331 in 1989 and .291 in 1990.[29] He was also embraced by teammates and fans, who came to appreciate his act as a West Virginia hillbilly.

In 1991 Krukker was on the verge of making big money as a free agent, but he refused to pressure the front office about a new contract. Instead, he remained noncommittal when the press began asking him about is future. "The Phillies pay me to play baseball, and if they don't want me, they have that option," he said. "I'll go somewhere else. Whatever they want to do is fine with me. If they want to talk during the season or after, it doesn't matter. That's not up to me, that's up to the front office. I don't pressure people."[30] In private, however, Kruk wanted to return to the Phillies. "I sure wanted to stay in Philly," he said in a 2001 interview. "I knew if we got everybody healthy, we could have a good team, and I really liked the clubhouse. I remember telling Lee Thomas in spring training that I wanted to stay. I just didn't want to go through all the hassles with the media constantly asking me questions about it. I wanted to get it done real quiet."[31]

In May, after Daulton and Dykstra were nearly killed in the car crash, Kruk realized just how much he loved his teammates and became determined to re-sign with the Phillies. Dykstra, on the other hand, remained unfazed by the incident or the injuries he sustained.

After the accident the two teammates were rushed to Bryn Mawr Hospital. According to a hospital supervisor, Daulton was a "perfect gentleman, who cooperated with all of us," but Dykstra was a "different story." "In the emergency room, his behavior was abusive," said the supervisor. "He cursed at doctors, spit on a nurse and punched hospital equipment." Only when his patient-care manager informed him that he was "under a lot of scrutiny" did the outfielder's behavior "improve significantly."[32]

When he was released from the hospital, Dykstra, having been placed on the sixty-day disabled list, completed a brief rehab assignment in the Minors and returned to the Phillies' lineup in August. He also resumed his late-night carousing and boorish behavior. Two weeks later he crashed into the unpadded outfield wall at Cincinnati's Riverfront Stadium, reinjuring his collarbone, and was out for the remainder of the season.[33] There was no remorse. Nails was going to live by *his* rules, and damn the consequences. According to teammate Tommy Herr, "Lenny didn't pay attention to man's law or to God's law. He did things his way."[34]

Once, the Phillies invited U.S. surgeon general Dr. Antonia

Novello to spring training to do a presentation on the dangers of chewing tobacco, one of Dykstra's obsessions. Nor was he alone. The Phillies were one of the "smokingist, chewingest clubs in baseball," according to Bill Conlin of the *Philadelphia Daily News*. After the thirty-minute presentation, Novello handed each player a package of bubble gum, a healthier alternative to the tobacco. Before the game Nails took the gum, wrapped it around a plug of chewing tobacco, and shoved it into his mouth.[35]

Lenny Dykstra was "macho." Excessively proud, he carried himself with a cockiness that exuded arrogance. He continued to dope in order to build muscle mass. He strutted when he walked, as if daring anyone to challenge him. Even his nickname—"Nails"—projected male toughness. But Dykstra's indulgent lifestyle exceeded the boundaries that even some of his other macho teammates were willing to accept. He genuinely believed, for example, that his status as a successful professional athlete entitled him to ignore baseball commissioner Fay Vincent's edicts; to engage in high-stakes gambling, excessive drinking, and promiscuous behavior; and to be excused for those indiscretions.

According to Phillies president Bill Giles, Dykstra "played the game the same way he lived." "Lenny was the kind of guy who took a lot of risks," said Giles in a 2009 interview. "On the field that approach helped us win. But he did the same thing off the field—womanizing, drinking, and gambling. Lenny was like Pete Rose in that he wasn't afraid of anything. Both of them also believed they were above the law."[36] While Dykstra's "no-holds-barred" playing style benefited the Phillies, his reckless off-field behavior didn't help him or the team. Sooner or later, it would catch up with him. In fact, by 1991 there were indications that Dykstra's gambling was spiraling out of control.

"Once, in Atlantic City, I saw Lenny lose $50,000 in twenty minutes on black jack," recalled Kirk Radomski, the Mets' clubhouse attendant who remained friends with Dykstra after his trade to Philadelphia. "On another trip to the casinos, I saw him lose $200,000 in a few hours. Then he got markers for another $150,000, and blew through that in no time." On both occasions Dykstra "got angry" and began "cursing, screaming, spitting tobacco juice on the floor and kicking the table." But the casino "put up with it" because he was a "bad gambler" who would "lose a lot of money."[37] Commissioner Fay Vincent heard rumors of Dykstra's high-stakes gambling and sent John Dowd, his special counsel, to investigate. When Dowd reported that the Phillies' center fielder was "running up some big poker debts" but "was not involved in betting on baseball," Vincent decided to meet with Dykstra out of a genuine concern for his welfare. He knew that Lenny was a candid individual and believed that he could deliver the point more forcefully if they met privately in an informal setting rather than at a formal hearing in his office. Dykstra agreed and declined the players' association's offer to have an attorney present at the meeting.[38]

In March 1991 Vincent traveled to Clearwater, Florida, to meet with Dykstra at the Phillies' spring-training facility. Phoning ahead, Vincent asked Lenny, "I don't want to make a big deal out of this, so can we meet and talk at the ballpark before a game?"

"Whatever you want," replied Dykstra.

When Vincent arrived at Jack Russell Stadium, he asked to meet privately, and Nails ushered him into a nearby men's room.

Before beginning his inquiry, Vincent asked, "Do you want a union lawyer present?"

"I don't need anybody but me," he said. "I'm happy to talk with you alone."

"Are you sure?" asked the commissioner.

"I don't need the union involved," said Dykstra. "This has nothing to do with that."

"Okay," said Vincent, "let me get right to the point."

Both men were surprisingly comfortable with each other, having established a degree of trust. It was exactly what Vincent had hoped would happen.

"Lenny, look, I know you've been making big-time poker bets and losing," he began. "You haven't violated any baseball rule, but what you're doing is not smart and I'm worried about you."

"I'm worried about you, too," Dykstra replied matter-of-factly.

Surprised, Vincent asked: "Why me?"

"I saw what you did to [Pete] Rose [for gambling on baseball],"
said Lenny. "You threw him out of the game. I'm scared because
I do *not* want that to happen to me. The reason I don't want the
union here is because I'll tell you anything you want to know. I
want to cooperate."

The commissioner was relieved. His plan was working. "I'm not
going to throw you out of baseball," he said. "But I do want to you
to stop running up poker debts. You're putting yourself in a very
vulnerable position. If you start owing any serious money to professional gamblers, they will ask you to do all kinds of things that I
don't want you to do. I'm sure you can see the risks involved there."

Before Vincent could complete the sentence, Dykstra assured
him that "you won't have to worry about me." "I'll do just what
you say. Nothing is going to get in the way of me playing baseball."

Satisfied with the response, the commissioner placed the outfielder on a year's probation and monitored his activities. Dykstra
proved true to his word, at least during his probation.[39]

Gambling was not Lenny's only problem, either.

Doping had also become an addiction. According to Kirk Radom-
ski, who supplied Dykstra with steroids and monitored his use,
"Lenny and I would meet whenever the Phillies came to New York.
We'd have lunch, or I'd go to the ballpark and we'd sit and talk, and
I'd make sure he was following up on everything.

"I explained what I was giving him, how to inject it and how
long to cycle (i.e., for a period of 4–6 weeks the user is actually
taking steroids, which should alternate with a similar period of
time off). I sold him two cycles, and I explained step-by-step how
to break them up into weekly doses. But I also emphasized that if
he wanted to get the best results, he had to continue weight lifting."[40] Dykstra's remarkable success in 1990, when he hit .325, with
192 hits, 89 walks, and 106 runs scored, gave Radomski credibility.
Nails continued to learn as much as he could about doping from
him. "The problem with Lenny," said Radomski, "was that he lived
life with the same intensity that he played baseball. For him, too
much was never enough. If a candle had three ends, Lenny would
burn all three of them. Between the steroids, the amphetamines

and the alcohol, he was a walking pharmacy. Lenny was the ultimate wild man."[41]

Dykstra squeezed all he could from his ability because he believed that he had "a short window of opportunity" and that he "needed to take advantage of it." "When my body's done," he said, "it's done."[42] In fact, Nails was so desperate to capitalize on that "short window of opportunity" that in addition to Radomski, he enlisted the help of Jeff Scott, a Florida bodybuilder.

During spring training in 1991, Dykstra met Scott at a Clearwater strip club and joked about the bodybuilder's bulging physique. Shortly after, Dykstra began consulting Scott on how to cycle and on what kinds of steroids to use. Scott was more accessible than Radomski, thus more valuable. Over the next eight years Lenny paid the bodybuilder $20,000 plus "special perks" to help him "bulk up." In return, Scott enabled Nails to prolong his career, pad his statistics, and, ultimately, to score a multimillion-dollar contract from the Phillies.[43]

Dykstra believed that his steroid use allowed him to "keep his weight up" and eliminated the need for "heavy workouts during the season." There was more to it than that, though. For Nails, doping was not just a matter of conserving energy, maximizing his playing ability, padding his personal statistics, or even the ego gratification that accompanied those things. "You gotta understand, there were only twenty-eight people who had my job in the whole world," he told Randall Lane, author of *The Zeroes: My Misadventures in the Decade Wall Street Went Insane*, in 2008, referring to the fact that in the early 1990s, there were only twenty-eight Major League Baseball teams and that each had only one starting center fielder. "Thousands of people wanted those jobs, and every year there were guys trying to take my job. So I needed to do anything I could to protect my job, take care of my family. Do you have any idea how much money was at stake?"[44]

"Financial security" was one of the primary reasons a Major Leaguer used PEDs. Increased production allowed marginal players to remain in the Majors and talented ones to obtain the multimillion-dollar contract that guaranteed a generous income for the rest of their lives. Besides, the risks were believed to be minimal in the early to mid-1990s. Few ballplayers, for example, knew about the immediate or long-term dangers doping presented to their health. Severe mood swings, rage, depression, suicidal tendencies, tendon and ligament tears, kidney and liver damage, impotence, heart disease, and cancer—all the health risks now associated with PEDs—had not been identified by researchers until the 2000s. Even then, those risks were often associated with megadoses of PEDs.[45]

What's more, Major League Baseball had no testing policy for anabolic steroids in place until 2003. Prior to that there was a very weak policy, which focused mainly on recreational drug use, so players could use PEDs without fear of getting caught. In fact, the owners and the players' union dragged their feet in negotiating a stronger drug policy because the offensive explosion that accompanied doping generated huge television revenues as well as exorbitant player salaries. Accordingly, the use of anabolic steroids, human growth hormone, and even steroid precursors like androstenedione and creatine, whose effects resembled those of steroids, were perfectly legal in baseball.[46]

Regardless of the steroid issue—or perhaps because of it—the Phillies' fortunes seemed to be finally changing for the better in 1991. After a 4-9 start, Nick Leyva was fired, and Jim Fregosi became the Phils' new manager. The team responded, pulling within three games of the .500 mark by the first week of May. With the loss of Dykstra and Daulton, the Phils fought even harder, going 5-4 on their first West Coast trip and 7-4 overall to get back to the .500 mark.[47] On May 23 Tommy Greene pitched a no-hitter against the Montreal Expos at Olympic Stadium, striking out ten hitters in the 2–0 shutout. It was his first complete game of the season, and it came in just his second start. Greene shut the Expos out again in his next start. He would extend his scoreless-inning streak to twenty-nine consecutive innings, finishing among the league's leaders in that category.[48]

In early June the Phils went into a tailspin, losing eight of eleven to fall out of the race. Dave Hollins, acquired by Thomas in the Rule Five draft the previous year, was recalled from Triple-A Scranton

Wilkes-Barre to provide some offensive punch. The Buffalo, New York, native didn't disappoint, either. Playing third base, Hollins hit .388 in July and led the team in homers and RBI that month. In August Mitch Williams, acquired from the Chicago Cubs on April 7, tied a National League record by winning eight games. Together with the five saves he recorded that month, Williams, the new closer, was instrumental in a thirteen-game winning streak the team rode into early August. By season's end he sported a 12-5 record with a 2.34 ERA and 30 saves. Although the Phils suffered a brief slump, they won eleven of their final eighteen games to finish in third place.[49]

Kruk had his best season ever in 1991. Not only did he lead the Phillies in runs (84), walks (67), triples (6), home runs (21), and RBI (92), but he also put together a fifteen-game hitting streak and was named to his first All-Star team. He also played as many different positions (first, left, center, and right) as he wore uniform numbers (11, 19, 28, 29) since arriving from San Diego in 1989. In fact, when asked what position he played at the midsummer classic, Kruk replied, "Hitter."[50]

The Phillies rewarded him with $1,125,000 raise, boosting his salary from $1,175,000 in 1991, to $2,300,000 for the 1992 season.[51] Kruk celebrated by purchasing a new house in Burlington, West Virginia. He also built an addition with a hot tub in the back of the house overlooking the rustic mountains of his native state. "Johnny and I were sitting in the hot tub that winter," recalled his boyhood friend Rick Rotruck. "It was deer season, and I saw a white-tail buck grazing in the backyard. Johnny got out of the tub, put on a pair of cowboy boots, found his gun, and went outside.

"It's freezing and he's dripping wet in just those cowboy boots. Well, he poked his head around the corner of the house, put the gun on his shoulder, and dropped the buck. Then he came back in, shivering, got back in the tub, and asked me, 'Now, who can we call to clean him?'"[52]

When his old Potomac State baseball coach, Jack Reynolds, heard the story, he chuckled and said, "That sounds like Johnny." "But to come out of a small town like Keyser, West Virginia, and make it to the Major Leagues and bat .300 in a ten-year career," he added, "well, that's pretty remarkable."[53]

What's more exceptional, however, is that despite his success and the wealth that accompanied it, the Krukker never forgot where he came from. He remained a small-town boy with a strong set of values, a kind heart, and a deep and abiding passion for baseball.

SIX

Fourth Estate

The year 1991 was a rare season for the Phillies. Although they didn't compile a winning record, their third-place finish was the highest since 1986 when they completed the season in second, twenty-one and a half games behind the New York Mets. The last time the Phils enjoyed a winning season was 1983, when they defeated the Los Angeles Dodgers in the National League Championship Series, three games to one, to capture the pennant.[1] Since then the team was a perennial loser. The only thing worse was reading about their pathetic performance in Philadelphia's newspapers every day.

For more than a generation, the city's sportswriters worked hard to earn—and to maintain—a well-deserved reputation for intrusive questioning and colorful reporting. Like the "Fourth Estate," many of the writers saw themselves as the shapers of public opinion when it came to professional sports and reveled in the controversy they created in the process.[2] Sometimes their behavior violated baseball's Code. Historically, newspapers and teams maintained a level of trust in their reciprocal influence on each other. The newspapers relied upon managers, coaches, and players for accurate and sometimes privileged information that might deal with an impending trade, the reasons for a player's release or a coach's firing, or troubled clubhouse dynamics. In return the team understood that the press was their direct conduit to the fans and relied on local newspapers for spinning a story to the club's advantage. The unspoken trust was reinforced by the Code, which requires beat writers to respect the clubhouse as the players' sanctuary and that "what is said and done in the clubhouse stays in the clubhouse." Nor should a writer *ever* report the private peccadilloes of the ballplayers. Sometimes, however, the temptation to do so is too great to ignore, especially when the beat writer has access to the clubhouse and travels with the team on road trips.[3] Although the Phillies and the press did not always enjoy a comfortable relationship when the club was losing, the beat writers tended to be more respectful of the Code when the team was winning.

In the 1990s there were only two daily newspapers in the city that covered the Phillies: the *Inquirer* and the *Daily News*. The *Inquirer*, published by Knight Ridder, was the least offensive in its coverage. Having won seventeen Pulitzer Prizes in the last eighteen years, the paper, which still maintains a liberal slant, was at the end of a golden era but continued to enjoy the largest circulation and staff of any newspaper in southeastern Pennsylvania. Under the leadership of executive editor Max King, the *Inquirer* was Knight Ridder's most profitable enterprise and the most influential paper in the region. Sports editor David Tucker maintained the same standards of professionalism emphasized by King, but also encouraged his writers to be more entertaining in their reporting. Jayson Stark had been the Phillies' beat writer since 1979, and Frank Dolson was the paper's regular baseball columnist. Both writers offered readers a healthy mix of history, analysis, and human interest. Frank Fitzpatrick, who came to the *Inquirer* in 1980 as a sports editor, was more daring when he became the beat writer in 1992.[4]

Fitzpatrick was ideal for the job at a time when sports journalism was rapidly changing. As a former editor he realized that the days of objective reporting were over. Readers wanted to know about the personalities of the players, their off-field antics, and clubhouse dynamics. At the same time Fitzpatrick knew that his responsibility as a beat writer was to focus on the events of the game and the players' on-field performance. "It was a compromise," he admitted in a recent interview. "I was more interested in the human side of the game. How the players interacted in the club-house, who they were as people, how they viewed the fans. I had access to that knowledge—the readers didn't—and it was every bit as important to me as the game summary." Generally, Fitzpatrick enjoyed a good working relationship with the Phillies. Team president Bill Giles would occasionally voice his displeasure when the beat writer described the team's performance as "dreary" or "dismal," but he never held a grudge. Nor did general manager Lee Thomas, though he didn't always appreciate some of Fitzpatrick's "tongue-in-cheek" humor. Still, Thomas would air his grievance, and "it'd be over." Manager Jim Fregosi was not as tolerant.

When Fitzpatrick began covering the Phillies in 1992, Fregosi regarded him as a "student." "Fregosi loved to pontificate," said the sportswriter. "He was going to show the beat writers how [to cover] his team." In early April Fitzpatrick interviewed utility infielder Wally Backman, who revealed that there was a divide in the clubhouse between the pitchers and some of the hitters. When Fitzpatrick used the remark as an explanation for why the Phils got off to such a poor start, Fregosi called him into his office to reprimand him. "He insisted that I was 'off the mark' and that if I wanted to find out about the clubhouse, I should talk to him and no one else," recalled the beat writer. "After that he was very careful about what he said to me. Fregosi could hold a grudge."[5]

Philadelphia's other newspaper, the *Daily News*, was a satellite of the *Inquirer* and was largely responsible for the infamous reputation of the local press. The *Daily News* was a sassy tabloid that made very little effort to cover national or international news other than what was made available by the wire service. Instead, the paper promoted itself as the "people's paper," catering to blue-collar workers, and concentrated on stories of local human interest with a strong emphasis on the city's professional sports teams. Often accused of sensationalizing the news, the paper's sportswriters tended to make ballplayers flashier—and often more controversial—personalities than they really were. Stan Hochman and Bill Conlin introduced the contentious style when they began writing for the tabloid in the 1960s.

Known as "chipmunks," Hochman and Conlin represented a new

breed of aggressive young sportswriters who went beyond the statistics and narrative description of the game to focus on the players' personalities and clubhouse controversy.[6] Hochman, the first of the two to cover the Phillies beat, was forced to adapt to television coverage, which eliminated the need to rehash the events of the game. Instead, he resorted to intrusive questioning in postgame interviews and scrutinizing the performances as well as the lifestyles of the players. His critical coverage of the Phillies and pointed commentary on racial issues were watersheds in local sportswriting from the earlier days when the beat writer could sit in the press box and wax eloquent about the game. Still, Hochman was respected by the players because of his voluminous knowledge of the sport and his perseverance in getting a story. Still, his provocative writing was mild by today's standards. Conlin, who assumed the Phillies beat in 1966, took the *Daily News*' baseball coverage to a new, more antagonistic level.

For Conlin, the outcome of the game was an afterthought. Instead, he focused on behind-the-scenes stories, lively opinion writing, and humorous barbs revealing the human frailties of the ballplayers. He savored controversy and often produced his own by re-creating profane locker-room conversations through typographical euphemisms like "fluffing" and "cough-sufferer." At six foot three and, for most of his career, more than three hundred pounds, Conlin refused to back down from anyone who challenged him, whether it was a ballplayer, manager, or even the owner of the club himself. Not surprisingly, the Phillies' brain trust considered him a "bully."[7]

"Bill's not afraid of controversy," said *Daily News* sports editor Mike Rathet in the mid-1980s. "I can count on him to stir the fur. If there's a hot issue, a lot of readers want to see what Conlin's take on it will be. He's my cleanup hitter."[8] Some national sportswriters considered him the "poet laureate" of the *Daily News* sports section because of his familiarity with good literature.[9] Conlin possessed an exceptional ability to integrate Shakespearean quotations and references from writers as varied as Hemingway, Dostoyevsky, and Tolkien into his writing. That talent would earn him the J. G. Taylor Spink Award, an honor bestowed by the

Baseball Writers' Association of America annually to a writer "for meritorious contributions to baseball writing," shortly before his death in 2011.[10]

By 1987, however, Conlin, who refused to speak with then manager John Felske, had worn out his welcome in the Phillies' clubhouse. As a result, the *Daily News* was forced to find another beat writer. The tabloid hired Paul Hagen of the *Fort Worth (TX) Star-Telegram*, who covered the Texas Rangers.[11] Although Conlin continued to antagonize the Phillies as a columnist, Hagen was a breath of fresh air for the team. He was a ballplayer's writer—fair, concise, and one who possessed a good, sound knowledge of the game. "I was excited to go to Philadelphia," he admitted in a recent interview. "I wanted to cover baseball in a market that mattered, and I felt like Phillies fans would be interested in what I was writing. It wasn't like Texas, where people lost interest in the Rangers once the [Dallas] Cowboys opened training camp."[12]

Hagen's writing style evolved during the late 1980s and early 1990s. While he continued to be fair and balanced in his coverage, he realized that the tabloid distinguished itself from the *Inquirer* with a more colorful style of writing than he had been accustomed to in Texas. Sports editor Mike Rathet encouraged the approach, giving Hagen more free rein than he ever enjoyed before. The new beat writer also benefited from *not* being Bill Conlin. The players trusted Hagen and welcomed him into their clubhouse. If he found himself in trouble for something he wrote, it was usually unintentional. Once, on May 24, 1990, for example, Hagen reported that Darren Daulton was in a hitting slump because "in a five day span, he flew from Philadelphia to Tampa to Houston to Tampa to Philadelphia." In fact, Daulton's pregnant wife, Lynne, was running him ragged. She demanded that he return home to Safety Harbor, Florida, near Tampa, on off days in case she gave birth. Hagen was too discreet to write something like that. But when the *Daily News* ran the piece, shortly after the couple's first child was born, the editor added the headline, "Wife Delivers, He Hasn't. Now Daulton Can Focus on Hitting."[13] Dutch was furious when he saw the headline.

FIG. 10. Dykstra, a media hound who knew how to handle the press,
had the Philadelphia sportswriters hanging on his every word.
Photo by Al Tielemans.

"When I walked into the clubhouse to explain what happened,
Darren got in my face and gave it to me good," said Hagen. "I
couldn't get a word in edgewise. He went on for a good ten minutes, threatening to cut me off from any more interviews. Finally,
Lenny Dykstra, a real media hound who knew how newspapers
operated, interrupted and explained to him that the editor writes
the headlines, not the beat writer. Then Darren calmed down."[14]

The *Inquirer* and *Daily News* weren't the only media outlets that
covered the Phillies, either. Beginning in 1987 the beat writers
were forced to compete with 610 WIP Sports Radio and their various hosts, who sensationalized the news. With the help of a steady
stream of former *Inquirer* sportswriters and veteran broadcasters,
the radio station was the sole landing spot for sports fans seeking
immediate news and information about their favorite teams. Originally, the hosts engaged callers with serious sports discussions,
but they were gradually replaced by others such as Howard Eskin

and Angelo Cataldi who were more like fans than experts. Station manager Tom Bigby was responsible for the change, believing that "sports talk alone won't survive," but if you did "sports entertainment, the possibilities are endless," because "you're reaching younger demographics."[15] Eskin, once a pudgy kid from Northeast Philadelphia, made his infamous reputation by breaking stories on his afternoon radio show and for stirring public opinion with his abrasive commentaries. Disapproving colleagues considered him boorish and self-serving. They called him a "jock sniffer" with ethical blinders to athletes with whom he cultivated personal friendships. "He drives the whole city nuts," said Pat Croce, a fitness guru and former president of the Philadelphia 76ers. "It's like having a toothache. You keep checking with your tongue to see if it's still there." Unlike many of his contemporaries in radio, television, and the press, however, Eskin worked harder, often putting in eighteen-hour days, and actually attended the games he talked about. "Whether you like him or hate him, people on both sides have come to respect his work ethic over the years and the fact that he is dogged," said Stephan Rosenfeld, former news director at KYW-TV, who later hired Eskin to do television sports.[16]

Angelo Cataldi, a former *Inquirer* writer, was another of the new breed of sports radio personalities. Cataldi, whose mantra was "entertainment first, sports second," immediately brought a comedic and witty personality to WIP. During his morning radio show, he engaged callers with extended periods of "guy talk," where the conversation focused on women, sex, and locker-room humor. Accordingly, Cataldi, along with cohost Al Morganti, established the annual "Wing Bowl" competition, where thousands of people crowded into South Philadelphia's Comcast Center to see which contestant could eat the greatest number of buffalo wings within a certain time period, while a bevy of semiattractive, scantily clad women paraded through the arena. Cataldi was also good at stirring controversy. He was known to mobilize his listeners against the owners of the city's sports franchises in order to effect changes in management and personnel. Jealous of Eskin, he waged a longstanding feud with him, ripping the afternoon host at every possible opportunity. But Cataldi also had a good heart. The proceeds from Wing Bowl as well as from another annual beauty contest he founded went to charity. Cataldi was also known to stuff ballot boxes during fan voting for the All-Star team so that deserving Phillies could appear in the midsummer classic.[17]

None of that, however, stopped Fregosi from voicing his opinion that "the only people who listen to WIP are men from South Philly who screw their sisters" and that those who work at the station "are just like the men from South Philly." Unfortunately for the Phillies' manager, Frank Fitzpatrick used a tape recorder to take notes and verified the remark when Howard Eskin later asked him about it. Eskin repeated Fregosi's statement on his radio show. After being excoriated by WIP's hosts on air as well as by the fans, the Phillies' skipper apologized for the remark, insisting that it did not "reflect [his] true feelings about the fans" and admitted that he was "embarrassed" by it. But when Fregosi added that he "didn't think he had to be careful in what I say in my own office," it was clear that he was sorrier that he got caught.

"Fregosi had an unwritten rule," recalled Fitzpatrick. "When the writers were in his office, everything was off the record until we took our notepads out and started writing. But I wasn't too good at shorthand, so I used a tape recorder and just left it running. Of course, Fregosi figured out how Eskin heard about his disparaging remark, and he just tore in to me. Even before that incident, it was clear to all the beat writers that he hated WIP because of the sarcastic remarks he made about the hosts. But after Eskin reported the remark, Fregosi was extremely careful about what he said when he knew he was being taped."[18]

To be sure, Jim Fregosi had strong opinions and was almost always in control of the conversation, whether it was in a meeting with an individual player or a press conference. His ego was so large that it became one of his nicknames: "Ego," instead of "Frego." The inflated confidence came from his playing days when he made six All-Star teams before the age of twenty-nine. An outstanding shortstop with the California Angels in the 1960s, Fregosi played eighteen seasons in the big leagues with the Angels, New York Mets, and Pittsburgh

JIM FREGOSI

FIG. 11. Jim Fregosi, a baseball lifer who made six All-Star
teams as a player, managed the California Angels (1979–82)
and Chicago White Sox (1986–88) before arriving in
Philadelphia. He was a players' manager who favored veterans
and the platoon system. Photo by Al Tielemans.

Pirates. He ended his playing career on June 1, 1978, and was hired
the very next day to manage the Angels, whom he led to the American League's Western Division title the following year. Fregosi also
managed the Chicago White Sox between 1986 and 1988 before
joining the Phillies as a special-assignments assistant for his former
Angels teammate Lee Thomas.[19] When Thomas chose him to replace
Nick Leyva as Phillies manager on April 23, 1991, Fregosi admit-

ted that he had "learned patience and gained experience" from his previous managerial stints and that he was "fortunate to have the opportunity to use that knowledge with the Phillies."[20]

Fregosi was better suited to managing a veteran team than a group of youngsters. He wanted the players to police themselves, to find their own leader, and to mentor the rookies. At the same time, Fregosi was highly regarded by players for his biting honesty, dedication to the game, and unwavering loyalty. He trusted his players to do their jobs, a quality that instilled confidence in them. "He had that special gift as a manager that made you want to get to the field and play your ass off for him," said Lenny Dykstra.[21] With the press Fregosi could be entertaining, regaling them with stories from his playing days, or he could be brutally honest, if not patronizing. Once, he was forced to start a journeyman pitcher, Mickey Weston, against the Montreal Expos. He was hit so hard that Fregosi lifted him in the second inning. In the postgame press conference the Phils' skipper was asked, "What was Weston's biggest problem?" "Too much contact," he deadpanned.[22]

After the Phillies' third-place finish in 1991, Fregosi was optimistic about the team's chances in 1992. In fact, he felt so good about himself and the Phillies that he decided to quit smoking, a lifelong vice. When he arrived at spring training in 1992, the Phils' manager announced that he had kicked the habit. Not once did he touch a cigarette during the team's six weeks in Clearwater. Then the team flew north for opening day.

On Tuesday, April 7, more than sixty thousand fans flocked to Veterans Stadium to watch the hometown Phillies open their season against the Chicago Cubs. The players looked resplendent in their new pinstriped uniforms, sporting a fire-engine-red script *Phillies* on the front with blue stars dotting the i. During his first at bat of the new season, Lenny Dykstra led off against Chicago's Greg Maddux in the bottom of the first inning. After a called first strike, Maddux threw inside to back the center fielder off the plate. The pitch hit Dykstra, fracturing his left wrist, and the Phillies went on to lose the home opener, 4–3.[23] Within the next few weeks Dale Murphy, Tommy Greene, and José DeJesús also went on the disabled list with injuries, and the ashtray in Fregosi's office revealed that he was chain-smoking again.[24]

The Phillies quickly fell to last place, where they remained for most of the season. They also set a club record for placing a total of seventeen players on the disabled list. Fregosi spent the season trying to find the right combination in his lineup. In the process he used forty-eight different players, nineteen of whom were rookies. But the team never jelled, finishing in the basement with a 70-92 record. Still, there were signs that positive things were beginning to happen.

Daulton, fully healthy for the first time in years, enjoyed a career year and became an All-Star for the first time. Dutch played in a career-high 145 games, hitting .270 with 27 homers, and had a .385 on-base percentage. He also led the National League with 109 RBI, joining Hall of Famers Roy Campanella, Johnny Bench, and Gary Carter as only the fourth catcher to achieve that feat. The exceptional performance earned him a Silver Slugger Award and a sixth-place finish for the NL's Most Valuable Player Award.[25] Once scorned as an "overpaid bum," Daulton emerged as the team's leader and a fan favorite. "It's nice to be cheered, and not booed," he admitted. "I've taken the brunt of jeering over the past few years, but I understand the fans better now. Philly is a blue collar town. They see what an athlete is earning, so they expect him to be good all the time. The problem is, they don't know if a guy is hurting. I've always given 100% when I've played, even when I was hurting. Now that I'm healthy, maybe I'm the player they expect me to be."[26]

In retrospect, Daulton's remarkable offensive production, his ability to sustain good health throughout the season, and his chiseled physique, as well as his close relationship with Lenny Dykstra, made him vulnerable to charges of steroid use by at least two sportswriters after his career ended.[27] PEDS increase the muscle mass and quick-twitch reflexes needed to produce the kind of power-hitting statistics the Phillies' catcher compiled in 1992. Considering that Dutch never hit more than 12 home runs and 57 RBI in a Major League season before that year, it's tempting to attribute the sudden offensive surge to steroid use.[28] Another side effect of PEDS is increased recovery time from fatigue and injury. Prior to

1992 Daulton, who battled through multiple knee surgeries, a fractured right clavicle, a broken right hand, an incomplete tear of the rotator cuff, and a broken eye socket, had spent more time on the disabled list than he did on the playing field in a checkered seven-year Major League career.[29] But in 1992 he played in 145 of 162 games without a single stint on the disabled list.[30] For a catcher with an injury-riddled career, that is an extremely difficult thing to do because of the punishing physical demands of the position.

It is just as tempting to believe the allegations of Daulton's steroid use when the catcher's highly sculpted body is considered. Dutch, the object of many a female's fantasies, gave the appearance of a Greek god when he removed his shirt. It takes a lot of hard work to maintain a physique like that. Daulton spent many hours lifting in the weight room with Dykstra, six days a week for two and a half hours each day, to build that kind of muscle. Such feverish weight training is not unusual for a bodybuilder. In fact, the vast majority of PED users are not athletes but bodybuilders primarily focused on personal appearance. They simply want to look leaner and more muscular. Thus, "lean mass builders," like Winstrol, are the most frequently used steroids among bodybuilders. Generally, these are anabolic drugs, a man-made synthetic derivative of the male sex hormone testosterone. Not only do these drugs increase muscle mass and reduce fat mass, but they also provide the endurance for grueling weight-training sessions.[31] For all these reasons, Daulton was vulnerable to allegations of steroid use. But there are other, more palpable, factors for his success as well.

Near the end of a miserable 1991 season, Daulton, who hit an anemic .196, was challenged by Phillies manager Jim Fregosi. Fregosi pinch-hit Ricky Jordan for the catcher late in games. After one particular benching Daulton stormed into the manager's office and told him that he was tired of being pulled in clutch situations.

"You want to stay in the game?" Fregosi asked. "You want to be a leader on this team?"

Stunned by the question, Daulton stood there with his mouth open. Wasn't it obvious that he was a leader? That he should expect to hit in clutch situations?

"Well, you have a lot of work to do," added Fregosi. "You know all those long 'home runs' you hit that go foul? Well, they don't count!"[32]

Fregosi had challenged his pride, and Dutch was determined to prove that he could be the team leader, both at the plate and behind it.

That off-season the catcher embarked on an extensive weight-training program and worked regularly on his hitting with Denis Menke. When he reported to spring training in February 1992, Dutch was in the best shape of his career and was hitting the ball better than ever. Able to place weight on his left leg, Daulton hit for power and could also spray the entire field instead of pulling the ball to right, as he had done in the past. Lee Thomas was so impressed, he told *Daily News* beat writer Paul Hagen, "This may sound crazy, but I can't think of another catcher in baseball I'd trade [Daulton] for. I think he's capable of hitting .260 with 20 homers and 80 RBI. In fact, I think he *will* do that this season."[33] In the end Daulton exceeded his general manager's prediction. Thomas rewarded him with an $18.5 million contract, making Dutch the highest-paid catcher in baseball.[34]

Other veterans were also productive. John Kruk posted a career-high .323 batting average and joined Daulton on the National League All-Star team. Mitch Williams continued to be a dominant closer, saving 29 games, just 1 less than the previous season. Mariano Duncan, who came over from the Cincinnati Reds, was an invaluable defensive replacement and spot starter. In 142 games he split time between the infield and outfield and batted .267, with 50 RBI and 23 stolen bases. The Phils also had some exciting young prospects. Third baseman Dave Hollins slammed 27 homers and 93 RBI. Outfielder Wes Chamberlain, who hit .331 at Triple-A Scranton, was promoted to the Phillies in midseason and displayed some impressive power at the plate. Between June 18 and August 18, Chamberlain batted .290 in 51 games, including a grand slam against Montreal, before he sprained an ankle, ending his season.[35] Mickey Morandini provided solid defense at second base and made history on September 20 by turning an unassisted triple play in a game against the Pittsburgh Pirates.[36] But the most pleasant surprise was the emergence of twenty-five-year-old Curt Schilling as the ace of the pitching staff.

FIG. 12. Curt Schilling, shown here with the Houston
Astros in 1991, was a journeyman pitcher until he came to
Philadelphia in 1992. National Baseball Hall of Fame
Library, Cooperstown, New York.

Acquired from the Houston Astros for pitcher Jason Grimsley
on April 2, Schilling was an unremarkable reliever who had a reputation as a "flake." The Astros were only the most recent team that
had given up on him. Before that Schilling pitched for the Boston
Red Sox and Baltimore Orioles. Similarly, Grimsley had failed to
live up to his potential with the Phillies. On the surface the trade
seemed like an even deal, neither team getting the upper hand.

Schilling began the '92 season in the bullpen, where he made 16 appearances, walking 11 and striking out 29. Then on May 19 he was placed in the starting rotation against his old team the Astros. It was his first National League start, and the six-foot-four, 225-pound right-hander won, 4–3. Schilling went on to complete 10 of his 26 starts that season, hurling 4 shutouts and a string of 29 straight scoreless innings. Opposing hitters batted a league-low .201 against him. By season's end Schilling enjoyed a 14-11 record, 147 strikeouts, and a 2.35 earned run average for a last-place team. Schilling together with southpaw Terry Mulholland (13-11, 125 K, 3.81 ERA, and a league-leading 12 complete games) formed an impressive righty-lefty starting combination that could easily change the fortunes of the club.[37]

When asked how he was able to turn around his career with the Phillies, Schilling admitted that the death of his father in 1988 had deeply affected him. "I was wandering aimlessly at that point in my life," he explained years later.

> I'll admit that I was a flake in the sense that I didn't approach things like conditioning as seriously as I might've, but I always respected and loved the game. When I was traded to Philadelphia, there were people who helped me turn things around. Lenny Dykstra took me under his wing and taught me a proper approach to the game. Terry Mulholland taught me how to prepare myself mentally to become a starter and how to pitch deep into a game. And [Phils pitching coach] Johnny Podres made me realize that the only limits in my life were self-imposed. I was truly fortunate to have those people in my life when I went to the Phillies.[38]

Despite all the talent, Lee Thomas knew that he needed more veteran experience to compete in 1993. That was made clear to him by Daulton, Dykstra, Kruk, and Williams when he called them into his office at the end of the season to ask for their advice. "It was, shall we say, an 'open discussion,'" said Williams. "Lee had a player's mentality. He was a hard-nosed bulldog. That's what I respected about him. We told him that we just didn't have the players to win. Then he lost his temper, and I lost mine. We were screaming at each other until he finally agreed to pursue some of the free agents on the market."[39]

During the off-season Thomas signed the kind of hard-nosed old-school players who complemented his team's budding character. He made a run at top free-agent pitchers David Cone, Greg Swindell, Greg Maddux, and Doug Drabek as well as power hitters Joe Carter and Kirby Puckett. But when he failed to land any of those prize free agents, Thomas decided to split his limited financial resources to improve his outfield and pitching. He began with Pete Incaviglia, once a premier slugger with the Texas Rangers. Although "Inky" struggled in his first year in the National League with the Houston Astros, hitting just 11 home runs in 113 games, Thomas was convinced that the burly outfielder would rebound and offered him a two-year $1.05 million contract. Thomas planned to platoon Incaviglia in left field with Milt Thompson, an excellent defensive outfielder who had previously played for the Phillies in the mid- to late 1980s. After the St. Louis Cardinals bought out his $300,000 option, Thompson agreed to return to Philadelphia for $1.4 million. The signing allowed the Phillies to move Mariano Duncan to the infield, where he would split playing time at second base with Mickey Morandini, and at shortstop with two highly prized prospects, Kim Batiste and Kevin Stocker.

With the left-field platoon of Incaviglia and Thompson set, Thomas upgraded right field. He signed free agent Jim Eisenreich after Ruben Amaro Jr. failed to hit his weight, and aging veteran Dale Murphy was granted free agency to complete his career with the expansion Colorado Rockies. Once considered one of baseball's best pure hitters, Eisenreich, who suffered from Tourette's syndrome, was believed to be a declining player after six seasons in the American League with the Kansas City Royals. As a result, Thomas was able to sign him for just $675,000, roughly $1 million less than the Royals paid him the year before. "Eisey" would platoon right field with rookie Wes Chamberlain.

Thomas also strengthened the team's pitching by adding left-hander Danny Jackson from the Pittsburgh Pirates in a trade for two prospects. Like Eisenreich, Jackson's stock had declined since

1988 when he won 23 games for the Cincinnati Reds and finished second in the Cy Young balloting. Thomas viewed Jackson as a solid number-three starter behind Schilling and Mulholland.

Realizing that the bullpen was also in need of veteran experience, the Phils' general manager signed Larry Andersen, a right-hander, for just $700,000 and David West, a left-hander, for even less at $315,000. Both of the pitchers could be used either in middle relief or as setup men for closer Mitch Williams. Andersen became one of the more colorful personalities on the team. The forty-year-old veteran kept the clubhouse loose with a variety of self-deprecating pranks like spraying hair-in-a-can, a foamy dust solution, across his receding hairline. His "Shallow Thoughts for the Day" were also popular among teammates, including:

"Why do you drive on a parkway and park on a driveway?"

"Why is there an expiration date on sour cream?"

"Why do fans sing 'Take me out to the ballgame' if they're already there?"[40]

Beneath the comedic facade, however, Andersen was a fierce competitor. David West shared the same winning mind-set, while his laid-back disposition also complemented the team dynamic Thomas was cultivating.[41]

The signings were hardly headline news on the Philadelphia sports pages, but they did address the club's needs. The only thing that remained to be seen is if this latest band of throwbacks would be able to transform those who preceded them on the roster into a pennant contender. No doubt, the Fourth Estate would be waiting to find out.

SEVEN
Spring Training

When Jim Eisenreich reported to the Phillies' spring-training complex at Clearwater, Florida, in February, he did not know what to expect. Since age six he struggled with Tourette's syndrome, a nervous disorder that causes tics, or repetitive, involuntary movements, and verbal outbursts. Eisenreich was a loner growing up and the object of constant ridicule. Even after a successful high school and college baseball career, the social pressures were so enormous that Jim retreated into himself.

Drafted by the Minnesota Twins in 1980, Eisenreich made it to the big leagues two years later. Playing center field he hit .303 in his rookie season. But he was so embarrassed by his tics that there were games when he had to come off the field in the middle of an inning. Jim soldiered on for two more seasons, not knowing if his difficulties were physical or psychological. Frustrated and undiagnosed, he left baseball after the 1984 season.

Over the next two years Eisenreich underwent constant testing until doctors finally identified the disorder as Tourette's. Jim, now able to control the condition with medication, returned to baseball with the Kansas City Royals in 1987. He spent the next six seasons with the Royals as an outfielder, but never really felt at home on the team.[1] Although constant tics and eye blinking no longer plagued him, Jim was embarrassed by his condition. Accordingly,

FIG. 13. John Kruk was proud of his sizable girth. He once
told a woman who chastised him for his huge appetite, "I ain't
an athlete, lady. I'm a ballplayer!" Photo by Al Tielemans.

when he signed with the Phillies after the 1992 season, the outfielder feared that his new teammates wouldn't accept him.

Mustering the courage to walk into the Phillies' clubhouse, Eisenreich discovered a menagerie of colorful—and profane—characters.
"Fuck this," muttered Lenny Dykstra, chewing a plug of tobacco
and scrutinizing a recently delivered box of new batting gloves.
"How come these gloves don't have red triangles on 'em? Where the

fuck's [clubhouse manager] Frank [Coppenbarger]? I want gloves with those fuckin' red triangles! Send 'em back!"

At another end of the clubhouse Daulton was holding court before a gaggle of sportswriters when he noticed Kruk enter the room. "Hey you fat fuck! Why didn't you call me all winter?" he cried out in mock derision. Mitch Williams, a novice golfer with putter in hand, was working on his short game when he saw Pete Incaviglia come through the door. "Inky!" he screamed, greeting his former teammate from the Texas Rangers. "That's all we need, another greaser." After all the pleasantries were exchanged, Curt Schilling switched on his boom box, and the rhythmic beat of "Two Princes" by the Spin Doctors came blaring through the clubhouse. The soundtrack would become the team's unofficial theme song.

Eisenreich wasn't quite sure of what to make of all the craziness. After locating his locker he quietly emptied his travel bag, took a seat, and wondered what he had gotten himself into.

"Hey, you're that guy with the whatcha-ma-call-it!" said the Kruk-ker, now sitting buck naked in front of his locker and snapping his fingers in a futile attempt to remember the name of the disorder.

"Tourette's," replied Eisey.

"Yeah, that," said Kruk, taking a drag on his cigarette. "Wel-come to the fuckin' nuthouse. You're the most normal guy here!"[2]

Speechless, Eisenreich just sat quietly with his head down.

Kruk wouldn't let up, though. The next morning during stretch-ing exercises, he started in on the outfielder again.

"Look at that guy," said the burly first baseman. "He doesn't flinch. He looks like a serial killer, staring like he wants to mur-der one of us. He looks like [mass murderer] Jeffrey Dahmer at his trial, not blinking at all."

The other players immediately went silent. Everybody knew Eisenreich had Tourette's syndrome and waited nervously to see how he would respond. Then Eisey looked up and smiled. It was the first time in his career that he felt like part of the team. After that Kruk began calling him "Dahmer." Other teammates started to do the same. Once, on the bus ride back to Clearwater from an overnight trip, Pete Incaviglia said, "Hey, Dahmer, thanks for not eating me last night." Without missing a beat, Eisey replied, "You're welcome, Lunch."[3]

Soon Eisenreich was doling out the wisecracks just as much as his teammates, who refused to tiptoe around him. "I loved it," he recalled in a recent interview. "From spring training on, it was the most fun year I ever had in baseball. The characters on that team were so crazy that I really did feel as if I was the most normal one or, at least, one among many crazies."[4]

At first glance "craziness" appeared to be the only thing the 1993 Phillies had going for them. The dreadful last-place finish of the previous season killed the interest of many fans and with good reason. Most preseason polls picked the Phils to finish in fourth or fifth place in the National League's Eastern Division. "That's all right," said Daulton, after learning of the predictions. "We'll show you something. You guys are underestimating us badly. We have a good group of major league players now. That's something we didn't have last year. But now we have Eisenreich, Thompson and Incaviglia. These are good, established big league players. That's what we need."[5]

To be sure, Daulton had reason to be optimistic. The new acquisitions gave the Phillies a much-improved offense with a strong mix of right- and left-handed hitters in the middle of the batting order, something the team lacked the previous year. Just as important, the addition of starter Danny Jackson and relievers Larry Andersen and David West gave some much-needed veteran experience to the pitching staff. Manager Jim Fregosi had also assembled an excellent coaching staff, and like his players he gave each one a specific role. Larry Bowa, the fiery shortstop of the 1980 world championship club, was the third base coach and base-running instructor. Bowa had managed in the San Diego Padres organization in the mid-1980s and returned to the Phillies as a coach in 1988. He was given a lot of latitude by Fregosi, who often relied on him to give the younger ballplayers a reality check.

John Vukovich, another member of the 1980 world champions, was Fregosi's dugout assistant and the team's defensive specialist. "Vuke" had already been a first and third base coach with the Chi-

FIG. 14. Johnny Podres, the Phillies' pitching coach, was
best remembered for hurling a shutout against the New York
Yankees in Game Seven of the 1955 World Series to give the
Brooklyn Dodgers their only world championship title.
Photo by Al Tielemans.

cago Cubs and was arguably the best teacher-coach on staff. Although
he could be just as tough on the ballplayers as Bowa, he was better at offering positive feedback. Players tended to work harder for
him because he understood the difficulty of playing at the Major
League level. Vuke was primarily a utility man during his playing
career. He had to learn as much as he could about the game just
to survive in the Majors. He also had an extraordinary work ethic,

one that endeared him to managers and coaches alike. Thus, his knowledge of the game as well as his ability to communicate with the players were better than any of the other coaches of the staff.

Johnny Podres, the pitching coach, enjoyed a distinguished playing career with the Brooklyn and Los Angeles Dodgers. Since 1970 "Pods" had been a pitching coach with the Dodgers, San Diego Padres, Boston Red Sox, and Minnesota Twins before joining the Phillies in 1991. He was exceptionally good with young pitchers, in knowing not only how to correct their mechanics but also how to motivate them. Veteran pitchers respected his playing background, so they also paid attention when he spoke.

Denis Menke, the hitting coach, played all or part of thirteen seasons in the Majors with the Milwaukee and Atlanta Braves, Houston Astros, and Cincinnati Reds. He was remarkably versatile, able to play first, second, third base, shortstop, and the outfield. When his playing career ended Menke managed in the Milwaukee and Toronto organizations before returning to the Astros as a hitting instructor. Like Vukovich, Menke, who had a lifetime batting average of .250, learned all he could about the offensive aspects of the game and was able to communicate exceptionally well with the players.

Mike Ryan and Mel Roberts rounded out the coaching staff. Ryan, the bullpen coach, was a former catcher who played for the Boston Red Sox and Phillies. He returned to Philadelphia as a Minor League manager and later a coach on the 1980 World Series champs. Roberts, the first base coach and outfield instructor, had also managed in the Phillies organization since 1970. He joined Fregosi's staff in 1992. Collectively, the coaching staff had nearly two centuries of experience in professional baseball and a strong loyalty to the Phillies organization.[6]

At the same time, there were still many questions to be answered as the Phillies opened spring training. One of the major concerns was the need to find a reliable shortstop. In 1992 five different players were tested at the position: Kim Batiste, Mariano Duncan, Joe Millette, Mickey Morandini, and Juan Bell. Each one had shortcomings, either offensively or defensively. Although Bell was slotted to start going into spring training, his weak hitting and prickly attitude suggested that he was not a long-term solution. Another major concern was the pitching staff. In 1992 the Phillies sent twenty-four different pitchers to the mound, fifteen of them as starters.

Entering spring training Terry Mulholland and Curt Schilling were the only certainties in the starting rotation. Tommy Greene, who showed great promise in 1991, was coming off a season plagued by shoulder problems. Danny Jackson was also questionable. Although he pitched effectively throughout the 1992 season, Jackson had landed on the disabled list seven times since 1989. As a result, general manager Lee Thomas invited an army of hurlers to camp, including Pat Combs, a former starter and number-one draft choice who was struggling in the Minors; Kyle Abbott, who compiled an embarrassing 1-14 record as a starter through most of the 1992 season; Tyler Green, another former number-one draft choice and highly prized prospect; veterans José DeJesús and Ken Howell; and youngsters Mike Williams, Cliff Brantley, and Brad Brink.[7]

The team would also have to find a reliable backup catcher who could assume a starting role if Daulton was hurt and a place in the lineup for Mariano Duncan's productive bat. "We have some things to iron out," Thomas admitted, "but I also think we're a lot better off now than we were a year ago at his time. These guys have a great attitude and want to win. I really like what we've got in camp."[8]

The Phillies opened the Grapefruit League by defeating the world champion Toronto Blue Jays, 9–7. Wes Chamberlain collected three hits, driving in two runs and scoring twice. Two days later the Phils thumped the Blue Jays, 10–1, with Mulholland pitching three scoreless innings. When the Phillies got off to a 5-1 start, the players began to believe in themselves. Veterans were given most of the playing time and performed extremely well at the plate. Dave Hollins hit .380, while Daulton was right behind him with a .378 average, 5 home runs, and 12 RBI. Thompson (.347), Morandini (.340), Chamberlain (.321), and Kruk (.302) also provided outstanding offensive, while Danny Jackson (4-1), Terry Mulholland (3-0), and Tommy Greene (1.96) performed well on the mound.[9] Conspicuously absent from the star performers was Lenny Dykstra, who had been among the league's leading hitters the previous two seasons. Nails, one of the most superstitious players in baseball, purposely limited his at bats in the Grapefruit League, fearing that he would "use up his hits" before the regular season began.[10]

On one steamy day Lenny actually tried to get thrown out of a game so he didn't have to play in the hot Florida sun. In the very first inning the feisty lead-off hitter began arguing balls and strikes with home-plate umpire Eric Gregg, a Philadelphia native who was often criticized by players for having too wide a strike zone.

When Gregg, who weighed more than 350 pounds, refused to eject him, Dykstra made the attack personal. The Dude called Gregg "Fat Albert," suggested he was so overweight that he couldn't see the actual strike zone over his considerable belly, and even recommended a weight-loss program.

Finally, Gregg halted the game, removed his mask, and said, "Lenny, I know exactly what you want me to do. You want me to run you out of this game. But if I got to stay in this heat, you got to stay in this heat, too. So it doesn't matter what you call me, or how many times you call me names. I'm not running you out of this game."

Realizing the ploy wouldn't work, Dykstra kept quiet and resigned himself to playing the game.[11]

The Phillies' front office had other concerns about their star center fielder, though. When Dykstra reported to spring training, he was noticeably bigger than the previous season. He was 30 pounds over the 167-pound playing weight listed on the Phillies' official roster. "There wasn't an ounce of fat on me," said Lenny. "I looked like a fucking Greek statue, and I walked onto the field like I had a fifteen-inch cock." In fact, Dykstra's muscle-bound torso gave him the appearance of the "Incredible Hulk," and he looked remarkably awkward for a player who was barely five foot nine.

"You've been working out," observed Thomas, being careful not to make any unwarranted assumptions.

"Yeah," admitted Dykstra.

"I just hope you're not doing anything that would hurt your health," replied the general manager.

Spring Training

FIG. 15. Lenny Dykstra arrived at spring training thirty
pounds over his usual playing weight. When asked about the
added muscle, he winked and said, "Good vitamins." Years
later the Mitchell Report revealed that he was taking
anabolic steroids. Photo by Al Tielemans.

"Everything is cool," said Lenny, dismissing the concern.[12]

Thomas, while genuinely concerned about his prized player's
health, was not about to challenge him. Front-office personnel were
careful not to pry into the personal lives of the players, fearing an
altercation with the players' union. Thomas was also handcuffed
by Major League Baseball's extraordinarily lenient drug policy.

Despite the fact that baseball commissioner Fay Vincent banned steroids from the game two years earlier, his June 7, 1991, memo to all the MLB clubs never said how juicers were going to be caught. There was no testing policy, and players with drug-abuse problems would be banned from the game only after unsuccessful rehabilitation efforts.[13] Vincent might as well have said, "Steroids are illegal now, but do us all a favor and just don't get caught, guys." The only way Dykstra would have been exposed was by a teammate, and that certainly wasn't going to happen.

Like Thomas, John Kruk may have also had his suspicions when he greeted Nails at Clearwater that March. "What the fuck did you do to yourself?" he asked, shocked by his teammate's increased bulk.

"Good vitamins," replied Nails with a wink and a smile.

Years later Kruk would deny any suspicion that his teammate was juicing. "If Lenny had been using steroids, he'd have no reason to lie to me," he insisted. "We were close. We talked about everything. And I wouldn't lie about it now. Besides, it wasn't illegal back then. It's not like it was going to ruin his career."[14]

But Kruk's remarks are colored by the omertà imposed on teammates by the Code, specifically the "clubhouse code." Simply put, "What is seen, heard, or said in the clubhouse stays in the clubhouse." For many players, the clubhouse is the only refuge they have to protect their privacy. There is an implicit understanding that teammates will respect each other's privacy. As teammates the players are all one big family, and loyalty is the bond that holds the family together. While not everybody in the family is going to get along with each other and there are going to be plenty of stresses and disagreements along the way, it is generally understood that the airing of dirty laundry to the press is strictly forbidden. Such matters are expected to be handled in house, behind closed doors.[15] If Kruk or any of his teammates voiced their suspicion publicly that Dykstra was juicing, they would have violated the clubhouse code. But according to Nails, they all knew about his steroid use.

In his recent autobiography, *House of Nails: A Memoir of Life on the Edge*, Dykstra insists that he "wasn't shy about [doping]."

Sometimes I'd drop trou and load up right in front of the other players. Because the shit was so thick I had to use a big gauge needle. There were times I would show up at the yard the next day, forgetting to take the Band-Aid off my ass. It didn't matter; everyone knew why it was there. But they didn't give a fuck. They wanted results. They wanted a win. And Lenny Dykstra *on* steroids was going to give the Philadelphia Phillies a much better chance to win than Lenny Dykstra *off* steroids.[16]

Dykstra arrived at spring training with the intention of having a career year. Due for a new contract at the end of the season, Lenny set his sights on being the highest-paid lead-off hitter in the game. But that would depend on being injury free. In 1992 Dykstra suffered three separate injuries, landing on the disabled list with each one for extended periods of time. By season's end his weight had plummeted to 170, and he was struggling to hit with power.[17] Doping would add the muscle mass he needed to drive the ball into the gaps and over the fence. Thus, the key to his success on the field, and later in contract negotiations, was juicing. That off-season Dykstra reportedly told Jeff Scott, his steroids dealer, "I want to put on some serious size, dude." To that end Scott "prescribed" a cocktail that blended several steroids, oral and injectable. "I injected him more times than I could count," admitted Scott. As Dykstra stepped up his steroid use, his January-to-April sidekick watched him explode to cartoonlike proportions. Then at the end of spring training, Scott sent Nails north with one hundred vials of Deca-Durobolin to sustain his muscle mass throughout the regular season.[18]

There were also reports that Dykstra was gambling again. Despite the fact that baseball had placed him on one year's probation for gambling in a high-stakes poker game, Lenny lost $50,000 at a baccarat table in an Atlantic City casino in December 1992 and had to be restrained from attacking another casino customer. After *Philadelphia Magazine* ran a feature on the incident in January 1993, Dykstra found more discreet ways to feed his gambling addiction.[19] Beginning that spring Nails reportedly asked Lindsay Jones, a Southern California friend and business partner, to bet an average of $2,000 per game on select Phillies games throughout the season, an act that would have banned him from baseball for life if discovered by the commissioner's office.[20]

In addition, Lenny routinely played Phillies broadcaster Rich "Whitey" Ashburn in high-stakes tennis matches. The sixty-six-year-old Ashburn was quite fit for his age and an excellent tennis player. Once, the two played each other at an exclusive club near Ashburn's Main Line home. Dykstra was losing bet after bet, venting his frustration in a steady stream of profanities. Ashburn noticed that two women on the next court were appalled by Lenny's behavior. On one of the line changes, the gentlemanly broadcaster apologized. "Ladies," he began, "I know the language you're hearing from my opponent is foul and indefensible, but I have to tell you that he suffers from Tourette's syndrome."

After explaining the disorder and the verbal outbursts that characterized it, Ashburn asked for their indulgence and then returned to his game. Of course, none of it was true, but the ladies felt sorry for Dykstra after that and simply ignored his boorish behavior.[21]

Ashburn could relate with Nails. A hard-nosed lead-off hitter and center fielder for the 1950 pennant-winning Whiz Kids, Whitey was one of the most talented, exciting, and popular players in Phillies history. He was a "ballplayer's ballplayer," who could curse, drink, and gamble with the very best. Not until 1963 when his playing career ended did Ashburn mellow. Although he yearned to manage the Phillies after he retired, Whitey joined the club's radio and television broadcast team instead. It was a job that not only allowed him to enjoy camaraderie with the players, but would eventually make him one of the most beloved personalities in Philadelphia sports. Ashburn's relaxed, low-key style and dry wit made him seem like a good friend, but he was at his best when the Phillies paired him with Harry Kalas, who joined the broadcast crew in 1971.

The chemistry between the two announcers was unique. Kalas's silky-smooth voice was ideal for doing play-by-play, while Ashburn's appreciation for the nuances of the game made him a superb color analyst. Both of the announcers also knew how to create the ambience of the ballpark for listeners, using downtime to allow the sounds of the crowd and the game to enliven the radio broadcast. Both men also created a number of signature lines. Ashburn uttered such memorable phrases as the following:

"Hard to believe, Harry."

"He looks hitterish."

"He looks runnerish."

"Right down the middle for a ball."

"You can bet the house on it, Harry."

Similarly, Kalas was known for "Swing . . . and a long drive, this ball is . . . outta here!" and "Swing and a miss! Struck him out!" "Harry the K," as he was more affectionately known by fans, also accentuated the names of individual ballplayers like "Michael-Jack-Schmidt" and "Mick-key More-an-DEE-nee." But some of the most memorable moments came when Kalas played straight man for Ashburn, whose on-air humor often popped up unexpectedly.

In one of their first radio broadcasts together, a player broke his bat.

"Richie, the game bat must be very important to a player," observed Kalas, creating an opening for his partner to offer the benefit of his own playing experience.

"It really is, Harry," Ashburn responded with a straight face. "In fact, when I was doing well with a certain bat, I wouldn't trust leaving it around the dugout or in the clubhouse. I used to take that bat back to my hotel room and go to bed with it. In fact, I've been in bed with a lot of old bats in my day."[22]

The 1993 team would become a special one for both Ashburn and Kalas. That season the Phillies broadcast 153 of the team's 162 regular-season games on television, more than ever before. Eighty-five of the games were anchored by Ashburn and Kalas and aired on WPHL Channel 17, with Andy Musser, Chris Wheeler, and Kent Tekulve rotating in. Another 45 games were televised on PRISM, a cable TV channel, with Chris Wheeler, Garry Maddox, and Jay Johnstone calling the action. And yet another 23 games were televised on SportsChannel Philadelphia, with Musser doing the play-by-play and Tekulve serving as color commentator. In addition, all 162 regular-season games were aired on wOGL-AM Radio 1210, which covered the tristate area of eastern Pennsylvania, Delaware, and southern New Jersey. Ashburn and Kalas also anchored the radio broadcasts, with other announcers rotating in every three innings.[23]

Because they spent so much downtime with the players on the road, Ashburn and Kalas got to know them very well. Whitey regularly set up blackjack games in the back of the plane where Daulton, Dykstra, Andersen, Kruk, and Williams could be found. Whenever Richie dealt, no matter what cards he turned up, the other participants inevitably heard him say, "Nothing there, nothing there, nothing there . . . Read 'em and weep, boys!"[24] The two broadcasters regularly joined players on the golf course. They ate together at restaurants. And they drank together. "Once we had a flight to Denver, and we were delayed three hours because of thunderstorms in Philadelphia," recalled Larry Andersen. "So we just sat at the end of the runway waiting for takeoff. We eventually ran out of beer, and Harry passed out. An hour later he woke up, and we're still sitting on the runway. He looked at me and said, 'Pretty smooth flying so far.' Harry had a very subtle way of saying things."[25]

"Everybody loved Harry," recalled Mickey Morandini. "Our respect came from how he broadcasted. He never ripped players. He saw it like it was. He never said anything behind your back, and we respected that."[26]

Both Kalas and Ashburn loved the '93 team because they could be raucous, funny, feisty, and nasty, but, most important, they could play the game of baseball as well as any other team that donned the Phillies' red pinstripes. They were, in Kalas's words, "a joy to be around."[27]

If there was a defining moment that spring, it came on March 21 in an exhibition game against the St. Louis Cardinals at Al Lang Stadium in St. Petersburg. It was about a week before the teams headed north to begin the regular season, a time when the players just want to avoid injury. The Phillies, who led the National League in hit batters with fifty-two the previous season, were particularly sensitive about that statistic. Believing that opposing pitchers disrespected them, the Phils were going to put a stop to any notion that their hitters were going to be pushed around in 1993.

In the first inning Cardinals pitcher Donovan Osbourne nailed Dave Hollins on the arm. Hollins, who had been plunked a Major League–high nineteen times in 1992, trotted down to first base, acting as if he didn't care. On the contrary, he had placed the Phillies' pitching staff on notice during the first week of spring training: "If you're not going to protect our hitters, there's going to be a problem between you and me. I'm going to be the first one to come after you if one of our guys gets hit and you don't do something about it."[28]

Tommy Greene was on the mound in the third when Osbourne stepped to the plate. Greene, one of the nicest players on the team, knew that he had to retaliate, and he was sweating bullets. He looked in for the sign, and Daulton gave him the middle finger, the universal signal to drill the batter. The very next pitch nailed Osbourne in the neck.

Ill-will was running high among both teams a few innings later when Cards reliever Paul Kilgus hit Ricky Jordan with a retribution pitch one batter after Duncan slammed a home run. Jordan charged the mound, initiating a rare spring-training brawl. Daulton, Incaviglia, and Hollins followed, throwing punches along the way. When the dust settled Jordan was ejected, but the Fightin' Phils served notice that they would no longer tolerate such abuse. "Enough is enough," said Jordan after the game. "That's not tolerable. We have to take a little more control."[29]

The incident established Hollins as one of the enforcers of the Code. When a pitcher throws at an opposing hitter, the Code demands retribution. It may take the form of the hitter charging the mound, a bench-clearing brawl, or the victim's pitcher defending him by throwing at an opposing batter. The retributive act makes the statement "We are not going to be pushed around or disrespected anymore. We are going to take a stand." Such retribution restores competitive balance to the game as well as respect between the two teams.[30] In this instance the bench-clearing brawl also solidified an "us-against-them" attitude among the Phillies that would continue to grow throughout the regular season. Not only did they embrace their underdog status, but they gloried in it. The fearsome demeanors and sheer physical bulk of players like Daulton, Dykstra, Hollins, Incaviglia, and Chamberlain discouraged opposing pitchers from even considering a brushback. "I'll tell you what," said Dykstra. "We've got a lot of mean and intimidating-looking guys on this team. I don't think too many teams are going to be eager to mess with us."[31]

A special chemistry was developing among the players. In the recent past spring training had been a time of meaningless exhibition games marred by ill feelings, constant complaints, and sniping at the manager. But the Phillies on this team appeared to genuinely like each other. The new arrivals had the same competitive spirit as the holdovers. All of them were throwbacks from other organizations who wanted to prove that they still had a lot of baseball left. They worked hard throughout spring training. The games were not only meaningful but essential to the bonding process that occurred in Clearwater.

The Phillies concluded their spring-exhibition season with a 16-10 record, winning six of their last seven games. It was the best the club performed in the Grapefruit League in many years.[32] "I don't know if you can call it chemistry or what the heck you call it, but you could sense it in spring training," said Kruk. "By the time we left camp, we knew we had an excellent line-up and some good starting pitching. It was the first time we really felt like we could win it all."[33] Before the Phillies broke camp, team president Bill Giles met with Darren Daulton, the last of the unsigned veterans, and gave him a four-year $18 million contract extension. The new deal guaranteed the thirty-one-year-old catcher an average of $4.5 million a year, while also providing the Phillies with an option for a fifth year (1998) at $5 million and a $500,000 buyout clause. Giles took a calculated risk by promising that kind of money to a player with a track record of injuries, but he felt that Daulton was worth the risk.

"Darren is very special to me," said the team president. "With all the injuries and the auto accident, he is a great example of what determination and hard work can do. The new contract means that the best catcher in baseball will be in a Phillies uniform for the rest of his career."[34]

When his teammates learned of Daulton's new deal, they couldn't resist goading him. "You know what you need to do now, Dutch?" said Kruk. "You need to build a big mansion, and we'll all live in it, party, have a good time and play ball."

Stealing a line from the popular film *Field of Dreams*, Incaviglia, who overheard the remark, cracked, "Yeah, if you build it, we will come!"[35]

Little did they know, the fun was just beginning.

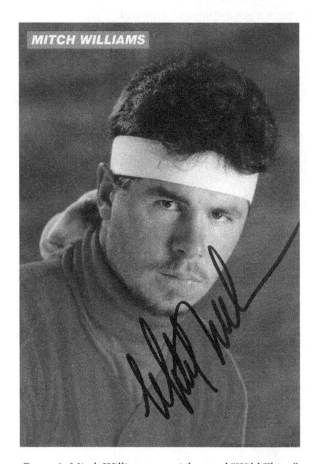

Fɪɢ. 16. Mitch Williams was nicknamed "Wild Thing" for his unorthodox delivery as well as for a proclivity for pitching into trouble before getting out of it. Teammate John Kruk once observed that Williams pitched "like his hair's on fire." Photo by Al Tielemans.

EIGHT
Wild Thing

The Phillies opened the 1993 season with a shocking sweep of the Astros at Houston's Astrodome. On Monday, April 5, Terry Mulholland won the opener, 3–1, against free agent Doug Drabek. The left-hander allowed only four hits in breaking the Phils' eight-year opening-day losing streak. The next day Curt Schilling scattered six hits over eight innings for a 5–3 win over Greg Swindell, Houston's other big free-agent signing. Mitch Williams notched his first save of the season. Although the Phillies were no-hit through six innings by Pete Harnisch in the getaway game, Darren Daulton homered in the seventh to put them on the board. Down by a run in the eighth, 3–2, Mickey Morandini stepped to the plate and blasted a solo shot to tie the game. Milt Thompson's three-run double in the tenth gave the Fightins a 6–3 victory and a clean sweep of the series.[1] "I think we'll look back on that home run by Mickey as a turning point in our season," said Schilling after the game.[2] If nothing else, the Phillies made history. The last time they opened a season with three straight wins was 1970, and the last time they accomplished that feat on the road was 1915, the year of the club's very first pennant.[3]

When the Phillies returned to the Vet for the home opener against the Chicago Cubs on Friday, April 9, they were greeted by the largest opening-day crowd in franchise history. The 60,985 fans who turned out to see the game were thrilled by Daulton's two homers and five RBI, but their hopes to see the Phils extend their win streak were dashed when the Cubs prevailed in the 11–7 slugfest. As a result, the Phillies fell out of first place for what would be the only time all season.[4] The Fightins redeemed themselves the next day when Williams notched his second save by striking out the side on eleven pitches in the ninth to cap a 5–4 win over Cubs. On Sunday, April 11, Schilling earned his first complete-game victory, 3–0, to close out the series.

The Phillies improved their record to 8-1 after a three-game sweep of the Cincinnati Reds at the Vet. Dykstra found his power stroke in the first game of the series, slamming a solo homer in the seventh to give the Phils a 5–4 win. Tommy Greene and Ben Rivera followed with back-to-back victories to close out the homestand.[5] With the Phils firmly in control of first place in the National League East, the city jumped on the bandwagon. "While the Phillies' fast start should come with a warning from the Surgeon General that excessive April euphoria can be hazardous to your health," cautioned Paul Hagen of the *Philadelphia Daily News*, "there is a building sense that something different is happening in the crumbling concrete doughnut at the corner of Broad and Pattison."[6]

No one was enjoying the party more than Mitch Williams. The Phillies' surprising reversal of fortune seemed to parallel his own. Williams struggled through a miserable exhibition season. In eleven and two-thirds innings of work, the usually reliable closer posted an 0-2 record with a wretched 10.03 ERA, surrendering 22 hits and 8 walks.[7] But now, nine games into the regular season, he was the proud owner of five straight saves in as many chances. If the Phillies were going to contend, they would have to count on Williams to close games in the ninth.

"I wasn't the least bit worried," the left-hander said years later, explaining his poor spring training. "I felt fine, physically and mechanically. All I had to do was add the adrenaline. When the regular season started, I took it up a notch. I just never got pumped up to pitch games that didn't count, and everybody knew I ran on adrenaline. After I got that first save against Houston in the opening series, I had all the confidence I needed to close for the rest of the season."[8]

Wild Thing

Better known as "Wild Thing," Williams had already earned the colorful nickname by the time he arrived in Philadelphia. Boasting a high-powered fastball, the closer's tendency to walk the bases loaded before striking out the side had become legendary—and intolerable—in Texas and Chicago, where he pitched earlier. It also drew comparisons to Ricky Vaughn, the closer for the Cleveland Indians in the popular film *Major League*. Vaughn had no clue where his next pitch was going, but it was going to get there with record speed.

"I loved it," said Williams of the punk pitcher played by Hollywood actor Charlie Sheen. "I guess I can see why they called me that. I wasn't exactly known for painting the corners of the plate. On the field, I pretty much let it all hang out. So it doesn't bother me a bit what people call me. Besides, there are a lot of worse things you can be called."[9]

Williams also possessed a highly unorthodox delivery, nearly falling sideways to the ground with every pitch. "He pitches like his hair's on fire," observed John Kruk.[10] In Philadelphia Williams was not only tolerated but embraced by fans for his high-wire act. Not surprisingly, his journey to the City of Brotherly Love was more of a roller-coaster ride than a steady ascendancy.

Born on November 17, 1964, in Santa Ana, California, Mitch Williams was the second of three sons. His parents divorced when he was twelve years old. Afterward, Mitch and his older brother, Bruce, lived with their father, Geoff, in West Linn, Oregon, outside of Portland. Since there wasn't much money, the brothers spent their time playing sports, which became the bond that united them with their father. "My dad was my greatest influence and my best friend," Williams admitted. "Sure, I got disciplined growing up, but I also got a lot more praise and a lot more encouragement than a lot of kids."[11]

Football was Mitch's favorite sport. At age seven he started playing quarterback in the Little Guy Football League on his father's team. He continued to play the position at West Linn High School. "I could throw a football 75 yards flatfooted, but I could not run a lick," recalled Mitch. "What I really wanted to do was play defense."

But at six foot two and just 136 pounds, Williams, as a sophomore, was too small to play on the defensive line or at linebacker. When he put on a few more pounds in his junior year, though, the coach allowed him be the long snapper on punts, mostly because he loved hitting people and was the only player who agreed to do it.

Williams also pitched for West Linn High School, following in his brother's footsteps. "We both threw hard, but all the scouts were interested in my brother because he was a year older," said Mitch. Scouts would call the high school and ask head coach Terry Pollreisz who was pitching. To make sure he was attracting attention for both brothers, Pollreisz would tell the caller, "Williams, show up." Naturally, half the time scouts would see Mitch and the other half Bruce. The ploy was successful. Bruce was signed by the Milwaukee Brewers after his senior year, in 1981, and Mitch by the San Diego the following year.[12]

As a starter Mitch went 42-5 for West Linn over three seasons. His most impressive performance came in 1982, his senior year, when the Lions went 26-4 and captured the Oregon state championship. Mitch posted a perfect 17-0 record, winning 65 percent of his team's games that season. It was also the best high school pitching performance in Oregon state history.[13]

Selected by the Padres in the eighth round of the 1982 draft, Williams signed for $18,000. He made his professional debut as a starter at Walla Walla, Washington, in the Class A short-season Northwest League, where he posted a 3-4 record with 66 K and a 4.78 ERA. In 1983 Williams began the season in Class A Reno of the California League but had control problems, compiling a 1-7 record with a 7.14 ERA. Demoted in midseason to low-A ball at Spokane, Wild Thing found his groove, improving his record to 7-6 while lowering his ERA to 4.48. He returned to Reno in 1984 and went 9-8 with 166 K and a 4.99 ERA. But that winter the Padres left Williams unprotected, and the Texas Rangers took him in the Rule Five draft.[14]

"I think a lot of people in the San Diego organization misinterpreted Mitch's confidence as being cocky, or arrogant," explained John Kruk, who also started his pro career with the Padres. "They

Wild Thing

wanted choirboys, and the only thing Mitch sang was country. They couldn't wait for me to get out of there, too. We just didn't conform to what they wanted, which were guys who stayed on an even keel, not guys who got angry, got fired up. Mitch and I belonged on an East Coast team that had passionate fans and appreciated passion in their players."[15]

The Rangers sent Williams to Salem, Virginia, in the Carolina League. It was still Class A ball, but he showed enough promise to be promoted to Double-A Tulsa in the Texas League, where he finished the 1985 season. Between the two teams Williams posted an 8-11 record, 175 K, and a 5.25 ERA.

Williams was in the right place at the right time. The Rangers were in the throes of a youth movement. Bobby Valentine had just replaced Doug Rader as manager, and Tom House, who had been a roving pitching instructor with the Padres, replaced Dick Such as pitching coach. Invited to big-league training camp by the Rangers in 1986, Williams enjoyed a golden opportunity. Reunited with House on a full-time basis, the twenty-two-year-old southpaw was able to develop the mechanics and proper mental approach to become a successful reliever.

"I was lucky I had Tom House when I got to the Rangers," recalled Williams. "He was the one who got me throwing enough strikes to have a career." House simplified Mitch's delivery by eliminating the useless motion in it. Operating strictly from the stretch and keeping his hands lower in the set position, Williams was able to deceive hitters by hiding the baseball longer. While most pitching coaches would discourage their hurlers from throwing across their body to avoid arm injury, House rejected that notion. Instead, he encouraged the practice, believing that it would allow Wild Thing to remain closed longer and, as a result, put less stress on his arm.[16]

As a result of the change, Williams was moved up to the parent club in 1986 and led the American League with 80 appearances, a Major League record for a rookie. He also lowered his ERA to 3.58 and recorded 8 saves and 90 strikeouts. The following season was even better as Wild Thing posted a 3.23 ERA and 129 K in 85 appearances.[17] Williams was enjoying life off the playing field, too.

In 1985 he met Dee Ann Grammer, an elementary schoolteacher and avid baseball fan, at Arlington Stadium. Williams called her the same night. Two weeks later he asked her to marry him. "I kept trying to fix him up with a younger friend of mine," said Dee, a thirtysomething divorcee with two children. "But he was just a real change from anyone I'd ever known before. He was so witty and hilarious, we kind of hit it off.

"I fought it at first, even though we were both falling in love. It wasn't the age difference that made me hold back. It was the side of him that was so silly. He reminded me of the kids I taught at school. He needs a lot of praise and encouragement. He needs people telling him how good he is all the time. If not, he gets down on himself."

Wild Thing wouldn't take no for an answer, and Dee finally agreed to marry him. So at the tender age of twenty-four, he was blessed with instant family. "I wanted kids," he admitted, "and now I have a 14-year-old son and a 6-year-old daughter, two of the best kids I've ever met. They both call me 'Dad,' and that, to me, is like a dream come true."[18]

In 1988 Williams posted 18 saves in 67 appearances for the Rangers, but he had an inflated 4.63 ERA and just 61 strikeouts. Management, tired of his high-wire act, decided to trade the six-foot-three 180-pounder to the Chicago Cubs in a package deal that included two left-handers, Jamie Moyer and Drew Hall, and promising outfielder Rafael Palmeiro, whose .307 batting average was the second best in the National League that season. The Cubs' need for a late-inning reliever was obvious. As a team they had the worst record in the Majors for squandering saves, and their primary reliever, Rich Gossage, had the worst record among all relievers with 20 or more save opportunities, with just 13 saves in 23 opportunities. Chicago, attracted by Williams's ninety-five-mile-an-hour fastball, believed he could develop into a top closer.[19]

The 1989 season was bittersweet for Mitch. On the one hand, Gossage, Williams's boyhood hero, was released in spring training, and he became the team's closer. On the other, Mitch enjoyed one of his best seasons, posting a 4-4 record with a 2.76 ERA, 67 strikeouts (in 76 appearances during the regular season), and 36 saves.[20]

FIG. 17. Mitch Williams, shown here in 1989, exhausted
the patience of his managers in San Diego, Texas, and Chicago
before landing in Philadelphia in 1991. During his three
seasons with the Phillies, Williams appeared in 207 games,
including 7 in the postseason, compiling a total of
105 saves. National Baseball Hall of Fame Library,
Cooperstown, New York.

Selected to the All-Star team for the only time in his career, Williams was a key figure in the Cubs winning the National League's Eastern Division title. According to Cubs pitching coach Dick Pole, "Williams is a natural reliever. He's too hyper to sit down for four days. But what sets him apart from other closers is his competitiveness. Some guys don't like to pitch in a blown-out game, or a game situation that's tight," said Pole. "Not Mitch. When you send him out on the mound, you know you'll get everything he has."[21]

Williams's impressive work ethic applied even when he was not on the mound. He was always the first Cub to report to the ballpark, often arriving with the dawn for an afternoon game. "I liked my situation in Chicago," he recalled after his retirement. "[Manager] Don Zimmer was awesome. After a loss he never said, 'You threw the ball good. You just got beat.' Even when I blew a save he didn't say anything. I'd rather have that than have a manager who blew smoke up my ass."[22]

But even Zimmer lost his patience with Williams the following season. Noting that his closer "did everything 99 mph," the Cubs' manager tired of Mitch's tendency to walk batters. At season's end Williams had just 16 saves in 59 appearances with a 3.93 ERA. Zimmer wanted him gone, and the Cubs dealt Wild Thing to Philadelphia for pitchers Bob Scanlon and Chuck McElroy at the start of the 1991 campaign.

The year 1991 was more productive. Wild Thing saved 30 games for the Phillies, while winning 12, and posted 84 strikeouts and a 2.34 ERA. The following season Williams saved 29 games for a last-place team while winning 5 of 13 decisions.[23] Williams credited Phillies pitching coach Johnny Podres for much of his success.

Podres spent most of his fifteen-year playing career pitching for the Brooklyn and Los Angeles Dodgers. He compiled a 148-116 record, with 1,435 strikeouts, a 3.68 ERA, and 24 shutouts in 440 games. But Podres was at his best in World Series competition. After losing his first World Series game in 1953, he won four straight decisions over the next decade, allowing only 29 hits in 38$^1/_3$ innings with a 2.11 ERA. He is best remembered for pitching a 2–0 shutout in the seventh game of the 1955 World Series against the New York Yankees. The victory gave Brooklyn their only world championship before the team relocated to Los Angeles in 1957. When his playing career ended in 1969, Podres served as the pitching coach for the San Diego Padres, Boston Red Sox, Minnesota Twins, and Philadelphia Phillies for twenty-three seasons between 1973 and 1996.[24]

"Pods knew everything there was to know about pitching," recalled Williams.

> But when he came out to the mound to talk with me he never said a thing about mechanics. If I got wild, I needed to stay back in my delivery and stay on top of the ball. I knew that, and he knew that I knew that.
>
> Instead, Pods always gave a positive message to keep me focused. Sometimes he made me laugh by saying something stupid, just to get my mind off my troubles. Other times he'd pump me up, make me feel good about what I was doing, no matter how bad the situation was. For me, that was the most effective approach a pitching coach could take.[25]

The Phillies continued their torrid pace throughout April. One of the reasons for their success was that Lenny Dykstra was getting on base consistently. Mired in a 1-for-25 slump at the beginning of the season, Nails found other ways to prove that he was still one of the top lead-off hitters in baseball by working walks, stealing bases, and scoring runs. In fact, Dykstra set the tempo for the Phillies' offense that season. In games where he scored one run that season, the Phils enjoyed a 35-27 win-loss record. In games where Nails scored two runs, the Phils were 25-2. And in games where he scored three or more runs, the Fightins were 9-0.[26] "Lenny can hurt you in so many ways," said manager Jim Fregosi. "All I want to do is put his name in the line-up as many times as possible. I can't think of another guy I'd rather have in the lead-off spot. He makes so much happen just by being there."[27] Dykstra was more objective. "Over the long haul, if you stick with the plan, you got a much better chance to be successful," he said. "You can't just go out there and hack away with no idea of what you want to do. If you're not hitting, you just try to get on base. I learned that from experience. And that's the way I approach the game."[28]

Another reason for the Phils' success was the misfortune of other teams in the National League East, especially in the winter and early spring. The Pittsburgh Pirates lost Barry Bonds and Doug Drabek to free agency in the off-season. Similarly, the Montreal

FIG. 18. Dykstra, receiving postvictory congratulations, was the Phillies' catalyst for scoring runs. In games where Nails scored at least one run, the Phils went 69-29. By season's end, Dykstra led the National League in runs scored, with 143, and accounted for 16.3 percent of the total number of runs the Phillies' offense scored in 1993. Photo by Al Tielemans.

Expos, another small-market club, said good-bye to many of their veteran players in an ongoing rebuilding process. The underachieving Mets fired manager Jeff Torborg and replaced him with former Phils skipper Dallas Green. And the Chicago Cubs lost Ryne Sandberg, their All-Star second baseman, to a broken wrist in the first

Wild Thing

exhibition game. As a result, it wasn't going to take one hundred wins to clinch the division, and the Phillies appeared to be solid enough, both offensively and defensively, to do it.[29]

On Friday, April 23, Schilling hurled a 2–0 shutout against the Dodgers, striking out a career-high nine. Danny Jackson followed the next day with a 7–3 victory over Los Angeles, and Greene gave the Phils a sweep in the final game of the series with a 5–2 victory.[30] But the final week of April defined the Phillies' season, and it began on the twenty-sixth, a cold, dismal Monday night at the Vet.

Trailing the San Francisco Giants 8–0, Wes Chamberlain hit a weak line drive back up the middle that was snared by pitcher Bryan Hickerson to end the fifth inning. In a barefaced show of machismo, the Giants' hurler spiked the ball into the artificial turf. It was a blatant violation of the Code, which forbids a pitcher from disrespecting an opponent by showing him up. Although Giants manager Dusty Baker insisted after the game that his reliever "didn't intend to show anyone up," the Phillies didn't interpret it that way.

"Unbelievable," said Milt Thompson. "I've never seen anything like that before. It ticked us off. And fired us up. We were destined to win after that." Dave Hollins echoed his teammate's feelings. "It fired up a lot of guys. It was one of those times when a team is sleeping and you don't want to try to wake them up. That got a lot of guys pumped on our bench."

Infuriated, the Fightins launched a comeback in the sixth inning. Morandini walked. Kruk singled him to third and then limped off the field. Hollins scored Morandini with a sacrifice fly. Daulton walked, and Incaviglia singled in pinch runner Jim Eisenreich, who remained in the game to play first base. Mariano Duncan followed with a double to score Daulton, making the score 8–3. The Phils scored another four runs in the seventh on three walks and an RBI single by Eisenreich, Thompson's two-run single, and an error by Giants second baseman Mike Benjamin. Morandini's triple with one out in the eighth and another RBI single by Eisenreich tied the score. Once again, the bullpen came to the rescue. Larry Andersen, in relief of ineffective starter Ben Rivera, shut down the Giants in the seventh, and David West struck out three and no-hit San Francisco in the eighth and ninth. In the tenth Juan Bell scored the winning run on a wild pitch by Gino Minutelli. The 9–8 victory took four hours and thirty-three minutes and put the Phillies ten games over the .500 mark for the first time since 1986.

Not only did the come-from-behind victory show that the Phillies were a scrappy bunch who refused to quit, but it also revealed the depth of the bench. Although Kruk was leading the National League in batting, Eisenreich, his replacement, came off the pine to deliver three hits, knock in two runs, and score two more.[31]

The bench came through again in a more dramatic fashion on April 29. It was Milt Thompson's turn to shine this time. Entering the game he was hitting just .185, but he found a way to contribute defensively. With two out in the eighth and the Phillies leading San Diego 5–3 at Jack Murphy Stadium, the Padres' Bob Geren hit what appeared to be a game-winning grand slam. Suddenly, Thompson came out of nowhere. He leaped at the base of the left-field fence, making a game-saving catch for the third out.

Pumping a fist, the usually mild-mannered outfielder jumped excitedly in the air as Dykstra ran over to bear-hug him. Teammates emptied the dugout to offer their congratulations on the game saver.

"I knew [Geren] hit it good," said Thompson after the game, "but I was still going to try to get it. I still can't explain how I caught that ball, I just did."

Williams came in to pitch the bottom of the ninth, quickly dispatching the Padres for his ninth save of the campaign.[32]

Wild Thing was at the center of a controversy the very next night when the Phillies played the Los Angeles Dodgers. Clinging to a fragile 7–6 lead in the bottom of the ninth, Williams loaded the bases with nobody out. He seemed to be having difficulty with his spikes, so he called time and walked off the mound and into the Phillies' dugout to get a new pair. As Dodger fans rained down a hailstorm of boos, L.A. manager Tommy Lasorda shot onto the field, approached the home-plate umpire, and argued that Williams should not be allowed to take any warm-up pitches when he returned. Of course, when Wild Thing took the mound a few minutes later, he immediately began throwing warm-up tosses. Lasorda threw a fit.

When play finally resumed, pinch hitter Mike Sharperson ripped a shot back through the box. Snatching victory from the jaws of defeat, second baseman Mickey Morandini stabbed the ball and doubled off Mike Piazza at second for an unassisted double play. "It was just one of those reaction plays," said Morandini, downplaying the feat. "I dove, and the next thing I knew the ball was in my glove. The thing I remember most was the look on Lasorda's face and the cuss words he was screaming from the dugout."

Williams then retired Brett Butler on a grounder to short to preserve the 7–6 win. It was his tenth save, and the third in as many days.[33]

The Phils ended April with a 16-5 record, their best ever.[34] It was also the first time they had been in first place on May 1 since 1964.

"Everything is breaking right for us," observed veteran reliever Larry Andersen. "You watch any team that wins. Good things happen. We're a good ball club now, but a lot of this is like fate, too."[35]

NINE

Lightning in a Bottle

The Phillies caught lightning in a bottle in May. With a record of 34-15, the Fightins ended the month in first place in the National League's Eastern Division, seven games ahead of the second-place Montreal Expos.[1] It was the best start in franchise history. Winning had become contagious. Gone were the gloom and negativity that polluted the clubhouse in seasons past. No longer did sullen and sulky players arrive at the Vet expecting to lose. Instead, this Phillies team was upbeat, loose, and funny. They couldn't wait to get to the ballpark. If someone hit a walk-off homer to win a game, he got a shaving-cream pie smashed in the face. Teammates regularly indulged in belching contests, rolled around on the clubhouse floor in impromptu wrestling matches, and danced to Tag Team's rap song "Whoomp! There It Is!"[2] It was like a Romper Room for incorrigibles. "Winning does that," said Dutch Daulton. "We expect to win every night, so when you come to the ballpark you know it's going to be fun."[3]

To be sure, the team's behavior would have been considered juvenile, at best, if they had been losing. But the sportswriters were using adjectives like *colorful*, *entertaining*, and *macho* to describe the ballplayers and their antics. "They actually reveled in that 'macho' image," said Frank Fitzpatrick, the beat writer for the *Philadelphia*

Inquirer. "The more we wrote about it, the more they reveled in it. And that team did have a certain swagger in the way they played."[4]

Dykstra, nicknamed "Dude" because he used the term when referring to others, disagreed with the various adjectives the press used to describe the team. "The media always likes to get hold of a different angle, but the bottom line is craziness and being macho doesn't win ball games," he explained to J. Edwin Smith of *The Sporting News.* "Yeah, we have fun, but you've still got to perform. You need a full team to do that—not just a couple of guys."

When Smith asked how accurate "Animal House" was to describe the Phillies' clubhouse, the Dude replied, "I don't know if you can call it 'Animal House,' but there are some people in here who are a little off balance."

"We're not bad people," John Kruk chimed in. "But you wouldn't want to have us over to your house for dinner."[5]

Nevertheless, the Phillies' "swagger," "machismo," "craziness," or whatever it was labeled was the result of a special chemistry that emerges when individual players do extraordinary things on the field, inspired by a genuine desire to contribute to something much bigger than themselves. These Phillies were not a team laden with star performers but rather a collection of good, solid ballplayers who cared about each other and placed team success above personal achievement. "Winning, and the chemistry that goes along with it, isn't always about superstars," Mitch Williams explained. "It's about guys who go out every day and leave it all on the field."[6]

The six players who best represented the team's take-no-prisoners approach to the game were Daulton, Williams, Lenny Dykstra, John Kruk, Dave Hollins, and Pete Incaviglia. The six veterans lockered together at the far corner of the Phillies' fraternity-like clubhouse in a cozy but cluttered area referred to by the players as "the Ghetto" and "Macho Row" by the more politically correct beat writers.[7] Here they boasted about their on-field exploits, scratched themselves, and talked baseball long after the game had ended. Nearby was the trainer's room, which provided a quick escape when one of the members wanted to avoid the intrusive press or enjoy an ice-cold postgame beer. Also in close proximity was a big blue chest labeled "Beavers." It was filled with a wide variety of adult magazines, reading material for the restroom that was just around the corner.[8]

Daulton, the leader of the motley crew, held court from a beat-up lounge chair wedged inside one of the lockers. He could be found there four hours before game time stretching his chronically stiff left knee, the result of annual surgical "cleanups."[9] Of the six veterans who lockered on Macho Row, Dutch asserted his authority most. "There was no one else on that team who even came close as a leader," recalled John Kruk. "But he did it the right way. He would pull people aside one-on-one. It was always private and very calm and casual. I heard him tell guys on our team, 'If you don't straighten out and start doing things the right way, I'm going to kick your ass.' And it got straightened out."[10]

"When Dutch speaks, everyone listens," observed reliever Larry Andersen, the team jokester. "There are three reasons for that. First, he's been here the longest. Second, he works harder than anyone else. And third, he's strong enough to beat us all up."[11] Daulton called the clubhouse meetings, made the speeches, and policed those who stepped out of line. A consummate professional, Dutch became so annoyed by outfielder Wes Chamberlain's habitual helmet throwing that he smashed one of the rookie's helmets into pieces with a bat right in front of him.

"If anyone but Dutch did that, the guys would get angry," said Phillies bullpen coach Mike Ryan. "With Dutch, everybody pays attention."[12] That included the veterans of Macho Row. Once, Mitch Williams stomped off the mound in disgust after Fregosi removed him from a game. A seething Daulton considered the act selfish, a personal affront to both himself and the manager. He confronted Williams the very next day and told him so. Dutch also warned the closer that there would be consequences if he ever did it again. "He was right," admitted Williams. "I acted like an idiot."[13]

"All I ask is that my teammates bust their tails for me the way I do for them," admitted Daulton, whose chiseled appearance discouraged anyone from challenging him. "If you're looking for softness, forget it," said his wife, Lynne. "Darren is tough-minded. He

FIG. 19. Daulton's finest season in baseball came in 1992 when he led the National League in RBI with 109, won the Silver Slugger Award, and made his first All-Star appearance. But his impressive leadership abilities allowed the Phillies to capture the pennant the following year.
Photo by Al Tielemans.

doesn't dwell on problems, he resolves them quickly. Nor does he complain, not even when he's in a lot of pain."[14]

"You look at all Darren's been through and you realize he's a tough individual," said Fregosi. "He's had some tough years here in Philly, the knee surgeries, playing with pain, having to sit behind other catchers. But now he's the premier catcher in baseball."[15]

Perhaps bench coach John Vukovich said it best when asked about Daulton's unique place among the many athletes who donned the red pinstripes. "I've played with better players," said Vukovich, a member of the 1980 world champion Phillies. "I've coached better players. But in thirty-two years I never saw a bigger leader. For me, he set the standard of being a man."[16]

While Daulton was the uncontested leader of the team, his buddies on Macho Row tended to lead by example or a quick sarcastic quip. They could be cantankerous, profane, and brutally candid. Masters of the one-liner and no-holds-barred zingers, the mem-

Lightning in a Bottle

bers of Macho Row could also be disarmingly funny, fiercely loyal, and remarkably insightful in their knowledge of the game. They were "old school" players who brought a fiercely aggressive style of play to the team and a loose, colorful—and profane—atmosphere to the clubhouse. Throwbacks to an earlier era, Daulton, Dykstra, Kruk, Williams, Hollins, and Incaviglia played the game hard and with a chip on their shoulders. It was a rough, sometimes ruthless edge that almost dared opponents to challenge them. Winning came first and the team an extremely close second.

Macho Row was a collection of "throwbacks" in another sense, too. "We're throwbacks from other organizations," explained Kruk. "No one else wanted us."[17] Kruk and Hollins had been rejected by the San Diego Padres, Dykstra by the New York Mets, Incaviglia by the Texas Rangers and Houston Astros, and Williams by the Chicago Cubs and the Rangers before that. Daulton was the only holdover who began his career with the same organization, and there had been times when he easily could've been dealt elsewhere. Rejection like that spawned an attitude that mocked the stylish, well-paid, and sophisticated stars of other MLB teams who would not dare keep company with such a collection of rogues.

Sports Illustrated's Leigh Montville observed that the rejection created a sense of "defensiveness and paranoia" among them. "The flush of success," he wrote, "is muted by their memories of failure, adding a quality of vulnerability to winning that doesn't exist in most places."[18] Perhaps that is why most of the members of Macho Row made a beeline for the trainer's room whenever the sportswriters entered the clubhouse. "It was not easy covering that team," recalled Bob Brookover, a beat writer for southern New Jersey's *Courier Post*. "Dykstra never had much time for the newspapers he deemed second-tier. Kruk was moody, and Hollins was often unapproachable. Macho Row was a 'no-go zone' if you were looking for some help on a story."[19]

But Paul Hagen, beat writer for the *Philadelphia Daily News*, disagreed. According to Hagen, Macho Row "could be very difficult for the national columnist who just dropped in or the local columnist who showed up two or three times a year. But to the beat writers, they were fine." In fact, Dykstra was very media savvy. When he was traded to the Phillies in 1989, Hagen approached him in the clubhouse to introduce himself. "I know who you are, dude," said Nails, looking the *Daily News* sportswriter straight in the eye. "I know who all of you are."

After that, Dykstra made himself very accessible to Hagen, going so far as to invite him to his Main Line mansion every January for a preseason story. As for players retreating to the trainer's room when the clubhouse was open to the sportswriters, Hagen dismisses that as "mythology," insisting that if any member of Macho Row—or any member of the team—did that to a beat writer, Daulton would hunt them down and tell them to "talk to us for a few minutes, that it was part of their job."[20] Hagen appears to be in the minority, though.

While Brookover agreed that Daulton was a "standup guy" and a "thoughtful gentleman who respected any writer who worked hard to get a story," he insisted that Dutch was "the exception." "The other members of Macho Row made my job hard to do," he added.[21] Similarly, Frank Fitzpatrick of the *Philadelphia Inquirer* recalled that Dykstra, Kruk, Williams, Hollins, and Incaviglia would "make the beat writers wait after a game while they lingered in the trainer's room." When they reappeared, Daulton was the only reliable interview; the others were "crapshoots, unless they had a big game and they knew they had to talk with you. A guy like Kruk was a real pain in the ass. You knew he was intelligent and could be real funny and accommodating when he wanted to talk. But interviewing him was a crapshoot." As a result, Fitzpatrick found alternatives. His "go-to guys" were Mariano Duncan and Mickey Morandini, who "always agreed to talk with [him]."[22]

Larry Shenk, the Phils' vice president of media relations, sympathized with Brookover and Fitzpatrick. "The 1993 team was the toughest to deal with from a PR standpoint," admitted Shenk, who had been with the club since 1964. "Macho Row was not exactly *Mister Rogers' Neighborhood*. You had to pick your spots when you needed to talk to a player who lockered there." After home games the members of Macho Row "squeezed into the trainer's room to rehash the game" while the clubhouse was "filled with media." When no one surfaced, Shenk was forced to "plead with Daulton" to give the writers some time. "Darren saved those of us in PR," he added.[23]

Considering the intrusive, if not arrogant, reputation of the Philadelphia media, it would not be surprising if the members of Macho Row tried to dodge their responsibility to talk to the sportswriters, especially if they had been burned by a particular writer before. Whether a ballplayer agreed to speak with a beat writer or not, or any sportswriter for that matter, seems to have depended on whether he liked or trusted him. Daulton appeared to confirm that assumption when asked about the issue years later. "When you play in Philadelphia, you become guarded with the media," he said. "You learn pretty quickly that the writers are a lot like the fans. The ones who support you when things are going good are the same ones who rip you when things aren't going so good. You don't like to think that, but it's true. When it comes down to the writers, you have to decide who's going to be fair to you."[24]

The Phillies opened May on the West Coast. After losing to the Dodgers, 5–1, the Phils took the getaway game, 9–1, behind a brilliant performance by Mulholland. The next night Dave Hollins's two-run homer in the twelfth inning gave the Phillies a 4–3 victory over the San Francisco Giants to preserve the Phillies' perfect 5-0 record in extra innings. One of the most amusing plays came in the seventh inning when John Kruk dove for a hard-hit grounder off the bat of Giants infielder Steve Scarsone. Larry Andersen ran over to cover first base. The Krukker's throw was high, and the forty-year-old reliever had to reach for the ball. Although he tripped over the bag, falling to the ground, Andersen somehow managed to hold onto the ball for the out.

"Dammit, take it yourself!" Andersen, tongue-in-cheek, snapped at the first baseman, who was chuckling at the sight of his teammate splayed out across the foul line. "I'm too fuckin' old for this shit!" That's when Kruk really lost it. He was laughing so hard that he almost had to call time.[25]

The Phillies ended their West Coast trip, splitting the two-game series in San Francisco. Returning to the Vet on May 7, the Fightins hosted a three-game series with the St. Louis Cardinals. After winning the first two contests, the Phils had designs on a series sweep, but they fell behind, 5–2, entering the eighth inning of the Mother's Day finale on May 9. Cardinal starter Bob Tewksbury recorded two quick outs. Then Daulton stepped to the plate and stroked a single to right. Chamberlain followed with a double into the right-field corner, sending Dutch to third. St. Louis manager Joe Torre decided to lift his starter and brought in Lee Smith, Major League Baseball's all-time saves leader. Lucky for the Phils, Smith hadn't pitched in nearly ten days, so he wasn't at his best. After walking Milt Thompson on five pitches, the Cards' reliever faced Mariano Duncan, who was hitting .533 lifetime against Smith.[26]

"After he walked Thompson, I didn't think he'd be throwing me any breaking balls," mused Duncan. "I was looking for a fastball on the first pitch." At third base Daulton and coach Larry Bowa were talking about the possibility of a momentum-turning grand-slam. Why not? So many other miraculous things had already happened in the young season, a grand slam seemed like a distinct possibility.[27]

Duncan got the first-pitch fastball he had anticipated and smashed it into the left-field stands, erasing the four-run deficit to give the Phils a 6–5 victory. "I knew it was gone as soon as I hit it," said the veteran infielder who started the season as a reserve but was playing himself into a starting role. "That was a special home run for me because it was Mother's Day. I called my mother in the Dominican Republic right after the game. She was so happy. She told me that was the best Mother's Day present I could give her."[28]

Thirty hours later Daulton repeated the performance in Pittsburgh to give the Phils a 5–1 come-from-behind victory over the Pirates. "Don't analyze it, boys," Bowa shouted to the players at the end of the game. "Just let it ride. We're in the zone."[29] The Atlanta Braves gave the Phillies a reality check, though.

Atlanta's Fulton County Stadium was sold out in advance of the three-game weekend series. The Braves, two-time defending National League champions, had no intention of surrendering their title to the roguish Phils. The Fightins dropped the opening game, 10–7. Starter Terry Mulholland lasted only two innings, giving up six runs on six hits and two walks. What made the loss so difficult was that the Phils jumped on Atlanta starter Tom Glavine for four runs in the top of the first.

Schilling threw a no-hitter for five and two-thirds innings the next night, but the Braves rallied to win, 5–3. Still, the Phillies earned the respect of the Braves and their tomahawk-chopping fans. Twice they came from behind in the middle of the game, and in the Sunday finale the Fightins rallied twice again to salvage a 5–4 win. They never backed down and left town believing that they were every bit as good as their Western Division rivals. Overall, the Phillies' starters were 17-8 with a 3.24 earned run average. That kind of pitching would take the team far.

"They're scary," admitted Braves manager Bobby Cox. "They've got the lumber, the arms, the defense. What they've done is no surprise to me. During the winter, I picked them to win their division. Don't look at last year to judge them; they were hurt then. But now they've got everybody healthy—Dykstra, Kruk and Daulton. That's a damned good ball club, believe me."

Atlanta third baseman Terry Pendleton agreed with his manager. "The Phillies are so much like we were in '91—they've got a good mix of veterans and young players and good pitching."[30]

On Monday, May 17, the Phillies pounded out seventeen hits in sinking the Florida Marlins, 10–3, their first game against the new expansion team that season. Kruk, whose .382 batting average placed him among the league leaders in that category, picked up another three hits. Tommy Greene blanked the Marlins, 6–0, the next day, with Kruk contributing another three hits. But Florida prevented a sweep by defeating the Phils 5–3 in the final game of the series.[31]

By now the Phillies' old-school style of play and the roguish appearance of many players had captured national attention. In National League cities increasing numbers of fans turned out to watch the Phils whenever they arrived to play the hometown team. "We didn't know we were so popular," said Kruk. "Every city we went to, the crowds were getting bigger and bigger. We'd walk down the street and cars would go by, and people would yell, 'Hey Kruk, you *friggin'* guys suck!' Hell, we liked that. It brought us together, kind of like twenty-five of us against the whole city."[32]

Kruk, the best natural hitter on the team, had perfected a country-boy image that captured the fancy of sportswriters and fans alike and made him one of the team's most popular players. Overweight, middle-aged softball players could relate with the Krukker because of his considerable girth, long hair, and unshaven face. Kids were in awe of his ability to stuff as many as twenty sticks of gum in his mouth during the course of a tense game.[33] Sportswriters were impressed by his dedication. Kruk made a habit of sleeping in the Phillies' clubhouse at the Vet after a Saturday-night game so he was sure to be on time for the Sunday-afternoon contest. Actually, he was just too lazy to drive his truck home to New Jersey just to turn around a few hours later and drive back to the ballpark.[34] Once, after a Saturday-night game, the Krukker played Wiffle ball in the clubhouse until seven in the morning with members of the grounds crew. Since he thought he was going to get a rest the next day, he insisted on pitching thirty innings. After the Wiffle contest ended, Kruk took a short nap. When he woke up he was so sore that he could hardly move. To make matters worse, he found out that he was starting at first base that Sunday. Somehow he managed to collect three hits.[35]

"Johnny was one of us," recalled Mark Carfagno, a member of the grounds crew better known as "Froggy." "In early April the Phillies had a game on a cold and windy night, and the grounds crew was freezing. We went out there with sleeveless shirts because we didn't have any heavy jackets to wear."

When Kruk saw his friends out there, he went directly over to Ralph Frangipani, the head groundskeeper. "What the fuck are you idiots doing out there half naked?" he asked indignantly. Frangipani explained that someone forgot to order jackets for his crew and that management told them to "tough it out."

"Tough it out, my ass," Kruk snapped. "Fuck that. I'm buying you guys new jackets right now!"

The first baseman marched into the clubhouse, found equipment manager Frank Coppenbarger, and directed him to collect the sizes of every grounds-crew member and to order new jackets. When told that the jackets would cost $155 each, Kruk dismissed

Lightning in a Bottle

him, saying, "I don't care. I'll pay for them. Give me the bill." The following day the new jackets arrived and were given to each member of the grounds crew.[36]

But not everyone appreciated Kruk. Once he was seated in a restaurant smoking, drinking, and eating a huge meal when a woman recognized him. Appalled by his vices, she berated him, saying that no professional athlete should indulge in those habits. "I ain't an athlete, lady," replied the Krukker. "I'm a ballplayer."[37] Nor did the Phils' first baseman endear himself to the Phanatic, the team's huge furry green mascot. When asked about what changes he would like to make to the game, Kruk said, "No mascots on the field. Shoot anything that looks like it escaped from *Sesame Street.*" Another suggestion was "the right to hit a reporter if he writes something stupid about you." "Set up a ring in the corner of the clubhouse," he explained. "But first, they'd have to sign a Jacoby & Meyers' waiver."[38] Of course, that didn't place him on the best terms with sportswriters.

On May 17 Pete Incaviglia impressed his teammates by hitting a 440-foot two-run homer in Miami. Inky continued his hitting prowess the next night in Montreal when he hit his fifth career grand slam in the first inning. By week's end the Ink Man would hit five homers in five days and drive in twelve runs. Attributing his success to Denis Menke, the Phils' hitting coach, Incaviglia explained that Menke "changed my hands a little bit and shortened my swing, allowing me to get to the pitch quicker and the results have been great."[39]

On May 18 Schilling pitched his third complete game, a 9–3 victory over the second-place Expos. Montreal took the next two games, 6–2 and 6–5, but the Phils split the four-game set by salvaging the finale, 14–7.[40] The next series against the New York Mets attracted 153,424 fans to the Vet. It was the largest attendance for a four-game series since 1982.[41] Tommy Greene improved his record to 6-0 with a 6–3 win in the opening game. Incaviglia belted two homers, and Hollins added a three-run homer in the fifth to clinch the victory. The next day Schilling threw a league-leading fourth complete game, 4–2, over the Mets.[42] New York salvaged the finale, 5–4, when the Mets rallied in the ninth. The Phils closed out the month of May with a sweep of the expansion Colorado Rockies in Denver.[43] The three-game series made Kruk appreciate his situation in Philadelphia. "I couldn't play here," said the colorful first baseman, referring to the Rockies' Mile High Stadium. "I wouldn't breathe, and if I can't breathe, I'm going to die. Denver is a nice city, but what the hell would you see of it when you're dead?"[44]

All three games against the Rockies were blowouts, with scores of 15–9, 6–0, and 18–1. In the 6–0 victory Mulholland struck out fourteen batters and improved his record to 6-4, statistics that suggest he was the ace of the pitching staff. In fact, the southpaw had been the Phillies' most productive pitcher in 1991 and 1992, winning thirty-eight games, including a no-hitter. But Mulholland, who had arguably the best pickoff move in baseball, resisted the label of "ace," preferring to be "one among many contributors" to the team's success.[45] His humility underscored the selfless attitude that characterized the team.

On Monday, May 31, the Phillies opened a three-game series against the Reds at Cincinnati. Curt Schilling, who started the game, was averaging fewer than two walks per nine innings. But he had problems with home-plate umpire Bob Davidson's strike zone, walking two of the first five batters he faced. Schilling continued to run deep counts, which was also unusual. By the third inning pitching coach Johnny Podres had had enough. On his way to visit the mound, Podres told Davidson that his strike zone was "horseshit" and strongly suggested that he "take his head out of his ass so he can see better."[46] Not surprisingly, Davidson tossed him from the game. After that Davidson seemed to have a vendetta against the Phillies.

In the sixth Daulton took a called third strike that appeared to be well off the plate. In the seventh Schilling was facing Reds shortstop Barry Larkin, and Davidson called two pitches that caught the corner for strikes balls. Daulton questioned those calls, but he remained in his crouch, making sure not to turn around to face the umpire. When Schilling came off the mound and asked where the pitches had been, Davidson told him, "Your catcher is screwing you."

Schilling was dumbfounded. "Basically, what Davidson was tell-

Lightning in a Bottle

ing me was that he's calling strikes balls because he's mad at the catcher," said Schilling after the game. "It was ridiculous. Does the home plate umpire have to be in a good mood for me to throw a good game? That was way over the line."[47]

In the eighth, with the Phillies leading by a run and Cincinnati runners on first and second with nobody out, Davidson called a balk on reliever Larry Andersen. Daulton went ballistic, bombarding the home-plate umpire with a fusillade of obscenities. Although manager Jim Fregosi ran out of the dugout to restrain his catcher, it was too late. By the time Fregosi got to home plate, Daulton was jabbing his finger into Davidson's chest and calling him a "motherfucker." No sooner had the profanity left his lips than the umpire tossed him. Fregosi, caught up in the heat of the moment, repeated his catcher's remark and soon followed him to the showers.[48] Cincinnati went on to score three runs and win the game.

To be sure, the Code maintains that there are proper and improper ways for a player to interact with an umpire. A player can curse but not directly at the ump. A catcher can question the home-plate umpire's calls, but he must not turn around to look at him. And never should a player talk about an umpire's mother. All of these are violations of the Code because they disrespect the umpire by showing him up. Even if an umpire makes a mistake, he will rarely ever admit it. If he does, the managers and players will ride him mercilessly and question each and every one of his calls. At the same time, each umpire has his own boiling point and will take only so much abuse before the ejections start to fly. Veteran managers know this and tend to see how far they can push the envelope. Sometimes they argue a call for the sole purpose of getting tossed in order to swing the momentum of the game their way or to give a wake-up call to their team.[49] This was not the case with Fregosi and Davidson, though.

Fregosi came out of the dugout to protect his catcher and prevent him from being tossed. He was aware that Davidson was punishing his pitchers because Daulton was questioning the umpire's strike zone. Daulton, on the other hand, crossed the line when he started poking Davidson in the chest. When he called the umpire a "motherfucker," Davidson had no choice but to eject him. It was a very rare ejection for Daulton, who had a reputation for respecting the umpires, even when he disagreed with their strike zones.

Seated in the trainer's room icing his knees after the game, Daulton called Davidson an "impact umpire." "We call him 'Balkin' Bob' because he's always waiting for an opportunity to make an impact on the game," explained the Phillies' catcher. "When an umpire is doing his job, you don't know he's there. He doesn't call attention to himself. But Davidson knew that this game was on ESPN and he couldn't wait to suit up and make an impact. He's one of those guys, if you go to his house, there are a lot of pictures of himself on the wall and none of his family."[50]

The Phillies lobbied furiously in the days immediately following the incident to be sure any punishment of Schilling or Daulton was minimal. While Schilling didn't receive as much as a reprimand from the National League president, Daulton was slapped with a four-hundred-dollar fine. For his part, Davidson acknowledged having "a little hoop-de-do" with Daulton, but denied it affected his calls. Because disciplinary action against umpires is not made public, it is not known what, if any, punishment was meted out. But it was not coincidental that Davidson was on vacation the next time his crew was assigned to umpire a series in Philadelphia in early July.[51]

Despite their winning ways, the Phillies committed a disturbing fifty-four errors by the end of May. Eighteen of those miscues came from the shortstop position. Fregosi finally gave up on Juan Bell and gave Kim Batiste and Mariano Duncan opportunities to take over the position, but both failed to do so. "I'd be willing to listen if anybody has a suggestion," grumbled Fregosi. "Somebody, sooner or later, has to step forward." General manager Lee Thomas finally resolved the matter when he placed Bell on waivers on May 30. Shortly after, the veteran shortstop was claimed by the Milwaukee Brewers. The move opened the way for twenty-three-year-old Kevin Stocker, who would be called up from Triple-A Scranton Wilkes-Barre a month later.[52]

On June 1 the Phillies defeated the Cincinnati Reds, 6–3, after losing a 3–1 lead in the seventh inning. The next day they won again behind the pitching of Ben Rivera, who posted a career-high nine strikeouts in the 5–2 victory. Returning to the Vet to face the Colorado Rockies, Terry Mulholland pitched a complete game, striking out a career-high fourteen, but the Phils lost, 2–1. Greene and Schilling followed up with back-to-back victories to close out the weekend series. After defeating the Expos in Montreal on June 14, the Phillies enjoyed an incredible 45-17 record and led the National League East by eleven and a half games. On June 23 they picked up their fiftieth win of the season against the Atlanta Braves, 8–3. Everything seemed to be going perfectly. Jim Eisenreich was hitting .351 with 18 RBI and was in the middle of a thirteen-game hitting streak. Incaviglia continued to provide the Phils with timely power hitting, leading the team with 21 RBI. Big Ben Rivera had the best June of any pitcher on the staff with a 5-1 record in six starts, and veteran reliever Larry Andersen didn't allow an earned run in eleven appearances during the month. Then the Phillies suddenly hit a wall.

Cleanup hitter Dave Hollins went on the disabled list for two weeks. He needed surgery on his throwing hand to remove a fractured hook in the hamate bone. On June 26–27 the Phils lost two straight to the Pirates before flying out to St. Louis for an important four-game series against the second-place Cardinals. It was a disaster. The Phillies lost the opener, 3–1. It was the team's third straight loss in as many games. They rebounded for a 13–10 victory the following day, but St. Louis was determined to win the showdown.[53] Like many opponents, the Cards weren't convinced that the Phillies could sustain their winning ways. "They're ripe for the taking," said St. Louis catcher Tom Pagnotti after the Phils dropped the opener of the series.[54]

Tommy Greene took the mound for the third game of the series. Greene started the month with an 8-0 record and a 1.92 ERA. Since then he had managed just one win in four starts, and his earned run average ballooned to 8.62. He was struggling, both mechanically and mentally. Cardinals hitters feasted on him, rapping out nine hits and six runs in five innings en route to a 9–3 victory. It was Greene's fifth consecutive bad start. The loss reduced the Phils' National League East lead to six and a half games.

The next night Curt Schilling was pummeled for eleven runs in just two and two-thirds innings. In the first inning after Schilling had surrendered the Cardinals' fifth run, Daulton called time and strolled out to the mound.

"Schil, you don't have shit today," he told his pitcher. "We're going to have to trick the hitters tonight."

No sooner had Dutch given his candid analysis than pitching coach Johnny Podres ambled out to the mound. Podres, known for encouraging his pitchers when they were getting hit hard, told the right-hander: "You've got great stuff. Just keep firing. You're looking good."

After Pods returned to the dugout, Schilling, confused, turned to Daulton and asked, "Which is it?"

"You ain't got shit," the catcher replied.[55]

The Cards went on to shellac the Phillies, 14–5, and pick up another full game in the standings. Now the Phils' lead had shriveled to just five and a half games.

"I embarrassed myself," Schilling said after the game, shell-shocked.

Daulton showed no sympathy for his batterymate in his postgame remarks to the media. "That was the most embarrassing game I've ever been part of," said the catcher. "I've been on some bad teams and I've been a very bad, very, very bad player. But that's the most embarrassed I've ever been."[56]

Dutch should have stopped there. The Code forbids a ballplayer from criticizing a teammate in public or in the newspapers. Not only does such behavior violate the trust and loyalty players must have for each other if they are to endure the inevitable crises of a 162-game season, but it challenges baseball's version of manhood.[57] Daulton didn't care. He had watched Greene and Schilling surrender and trudge meekly off the mound with their heads down in an ignominious retreat. If this was the way the two starters responded to pressure, the Phillies were in trouble. Dutch knew that he had to deliver a message. It was probably the only time in his career that he voiced his displeasure with teammates to the media rather than to address it privately with the offenders.

Lightning in a Bottle

FIG. 20. Mentored by Phillies pitching coach Johnny Podres
and catcher Darren Daulton, Curt Schilling became one of
the most dominant pitchers in Major League Baseball. After
being traded in 2000, Schilling was instrumental in pitching
the Arizona Diamondbacks to a World Series title in 2001 and
the Boston Red Sox to two world championships in 2004 and
2007. At the end of his twenty-year Major League career in
2007, Schilling compiled a 216-146 win-loss record,
3,116 strikeouts, and a 3.46 earned run average.
Photo by Al Tielemans.

"It's only July 1, and I don't think there's any need for pressure," he began, referring to the stress that comes with a pennant race. "But I think a couple of guys might have felt it. I would not think that four games against a contending team would cause guys to change the way they've been going about things, but maybe it has. And I'm not talking about everybody."

Daulton didn't have to name names; it was clear that he was referring to Greene and Schilling.

"We've got one guy who was 8-1, and in his last five decisions he hasn't shown up," Daulton continued. "The other guy . . . I don't know if they're tired, nervous, scared, worried, feeling the pressure or what. But I don't think this is the time for it."[58]

Usually such a verbal lashing calls for retaliation. Instead, Greene and Schilling accepted the criticism and agreed that their catcher had a valid point. "What could I say?" Schilling confessed in a recent interview.

> Darren was right. I lost focus. I was 8-1 at the beginning of June, and I thought about how nice it would be to get selected to the All-Star Game. I had gotten off the beaten path with that kind of thinking. It was irrelevant. Then I began pitching poorly, and by the end of the month I went 0-5. So when the writers asked for my response, I told them that everything Darren had said was absolutely right. Of course, I would rather not have been embarrassed. But Darren knew me, like he knew all the pitchers, and he knew how to get to me.[59]

Daulton confirmed that point. "I wasn't trying to inflame the situation," he said years later. "I was just trying to get the best out of them. As a catcher that was my responsibility. I had to know which buttons to push. To their credit, they learned from it, and they both pitched well for the rest of the season."[60]

On July 2, after the team returned to Philadelphia, Daulton and Kruk met privately with Schilling. "We told him that his pitching was the most important thing," recalled the Phillies' first baseman. "I think he just got caught up in too much stuff," like "calling the talk radio shows," "building an $800,000 house," and "[buying] a $200,000 Lamborghini." The two veterans convinced him to straighten out his priorities. They told Schilling that he had to decide whether he wanted to "pitch good just to make money to pay for the [luxuries] he bought" or to "help the team win."[61] Later that day Daulton called for the first closed-clubhouse players-only meeting of the season. His message was simple: "Play fearless, intimidating baseball. Take it a game at a time, and stop thinking about the pennant race."

After the thirty-one-minute meeting ended, a dozen reporters gathered around his locker to get the story. But by that time Daulton had realized that he had already said too much to the press. It would've been better to issue the tongue-lashing to the two pitchers in private. "You know guys, I really don't want to talk about the meeting," he said, dismissing the subject once and for all. "It was just a little regroup, and that's all I have to say."[62]

Schilling and Green righted themselves quickly. They began pitching inside to hitters, challenging them with their fastball, and intimidating those who once owned them. Instead of hanging their heads after a defeat, the two starters showed renewed determination. And the Phillies returned to their gloriously malevolent selves.

FIG. 21. Third baseman Dave Hollins played baseball with
the intensity of a football player. "If you had twenty-five guys
on the team like Hollins, they would have all killed each other
by the third week of the season," remarked third base
coach Larry Bowa. Photo by Al Tielemans.

TEN
Mikey

Dave Hollins sat in front of his locker and stewed. Since returning from the disabled list on June 28, he had been struggling at the plate and in the field. It was now mid-July, and his average had dropped from .288 to .266. In one twenty-game stretch the Phillies' third baseman committed nine errors and made at least another dozen wild throws. It got so bad that manager Jim Fregosi was using Kim Batiste as a late-inning defensive replacement.[1]

Did Hollins come back too soon from hand surgery? Were his hitting woes related to poor mechanics? Was it a mental thing? It was bad enough that he wasn't contributing, but he felt that his lack of offensive production was adding to the Phillies' recent woes.

Hollins took losing personally. The humiliating series against the Cardinals left him reeling. The more he thought about it, the more he stewed. Picking up a bat, the twenty-six-year-old third baseman started wringing his hands as if to squeeze sawdust out of it. Then he put the bat down and cursed. He glared at the uniform he just took off, cursed again, and then picked up an empty beer can and threw it in his locker.

Hollins couldn't help himself. "Mikey" had taken control. "Mikey" was the alter ego to Dave's evil twin. *Dave* was a normal guy, the "Dr. Jekyll" to *Mikey*'s "Mr. Hyde." Dave was a wonderful teammate who hustled on the field, respected the manager and his coaches, and was eager to talk baseball with fans. But Mikey was downright dangerous. "You stay away from Mikey," said Daulton. "He'll kill you, just as soon as look at you!"[2]

With the physique of the Incredible Hulk, Hollins could be frightening when he was angry. Once, after striking out with the bases loaded in a game against the Chicago Cubs, he took a bat to the clubhouse toilet, smashing it to pieces. "I wasn't the kind of player who would blow things off, and say, 'We'll get 'em tomorrow,'" he admitted. "If you start to accept losing, you will lose. And losing was so unenjoyable to me. I didn't want to be on a losing team. I let everybody around me know that, too. If you're not playing hard and trying to win for the team, then you were going to have a problem with me."[3] That's why the third baseman threatened to go after the Phillies' pitchers if they didn't protect the hitters.

After leading the National League in hit by pitches with nineteen in 1992, Hollins was fed up. He vowed to even the score with opposing pitchers, especially with Atlanta's Greg Maddux, who hit him four times. During the off-season, Dave ran into Maddux at a charity event in Las Vegas and confronted him. "Listen, if you ever hit me or any of my teammates again, I'm going to kill you," he snarled at the Braves' ace. Then he turned and walked away. John Kruk, who was also at the event, saw Maddux the next day. When the Atlanta starter asked him if the third baseman was serious, Kruk replied, "He's as serious as a heart attack."[4]

Hollins also put the Phils' pitchers on notice at the beginning of spring training. "Whenever I got hit by a pitch, I acted as if it didn't bother me, so our pitchers thought I didn't care," he explained. "They figured it was no big deal if I got hit or not. Well, that wasn't the right message to send your teammates or the other team, so I addressed it. I just told our pitchers, 'If you're not going to protect the hitters, there's going to be a problem between you and me. I'm going to be the first one to come after you if one of our guys gets hit and you don't do something about it.' There was no problem after that. All the pitchers fell in line."[5]

Hollins was an old-school ballplayer who believed that everyone on the club had a responsibility to each other, and if they refused to follow through, he would make them accountable. It was a matter of respect as well as custom. Pitchers intentionally throw at batters to disrupt their timing, to back them away from the plate, to punish them for hitting a home run, and especially to retaliate after a teammate has been hit. "Retaliation" is an essential part of the Code. If a batter is hit, his pitcher has a duty to strike an opposing batsman in return. It's a subtle way of protecting your teammate and restoring respect as well as a competitive balance to the game.[6]

There were times, however, when Hollins went overboard. Once, in a spring-training game at St. Petersburg, manager Jim Fregosi sat the six-foot-one, 205-pound third baseman, and on the bus ride back to Clearwater Mikey was fuming. "When I get off this bus, I'm going to kick Fregosi's ass," he told Kruk. "I'm going to kill that motherfucker."

"You can't kill the manager," replied Kruk. "I don't care what you do, but you're not going to kill the manager. It don't work that way."

"I don't give a fuck," snapped Mikey. "I'm going to kill him."

Eventually, the Krukker got Hollins to calm down and give the Phils' manager another chance.[7]

"Dave is the most intense player I've ever seen," said third base coach Larry Bowa, who was pretty intense himself during his playing days. "If you had 25 guys on the team like Hollins, they would all kill each other by the third week of the season."[8] "Intense" was an understatement. Hollins played the game with reckless abandon, refusing to give an inch to the opposition. At the plate Dave, a switch hitter who could drive the ball with power from either side, never shied away from a brushback pitch. On the base paths he barreled over middle infielders like an NFL linebacker to break up a double play. At third base he knocked hard-hit line drives down with his body if he couldn't field them.

While team leader Darren Daulton respected Hollins's intensity, he did not tolerate the third baseman's selfish behavior. When the Phillies swept the Astros in Houston to open the season, Hollins went 0 for 3 in the last game of the series. Infuriated by his performance, the young third baseman became sullen. While his teammates were celebrating the sweep on the plane ride back to

Philadelphia, Hollins continued to brood. When Dutch approached him and asked if he was all right, he ignored the catcher. Now Daulton was angry. Hollins's behavior indicated that he cared more about his own performance than the success of the team. It was pure selfishness.

When Hollins walked into the clubhouse the next day, Daulton was waiting for him. "After the cold shoulder you gave me yesterday, I stayed up all night thinking about how I was going to beat the shit out of you," said Dutch. "Let's get one thing straight—the team comes first, no matter how good or how bad you do. There were plenty of times I struck out three or even four times in a game, but it didn't matter because we won. You better learn to deal with it. Don't ever do that to me again, or I *will* beat the shit out of you!"[9] His message delivered, Daulton turned and walked away.

Today, Hollins laughs about the "Jekyll-Hyde" characterization. "It was just the way I played the game," he said in a recent interview.

> It was the way I needed to prepare for a game and the way I reacted to a bad performance. I would've loved to have had a blast, sing, and be happy all the time. But that didn't work for me. Whenever I relaxed it seemed I got kicked in the ass. I was still a young player, and I thought I was letting the people around me know how serious I was about winning. But I didn't always come across that way. Dutch taught me an important lesson. He taught me that I could still play hard, but that it shouldn't interfere with putting the team first.[10]

That Hollins played baseball with a football mentality is understandable. Growing up in Orchard Park, New York, a suburb of blue-collar Buffalo, Dave dreamed of being an NFL player for the hometown Bills. But his father had other plans for him.

Born on May 25, 1966, Dave was the sixth of Ronald and Florence Hollins's seven children. Like most of their neighbors, the Hollinses were hardworking, proud, and independent parents with a strong sense of right and wrong. Florence worked as a registered nurse at South Buffalo Mercy Hospital and Ronald for the state in the sales-tax department. To make ends meet, he also worked at a sporting-goods store. "My parents worked hard for what we had," recalled the Phillies' third baseman. "They worked all the time, pulling in $20,000 or $25,000 a year. We weren't in poverty or anything. There was always food on the table. But we were just getting by. And when you have seven kids and you're just getting by, there's no social life. After work, my dad came straight home and he made sure that extra 15 or 20 bucks went to the family instead of dropping it at the gin mill or going out somewhere with the guys."

Ronald's true passion, however, was baseball. In the 1940s, before he got married, he was good enough to earn twenty-five dollars a game in the semipro leagues at a time when a worker at the local Bethlehem Steel plant might make thirty-five dollars a week. That's why he encouraged Dave to play ball instead of getting a job in the summer. "You can work your whole life, 40 or 50 years after you get out of college," Ronald told his youngest son. So Dave played seven days a week in three different leagues. At the same time, Ronald had certain expectations for his sons. Playing baseball wasn't just fun and games, and Dave understood that from the beginning. "If I came home from a bad game and took it lightly, well, that wasn't something that was accepted around the house," he said. "Even in Little League sports was taken very seriously. To blow it off, to say you'd get them next time, just didn't cut it. That's just the way I was brought up. If you take things too lightly, you tend to get comfortable with losing."[11]

At Orchard Park High School Dave was a highly recruited quarterback who could've played at several Division I colleges. But he also played baseball for Bob Barrows, a local legend who coached the Quakers to 643 victories, including 24 ECIC division titles, seven Section 6 championships, and a New York state crown in 1988.[12] "Coach Barrows had a feel for the game and a passion for it, too," said Hollins. "Guys responded to him. He had his own unique personality. When things went wrong, he addressed it, then let you play. He was no brow-beater. That wasn't his style."[13]

Dave earned "All Western New York" baseball honors in 1983 and 1984. Named the region's "Player of the Year" in 1984, he is still considered the best baseball player to come out of that part of the state.[14] "I was a better football player than baseball player in high school," Hollins admitted. "I didn't have the same baseball skills as other kids who were getting drafted. I had to work harder. I guess that's where the football mentality tied in."[15]

Two of Hollins's brothers—Steve and Paul—signed professional baseball contracts. Steve, a five-foot-nine second baseman, played in the Phillies organization in 1990, but never made it higher than rookie ball at Princeton in the Appalachian League.[16] Paul, a six-foot-two, 195-pound outfielder, played in the New York Mets, Seattle Mariners, and Detroit Tigers organizations in the 1980s. Paul, who is seven years older than Dave, was supposed to be the star. "I'm on the record as saying that Paul Hollins is the best athlete I ever had," said Orchard Park High School coach Bob Barrows. "But I always thought he got a raw deal. I never understood what the knock on him was."

"You not only have to have talent, you've got to have the breaks," said Dave when asked about his brothers' professional baseball careers. "They got no breaks. Paul was an All-American at South Carolina. He hit .400 his senior year, 15 homers, went to the College World Series. But he didn't even get drafted. He had to sign as a free agent with the Mets. His last three years in the minors he averaged 21 homers a season, but he could never get above Double A. He never got a shot to go to Triple A. But everything clicked for me, just the opposite of what happened to my brothers."[17]

When he wasn't selected in the June 1984 draft, Hollins accepted a baseball scholarship to the University of South Carolina, a stellar NCAA Division I program. Selected by the San Diego Padres in the sixth round of the 1987 amateur draft, the hard-nosed third baseman spent two seasons in Class A ball and a third in Double A. During that span he compiled a .292 batting average with 20 home runs and 215 RBI.[18] Hollins was just twenty-three years old when Phils general manager Lee Thomas stole him from San Diego in the Rule Five draft in December 1989. Because he never played higher than Double-A ball, the Phillies had to keep the promising third baseman on the twenty-five-man Major League roster for the entire 1990 season or return him to the Padres at half the salary.

Despite the fact that Hollins was not yet ready for the Majors,

FIG. 22. Hollins was a hard-nosed third baseman who often played
through injuries. Photo by Al Tielemans.

Thomas recognized his tremendous talent and retained him. He
appeared in seventy-two games during the 1990 campaign, batting
just .184 with 5 homers and 15 RBI. In 1991 Hollins played regularly in the second half of the season, boosting his average to .298
in 114 at bats.[19]

"I always tell myself how fortunate I am," said Hollins. "I got out
of the San Diego organization at just the right time. I was having
my best month at Triple A [Scranton Wilkes-Barre in 1991] when
the guy at third base in the big leagues [Charlie Hayes] cooled off,
so I got called up. If he doesn't cool off, if I'm not playing well, I
don't get called up and have a chance to play every day."[20]

The year 1992 was Hollins's breakout season. Named the starting third baseman at the beginning of the season, Hollins played
in 156 games. He hit .270 with 27 home runs, 93 RBI, and 104 runs
scored. The productive offense made up for his defensive shortcomings, having committed 18 errors at the hot corner.[21] Still,
the Phillies were so impressed with Hollins's offensive production
that they broke from their policy of not giving multiple-year contracts to players not yet eligible for arbitration. As a result, Hollins
received a two-year deal worth $600,000 for 1993 and $2 million

for 1994.[22] At the same time, the big contract added more pressure on the third baseman to perform.

During the off-season the pressure increased when Hollins discovered that he had diabetes. The condition led to a dramatic 15-pound weight loss, something the Phils' cleanup hitter could ill afford. Hollins struggled to get back to his 205-pound playing weight for the '93 campaign. According to Jeff Scott, the bodybuilder who was supplying Lenny Dykstra with steroids, the third baseman began visiting his apartment to find out more about Androstenedione, a prohormone that increases muscle mass. While Hollins denies ever being in Scott's apartment, another source insists that the Phils' power hitter often visited there.[23] Because Hollins inquired about the drug does *not* mean that he was using it. But there is the suggestion that Dykstra was not the only member of the Phillies who was linked to PEDS.

In addition to Nails, Daulton, Incaviglia, and Hollins have long been suspect, and Todd Pratt, the Phils' backup catcher, was even identified as a PED user in the Mitchell Report.[24] In fact, Jeff Cooper, the Phils' trainer, admitted to Todd Zolecki of the *Philadelphia Inquirer* in 2007 that there was at least one other player aside from Dykstra whose PED use was "obvious." When Cooper approached the player on the steroids issue, he was told to "mind his own business," and "the matter went no further."[25]

Regardless, Hollins was concerned enough about his offensive production during the spring of 1993 that he returned early from hand surgery in late June in order to replicate his impressive home run and RBI totals of the previous year.

"It's not a fun time to be playing," Hollins said of his slump. "No one wants to go out and play poorly." But manager Jim Fregosi believed it was necessary to have his regular third baseman in the lineup. "He has to play through it," said the skipper.[26] So when the Phillies returned home from St. Louis with their tails between their legs and their lead reduced to five and a half games, Hollins was in the starting lineup.

On Friday night, July 2, the Phils faced the San Diego Padres in a twilight doubleheader. The first game was scheduled to start at 4:35 p.m. but because of a sudden shower, it was to 5:45 p.m. when Terry Mulholland finally took the mound. A second rain delay occurred in the bottom of the fourth at 6:29 p.m. and lasted almost two hours. Play resumed at 8:25 p.m., but not for long. A torrential downpour halted the game again in the bottom of the fifth inning. The wind and rain were so fierce that the outfield fence was barely visible from home plate. It was midnight by the time the rain stopped and the tarpaulins removed from the infield. Finally, at 1:03 a.m., the first game ended in a 5–2 Phillies loss.[27]

In the Phils' clubhouse, Pete Incaviglia was undressing, anticipating a warm shower, when bench coach John Vukovich told him that the second game of the twin bill would be starting in twenty minutes.

"I couldn't believe it," said Inky. "I had no clue."[28]

Up in the radio booth Richie Ashburn, the Phils' color commentator, tried to make the best of the situation. Kidding his sidekick and fellow broadcaster Harry Kalas, Ashburn said, "Harry, I'm expecting a great game out of you tonight. This is the shank of the evening for you. You're usually just getting started at this hour."[29]

Although the first game began with 54,617 people in the stands, only 6,000 stayed on through the three rain delays, which totaled five hours and fifty-four minutes. But as the bars let out and night shifts ended, others learned that the second game was going ahead as planned, and the attendance increased by another 3,000.[30] When the second game finally began at 1:28 in the morning, the Phils and Padres had set a record for the latest Major League game ever started.[31]

The Fightins continued to struggle, though. Falling behind 5–0 by the top of the third inning, they were listless at the plate, able to generate only a few hits. Padres starter Andy Benes, who had the lowest ERA in the league at the time, worked effortlessly until the eighth when the Phils battled back to tie the game. With the scored still knotted in the bottom of the tenth, Pete Incaviglia led off with a walk. Eisenreich advanced him to second with a single to right. Mitch Williams was slated to pitch the eleventh, and with no pinch hitters left on the bench, Fregosi had no choice but to hit him. As Wild Thing strolled to the plate to face San Diego closer Trevor Hoffman, Incaviglia, standing on second base, looked on in disbelief. "I knew if that little SOB got a hit, we'd never hear the end of it," said the burly outfielder.[32]

After fouling off Hoffman's first offering, Williams, at 4:40 a.m., singled to left to score Inky with the winning run, ending a twi-nighter that began twelve hours and five minutes earlier.[33] Everyone was surprised by the come-from-behind win, except for Eisenreich, who smirked, "I knew we'd win. Our guys were used to watching the sun come up. If they weren't out here at the park, they'd have been watching it come up anyway, just from some other part of the city."[34]

Eisey had a point. His teammates partied just as hard as they played, and Macho Row was the wildest of the bunch. In fact, Daulton, Dykstra, Kruk, and Williams often joked about their mantra, "If they only knew."

"Some wild things happened on that team that the fans never heard about," admitted Daulton years later.[35] When asked to elaborate, Dutch referenced the Code, replying, "You know what they say: 'What goes on in the clubhouse stays in the clubhouse.'" But the Phils' catcher was willing to share one story.

> We were playing in Chicago, and Lenny, Inky, Jake [John Kruk], and I were asked to do an appearance at a Las Vegas casino. The [casino] owner offered to fly us out after the Cubs' series ended and pay for our hotel rooms and all our meals.
>
> I wasn't sold on the idea because we had to play the Mets in New York the following night. But Lenny, who loved to gamble, talked us into it. Needless to say, we had a blast for ourselves and barely made it to Shea [Stadium] the next night. Now that might sound pretty irresponsible, but my philosophy as a player was pretty simple: "You only live once, so give it all you've got!"[36]

Dykstra was more candid. In a recent interview with Josh Innes of WIP Sports Radio in Philadelphia, Nails said that the 1993 Phillies put the 1986 Mets "to shame" in terms of their off-field antics. "We took it to new levels," he declared, including "some monumental benders" and "dropping trou [going naked] with a couple of twenty-five-year-old chicks in a Jacuzzi" after a game in Houston.[37]

Some of the partying was good public relations, though. The '93 Phils were arguably the most fan-friendly team in the organization's history. "I loved Philly when I played there," said Lenny Dykstra. "It was a great sports town, and the fans know baseball."[38] It was not uncommon for Macho Row members, in particular, to be found in local bars having a beer and talking baseball with a group of admirers. "I really enjoyed my relationship with Phillies fans," recalled Incaviglia. "We'd go out for dinner and the fans would come up to say hello, and they'd always want to buy us a drink. We'd buy them drinks, too. Sometimes that made for a pretty long night. But you knew they really cared about the team."[39]

If Phillies fans cared about their players, it was due to the fact that they reminded them of themselves. That fact was not lost on John Kruk, who *always* made time for the faithful. "Phillies fans could relate to us," he explained.

> We weren't high draft picks. We weren't bonus babies. Most of us came from other organizations that didn't want us. Plus, we had everything—a good-looking catcher, a fat first baseman, a tobacco-chewing center fielder, a hundred-year-old setup guy [Larry Andersen], and a hairy left fielder [Incaviglia].
>
> The fans also had the chance to see us and talk to us somewhere other than the playing field. We made ourselves accessible to them. That's important. That's when they know you care.
>
> So when I hear players say Philly is a tough place to play because of the fans, I know those players didn't have the guts to succeed here. Once you're in with the fans, you're like family. It doesn't matter if you played here one year or twenty years. Phillies fans don't forget.[40]

But making time for the fans, all the partying and the camaraderie of the clubhouse, took its toll on several players. "There were eight, ten, twelve players most nights sitting around the clubhouse after the game, having a beer and talking baseball," said reliever Larry Andersen. "Other nights we were out, often with the fans. I think there were seven divorces from that team because of it, and I was one of 'em. I tried to tell my wife that drinking after the game with teammates and being accessible to the fans was a part of my job description, but it didn't fly. Still, it's what I thought baseball should be, and it took me twenty-four years to have the opportunity to play on a team like that. It was really special, and I wouldn't have traded it for anything."[41]

Although the Phillies were still in a losing funk, the come-from-behind victory against the Padres in the early-morning hours of July 3 reignited Lenny Dykstra. On Sunday, July 4, in the finale of the series, Dykstra collected three hits and scored three runs, propelling the Phils to an 8–4 victory over the Padres. He continued his hot streak when the Los Angeles Dodgers came to Philadelphia for a three-game series. In the opener Nails scored three more runs in the Phillies' 9–5 romp. Tommy Greene earned the victory, making him the first Phils starter to record ten wins before the All-Star Game. Although the Phillies lost the second game, 7–5, Dykstra hit his twelfth career lead-off home run. Finally, in the rubber match, Lenny's two-run double in the bottom of the twentieth inning gave the Fightins a 7–6 win over Los Angeles in another marathon game that lasted six hours and ten minutes. Nails would continue his hot hitting throughout July, posting a .374 batting average and scoring twenty-five runs in twenty-eight games while leading the team with five homers that month.[42]

Nearly two decades later Dykstra admitted that his use of steroids allowed him to perform at such a high level for a prolonged period of time. Being in the final year of his contract in 1993, the thirty-year-old center fielder "did what he had to do" to enhance his statistics. "Remember, I had a chance to make millions of dollars, but only if I could perform," he told WIP Sports Radio host Howard Eskin. "If you can't perform, they fire you. There's always someone else ready to take your job. I needed to protect my job, take care of my family. So whatever you have to do, you do because the window of opportunity to earn that kind of money is so small." In fact, Nails was so determined to become "the highest-paid lead-off hitter in the game" that he was careful to protect his secret.

Although Major League Baseball did not have any drug testing at the time, baseball commissioner Fay Vincent put steroids on MLB's banned-substance list in 1991. But Dykstra didn't care. He admitted that he was "so far ahead of the curve" in terms of camouflaging his use that he "wasn't worried" about getting caught.[43]

To be sure, steroids allowed Dykstra to have a career year in 1993. PEDs improved his recovery time, enabling him not only to survive the grueling 162-game schedule, but also to heal faster from muscle fatigue and injury. As a result, Nails, who played in fewer than 100 games in each of the previous injury-ridden two seasons, made 773 plate appearances in 161 games, more than anyone in Major League history. Steroids also augmented the quickness essential to his swing as well as to stealing bases and the muscle mass necessary to hit with power. Not surprisingly, Dykstra, in 1993, led the National League in hits (194), walks (129), and runs (143). In addition to batting .305, Nails set career highs in home runs (19), doubles (44), RBI (66), stolen bases (37), and on-base percentage (.420).[44] In retrospect, Dykstra would have been hard-pressed to achieve those statistics without the advantage of PEDs.

Despite Dykstra's hot streak, the Phillies continued to flounder. On July 8 the San Francisco Giants, who sat atop the National League's Western Division, came to the Vet for a four-game series. The only bright spot came in the third game, when Mickey Morandini smashed a grand slam, powering the Phils to an 8–3 victory on national television. San Francisco won the other three games by scores of 13–2, 15–8, and 10–2. After the dust cleared, the Giants had outscored the Phillies 41–20 in the four-game set. The starting pitching, so dominant a month ago, was shabby. The three losing starters in the series—Danny Jackson, Ben Rivera, and Curt Schilling—allowed thirty-four hits and twenty-six runs in nine and a third innings. Schilling was especially bad. He lasted just three and two-thirds innings in the finale and was blowtorched for eleven hits and six earned runs. This time, however, team leader Dutch Daulton was more careful in his postgame analysis. "I know everybody wants me to rip [the pitching]," he said. "But I've done that enough. They're young and this is part of their learning process. They're taking their lumps. But for us to win, they're going to have to get out of it."[45]

Heading into the All-Star Break, the Phillies had lost fifteen of twenty-seven games they played since their National League East lead was at eleven and a half games on June 14. The slump was understandable, though. For most of the first half, the Fightins had been playing exceptional baseball with a winning percentage of .684 or better.[46] They were due to cool off. The three-day break would allow them to recuperate. That is, with the exceptions of Daulton, Hollins, Kruk and Mulholland, all of whom were selected to the National League All-Star team, and manager Jim Fregosi, who was selected as a coach.

The sixty-fourth Major League All-Star Game was played on July 13, at Oriole Park at Camden Yards in Baltimore. Mulholland, who was 9-6 at the break, started for the National League, facing Mark Langston of the California Angels, the American League starter. In the top of the first, Barry Bonds of the San Francisco Giants doubled with one out, and Gary Sheffield of the Florida Marlins belted a homer to left, giving the NL a 2–0 lead.

Mulholland, who pitched the first two innings, allowed one base runner in the first when Paul Molitor of the Toronto Blue Jays walked with one out. In the second Kirby Puckett of the Minnesota Twins homered with one out to dead center field, reducing the NL lead to 2–1. Wade Boggs of the New York Yankees followed with a two-out walk, but was stranded on base when the Phils' southpaw retired the side. "I didn't feel shaky or anything like that," said Mulholland of his first All-Star appearance. "I thought I might, but I really didn't. I threw the first pitch high but, after that, I just said, 'Here I am. Let's get things going.' And I took it from there."[47]

Kruk, who was making his third All-Star appearance, arrived in Baltimore under the impression that he was going to be used as the designated hitter. But NL manager Bobby Cox inserted him at first base because that's where he had been voted in by the fans. That was fine with Kruk. He reasoned that the DH might end up playing the whole game. "And they might bring in [Seattle Mariners ace] Randy Johnson," he pointed out. That thinking backfired when AL manager Cito Gaston brought Johnson in to pitch the third inning. The face-off provided fans with some great theater.

The Phillies' first baseman, who was batting cleanup, faced Johnson, a six-foot-ten flamethrowing left-hander, with two outs and nobody on. The first pitch was a 95 mph fastball that sailed ten feet over Kruk's head. Backing out of the batter's box with a nervous grin on his face, the Krukker patted his heart dramatically and stepped into the box again. He was even more tentative now as he watched the next pitch sail right down the middle of the plate. Johnson dropped down for the next two deliveries, and Kruk, bailing badly, swung and missed. Both benches were laughing along with the Krukker by now.

"That was fuckin' hilarious," said Hollins.

"No, that was vintage John Kruk," said Mulholland, correcting his teammate. "Throughout his career, Johnny has been the master of self-preservation. This was the ultimate test."

Kruk bowed to Johnson, who winked at his strikeout victim as he strolled off the mound.

"When I first stepped into the box, I just wanted to make contact," admitted Kruk, who went 0 for 3 with two strikeouts. "After the first pitch, I just said, 'Here, the plate is yours. Go ahead and take it.' And he did. I was bailing out like a little kid. I was never so happy to strike out in my life. He's going to kill somebody. I wanted to live. And I lived. So it was a good at-bat."[48]

San Diego's Andy Benes came in to pitch the third for the NL, and, two pitches later, the score was tied, 2–2, when Roberto Alomar of the Blue Jays homered to right. After that it was all American League. Puckett, who was named Most Valuable Player of the game, hit a run-scoring double in a three-run fifth-inning rally that broke a 2–2 tie and sent the American League to its sixth straight victory by a final score of 9–3.

Dave Hollins, who made his first All-Star appearance, was inserted after the NL climbed to within 5–3 in the sixth. He was the only Phillie to pick up a hit, with a double to right in the eighth. Daulton, a two-time All-Star, went 0 for 3 and spent a portion of the sixth inning rolling around the dirt, chasing the pitches of John Smoltz of the Atlanta Braves.[49]

The Phillies started the second half of the season with a four-game lead in the NL's Eastern Division. Fans and management hoped that the three-day respite of the All-Star Break gave the players the rest they needed to return with a renewed determination to win. Only time would tell if they could recapture the magic that had prevailed during the spring.

ELEVEN
Dog Days

On July 15 the Phillies began an eleven-game West Coast trip with a 5–2 loss in San Diego. The following night the Padres won again, scoring five runs in the seventh inning to defeat the Phillies 5–3, who wasted two homers off the bat of Darren Daulton. The third game of the series was not much better. For the second straight night, San Diego rallied with three runs in the seventh for a 4–2 victory. The loss was the fourth in a row for the Phils, the longest losing streak of the season. Now their lead in the National League East was cut to three and a half games.[1] Patience was running thin. It was to be expected.

July and August are baseball's "dog days," that sultry period of summer when temperatures are the hottest. Tempers also tend to be hot, especially when a ball club is not performing to its expectations. No temper was hotter than Danny Jackson's after the Phillies dropped the third straight game to San Diego on July 17. On the bus ride from Jack Murphy Stadium to the team's hotel, the veteran southpaw became agitated by all the excuses for losing he was hearing from some of the younger players.

"The umpires aren't cutting us any breaks."

"Other teams in the NL East are too hot right now."

"Our pitching is too inexperienced to compete in a pennant race."

A ten-year veteran, Jackson was one of the few players on the team with postseason experience, having pitched for two world championship teams, the 1985 Kansas City Royals and the 1990 Cincinnati Reds. He knew what it was like to compete in a pennant race, and making excuses was not part of the winning formula. Thus, Jackson was growing angrier by the minute as the alibis continued. Suddenly, he snapped. Taking to his feet, the six-foot, 205-pound pitcher head-butted the luggage rack above his seat and then began screaming: "Stop all the bitching!" he thundered.

No one uttered a word. All eyes were glued to Jackson, his forehead now streaming with blood.

"Just shut the fuck up!" he ranted. "If the umpire blows a call, screw it! Hit the next fucking pitch! Who gives a fuck what team is hot! We can't control that. Control the things we can control like the way we play!"[2]

The gash on Jackson's forehead would require seven stitches, but his tirade registered with the youngsters. The next day Curt Schilling defeated the Padres, 6–3, picking up his first victory since July 11 and putting a halt to the Phillies' skid. Williams came on in the ninth for his twenty-fourth save. Moving on to Los Angeles, the Phils swept the Dodgers in three games, with Jackson recording his eighth victory and every position player collecting at least one hit in the series.

Returning to Philadelphia on July 27, the Phils hosted the St. Louis Cardinals for three games.[3] They had an additional incentive to beat the Redbirds after Mark Whiten, the Cardinal right fielder, was quoted on ESPN as saying, "It's nice to sit back and watch the Phillies fall flat on their face." But it was St. Louis who fell to the Phils in the three-game series. Kruk collected five hits in the opener to pace the 10–7 romp as the Phils extended their division lead to five games. The next night Todd Zeile hit a first-inning grand slam to give the Cards a quick 4–0 lead. But the Fightins rallied, with Daulton driving in six runs. The easy 14–6 victory gave Terry Mulholland his tenth win. The Phils swept the series the next afternoon, 6–4, to take a seven-game lead over the second-place Cardinals. Afterward, Daulton warned his teammates to learn from Whiten's example. "Let sleeping dogs lie," he warned his teammates. "Don't say anything stupid to the press that's going to come back and kick us in the ass tomorrow."[4]

To be sure, the Phillies were superstitious bunch, and it started at the top. Team president Bill Giles and other members of the brass, watching home games from the executive box on the 400 level of the Vet, would flip their neckties over their shoulders in the late innings to help start a rally if the Phillies were behind. Manager Jim Fregosi always wore his red satin jacket in the dugout, even when temperatures exceeded ninety degrees. Kruk, the most slovenly member of the team, never cleaned his batting helmet, and he would wear the same socks and same T-shirt if he was in the midst of a hitting streak. Larry Andersen wore the same cap until it smelled so ripe that Mitch Williams set it on fire.[5] But the most superstitious Phillie was Lenny Dykstra.

Nails would go through more than six hundred batting gloves each season. If he made an out, he stripped off the batting gloves, spit tobacco on them, and threw them away. If he was in a slump, he changed batting gloves every game. In fact, Dykstra discarded so many pairs of gloves that bench coach John Vukovich supplied his son's Little League team with the throwaways for three seasons. Nor was the idiosyncrasy limited to batting gloves.

If Nails made an out, he spit out the plug of tobacco he was chewing and inserted a fresh one in his mouth. Similarly, he was known to change his uniform during the game if he was hitless or if he struck out. Once, Lenny trashed an entire shipment of bats because the company's label was not lined up with his signature on the barrel. He believed that the misalignment threw off his balance when he stared down the barrel of the bat. On another occasion he threw out another shipment of bats because his name was printed—not signed—on the barrel. Although the Phils' clubhouse attendants were responsible for placing each player's initials on their equipment, Dykstra insisted that Frank Coppenbarger, the Phils' equipment manager, was the only person allowed to touch his belongings. "Dykstra liked the way I printed his initials," recalled Coppenbarger. "If one of the other clubbies tried marking his stuff, the Dude would go ballistic."[6]

The superstitions might have played a role in the Phillies' reversal of fortune, but there were other reasons for their improved play, too. Shortstop Kevin Stocker was summoned from Triple-A Scranton Wilkes-Barre and immediately stabilized the infield. After going 0 for 6 in his first game on July 7, the twenty-three-year-old rookie went 9 for 18 over the next two weeks and enjoyed two ten-game hitting streaks in late July and mid-August. Stocker's on-field demeanor earned high praise from manager Jim Fregosi, a former shortstop himself. "Kevin has a good field presence and remarkable instincts," observed Fregosi. "He knows exactly how to position himself at the right place and at the right time." Third base coach Larry Bowa gave Stocker his ultimate compliment, however, when he said the young shortstop "reminds me of a young me." "He makes all the right moves," added Bowa, who was never known for modesty.[7] Even the veterans of Macho Row were impressed. "Stick him right in the ghetto with us," demanded Pete Incaviglia. "He's got thick skin. This is where he belongs."[8]

In addition, third baseman Dave Hollins had rebounded from his three-week slump after returning from hand surgery. His hand stronger, Hollins's throws were much less erratic, and his long-ball swing returned. "The reason I rushed back is because, in early August, I wanted to be where I'm at now," explained Hollins, who collected 15 RBI and a .388 average between July 27 and August 12. He also enjoyed the National League's fourth-best at-bat-per-RBI ratio (5.2) and was among the league leaders in runs scored, RBI, and walks during that span. In fact, Hollins, despite missing fifteen games on the disabled list, was on pace to knock in 102 runs. "I knew I had to battle through it and that it would take time to get my timing back. But if I didn't come back when I did, I wouldn't have been any good to the team until late August."[9]

One of the things that helped the moody third baseman was the antics of teammate Danny Jackson, who, in addition to a penchant for head-butting, often indulged in a hilarious "Incredible Hulk" imitation. "The whole thing actually started when Dave returned from the disabled list," explained Jackson. "He was really getting down on himself because he wasn't hitting. So I just tried to make

FIG. 23. Pitcher Danny Jackson did his imitation of the Incredible Hulk by ripping off his jersey whenever his teammates needed to be "pumped up." Photo by Al Tielemans.

him laugh, to cheer him up a bit." Returning to the clubhouse from his workout in the weight room, Jackson spotted his younger teammate seated next to his locker brooding.

"Hey, Mikey, you're going to have a great game today," exclaimed the zany pitcher. "Wanna know why?"

Startled at first, Hollins looked up from his locker and replied, "No, why?"

"Because I'm here to pump you up!" shrieked Jackson, who tore off his T-shirt and began flexing his biceps.

Hollins was laughing so hard he began to cry. "You're nuts!" he said, barely able to get the words out between the laughter and tears.

"That's what they tell me!" roared Jackson as he continued to flex his ripped arms.

Hollins went 3 for 5 that night, pacing the Phillies to a 10–2 victory over the Pittsburgh Pirates and helping Jackson to his second complete game of the season. When teammates heard about the pitcher's crazy motivational technique and how it restored Hollins's hitting, they began egging him on to "pump them up!" The stunt became so popular that it actually helped to define the colorful nature of the team.[10]

Another reason the Phillies were successful was because of their reliable middle-relief corps. Larry Andersen and David West had been questionable at the beginning of the season. The Phils didn't know if Andersen, a forty-year-old veteran, had the stamina to endure another 162-game season, and West's career statistics prior to 1993 (16-20, 5.45 ERA) were not that impressive. But both relievers turned out to be extremely successful setup men for closer Mitch Williams. Andersen and West each strung together thirteen-and-a-third-inning scoreless streaks during the season and tied each other for the lowest ERA (2.92) on the staff. West, who was averaging nearly a strikeout per inning at one point, credited his success to pitching coach Johnny Podres, who allowed him to be a power pitcher. "Pods let me rely on my fastball," he said. "He respects my natural ability instead of making me a carbon copy of the other pitchers on the staff. That's what they tried to do to me in Minnesota, and it just didn't work. Here, they respect individuality, probably because so many of the veterans have fallen out of favor somewhere else. We're all misfits, who've found a home here."

The other middle relievers also surpassed expectations. Roger Mason, acquired by the Phillies on July 3 from the San Diego Padres, pitched forty-nine and two-thirds innings and recorded five victories. Bobby Thigpen, acquired on August 10 from the Chicago White Sox, went 3-1. Donnie Pall, acquired on September 1 also from the White Sox, allowed just 5 earned runs for a 2.55 ERA in the seventeen and two-thirds innings he worked. Because manager Jim Fregosi didn't want Williams, his closer, to pitch before the ninth inning, or to bring him into a game with runners on base, the middle relievers were crucial to the Phillies' success as well as to Williams's forty-three saves that season.[11] Wild Thing knew it, too.

"I will say till the day I die that the seventh and eighth innings are harder to pitch than the ninth because you have to make quality pitches," admitted Williams. "In the ninth inning, hitters don't have a safety net; they don't have that many batters coming up after them. The guys who pitch the seventh and eighth innings don't have that much margin for error. They get the important outs. I got all the recognition for the save. Well, a lot of times that season, the save happened in the seventh or eighth inning. Those guys made my job a hell of a lot easier."[12]

To show his appreciation, Wild Thing bought expensive gifts for everyone in the bullpen. "Mitch was a very generous person as well as an effective closer," recalled Mason.

> When the Phillies were in Houston in late August, he came up to me and asked for my shoe size. I'm thinking, "Okay, this is my initiation to the team. He's going to buy me a pair of really stupid-looking shoes, steal the dress shoes from my locker, and force me to wear these things in public."
>
> Well, the next day I show up at the Astrodome and I see these six-hundred-dollar pair of ostrich boots in my locker. It turns out that Mitch bought a pair of those boots for everyone in the bullpen. Another time he bought all of us these fancy leather belts with real expensive buckles on them. I'd heard of things like that before, but I'd never been a recipient. So, I was really taken by Mitch's generosity.[13]

Finally, the Phillies returned to their winning ways because Curt Schilling began pitching with confidence again. After losing five straight games and having his mental toughness publicly challenged by Daulton, Schilling turned his season around on July 18 when he defeated the San Diego Padres, 6–3, to snap the Phillies' four-game losing streak. He went on to win seven of his last eight decisions to finish the regular season with a 16-7 record.[14] Schilling combined a hard, rising fastball with a devastating split-finger fastball. When he pitched inside to hitters and located his pitches, rather than trying to overpower every hitter with his fastball, he was unbeatable. If he had been able to make those adjustments earlier in the season, he might have avoided his slump and won as many as twenty games that year.

Despite his success Schilling did not endear himself to the members of Macho Row. "Curt wants to be one of us, but we won't let him in," admitted Kruk. "Don't get me wrong. Schil has done a great job and I'd have to say he's our best pitcher. But I think sometimes he says too much to the press. That's when he gets into trouble. He should just worry about his job."[15]

Schilling's proclivity for airing his opinions wasn't the only thing that disturbed his teammates, either. He thought it was funny, for example, when during the playoffs he sat in the dugout with a towel over his head when Mitch Williams pitched in relief. The act suggested that it was too nerve-racking to watch Wild Thing attempt to save the game when he could just as easily lose it with his erratic pitching. Williams didn't appreciate the stunt. "It would've been fun to kick the shit out of him when he did that," he confessed years later. "The towel thing was the main issue I had with him. Don't get me wrong. If we had a big game to win, I'd want Schilling on the mound because he knew how to battle. But at some point you have to act like a man, and that was just childish."[16] Daulton was more succinct: "Every fifth day, Schil is our horse. The other four days he's a horse's ass."[17]

When recently asked about the towel incident, Schilling insisted that he "regretted it" and "stopped the practice immediately after Dave Hollins told me how it was being perceived by teammates." "I had no idea I was showing him up," said the former Phillies ace. "I was just nervous. In fact, I went straight to Mitch and apologized." According to Schilling, Williams said, "Dude, I'd wear a towel over my head, too, if I had to watch myself pitch." Wild Thing allegedly reinforced the point by having buttons made that read: "I survived watching Mitch pitch in the 1993 postseason."[18]

At the time, however, Schilling appeared to be oblivious to all the criticism. Instead, he was extremely positive when asked about his teammates on the '93 Phillies. "These are the 25 most important guys in my life," he insisted as the dog days of August ended and the team headed into the pennant race. "A lot of times you see teams where guys can't wait to get away from one another after the game. But I don't think the players here feel that way at all. This is as fun an atmosphere as I have ever been around, and I wouldn't trade my teammates for anything in the world."[19]

There's no question that the six-foot-five, 200-pound right-hander was happy to be part of a team that went from worst to first in one season and had fun doing it. Before arriving in Philadelphia in 1992, Schilling was a journeyman reliever for the Boston Red Sox, Baltimore Orioles, and Houston Astros. In the four seasons he pitched in the Majors, he had compiled a 4-11 win-loss record with 11 saves and a very unimpressive earned run average of 5.60.[20] There were flashes of the dominant pitcher Schilling would eventually become, but no sustained success and a work ethic that was mediocre at best. The premature death of his father left a huge void in his life.

Clifford Schilling was an army sergeant and a paratrooper who grew up in Somerset, Pennsylvania, where he played football in high school. But baseball was his passion, and he shared it with Curt, his only son. After serving in the military for two decades, Cliff worked as a night auditor for Ramada Inn, but open-heart surgery in 1977 forced him to retire. Afterward, he devoted himself to his son and two daughters. Cliff was especially committed to helping his son realize his dream to become a big-league pitcher. When Curt pitched at Yavapai Junior College, a two-hour drive from the Schilling home in Phoenix, his father never missed a game. When Cliff died of a heart attack at age fifty-five in 1988, his son lost direction.

"Curt thought of his dad all the time, particularly early in his career when he wasn't doing so well," said Shonda Schilling, his wife. "Cliff was the person he would always talk to. He'd always know what to say. Cliff was the one who saw all the development, but he never saw Curt pitch in a major-league game." That is why Schilling, during the regular season, signed a sheet before each of his starts, leaving his father's name on a list for a courtesy pass. If Cliff couldn't attend the game in person, his son wanted him there in spirit. It became a symbolic inspiration to help him succeed.[21]

"After my dad died, I kind of did my own thing," Schilling admitted. "I did the minimal amount of work and relied almost solely on my natural ability, which got me to Triple A and a couple of shots in the big leagues."[22] But during the summer of 1993 he was becoming the ace of a first-place team that had captured the attention of baseball fans across the nation. It would be difficult not to enjoy a team like that. Still, Schilling, at the age of twenty-six, did not have the maturity he demonstrated later in his career.

"Maturity was part of the problem," Schilling recently admitted. "I was a young player then, and I just didn't fit on the [1993 Phillies] team in terms of personality." But he also emphasized that he "didn't have much in common" with his veteran teammates, "especially those on Macho Row." "I liked to read books, and they didn't," he said. "I liked to talk about things other than baseball, and they only talked about the game. I loved my wife and wanted to stay married, and they liked to party. I voiced my opinions to the media, and they ran away from the press. That's really what made me an outcast, someone to pick on." But Schilling insisted that he was "okay" with the dismissive treatment of his teammates. "I knew I was there to pitch," he said, "and I wanted that to be the thing that did the talking."[23] To be sure, the budding ace *did* let his pitching do the talking.

On August 10 Schilling held the Montreal Expos to five hits and struck out seven to lead the Phillies to a 5–2 win at the Vet. Five days later in New York, he put the Phillies in a 4–0 hole in the first inning, but stymied the Mets' offense for the rest of the game as his teammates bailed him out. With the score 4–1, Dykstra led off the eighth inning with a walk off Mets starter Eric Hillman. Duncan struck out, but Kruk followed with a towering homer, cutting New York's lead to one run, 4–3. "Once Kruk hit that home run, you knew we were going to win," said Schilling after the game.

Mets manager Dallas Green went to his bullpen, bringing in Anthony Young, who retired Incaviglia on a fly ball to left for the second out of the inning. But Daulton resumed the Phils' rally, belting a 3-2 fastball down the third base line for a double. Chamberlain knocked him in with a single to right and took second on the throw to the plate. Kim Batiste, who entered the game as a late-inning defensive replacement at third, plunked an 0-1 slider into left-center for a game-winning single. "There's something special going on here this year," chirped Schilling. "We just know that somehow we're going to find a way to win. That's how it's been all year."[24]

On August 17 the Phillies began a six-game road trip to Colorado and Houston. In the opener of the three-game set at Denver, the Phils survived two late-inning rallies to defeat the Rockies, 10–7.

FIG. 24. Phillies starting pitchers dressed as cowboys.
Photo by Al Tielemans.

Dykstra, who smacked his fourteenth homer of the season, provided
the game winner. A crowd of 63,194 spectators came out to watch
the game, the largest crowd to see the Phillies play that season. The
next night the Phils' road attendance surpassed the 2 million mark,
making them the biggest draw in the National League. Kruk hit two
homers; Stocker, batting .324, drove in three of the sixteen runs
he would record that month; and Wild Thing closed out the 7–6
win with his thirty-fourth save of the season. While the Phils lost
the getaway game, 6–5, and dropped two of three at Houston, they
still enjoyed an eight-game lead over the second-place Cardinals.[25]

Returning to Philadelphia on August 23, the Phils lost to the
Rockies, 3–2, in thirteen innings. The next night Jackson won his
tenth game, 4–2, before a crowd of 43,419 raucous fans. In doing
so he became the fifth Phillies starter to record ten or more victories, joining Tommy Greene, Terry Mulholland, Ben Rivera, and
Curt Schilling. Williams also notched his thirty-sixth save, match-
ing his career high and putting him alone in second place on the
Phillies' all-time-save list, with ninety-five. Schilling won the final

game of the series, defeating the Rockies 8–5. While he posted a career-high nine strikeouts, Schilling was aided by backup catcher Todd Pratt's two-run homer (one of ten hits he collected that month, including four doubles and three home runs) and Mariano Duncan's two RBI. The victory boosted the Phils' lead to eleven games in the National League's Eastern Division. The Cincinnati Reds followed for a three-game series. The Phillies came back from a 4–1 deficit in the opener with a four-run sixth, but Williams blew his thirty-seventh save opportunity in the ninth, giving the Reds an 8–5 win. The next night Pete Incaviglia hit his eleventh home run, and Dykstra stole a base to set a new career high, thirty-four, but the Reds still won, 9–5. The Phillies broke their two-game losing streak in the finale. Jackson struck out eight and combined with Roger Mason on a six-hit shutout, thrashing the Reds 12–0. The big bats belonged to Morandini, who collected four RBI on two triples; Chamberlain, who also drove in four runs; and Ricky Jordan, who hit a double and two singles, knocking in two more runs.[26] It seemed like a different player came through in the clutch every night, underscoring the fact that winning was truly a team effort.

Despite the grueling demands of a 162-game schedule, the individual players also made time for the community off the playing field by hosting a variety of special events and charitable fundraisers. This is also part of the Code, specifically that players must be courteous to the fans and give back to the less fortunate. Ball clubs call it "community service," but it's actually the players' way of expressing their gratitude to those who ultimately pay their salaries.[27] Since 1984 Phillies' Charities raised more than $1.5 million for amyotrophic lateral sclerosis research. In 1993 Curt Schilling became the face of the organization's campaign to strike out ALS, known as Lou Gehrig's disease. Not only did Schilling pledge $100 for every complete game he pitched, $500 for every win, and $1,000 for every shutout, but he and his wife, Shonda, served as spokespersons for the cause. Other players made similar commitments to other causes: Danny Jackson contributed $500 for each of his victories and $100 for each strikeout to Philadelphia's Emergency Center for Homeless Women and Children; Terry Mulholland contributed $2,000 for every win to Philadelphia's Department of Recreation to start a Rookie League baseball program for more than fifteen hundred kids at fourteen inner-city rec centers; Mitch Williams donated $100 to the American Cancer Society for every save; Darren Daulton contributed $100 for every one of his RBI to the city's Committee for the Homeless; and Ricky Jordan donated $100 for every one of his RBI to the American Diabetes Association.

Still other players and their wives purchased tickets to Phillies home games for children with Tourette's syndrome (Eisenreich's), cancer (Kruk's), physical disabilities (Morandini's), and at-risk backgrounds (Thompson's). The couples also raised money for their respective causes, met with the children before games, and hosted other events for them. And Larry Andersen and Dave Hollins donated their time to visiting children at city hospitals.[28]

While many professional athletes use charitable contributions as a tax shelter, these Phillies saw their involvements as more than just giving money. For some, it meant using their celebrity status to draw attention to the needs of the less fortunate. For others, it meant giving of themselves to others in a discreet way with no expectation of publicity or financial gain. It was yet another way the '93 Phils endeared themselves to the city and their fans.

The Phillies ended August on the road in Chicago, splitting the last two games of the month with the Cubs. Dykstra led off the first game with his fourth home run of the month. Kruk and Hollins hit back-to-back homers in the third, giving the Phils a 6–3 lead. But it wasn't enough with the wind blowing out in Wrigley Field. After an hour rain delay, the Cubs rallied on a grand slam by catcher Rick Wilkins, and Chicago stole a 7–6 victory. The next day Ben Rivera blanked the Cubs on four singles and matched a career-high nine strikeouts to give the Phillies a 7–0 win.[29]

The Phils entered September with an 82-50 record and a lead of nine and a half games over the second-place Montreal Expos, who had overtaken the St. Louis Cardinals. It marked the first time in club history that the Phillies led their division on the first of each month from May to September.[30]

FIG. 25. Burly Pete Incaviglia, shown here as a Houston Astro in 1992, supplied some right-handed power to an overloaded left-handed lineup as well as some witty one-liners to a bawdy clubhouse. One teammate described "Inky" as the "strongman who fell off the wagon when the circus came to town." National Baseball Hall of Fame Library, Cooperstown, New York.

TWELVE
Inky

Pete Incaviglia was one of the most popular platoon players in Philadelphia. After coming to the Phillies from the Houston Astros on December 8, 1992, "Inky" quickly won over the fans because, in the parlance of the game, he "left it all on the field." He crashed into walls, drove in timely runs, and hit tape-measure shots, especially down the stretch drive.

"Like a pudgy snake that suddenly decides to try flying," wrote *Philadelphia Inquirer* beat writer Frank Fitzpatrick in his September 7 column, "Pete Incaviglia went airborne 15 feet from first base, diving headfirst, his arms extended in a frantic effort to beat the throw from second, a throw that would have converted an inning-ending double play. And he made it, gobbling up a big mouthful of dirt as he touched the bag."[1] Not only did the awkward dive allow the Phils to score one more run in a 5–3 victory over the Chicago Cubs, but it inspired Fitzpatrick's blue-collar metaphor for a team-first approach to baseball that had propelled the Phillies into first place in April and kept them there for the remainder of the season. Four days later, on September 10, Inky put on a showcase against his old team the Houston Astros.

With the score tied, 1–1, in the bottom of the second, Darren Daulton singled to start the inning. Incaviglia stepped to the plate and slammed a drive just out of the reach of lunging right fielder

Eric Anthony and off the right-field wall. Daulton scored, and the Phils had a 2–1 lead off left-hander Greg Swindell. Inky scored on an RBI single to left by hot-hitting Kevin Stocker to increase the Phils' lead to 3–1. Incaviglia teamed up with pinch hitter Jim Eisenreich in the eighth inning to knock in two more runs, giving Curt Schilling and the Phils a 4–2 victory.

Although the burly outfielder strained his left knee after slamming into a wall in a game against the Chicago Cubs earlier in the week, it didn't appear to affect his hitting. He was batting .451 in his last sixteen games. On the season the Ink Man was the owner of 95 hits and 86 RBI in just 331 at-bats. "I'm the type of guy who needs to play—whether I'm 80 percent or 100 percent," Incaviglia said when asked about his sore knee. "I need to be out there. If I thought I was a detriment and couldn't run, I wouldn't go out there. But I can cut and turn in the outfield, and I have no problem hitting."[2]

In fact, Incaviglia, like the rest of his teammates on Macho Row, believed in playing hurt, particularly in the heat of a pennant race. It is part of the Code. During the course of a 162-game season, injuries are inevitable. It's up to the players to stay healthy. They owe it to the team and to the fans. When an injury occurs, those who work hard on their rehabilitation are respected. Those who ignore treatment and stop showing up at practice are not. In fact, the shirker runs the risk of developing a negative reputation as a "clubhouse cancer." The Code requires every ballplayer to play through his injury while working on rehabilitation to return to full strength.[3] The '93 Phillies took that part of the Code very seriously.

"We had a talk early in the season, and we decided that we couldn't afford injuries," admitted John Kruk. "If you were hurt or on the disabled list, it was like you had the plague. No one talked to you." There was added pressure on the members of Macho Row. "When Pete Incaviglia hurt his knee, we rode him hard and he came back a little quicker than he probably should have," said Kruk. "But when you have one guy playing hurt, it becomes contagious." Take the case of Dave Hollins, who came back early from hand surgery.

"Hollins had stitches and they broke open," recalled Kruk. "The incision is bleeding and he's taping it up and going back out there. You think, 'Shit, if he can play with that, I can sure as hell play with [my injury].' You might miss a game or two when it normally would have been four or five. But with the kind of money major league ballplayers make, I think we owe the team and the fans a full effort."[4]

Not only did Incaviglia observe the Code, but he also teamed up with Hollins to enforce it when teammates went astray. "If there were any problems in the clubhouse, Hollins and I were usually in the middle of it," said the muscular outfielder. "We made sure that everyone was accountable to the team. The gist of it was: 'Hey man! What's going on? You need to pick it up! We want to win a championship here. You're either in, or you're out.'

"But make no mistake—Dave and I were just considered the enforcers," he added. "Dutch and Lenny were the leaders on the team. They were the guys who made us go."[5]

To be sure, Incaviglia enjoyed the role of enforcer. His father prepared had him for it. Born on April 2, 1964, at Pebble Beach, California, Peter Joseph Incaviglia was the third son of Tom and Doris Incaviglia. Tom, a Brooklyn Dodger farmhand, raised his sons to become ballplayers. In fact, Tony, the eldest son, set a good example for Pete when he was signed by the San Diego Padres.[6] "My father taught us that the three most important things in life are family, hard work, and accountability," recalled Inky. Tom was a blue-collar worker, and after his baseball career ended, he took a job in the post office and later owned a liquor store. "My dad worked more hours than he slept," said Pete. "Working hard, being accountable, and being grateful to my family for what I had were instilled in me at a very early age. So when I became a ballplayer, I never took anything for granted. Everything I ever got in baseball I worked hard to achieve it."[7]

The work ethic began at an early age. Incaviglia suffered from asthma as a child and, at age twelve, began lifting weights to strengthen his lungs.[8] By his sophomore year of high school, he was so strong that his extraordinary power hitting earned him "California High School Player of the Year" honors for three straight years. Recruited by Oklahoma State University, Inky quickly embraced head coach Gary Ward's "take-no-prisoners" philosophy. Ward promoted the art of intimidation. He forbade his players from shaking the hands of opponents after a game, win or lose. He demanded an aggressiveness that bordered on ruthless, both at the plate and on the field. Inky became a prized pupil, developing a swagger that went unmatched in Division I baseball. Often he stood in the batter's box to watch his prodigious home runs clear the fence. On those rare occasions when he struck out, the six-foot-one, 200-pound slugger would glare at the pitcher, daring him to try it again. He could be just as intimidating on the base paths. Once, Incaviglia barreled into home plate so hard that he broke the catcher's leg. By the end of his collegiate career, Inky had led the Cowboys to the College World Series in each of his three seasons and set NCAA career records for home runs (100) and slugging percentage (.915). His final season was his most impressive. In 1985 Incaviglia set NCAA single-season records with 48 homers, 143 RBI, and a 1,140 slugging percentage and won the Player of the Year Award.[9]

Selected by the Montreal Expos in the first round of the 1985 amateur draft, Incaviglia refused to play in the Minor Leagues, insisting that he was ready for the Majors. Determined to get his way, the Oklahoma State standout forced the Expos to do something that had never happened before in the history of Major League Baseball: to trade a draft pick to a team of his choice. Unable to reach an agreement, Montreal had no choice but to sign Incaviglia and immediately trade him to the Texas Rangers for Minor League pitcher Bob Sebra and journeyman infielder Jim Anderson. The signing was contingent upon the trade. The deal prompted MLB to revise its rules on amateur draft picks. In the future organizations would be prohibited from trading picks until they had been professionals for one year, a decision known today as the "Incaviglia Rule."[10] Texas granted Inky his demand, making him only the fourth player in MLB history to debut in the Majors without ever playing Minor League ball since the draft began in 1965. He was an instant success, too. In 1986 Incaviglia hit thirty home runs, setting a Rangers club record. But he also developed some humility.

Having never played a single day in the Minors, Inky was gullible and open season for any vet who wanted to pull a prank. Once, Bobby Jones, a veteran outfielder who had signed with the club in 1967 when they were the Washington Senators, offered a challenge to no one in particular: "Ya know, I bet I can lift those three guys this year."

Realizing the ploy, the other veterans chimed right in: "No way. I'll bet you $100 you can't do it."

To make the proposal sound more convincing, Jones added, "No, really. I almost did it last year, and I've been working out."

"I'll bet you a thousand you can't," said another vet, piquing Incaviglia's curiosity.

"What are you talking about?" the rookie asked Jones, who was now prepared to feed him the bait.

"Okay, Inky, you're a big guy," replied the veteran outfielder. "You go pick any two guys in the clubhouse, and we'll lay you all down on the floor. You'll get all locked up. Then I will pick all three of you off the ground, up to my waist."

"No way!" insisted Incaviglia.

Meanwhile, all the other veterans were increasing the wager, and Jones was taking all the bets.

The gullible rookie, dressed in complete uniform since it was only five minutes away from game time, found the two biggest players on the team, Larry Parrish and Gary Ward, both of whom weighed about 220 pounds. Since Inky weighed about 240, he figured that he had won the bet.

All three of them got down on the floor. Incaviglia, who was purposely placed in the middle, was told to put his hands behind the heads of the other two teammates. Then they locked legs and clamped him down. After Inky was completely immobilized, Jones asked, "Are they ready?"

When he gave the nod, all the other players hurried to find shampoo, liquid soap, after-shave lotion, mayonnaise, ketchup—or anything else that squirted—and showered Incaviglia. Before they let him go, his teammates emptied the clubhouse spittoons, filled with used tobacco and kitty litter.[11]

The prank might have taught Incaviglia to keep his curiosity in check, but he still had a lot to learn about respecting the game. While he continued to work hard at his hitting and fielding, the swagger that he had developed at Oklahoma State did not prepare him for the burdensome realities of Major League Baseball. Inky was thin-skinned. He argued with umpires, shunned autograph requests, failed to show up for public appearances, scowled at the fans, and vowed to beat up sportswriters if they crossed him. One season he even threatened to hold out. Rangers fans booed him mercilessly. Some even threw coins at him in the outfield. Even when Inky was on his best behavior, the fans criticized his "free-swinging, all-or-nothing" approach.[12]

During his first three seasons in Texas, Incaviglia led the American League in strikeouts once, tied for the lead once, and ranked second once. He also batted a career-low .236 in 1989.[13]

"Looking back, the first couple years with the Rangers were tough," he admitted. "I didn't have many friends on the club. There were teammates who were upset that I didn't have to go through the various levels of Minor League ball like they did. But if they were jealous, I think I eventually earned their respect because of my ability and by the way I played the game."[14]

Texas released Incaviglia ten days before the start of the 1991 season. He scrambled to get a job with the Detroit Tigers as a part-time player. Depressed and struggling to recapture his power swing, his weight ballooned to 260 pounds. The Tigers released him before the 1992 season, and Incaviglia scrambled again to find a job. Montreal, Pittsburgh, Seattle, Minnesota, and Houston made Minor League offers with invitations to big-league spring-training camp. He eventually signed with Houston because it was near his Arlington home.[15]

According to Philadelphia sportswriter Asher B. Chancey in a revealing article titled "The Bagwell Conspiracy," Incaviglia, in a desperate effort to revive his declining career, began to use steroids after he joined the Astros. Impressed by the remarkable offensive production of Astros teammates Jeff Bagwell and Ken Caminiti, Incaviglia allegedly "convinced Bagwell to share his magic potion." He also began to participate in the same extreme weight-lifting

FIG. 26. Incaviglia being congratulated by teammate Dave Hollins after a September 1993 home run. Photo by Al Tielemans.

workouts as Bagwell, with an eye on the following season.[16] At the same time, Incaviglia, according to Houston pitcher Jason Grimsley, was using amphetamines, probably to reduce the excess weight he had gained over the previous two seasons.[17] Released by the Astros that winter, Inky signed with the Phillies in December 1992. Bagwell allegedly continued to supply Incaviglia with steroids during the 1993 season when he was with the Phillies.[18]

By the time Incaviglia arrived in the City of Brotherly Love, he had shed his brash persona. His failure to realize the high expectations placed on him by the scouts coming out of Oklahoma State as well as suspicions of steroid use inside the game made him an outcast. But in Philadelphia he reinvented himself as a down-to-earth Italian kid with a massive build and a blue-collar attitude. The fans loved him for his huge heart and desire.[19] Inky's remarkable offensive production after two subpar years in Detroit and Houston also helped. In 1993 Incaviglia platooned in left field with Milt Thompson and still managed to hit 24 home runs and 89 RBI with a .274 batting average.[20]

When asked about the impressive power numbers he put up with the Phillies after his offensive struggles the previous two seasons, Incaviglia, in a 2009 interview, attributed his success to "better hitting mechanics." "When I came to Philadelphia, I had a reputation as a power hitter," he explained. "I was expected to hit twenty-five to thirty homers and drive in eighty to a hundred runs every year. But [Phillies hitting coach] Denis Menke made me a better hitter. We started tinkering with my mechanics and found a happy medium. I still had the same power, but I was also putting the head of the bat on the ball more often than not. At one point in the season, I had more RBI than hits. It was kind of a joke on the team that I couldn't get a hit unless someone was in scoring position."[21]

Once described by pitcher Terry Mulholland as the "strong-man who fell off the wagon when the circus came to town," Incaviglia was also one of the more colorful characters of Macho Row. "It was a once-in-a-lifetime team," recalled the Ink Man. "We had more fun than what should be allowed." But the 1993 Phillies also got the very most from the talent they possessed because they put the team first.

"The special thing about that team was that the players were unselfish," Incaviglia explained.

> I platooned with Milt Thompson in left. Jim Eisenreich platooned with West Chamberlain in right. There were a bunch of guys who played shortstop that season, including [Juan] Bell, [Mariano] Duncan, and [Kevin] Stocker. None of us were bothered by the platoon system. When we sat, we sat. There were no complaints. When we played, we found a way to deliver. Even the regulars weren't interested as much in personal statistics as winning a championship. It was like that from day one, and if anyone got off the page, Dutch [Daulton] was there to remind them that the team came first. That kind of unselfishness was rare back then in the Majors and almost impossible to find these days.[22]

Jim Fregosi's management style was another major factor in the team's success. Everyone understood their specific role, and he allowed them to do their job without any interference. Instead, Fregosi limited his involvement to making the necessary moves during a game that would put the team in the best position to win. Nor did Fregosi police the team. He relied on catcher Darren Daulton to assert that kind of leadership because he understood that it would have a greater impact coming from a veteran player rather than himself. Such an approach allowed the Phillies to "play loose and with confidence," according to Mitch Williams. It also placed the burden of responsibility on the team rather than on himself or the coaches.[23]

Fortunately, the team-first approach allowed the Phillies to escape the ghosts of 1964. Like those infamous Phils, who were up by six and a half games with twelve left to play and lost ten straight to gift-wrap the pennant for the St. Louis Cardinals, the '93 team entered September with a nine-and-a-half-game lead in the division and watched it slip away. Between September 6 and 17, the Fightins lost six of twelve contests to see their lead reduced to just five games ahead of the surging Montreal Expos.[24] Frank Fitzpatrick began to evoke nightmares of the Phillies' forgettable past on September 10, after an 8–5 loss to the Chicago Cubs at Veterans Stadium. This time Incaviglia was the goat instead of the hero.

In an ending as swift as it was eerie, the Cubs' fatal rally evoked not only the dismal reminder of 1964 swoon, but the "second-most haunting event in modern Phillies history as well," wrote Fitzpatrick. "Just like [left fielder] Greg Luzinski in the 1977 Black Friday playoff game against the [Los Angeles] Dodgers, Pete Incaviglia retreated awkwardly toward the leftfield wall for a long fly ball. Like Luzinski, the burly outfielder slammed into the fence. Like Luzinski, he missed it, and the game was lost.

"Then, from someplace unseen, a disembodied voice, like that of some long-dormant ghost, hoarsely bellowed the most dreaded words in this city's sports history.

"Nineteen sixty-four," it screamed.[25]

On Friday, September 17, the Phillies headed to Montreal for a three-game showdown against the red-hot Expos, who had won thirteen of their last sixteen games. One Expo fan dangled a large yellow noose over the visitors' dugout at Olympic Stadium and waved it frantically whenever a gaggle of Phillies walked by before the game.

"Hey Phillies," he screamed. "It's 1964 all over again!" The *Montreal Gazette* was more tactful. The newspaper's lead story was headlined "EXPOS-PHILLIES SERIES ISN'T BASEBALL, IT'S WAR." "Philly will fold," predicted Montreal pitcher John Wetteland. "They have to hit the skids at some point the same as everyone else does."[26]

In the opener Montreal took a 1–0 lead in the fourth when Phils starter Ben Rivera loaded the bases on a single and two walks before walking pitcher Dennis Martinez for the first run of the game. Rivera continued to have problems finding the strike zone in the fifth, when he opened the inning by walking Delino DeShields and then watched as the speedy infielder stole second base. DeShields scored on a single by Larry Walker before Rivera was sent to the showers. Roger Mason came on and surrendered a sacrifice fly, increasing the Expos' lead to 3–0. The Phils tied the game in the sixth when Daulton smashed a three-run homer. Before the inning was over, the Fightins rallied to take a 7–3 lead. But the Expos chipped away at the Phils' lead to tie the game and send it into extra innings. Mitch Williams came in to pitch the twelfth and promptly surrendered a double down the right-field line to Marquis Grissom. "It was a fast-ball about a foot outside," said Williams. "He's a pull hitter, and I tried to stay away from him. There's nothing I can do about that."

Delino DeShields stepped to the plate next. Dave Hollins repositioned himself in front of the third base bag to guard against a bunt, but the strategy backfired when Grissom stole third. Now the 45,757 fans at Olympic Stadium were on their feet, anticipating a victory. DeShields flew out to Dykstra in center field, but the damage had been done, as Grissom scurried home with the winning run. Montreal's come-from-behind 8–7 victory reduced the Phils' lead to just four games.

The Phillies evened the series the next day when Tommy Greene posted his fifteenth win. After the Fightins jumped in front 5–1, it appeared that they would coast to victory. But two broken-bat singles and Will Cordero's three-run homer gave Montreal a chance to steal the game for a second straight night. David West entered the game in the eighth and retired the side. But Mitch Williams made things interesting in the ninth. Wild Thing faced Larry Walker to open the inning and put him on base with four straight balls. Walker advanced to second on an errant pickoff throw and stole third before Williams struck out Mike Lansing and induced a fly ball to secure the 5–4 win. The victory boosted the Phillies' lead back up to five games.

"If you can't get it pumping in a situation like that," said Wild Thing, who notched his thirty-ninth save, "then there's nothing pumping inside you. We had to have that game, and we got it."

The finale on Sunday, September 19, was also decided by a one-run margin. The Phils took a 5–2 lead in the fifth off RBI singles by Darren Daulton and platoon players Ruben Amaro, Jr. and Wes Chamberlain. Once again, however, the Expos fought back, scoring two runs off starter Danny Jackson in the bottom of the inning. The Phillies clung to a 5–4 lead in the ninth, hoping that Wild Thing would prevail.

With one out and Expo runners on first and second, Larry Walker hit a chopper to inside the first base bag. John Kruk bobbled the ball before tossing it to Williams, who arrived at the base almost simultaneously with a head-first-sliding Walker. Umpire Charlie Williams called him safe, sending Williams into a tantrum.

"There's no way in the world he's safe," argued Williams after the game. "If [umpire Charlie Williams] is doing his job, there's no way he can miss that call. Impact umpiring. That was brutal."

What made matters worse for the Phillies was that Sean Berry, Montreal's next hitter, popped up to Kruk for what would have been the final out of the game. Instead, Will Cordero slapped a single to left to win the game for Montreal, 6–5, and once again the Phillies' lead was reduced to four games with thirteen left to play.

"We're in a good position," Daulton reasoned, "but I wouldn't say it's comfortable."[27]

After the Phillies dropped two of three games to the Expos, Bill Conlin of the *Philadelphia Daily News* skewered Mitch Williams, who was responsible for two blown save opportunities: "Williams has gone 1-2-3 just fourteen times this season. But that's an improvement on last season, when he did it just eight times. On the other hand, Mitch doesn't hold runners; he puts them in a half-way house.

FIG. 27. Williams's unorthodox delivery allowed him to set a new Phillies club record of 43 saves in 1993, including 13 straight between July 18 and August 24. Photo by Al Tielemans.

They are now 8-for-8 against him, including Delino DeShields' crucial one-out steal in the ninth yesterday. To say that Wild Thing is responsible for more civic anguish in Philadelphia than the wage tax would be an understatement."[28]

When Fregosi defended his closer, insisting that his team "didn't make the routine plays," Conlin seized the moment to evoke the ghosts of 1964. While the Phils' skipper was noticeably agitated with the suggestion that his team would also fold under the pressure of a pennant race, the Phils accepted the challenge and swept the Florida Marlins at Veterans Stadium. Curt Schilling's 7–1 victory on September 20, the first night of the home stand, silenced all the doomsayers. It was his fifteenth victory of the season as well as his seventh straight win.

"This is what you dream about as a kid," a giddy Schilling said after reaching a career high in victories. "I was almost as excited as I was for my first big league start. If you can't get pumped up for a pennant race, you never will."[29]

Schil gave the Phillies the momentum they needed to sweep

Inky

the Marlins. Donnie Pall, a late-season acquisition, earned his first victory as a Phil the following night when he was credited with the 5–3 win. Roger Mason, another midseason acquisition, won his fifth game of the season in the finale in extra innings. With the score tied at 1–1, Pete Incaviglia, making his first appearance since injuring his leg, led off the twelfth inning with a four-pitch walk off Marlins ace reliever Bryan Harvey. Tony Longmire came in to pinch-run for the Ink Man. Dykstra followed with a single to right, sending Longmire to third. Richie Lewis, who came in to relieve Harvey, plunked Mickey Morandini to load the bases with no one out. After Kruk struck out, Dave Hollins smacked an 0-1 pitch down the right-field line to score Longmire from third, giving the Fightin' Phils a 2–1 win. While the Phillies' lead over the second-place Expos remained at five and a half games, the victory reduced the magic number (that is, the number of wins, paired with the same number of Montreal losses, needed to clinch the division) to six.[30]

The Phillies enjoyed a rare day off on Thursday, September 23. John Kruk used the opportunity to make an appearance on CBS's *Late Night with David Letterman*. It was actually his second appearance. The Krukker appeared on the show the previous season. On that occasion he was a bit apprehensive because late-night TV "wasn't the kind of thing [he'd] normally do." But Lenny Dykstra encouraged him to go, so Kruk cleaned himself up and dressed in a nice burgundy shirt and a pair of dark slacks. Letterman quickly put him at ease, and the Krukker actually had fun. So when the producers invited him again, the Phillies' first baseman agreed. This time, however, he did *not* get a haircut or shave. Nor did he dress in a nice shirt and slacks, preferring to wear a pair of jeans, a Steely Dan T-shirt, and a Sawyer Brown baseball cap instead.[31] Letterman seized the opportunity to chide him:

"Well, John," he began, "thanks for fixing yourself up tonight."

Kruk explained that he had recently "had a couple of Diet Cokes with Steely Dan, and they told me to wear this shirt." "And the week before it was Sawyer Brown."

"You're a lucky man—free clothing," said Letterman, continuing the repartee. "Tell me about the gum," he asked changing the subject. "How much gum do you enjoy during a ball game?"

"Four to start the game, four after our first inning, [and] with our pitchers it lasts a long time, so the gum's usually pretty much gone by then."

"Do you not use tobacco when you're playing?" asked Letterman.

"Oh, I used to, but the dentist keeps pulling teeth, you gotta get rid of something. So I just figured the sugar was doing less damage than the tobacco."

One of the funniest exchanges occurred when Letterman asked the Phillies' first baseman if he liked playing against the Colorado Rockies in Denver:

KRUK: "Oh, no."

LETTERMAN: "What's the problem?"

KRUK: "There's no air. I got on base, and there was a three-and-two count, two outs, so they made me run [Letterman laughs]. And Dave Hollins kept fouling balls off, and I kept getting more tired, and I told the first base coach, 'I'm not going.' And he said, 'Well, you have to,' and I said 'The hell I do.'"

LETTERMAN: "That's kind of the way the game is played I think, isn't it?"

KRUK: "Yeah, but I was gonna bend the rules there for a while. So, then [Hollins] hit a ball in the gap, and I had to try to score. I slid into home, but it wasn't really much of a slide because I had no momentum left; it was just kind of a stick. I was safe, and Darren Daulton had to pick me up and help me back to the dugout.

LETTERMAN: "That's an inspirational story for all you Little Leaguers out there. If you don't feel like running, you don't necessarily have to make the turn at first.

Letterman ended the interview by asking Kruk why he changed his uniform number from 28 to 29. Krukker explained that when the Phillies acquired Mitch Williams, he wanted number 28 because "his wife had a bunch of jewelry with number 28 on it." Having heard that Rickey Henderson of the Padres gave another player twenty-five thousand dollars for his number, Kruk thought he would make a deal. "Mitch got number 28, and I got two cases of beer," he explained. "The thing about it is, Mitch got divorced. Now he wears number 29. And the two cases of beer are gone."

"Oh, that's too bad," remarked Letterman.

"It's a sad story," said Kruk, shaking his head as the audience erupted with laughter.[32]

On Friday, September 24, the red-hot Atlanta Braves came to town to close out the home season at the Vet. Since the All-Star Break, Atlanta, comfortably entrenched in first place in the National League's Western Division, had compiled a remarkable 48-16 record. Since August 8 they were even more impressive, going 24-6. They performed even better on the road, with a 27-5 record since July 23. But none of that appeared to affect Tommy Greene, who overpowered the Braves, permitting just three base hits in eight and a third innings for a 3–0 win.

"You have to feel something extra in a game like that," said Mitch Williams, who closed the game and notched his forty-first save of the season. "Not just because we're facing the Braves, but because we're getting so close to the end."

A sellout crowd of 57,176 packed Veterans Stadium for the second game of the series. But they went home disappointed by the 9–7 loss. It wasn't much better for the Phils the next afternoon when Curt Schilling lost his only game since the All-Star Break, 7–2. Despite losing to the Braves in the last two games of the series, the Phillies' magic number was reduced to three as the Expos cooled off.[33]

On September 27 the Phils began a four-game series at Pittsburgh's Three Rivers Stadium. Hollins collected four hits, and Mariano Duncan slammed a homer to give the Phillies a 6–4 win in the opening game. When the Expos lost to the Marlins later that night, the magic number stood at one. The clincher would come the next night, on Tuesday, September 28.

Mike Williams started the game for the Phillies. He was knocked out in the sixth when the Pirates took a 4–3 lead. But the Phils would not be denied, exploding for six runs in the seventh. Daulton opened

FIG. 28. Mariano Duncan called his division-clinching grand slam against
the Pittsburgh Pirates on September 28 the "biggest hit of my life."
Photo by Al Tielemans.

the inning with an infield single. Eisenreich followed with another
single. With two runners on base and no outs, Milt Thompson laid
down a sacrifice bunt. Pirate reliever Rich Robertson decided to
throw to third, but he was too late to get Daulton. Kevin Stocker
followed and singled in the tying run.

When Pete Incaviglia stepped up to the plate to pinch-hit, Pittsburgh manager Jim Leyland went to his bullpen. Blas Minor came
in to strike out Inky, and then Leyland summoned Denny Nea-
gle to face Dykstra. The strategy backfired when Nails drew his
127th walk of the season, putting the Phillies ahead to stay, 5–4.
Duncan put the game out of reach when he followed with a grand
slam to deep left field he later called "the biggest hit of my life."
It was his second grand slam of the year and a club-record eighth
for the season.[34]

In the visitors' clubhouse Phillies equipment manager Frank Coppenbarger rolled down the plastic in front of the lockers, pulled out
the cases of California champagne, and ripped open the cardboard
boxes containing hats and T-shirts that read "National League East

FIG. 29. Kruk celebrates the Phillies' division-clinching win against Pittsburgh. Photo by Al Tielemans.

Champions."[35] Two innings later reliever Donnie Pall squeezed first baseman John Kruk's toss to record the final out of the Phillies' 10–7 victory, setting off a raucous celebration that continued in the champagne-drenched visitors' clubhouse long into the early-morning hours.[36]

"It's 1993, baby! It ain't 1964," howled Wes Chamberlain, putting to rest the sportswriters' recurring references to the Phils' infamous swoon twenty-nine years before. "Where are those ghosts now?"[37]

Kruk, standing in the middle of the clubhouse with a beer in one hand and a champagne bottle in the other, admitted that "it just got sickening, watching everybody else celebrate every year." "You get jealous," he explained. "You want it to be your turn. Now, finally, it is." Then, after a few sips of champagne, the Krukker said, "Too sweet. I'm going with the beer."[38]

Perhaps Milt Thompson said it best when he described the season as a "roller-coaster ride," but "we rallied around each other to make the postseason and that's all that really counts."[39]

At the other end of the clubhouse, Bill Giles was giving a postgame television interview. "We've been down so long," said the team president as he was being doused with champagne, "I had kind of gotten used to us winning from 1976 to 1983. Now we have been down so long that this one is very rewarding to our fans and particularly to me." Before he could complete the statement, Curt Schilling smashed a chocolate pie in his face. "I don't even like chocolate" was all the dazed Giles could say.[40]

Chris Wheeler, the Phillies' broadcaster who was doing the interview, tried to break loose. But several Phillies caught him and began stuffing huge handfuls of chocolate pie down his pants.[41]

When the beer ran out, players pooled together some money and sent the clubhouse attendants down to a local bar to buy five more cases. Before the celebration ended, broadcaster Harry Kalas gathered the players in the trainer's room and said, "Gentlemen, thank you for giving me the best year of my life." Then he led them in a rendition of his favorite song, "High Hopes."[42]

"I'll never forget that," recalled Mickey Morandini years after his playing career ended. "The glow in the players' eyes, and the respect we all had for Harry, was obvious. It was a magical moment."[43]

The Phillies completed the regular season by winning just one of their last five contests. They finished three games ahead of the second-place Montreal Expos with a final record of 97-65. The ninety-seven victories were the third highest in team history to that point.[44] What's more, the 1993 Phillies rejuvenated the enthusiasm of the fans, who turned out in record numbers to watch the team play. In fact, the Phillies drew more than three million in attendance with an average of thirty-nine thousand at home games.[45]

But none of that seemed to matter to the motley band of gypsies, tramps, and thieves who had gone from worst to first in one year and, in the process, won the respect of the baseball world.

THIRTEEN

Hide the Women and Children!

The Phillies faced the defending National League champion Atlanta Braves in the playoffs. After trailing the San Francisco Giants for most of the season, the Braves eked out a third consecutive Western Division title by one game with a 104-58 record.[1] Still, they were confident that they enjoyed the momentum and the experience to defeat the Phillies in the National League Championship Series. In fact, Atlanta, after losing the World Series to the Minnesota Twins in 1991 and to the Toronto Blue Jays in 1992, was determined to win it all in 1993. On paper the Braves were the favorites.

Atlanta's starting rotation was anchored by Greg Maddux, a 20-game winner who led the league in complete games (8), innings pitched (267), and earned run average (2.36). Maddux, a future Hall of Famer, won the Cy Young Award with the Chicago Cubs in 1992 and would have a lock on the prestigious award for the next three years.[2] Tom Glavine, regarded as the number-two pitcher of the staff, won 22 games and led the league in starts with 36. Glavine, another future Hall of Famer, won the Cy Young Award in 1991 and would later capture the award again in 1998.[3] Steve Avery (18-6, 125 K, 2.94 ERA) and John Smoltz (15-11, 208 K, 3.62 ERA) rounded out the starting rotation. Atlanta also had a reliable closer in Greg McMichael. Although he inherited the role on July 28 after Mike Stanton began to struggle, McMichael earned 19 saves during the second half of the season to ensure another post-season berth for the Braves. Overall, Atlanta's pitching staff had the National League's lowest ERA, at 3.14.[4]

Offensively, the Braves were led by All-Star right fielder David Justice (.270, 40 HR, 120 RBI) and left fielder Ron Gant (.274, 36 HR, 117 RBI). In addition, All-Star shortstop Jeff Blauser (.305, 15 HR, 73 RBI) and third baseman Terry Pendleton (.272, 17 HR, 84 RBI) provided timely hitting. But the difference maker was first baseman Fred McGriff, who was acquired from the San Diego Padres on July 20 when the Braves were just 12 games over .500 and 9 games out of first. By season's end McGriff's 19 home runs and 55 RBI allowed the Braves to come charging back to win the Western Division.[5]

While the Braves had better pitching, more talented players, and greater postseason experience, the Phillies led the National League in runs scored (877) and were second in team batting average (.274). The two clubs also split their regular-season matchups, with each team winning 6 of the 12 contests they played.[6] However, Ted Turner promoted his team to the American public beginning in the 1980s by broadcasting Braves games nationwide on his TBS cable station, so Atlanta was billed as "America's team" and the Phillies viewed as "underdogs." In fact, baseball fans either loved or hated Atlanta; there wasn't much middle ground. Phillies fans, in particular, despised the Braves, viewing them with the same contempt as the Dallas Cowboys and the New York Yankees, organizations that were infamous for their elitism and arrogance.[7] It was that same arrogance coupled with the belief that the Braves could dispatch the Phillies in four straight games that resulted in Atlanta's downfall.

The NLCS opened in Philadelphia on Wednesday, October 6. The City of Brotherly Love was swept up in Phillies fever. People throughout the region donned Phillies T-shirts, hats, and other team paraphernalia. When Philadelphians greeted each other on the streets, in stores, or at work, they flashed the "We're No. 1" sign to each other. Billboards and buses sported signs wishing the hometown team luck. Even William Penn, the huge thirty-seven-foot statue of Philadelphia's founder perched atop city hall, donned a bright-red Phillies cap for the occasion. Extending his right hand,

Hide the Women and Children!

FIG. 30. The city of Philadelphia placed a Phillies cap on William Penn's statue atop city hall in the hope of ending the so-called Curse of Billy Penn. The curse was used to explain the failure of Philadelphia's pro sports teams to win championships since the March 1987 construction of the One Liberty Place skyscraper, which exceeded the height of the statue, in violation of a "gentlemen's agreement" that no building would rise above the brim of Penn's hat. Photo by Al Tielemans.

he appeared to give his blessing—"And thou Phillies, champions of the NL East, my soul prays to God for thee that thou may stand firm in the day of trial, that thee may be blessed with another pennant . . . even if it takes seven to clinch!"[8]

Veterans Stadium was decked out in red, white, and blue bunting. Scoreboard lights were changed. Seats were scrubbed, and the windows to the press box were cleaned. "Video Dan" Stephenson worked feverishly on Phillies highlight films to flash on Phan-o-Vision between innings of that night's opening game. When the gates opened at 6:00 p.m., the Vet was just as resplendent as the last time it hosted a postseason game a decade earlier.

Curt Schilling faced Atlanta's Steve Avery before a crowd of 62,012. Only seat 9, row 4, section 314 remained empty throughout the game. Schilling had saved the seat in honor of his father, Clifford, who died in 1988 of a heart attack at age fifty-five. "He'll be with me in spirit," said the Phils' right-hander before the game. "Pitching in the postseason was something we both dreamed about for a long time. It just doesn't feel right that he won't be here with me."[9]

Throwing consistently in the mid-90s, Schilling set a playoff record by striking out the first five batters he faced. Otis Nixon, Jeff Blauser, and Ron Gant went down swinging in the first inning, and Fred McGriff and David Justice were called out looking in the second before Terry Pendleton grounded out to shortstop Kevin Stocker to retire the side.

The Phillies took a 1–0 lead in the bottom of the first when Dykstra lined a double to left-center. Duncan followed with a single to right, advancing him to third. Kruk grounded to second for the first out of the inning, but Nails scored on the play. The Braves tied the game in the third. With two outs pitcher Steve Avery doubled down the left-field line and scored on Nixon's two-bagger over the head of Pete Incaviglia in left field. Atlanta added another run in the fourth when Schilling walked Gant, who advanced to third on a single by McGriff and scored on a sacrifice fly to left by Justice. The Phils answered in the bottom of the inning when Avery tried to sneak a 3-2 fastball past Incaviglia, who tied the score with a towering 423-foot homer to center field.

The Fightins went ahead in the sixth when they loaded the bases on a walk to Kruk, a double to right by Hollins, and an intentional walk to Daulton. With Incaviglia at the plate and a 2-1 count, Avery

Hide the Women and Children!

FIG. 31. Incaviglia homers in the fourth inning of Game One of the
National League Championship Series against the Braves on
October 6. Photo by Al Tielemans.

threw a wild pitch past catcher Damon Berryhill, and Kruk scored
the go-ahead run. Braves manager Bobby Cox lifted Avery for reliever
Kent Mercker, who retired the side.

Schilling, on the other hand, completed eight strong innings, giving up just two runs on seven hits with ten strikeouts. When manager Jim Fregosi told him his night was over, the twenty-six-year-old
right-hander pleaded to finish the game. "He is such a competitor
that he wanted to stay in there," said Fregosi. "But he had thrown
140-some pitches by then, and he had to be tired."

Instead, the Phils' skipper went to Mitch Williams to preserve
the 3–2 lead in the ninth. Schilling, arguably the most self-absorbed
player of the team, dreaded the decision. Not only did the two players dislike each other, but Schil had grown tired of Wild Thing's
high-wire act, especially when he was closing one of his own games.
It was difficult for Schilling to watch. To the dismay of teammates,
he took a seat in the dugout and placed a towel over his head and
sweated out the ninth.

Kim Batiste also came into the game as a defensive replacement for Dave Hollins at third, a move Fregosi routinely made during the regular season in the late innings of close games. Batiste had earned his manager's confidence by not making a single error all season. But this time the strategy backfired.

Wild Thing promptly walked Bill Pecota, the first batter he faced. Mark Lemke followed with a hard ground ball to third. Batiste fielded the sure-fire double-play ball and side-armed it past second base into right field, setting up the Braves' tying run. Pinch hitter Rafael Belliard followed with a sacrifice bunt, moving Pecota to third, and he scored on Nixon's grounder to short to tie the game, 3–3.

"After that error, I felt terrible," Batiste admitted. "When I got back to the dugout, I was just sitting there, talking to myself, saying, 'What are you doing? Where were you throwing that ball?'"[10]

Milt Thompson led the parade of veterans who consoled the young infielder. "Hey, it's over with," they told him. "Don't worry about it now. You may just get the chance to win this thing for us."

Batiste's opportunity to redeem himself came in the tenth inning with one out and John Kruk, who had just doubled, standing on second base. Atlanta closer Greg McMichael threw him a 1-2 change-up, and Batiste smacked the pitch into the left-field corner for a game-winning double. Suddenly, there was a mob scene of Phillies at second base, all pounding Kim Batiste on the chest, then lifting him onto their shoulders and carrying him off the field.[11]

"It was a real emotional thing," said Thompson, who hoisted Batiste onto his shoulders. "We all felt so good for him, coming back after the error the way he did."[12] "Just like that," Jim Fregosi added, "Batty went from the shithouse to the castle," as the Phillies secured a 4–3 victory in Game One.[13]

Although Schilling didn't get the win—which went to Mitch Williams—he did set the tone for the NLCS. His visible passion and overwhelming fastball put the Braves on notice that the Phillies would not be as easy to dispatch as they once believed. At the same time, Schilling created some hard feelings among teammates for the towel incident. Clearly, Williams didn't appreciate the stunt, but he made light of it after the game. "Schil is probably the only one who has the nerve to put a towel over his head,"

Hide the Women and Children!

he said to the media. "The rest of them watch, but they'd rather be under the towel with him."

John Kruk was more candid. "I thought it was disrespectful to Mitch," said Kruk. "I mean, Mitch is the same kind of competitor as Schil. He was out there giving it everything he had."[14]

Schilling loved the camera. He loved doing interviews with the media. And he especially loved all the national publicity he was getting. "October was my time to shine," he admitted in a 2009 interview. "I felt that in one night I could make people remember a game for the rest of their lives. I was able to maintain that kind of attitude in the postseason throughout my career, something that a lot of pitchers can't do. I also liked talking to the media, especially in October. I know that bothered a lot of teammates, but I am the kind of person who likes to voice his opinions."[15]

According to Angelo Cataldi, the morning host at WIP Sports Radio, Schilling was "on hold every day at 6:00 a.m. waiting to go on air with us at WIP." "Listeners thought it was pre-arranged," explained Cataldi. "But honest to God, it wasn't. And he'd stay on the air as long as possible. We couldn't figure out why he did it because none of the other Phillies ever bothered with us."[16]

Schilling also captured the spotlight when he began placing a towel over his head in the dugout while he white-knuckled his way through Williams's unpredictable pitching. Once he was told that it disrespected Williams, he stopped. But the incident took on a life of its own and would eventually result in the estrangement of the two pitchers. Nevertheless, Phillies fans had an excuse to join Schilling under that towel the next night when the Braves hammered Phillies pitching for sixteen hits, including four home runs, in a 14–3 rout.

Tommy Greene started Game Two for the Phils and was knocked out in the third inning after surrendering seven earned runs. Fred McGriff began the assault in the first inning when he hit a 438-foot two-run homer into the upper deck in right field. The mammoth blast, only the seventh ball ever hit to that area of the Vet, gave the Braves a 2–0 lead. Greene gave up five more runs in the third before Thigpen relieved him with one out and two runners on base. But it didn't get much better.

FIG. 32. From goat to hero. Kim Batiste is carried off the field by teammates after hitting a game-winning double in the tenth inning to give the Phils a 4–3 victory over the Braves in Game One of the National League playoffs. An inning earlier Batiste's throwing error allowed the Braves to tie the score, 3–3. Photo by Al Tielemans.

Thigpen proceeded to issue a three-run homer to Damon Berryhill. The Braves went on to add another run in the fifth on a solo shot by Terry Pendleton off Ben Rivera, the Phils' fifth starter who agreed to work out of the bullpen in the playoffs. The ugly assault continued in the eighth, with David West giving up four more runs.

The Phillies, on the other hand, managed only three runs. Two of those runs came off Braves starter Greg Maddux in the fourth, when Kruk singled and Hollins followed with a two-run homer. Aside from that the Fightins were able to put runners in scoring position only twice against Maddux, who gave up just five hits over seven innings and struck out eight. The Phils' third and final run came in the ninth, when Dykstra homered off Braves reliever Mark Wohlers.[17]

When asked about the Phils' embarrassing performance in a postgame interview, Daulton shrugged his shoulders and said, "We got the shit kicked out of us tonight. That's all there is to it."[18]

Braves fan Stuart Babe, thirty-three, could relate. Having flown

Hide the Women and Children!

up from Atlanta for Games One and Two, Babe nearly received the same treatment from the Boo Birds, who became resentful after the Phillies quickly fell behind. "I've had this cleaned twice," he complained, grabbing his Braves jersey. "I had people take mustard from a hot dog and smear it—grind it!—all over my jersey. When I left the stadium, I had to have police around me. Lord, were we abused!"[19]

Apparently, the city of Atlanta considered the Phillies just as incorrigible as the Boo Birds. When the NLCS shifted south for Game Three on Saturday, October 9, the *Atlanta Constitution-Journal* warned residents: "HIDE THE WOMEN AND CHILDREN, ATLANTA: AMERICA'S OTHER TEAM IS COMING TO TOWN!"[20] The scandalous headline acknowledged that the colorful Phillies had captured the imaginations of fans across the country and in so doing challenged the Braves as "America's team." But it was also intended as a humorous insult. Other newspapers described the Phils as "long-haired, pot-bellied and snarly-lipped" as well as a "motley crew of hairy, beer-soused brutes."

Pete Incaviglia had a simple response to all the ridicule: "This ain't no fuckin' beauty contest. It's baseball. All the other stuff doesn't mean shit."[21]

The Phillies started Terry Mulholland against Tom Glavine in Game Three at Atlanta's Fulton County Stadium. Phils manager Jim Fregosi was asking a lot of the southpaw. After the All-Star Break, Mulholland slumped, going 3-3. He missed twenty-four days in September with a severe hip strain and couldn't pitch until the final game of the regular season. But Mulholland still enjoyed the best earned run average (3.24) of any Phillie starter, so Fregosi had to pitch him.

For five innings Mulholland rose to meet the challenge, holding the Braves' explosive offense to just five hits. The Phillies gave him a 1–0 lead in the top of the fourth when Duncan and Kruk hit back-to-back triples. The Phils increased their lead to 2–0 in the top of the sixth when Kruk hit an opposite-field home run. But the Braves came storming back in the bottom of the inning.

Jeff Blauser opened the Braves' five-run assault by bouncing a hard grounder off Mulholland's glove for an infield single. Gant walked and McGriff and Pendleton followed with back-to-back singles, which tied the score at 2–2. Justice knocked in the go-ahead run on a double to left-center, his first hit of the series.

"Mul just ran out of gas," said Fregosi, who brought in middle reliever Roger Mason. But Mulholland refused to use his hip injury or the long layoff that followed as an excuse. "I just kept throwing balls in the wrong spot," he explained. "You can't let up on those guys. Make a mistake, and they're going to hit it."[22]

Braves fans suddenly came to life. Fifty-two thousand loyalists began doing the "tomahawk chop," led by owner Ted Turner, who was seated in the first row with his then wife, actress Jane Fonda. Even former president Jimmy Carter, a native Georgian, got into the act. Some diehards painted their faces like Indian warriors. Others engaged in trash-talking:

"What is wrong with the Phillies?" demanded Terry Dunn, age forty, wearing her 14-carat tomahawk earrings and a baseball jersey with *Braves* spelled out in rhinestones.

"Thugs!" sneered her friend Wanda Jarrett, forty-four.

"They've got scraggly beards and they weigh 300 pounds," added a third, Jennifer Boggus, twenty-seven. "And how much gum can you chew?"

"Every base has got spit wads all around it," Jarrett continued. "And if they're not spitting, they're scratching."

"God is a Braves fan," she insisted smugly. "They're chopping in heaven right now. We're going to take it, you know we are. We're America's team!"

Phillies fan Chris Graci, twenty-two, believed otherwise. "Somebody grabbed me by the throat in the second inning," said Graci, who flew down from Philadelphia for the game. "The security guard pulled him off me. The third inning comes, and I'm in my seat cheering: peanuts, beer and soda all over me. And we paid $300 to come here."[23]

Graci didn't have much to cheer about. By the end of the sixth, the Braves had increased their lead, 5–2. Atlanta starter Tom Glavine was now determined to keep the Phils off the board. In the seventh he retired Daulton, Incaviglia, and Chamberlain in order before

Hide the Women and Children!

turning the game over to the bullpen. "I just decided to be more aggressive with them," said Glavine. "I really went after them. I figured if they're going to beat me, it has to be with my best stuff."[24]

Atlanta added four more runs in the seventh off Larry Andersen and David West to make the score 9–2. But the Phillies refused to fold. Duncan hit another triple in the eighth and scored on Kruk's ground out to short. They added a fourth and final run in the ninth when Chamberlain doubled to left-center, went to third on a single up the middle by Stocker, and scored on a double to right by pinch hitter Jim Eisenreich. Unfortunately, it wasn't enough, as the Phils dropped Game Three, 9–4, to the Braves.[25]

"We're just not clicking on all cylinders," said John Kruk, whose triple, homer, and three RBI provided most of the Phils' offense against Tom Glavine. "We're not in synch. And you've got to have it all going against these guys."[26]

Down two games to one, the Phillies sought to redeem themselves in Game Four. Danny Jackson took the mound against Atlanta's John Smoltz and responded brilliantly. Not only did he pitch the Phillies to a 2–1 victory, but he also drove in the winning run in the fourth when he singled home Milt Thompson. By doing so Jackson vindicated himself for his poor showing against the Braves in the 1992 NLCS when he pitched for the Pittsburgh Pirates.

"Nobody gave me a chance," recalled Jackson many years later.

All I kept hearing about was the bad game I pitched in the NLCS against the Braves in 1992. I was mad. There were a lot of good games I threw in the postseason, too.

The media seemed to forget that when I was with the Royals in 1985 and we were on the brink of elimination, I tossed a complete-game shutout. Two weeks later when we were trailing the St. Louis Cardinals three games to one in the World Series, I won Game Five. Nor did anyone seem to remember that I won Game Three of the NLCS for the Cincinnati Reds in 1990, beating the Pirates 6–3. When you hear time and again that you're no good, or that you're washed up, it kind of puts you off. But I believed in myself, and my teammates believed in me.[27]

FIG. 33. Danny Jackson held the Braves to one run in $7^{2}/_{3}$
innings to give the Phillies a 2–1 win in Game Four of playoffs.
Photo by Al Tielemans.

Jackson used a crisp fastball and a devastating slider to hold the
Braves to one run in seven and two-thirds innings. Atlanta stranded
five runners in scoring position before yielding to Mitch Williams
with two outs and two runners on base in the eighth.

"I had a blast that game," said Jackson. "I loved being the guy
who was being counted on. I just told myself, 'Focus on your game.
Don't worry about anything else. Don't let anything distract you.'
And I stuck to that plan."[28]

Hide the Women and Children!

Wild Thing wasted no time in creating some excitement. The first batter he faced was Mark Lemke, who smacked a long liner to the wall in left. But Milt Thompson snagged the ball with a leaping catch. Williams created some more thrills in the ninth when he surrendered a bloop single to pinch hitter Bill Pecota and then committed an error on Otis Nixon's sacrifice bunt.

Anticipating another bunt, Williams called time and told Kim Batiste, a late-inning defensive replacement, that if the bunt came his way, he was going to third. That's just what he did when Jeff Blauser laid down the sacrifice. But Wild Thing didn't get a firm grip on the ball, and Batiste had to stretch as far as he could while holding the bag to get the out. With one out Ron Gant stepped up to the plate and hit a sharp grounder to Morandini, who fielded the ball, stepped on second, and threw to Kruk at first to seal the Phillies' 2–1 victory.[29]

"They never give up," Braves starter John Smoltz said of the Phillies. "I thought I had good enough stuff to win that game, 1–0, but it didn't work out that way." Smoltz's "stuff" was good enough to strike out ten Phillies, and after reliever Mark Wohlers fanned five more, Philadelphia had tied a National League Championship Series record with fifteen strikeouts. The Fightins also stranded fifteen base runners.[30] None of that mattered, though, because the Phillies, on the strength of Jackson's pitching, had evened the series at two games apiece.

When asked by the sportswriters about his inspiration after the game, Jackson, still reeling from all the negative publicity about his poor showing in the NLCS the previous year, responded bluntly: "I wanted to go out and stick it up your [the media's] ass."[31]

Schilling went to the mound against Steve Avery for Game Five on Monday, October 11. It would be the third and final game of the series played in Atlanta. The Phillies took an early lead with a run in the first on a single by Mariano Duncan and a double by Kruk. They added a second run in the fourth when Pete Incaviglia hit a deep drive off the left-field wall. Ron Gant failed to jump for the ball and was charged with a three-base error. Inky scored on a sacrifice fly by Wes Chamberlain. Daulton added a solo homer in the top of the ninth to give the Phillies a 3–0 lead.[32]

FIG. 34. Phillies second baseman Mickey Morandini turns a double play to end Game Four of the National League playoffs and preserve the Phillies' one-run victory. Photo by Al Tielemans.

Wes Chamberlain and Pete Incaviglia played outstanding defense early in the game. In the first Chamberlain held Braves second baseman Jeff Blauser to a single by cutting off a ball headed for the right-field corner. Later in the inning Fred McGriff rocketed a ball that caromed off the right-field wall. The rookie outfielder played the ball perfectly and hit the cutoff, Kevin Stocker, who nailed Blauser at the plate for the final out of the inning. Chamberlain also threw out Atlanta catcher Damon Berryhill, who tried to stretch a single into a double in the second inning. On the play

Hide the Women and Children!

FIG. 35. Dykstra homers off Atlanta's Mark Wohlers in the tenth inning of
Game Five to give the Phillies a 4–3 win. Photo by Al Tielemans.

before that, Incaviglia made a remarkable sliding catch to rob Terry
Pendleton of extra bases.[33]

The sparkling defense allowed Schilling to settle down and find
his groove. After the second Schil surrendered just one of the four
hits the Braves collected off him and struck out nine in eight strong
innings. He finally came out in the ninth after giving up a lead-off
walk to Blauser and a sure-fire double-play ball that Batiste booted.

Williams came on in relief with a 3–0 lead and almost blew the
game. With no outs and two runners on base, Wild Thing served
up an RBI single to McGriff to put the Braves on the scoreboard.
Justice followed with a sacrifice fly, making the score 3–2. Pendleton singled to put runners on first and second, and pinch hitter
Francisco Cabrera tied the game with a single. Now the game was
tied, 3–3, with the winning run on third and just one out.

Schilling was noticeably agitated. "I can't tell you what I was
thinking," he said later. "There were too many things going through
my head at the time."[34] No doubt, none of them was very compli-
mentary of Williams's nerve-racking performance.

Fregosi brought the infield in with the hope of cutting down the winning run on a grounder. But all the Braves needed was a well-placed ground ball through the infield or a deep fly ball to prevail.

Mark Lemke stepped up to the plate and laced a 1-1 fastball down the left-field line just foul. Williams struck him out on a nasty breaking pitch and then retired pinch hitter Bill Pecota on a fly to shallow center. But the damage had been done. Williams's blown save sent the game into extra innings.

Dykstra put the Phils back on top in the top of the tenth. He came to bat against Braves reliever Mark Wohlers with one out and ran the count to 3 and 2, waiting to jump on the full-count fastball he knew was coming. When Wohlers released the pitch, he knew it was gone; he didn't bother to turn around to see the ball crash off the seats below the right-field scoreboard. It was the Dude's sixth postseason home run of his career.[35] "I just like to play in these types of situations," said Dykstra after the Phils' 4–3 victory. "To want to be out there in those games, you can't teach that. Some people are scared to be out there. But I thrive in situations like this. So I expected to do what I did today."[36]

Schilling's performance was just as critical to the team's success. After sixteen brilliant innings in Games One and Five, he struck out nineteen Braves and allowed just three earned runs (a 1.69 ERA). Although the right-hander left both games in the ninth inning with a lead, the bullpen choked, costing him two victories. Nevertheless, Schilling put ego aside when asked how satisfying it had been to pitch in the postseason, even though he hadn't won either of his starts. "It feels great—because we won both of them, and that's the bottom line," he replied. "As long as we walked off the field with a 'W,' that's all I cared about."[37]

The NLCS returned to Philadelphia for Game Six, a rematch of the second game between Tommy Greene and Greg Maddux. Only this time the outcome would be different. The Phillies played with a cool confidence in defeating the Braves 6–3 to win the series, four games to two. Greene, pitching before a raucous crowd of 62,502 fans, gave up just five hits and three runs over seven innings. But the unsung hero of the game was Mickey Morandini, who helped the Phillies' offense most when he lined a hard shot off Maddux's leg in the first inning. Although Maddox remained in the game for five and two-thirds innings, he was not nearly as effective as he had been in his earlier start, surrendering six runs on six hits and four walks.

"I think that took some pressure off," said Morandini, understating the significance of his comebacker.

Morandini also robbed David Justice of two hits on spectacular defensive plays in the second and fourth innings and started a crucial inning-ending double play in the second.

The Phillies got on the scoreboard in the third when Greene walked, Dykstra singled, and Hollins walked to load the bases with two outs. Daulton followed with a double down the right-field line to give the Phils a 2–0 lead. Although the Braves managed to score a run in the top of the fifth, Hollins increased the Phillies' lead to 4–1 with a two-run homer in the bottom of the frame.

In the sixth the Phils added two more runs when Morandini tripled into the right-field corner after a single by Milt Thompson and an intentional walk to Dykstra. Atlanta narrowed the score to 6–3 in the top of the seventh on a two-run homer by Jeff Blauser. Greene, exhausted, managed to retire the side, but was pulled at the end of the inning. David West retired the Braves in order in the eighth, setting the scene for Williams, who came in to pitch the ninth.[38]

Wild Thing quickly dispatched the side. He struck out catcher Damon Berryhill on four pitches and used another four deliveries to induce a pop-up to center field from second baseman Mark Lemke before facing pinch hitter Bill Pecota. Philadelphia's mounted police readied themselves behind the outfield fence, preparing to discourage any attempt by fans to charge the field.

After working a 3-2 count, Williams toed the rubber and delivered one more fastball to Pecota, who swung and missed for the final out of the Phillies' 6–3 victory.[39] "Of all the improbable endings to this season," screamed CBS color commentator Tim McCarver, "the most improbable is Mitch Williams having a one-two-three inning."[40]

McCarver was partially correct. More improbable was that the Phillies, a last-place team the year before, defeated the nearly invincible Atlanta Braves, four games to two, in one of the biggest upsets in baseball's modern history.

F IG. 36. Closer Mitch "Wild Thing" Williams celebrates the
Phillies' 6–3 pennant-clinching victory against the Braves in
Game Six of the N LCS after striking out Atlanta's Bill Pecota.
Photo by Al Tielemans.

It was 11:17 p.m. Wild Thing pumped his fist and leaped into the
air as the wildly enthusiastic crowd of 62,502 erupted in cheers.
The image was captured by *Philadelphia Daily News* photographer
George Reynolds, and it graced the front page of the next day's
edition with a headline that screamed "WILD!" To reinforce the
point, the *Daily News* ran another Reynolds photo on the back page,
showing pitcher Danny Jackson ripping off his shirt while "pumping up the fans" during the on-field celebration that immediately

Hide the Women and Children!

followed. True to form, the rag headlined the back page "WHO'S UGLY NOW?" It was a spiteful retort to the Braves and their arrogant fans, who criticized the slovenly appearance of the Phillies throughout the series. And why not?

The Phillies had achieved the impossible. Not only did they go from worst to first in a single season, but they defeated baseball's version of a juggernaut that had been nearly invincible to capture the National League Championship. Across the City of Brotherly Love, hundreds of screaming, beer-swilling Philadelphians in cars and pickup trucks began honking their horns. Impromptu celebrations broke out in row houses and taverns, and a generation of fans too young to remember the Phillies' first world championship thirteen years earlier took to the streets to whoop it up.

Inside Veterans Stadium fireworks exploded, mounted police rode their horses onto the field, and thousands of fans stood, cheered, and mocked Atlanta's annoying tomahawk chop. When a few fans dashed onto the field, police quickly tackled them before escorting them out.[41]

In the midst of the celebration was Darren Daulton, who had waited the longest for a pennant and suffered the most. The feelings were so overwhelming, he appeared to be dazed. "I never had a feeling like that on a baseball field," Dutch gushed, trying to find the words to describe the exhilaration. "I saw the house [Veterans Stadium] rocking, and to know that we've done something that means so much to so many fans, it is just an unbelievable feeling."[42]

Curt Schilling was named the Most Valuable Player of the NLCS. Although he did not record a win in his two starts, Schilling's outstanding performances set the tone for the Phillies. While his penchant for burying his head in a towel whenever he was relieved by Williams may not have been appreciated by Wild Thing, winning the pennant appeared to quell whatever hard feeling existed.

"I couldn't be happier for Curt [winning the MVP] than I am," a champagne-soaked Williams told Les Brown of the *Daily News* during the Phillies' boisterous postgame celebration. "No one felt worse than I did that he didn't get the two wins he should have got. I got 'em he shoulda got 'em. But I'm glad he ended up being the MVP.

"Who else? I mean it was a team effort, but if you had to pick one guy who did something that was unbelievable, it was Schilling. He threw the crap out of the ball."[43]

At another end of the clubhouse, Schilling was standing on a platform holding his MVP Award and being interviewed on national TV. When asked how difficult it was to watch the ending of the two games he pitched, Schilling was gracious. "Well, I was just looking for an easy ending to tonight's game," he told McCarver of CBS Sports. "Mitch is a strange pitcher sometimes, but he gets it done. The bottom line is we won both of the games I started. I'm just glad he saved his 1-2-3 for tonight."

When McCarver asked Schilling what he thought of the Braves, the Phillies' ace said, "I take my hat off to them. They are a bunch of classy guys."[44] Teammate John Kruk was less generous, though.

When the national sportswriters swarmed around his locker to ask how such a band of outcasts with little playoff experience could defeat a star-studded Braves team that regularly played in the post-season, the burly first baseman was blunt: "The Braves are the most arrogant people in the world. But we didn't care who they were or what they thought. Our feeling was they could just kiss our asses."[45]

With such opposing viewpoints, it was left to Lenny Dykstra to put the Phillies' success into perspective. "We never quit," he explained. "We never died all year. Everybody thought we were down when the Braves blew us out in Games 2 and 3, but we answered right back. We got great pitching performances from Jackson and Schilling, and another from Greene tonight. We got some big hits and we had a total team effort.

"Sometimes, you just can't control what's meant to be," the Dude added. "And this was meant to be since spring training."[46]

Now, only the Toronto Blue Jays stood in the way of the Phillies fulfilling their destiny.

Hide the Women and Children!

FOURTEEN
The Series

The Toronto Blue Jays were the best Major League Baseball team that money could buy. They were a collection of free agents and well-paid veterans coldly efficient and methodical in dispatching their opponents. Since 1989 the Jays had appeared in five American League Championship Series and won the 1992 World Series against the heavily favored Atlanta Braves. Determined to repeat as world champions, Jays general manager Pat Gillick improved the roster by adding free agents outfielder Paul Molitor and starting pitcher Dave Stewart. He also acquired Rickey Henderson from the Oakland A's and reacquired former Blue Jays shortstop Tony Fernández from the New York Mets. In 1993 the Jays were the best team in Major League Baseball. Posting a record of 95-67, Toronto finished the regular season seven games ahead of the New York Yankees and went on to defeat the Chicago White Sox in six games for the pennant.[1]

Toronto was an offensive powerhouse with an American League–leading .279 batting average and the second most runs scored in the league, with 847. The Blue Jays' lineup featured the AL's top three hitters: John Olerud (.363 batting average), Paul Molitor (.332), and Roberto Alomar (.326). Olerud, Molitor, and cleanup hitter Joe Carter also collected more than one hundred RBI each that season. The Jays' pitching wasn't as overpowering but was still

Fig. 37. Schilling started Game One of World Series against
the Toronto Blue Jays, but surrendered seven runs on eight
hits before being lifted in the seventh inning. The Jays
won the game, 8–5. Photo by Al Tielemans.

impressive. Led by nineteen-game winner Pat Hentgen, the starting rotation also featured fourteen-game winner Juan Guzmán
and twelve-game winner Dave Stewart. Duane Ward, the closer,
boasted a league-leading forty-five saves.[2]

Like the Atlanta newspapers, Toronto's sportswriters chided the
Phillies about their infamous appearance and sophomoric behav-

ior. The *Toronto Star* described the Fightins as "a motley crew of hairy, beer-soused brutes who haven't a hope of beating our beloved Boys of Summer."

"Oh, they be bad," wrote columnist Rosie DiManno. "They be bold. They be ballsy. Most of all, they be comely as a baboon's butt, which might be considered a compliment in that particular club-house. They chew, they spit, they cuss, and belch. They are a species that could be found tippling brewskies in any Legion hall, a slo-pitch team sponsored by Billy Bob's hardware perhaps, except this particular group of hardy 'n' lardy sportsmen have made it to the World Series."[3]

The *Globe and Mail* was kinder, reporting, "Enough of the Phillies are round and lumpy and mangy—enough of them are crude—enough of them have nicknames like 'Nails' and 'Wild Thing,' that in the otherwise prefabricated world of professional sports, they stand out." And the *Toronto Sun* ran a contest, *"The Phillies are so ugly that . . ."* The eventual winner was: "the turf spits back."[4]

Far from being offended, the Phillies played up their motley image. Kruk told one Toronto sportswriter, "Honest, we're not bad people. But you wouldn't want us in your home." When the TV show *America's Most Wanted* learned that Schilling had dubbed the Phillies "America's Most Wanted Team," the producers shipped the team forty baseball caps bearing the show's name. Delighted with the gift, the Phillies wore their new caps during the pre-Series workout at the SkyDome. The TV show played along, telling the Toronto media, "We're not aware of any outstanding warrants, but we'll be looking very closely at tattoos."[5] Despite all the high jinks, the Phillies proved to be a worthy opponent in the Fall Classic.

The Series opened at Toronto's SkyDome on Saturday, October 16. Curt Schilling faced Juan Guzmán before a sellout crowd of 52,011. After two stellar outings in the NLCS, Schilling was disappointing. The game proved to be a seesaw battle, with the lead changing nearly every inning. Although the Phillies spotted Schilling a 2–0 lead in the first inning on run-producing singles by John Kruk and Darren Daulton, the right-hander surrendered four hits and two runs in the second, and the Blue Jays tied the game, 2–2.

Mariano Duncan put the Phils back in front in the top of the third when he singled, stole second, and scored on a single by John Kruk. But Toronto tied the game in the bottom of the frame when Devon White hit a routine fly to left-center. Milt Thompson and Lenny Dykstra went after the ball and just missed colliding as the ball deflected off Thompson's glove. The bungled play allowed White to advance to third, and he scored on Joe Carter's sacrifice fly.

Duncan came to the rescue again in the top of the fifth when he tripled off the left-field wall and scored on a wild pitch to give the Phillies a 4–3 lead. But Schilling gave up a solo home run to White in the bottom half of the inning, and the game was tied again, 4–4.

Although the Phillies tried to answer in the sixth with three hits by Ricky Jordan (who was added to the lineup as a designated hitter), Dykstra, and Duncan, the rally was cut short when Thompson hit into a double play and Kruk fanned to end the inning.

The Blue Jays took the lead for good in the bottom of the sixth when Schilling surrendered a 373-foot solo homer to John Olerud. Toronto erupted for three more runs in the seventh on one-out singles by Pat Borders and Rickey Henderson, sending Schilling to the showers. David West came in and promptly surrendered back-to-back doubles to White and Roberto Alomar before Larry Andersen ended the rally.

Trailing 8–4 in the eighth, the Phillies had an opportunity to narrow the deficit when Kevin Stocker singled and Dykstra reached first on an error by Alomar. But the Fightins folded, managing to score just one more run on a two-out RBI single by Jim Eisenreich in the ninth.[6]

"I thought Schilling had good enough stuff to win," said manager Jim Fregosi after the 8–5 loss. "He just didn't make enough good pitches when he needed to. If you get the ball up and over the plate, they're going to hit it, and that's what happened."[7]

The Phillies were not the only ones seeking revenge in Game Two. Dave Stewart, Toronto's starting pitcher, had spent two seasons with the Phils before they sent him packing. In May 1986 Stewart, then a twenty-nine-year-old veteran middle reliever who was just coming off arm surgery, was trying to make a comeback. He was teaching himself a split-finger fastball, but the Phillies wouldn't allow him to use it in the four games he pitched that spring. Stewart struggled, posting a 6.23 ERA, and the Phillies released him at the end of the month.

Believing that he could still pitch, Stewart returned home to Oakland, where he signed a Triple-A contract with the A's. After appearing in one game for Tacoma, the tall right-hander was promoted to Oakland, where he finished the 1986 season with a 9-5 record. During the next four years Stewart was the ace of the A's staff, winning at least twenty games a season and compiling a 10-3 postseason record. His most effective pitch was the split-finger fastball.[8]

Now Stewart was being given the opportunity to make the Phillies pay for their mistake. But after two scoreless innings the Phillies' offense went to work on him. Sending eight batters to the plate, the Fightins scored five runs on RBI singles by Dykstra and Dave Hollins and a three-run homer by Jim Eisenreich.

Although Phillies starter Terry Mulholland had control problems, he did not surrender a hit until the third. Nor did he give up any runs until the fourth, when Joe Carter blasted a two-run homer into the short left-field bleachers. But when Alomar singled and scored on a Tony Fernández double in the sixth to narrow the Phils' lead to 5–3, Fregosi, not wanting to take any more chances, lifted Mulholland.

Stewart was pulled by Jays manager Cito Gaston after the sixth. Reliever Tony Castillo, making his first appearance in the World Series, was given a baptism by fire when Dykstra led off the seventh with a home run over the Phillies' bullpen in right field. For the Phils Roger Mason entered the game in the bottom of the inning and retired the side in order. After recording the first out in the eighth, Mason gave up a double to Molitor.[9] The Jays' designated hitter later admitted that he was relieved to hit the double. "If it had been a single, I'd be stuck at first base having to listen to Kruk," he said. "John talks non-stop. Basically, he tries to convince you that you were lucky to get a hit. Then he spits on your shoes."[10]

One out later Fregosi elected to go to his closer, Mitch Williams. Paying no attention to Molitor on second base, Wild Thing allowed

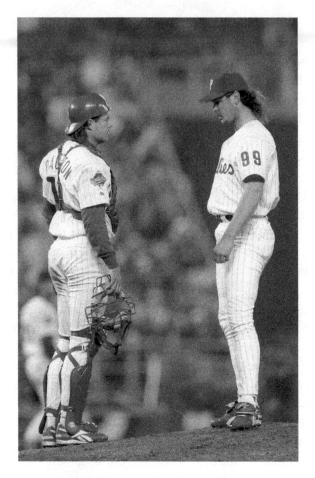

FIG. 38. Daulton, in one of many mound visits to closer
Mitch Williams, kept the Phillies' pitchers focused through
most of the postseason. Photo by Al Tielemans.

the base runner to steal third. Olerud followed with a sacrifice
fly, and suddenly the Phillies' lead was reduced to two runs, 6–4.

Inside the Phillies' dugout, Curt Schilling could not bear to watch.
He found a towel and hung it over his head as he had done throughout the postseason whenever the closer entered a game.

If Williams saw the insulting action, he chose to ignore it. Instead,
he proceeded with his high-wire act, walking Alomar, who promptly

The Series

stole second. Wild Thing had had enough. When Alomar broke for third base, Williams, in the middle of his delivery, wheeled and threw to Hollins to nail the Jays' speedy second baseman, and the inning was over.[11]

"Roberto is an excellent baserunner," said Jays manager Cito Gaston. "Normally he wouldn't do that."

Indeed, Alomar knew better. He could have scored from second on a base hit, and it still wouldn't have tied the game. But Fregosi was not surprised. "They've been watching us," said the Phillies' skipper. "They know that they can run on Mitch with that big leg kick of his."[12]

Unable to score in the top of the ninth, the Phillies sent Wild Thing back to the mound to seal the game. True to form, Williams issued a lead-off walk to Fernández. Third baseman Ed Sprague followed with a hot shot to Kim Batiste, who just entered the game as a defensive replacement at third base. It was a sure double-play ball, but Batty threw low to second base. Luckily, Mariano Duncan was able to salvage a force-out by short-hopping the throw.

Pat Borders grounded to Kevin Stocker to begin a 6-4-3 double play that ended the game and sealed the Phillies' 6–4 victory in Game Two.[13]

"I've saved 80% of the games I've been brought in to save," Williams told Mark Newman of *The Sporting News* after the game. "That's what's important to me. I don't care how I save it. As long as I get it done, that's all that matters."[14]

Having the respect of his teammates was also important to Wild Thing, and he had had enough of Curt Schilling's towel act. When Williams reached the visitors' clubhouse, he made a beeline to Schilling. Wild Thing respected his teammate's pitching ability, but his patience had worn thin with his towel act. "You're a great pitcher," he told Schilling. "But sooner or later, you won't be able to pitch anymore, and you'll have to be a man. And right now, you aren't acting like a very good one."[15]

The Series shifted to Philadelphia for Game Three on Tuesday, October 19. Veterans Stadium was packed with 62,689 raucous fans, who waited out a seventy-two-minute rain delay to see Toronto dispatch the Phils, 10–3. Danny Jackson started the game surrendering three runs in the first and a solo homer by Paul Molitor in the third before being relieved by Ben Rivera in the sixth. Rivera didn't fare much better, surrendering four more runs on four hits and two walks in the one and a third innings he pitched.

"The rain delay had nothing to do with it," said Jackson afterward. "I've had a delay before. I had too much rest between starts. I was too strong, and when I'm too strong I just don't get the pitches where I want them."[16]

Meanwhile, Jays starting pitcher Pat Hentgen stymied the Phillies' offense through six innings. After giving up one-out singles to Duncan and Kruk in the first, Hentgen bore down. "When Hollins came up to bat I was definitely going for a strikeout," said the Jays' starter. "I got two strikes on him and then made a real good pitch up and in to fan him."[17] Daulton struck out on a similar pitch to end the inning.

The Phils stranded seven runners over the first five innings. Not until the sixth did they score their first run, on an RBI single by Jim Eisenreich. The Fightins managed three more hits against Danny Cox, who came in to pitch for the Jays in the seventh, but were able to generate only one run off an RBI single by Duncan.

Toronto scored two more times off Larry Andersen in the top of the ninth, and the Phillies added another run on a Milt Thompson homer in the bottom of the inning before losing, 10–3.[18]

"I don't think you have to make any more of this [the loss] than what it is," said Daulton. "We can't panic now. We've had a lot of games like this before and we've come back and got the job done."[19]

The heartbreaker came the following night in a sloppy, rain-delayed Game Four. There was also an entertaining sideshow to the game thanks to Philadelphia mayor Ed Rendell.

Rendell, a sports junkie, initiated a verbal feud with Toronto starting pitcher Todd Stottlemyre, whose father, Mel, pitched for the New York Yankees in the 1960s. Before the Series began the mayor was asked about the possibility of a Blue Jays sweep. Rendell said that he doubted that possibility because he "didn't think Stottlemyre could beat the Phillies." "I saw that 430-foot homer Frank

Thomas hit off him [in the American League Championship Series against the Chicago White Sox]," he explained. "I think I could hit the ball 270 feet off Stottlemyre, and that's a pretty good shot for me."

Naturally, the national press fanned the flames. David Letterman invited Stottlemyre on his show and asked him what he thought about Rendell's remarks. "I'll tell you what," said the young hurler. "When this thing is over, I'll fly to Philly. Tell the mayor to put a uniform on, and we'll see what happens."

"How will you pitch to him?" asked Letterman.

"I'll probably put the first three behind his head, then paint the outside corner," replied Stottlemyre.

When Rendell learned of the challenge, he said, "I'm happy to do it. But he's got to throw me the same hanging curve he threw Frank Thomas. If he can throw that exact pitch to me over and over again, in the same location and at the same speed, and if I don't hit one of them 270 feet, then I'll give him $250 for the charity of his choice."[20]

Although the challenge was dropped after that, it did provide an interesting backstory for Game Four.

With a chance to even the Series, the Phillies blew leads of 6–3, 12–7, and 14–9 only to lose 15–14. Played on a foggy night in a constant misting rain, the game was one of the most bizarre contests in postseason history. Neither Tommy Greene, who started the game for the Phillies, nor Todd Stottlemyre, the Jays' starter, lasted three innings. Toronto pounded Greene for three runs in the first, but the Phils took a 4–3 lead in the bottom of the inning by taking advantage of Stottlemyre's four walks and a bases-loaded triple by Milt Thompson. The Phillies increased their lead by two runs after Dykstra nailed a two-run homer. Stottlemyre, who gave up all six runs on three hits and four walks, was lifted for reliever Al Leiter, who retired the side. Greene was sent to the showers in the bottom of the third when Toronto routed him, scoring four more runs to take a 7–6 lead. Mason entered in relief and retired the next three hitters.

In the fourth Dykstra doubled and scored on a single by Mariano Duncan to tie the game, 7–7. An inning later the Phils pounded

FIG. 39. Schilling acknowledges Phillies fans after his complete-game victory, 2–0, in Game Five on October 21. Photo by Al Tielemans.

the Jays' bullpen, batting around and scoring on two-run homers by Daulton and Dykstra and an RBI double by Thompson.

Phils middle reliever David West entered the game in the sixth with a 12–7 lead and promptly surrendered two more runs to the Jays. But the Phillies answered with single runs in the bottom of the sixth and seventh innings.

The Phillies held a comfortable 14–9 lead going into the eighth, when the game spiraled out of their control. After reliever Larry Andersen retired Roberto Alomar, Joe Carter singled and John Olerud walked. Paul Molitor followed with a hard grounder to third that handcuffed Dave Hollins, allowing a run to score.

Mitch Williams entered the game. After a run-scoring single by Tony Fernández and a walk to Pat Borders, Wild Thing gave up an RBI single to Rickey Henderson and a two-run triple to Devon White. Before the dust settled, Toronto held a 15–14 lead. Deflated, the Phillies went down quietly in the eighth and ninth. It was bad enough that the hitters were retired in order in each frame, but four of the six batters went down on strikes.[21]

"I stunk," said Williams. "I've stunk before except tonight it was on national TV in front of the whole country instead of our little cable TV station here in Philadelphia. That was the only difference."[22]

"That was a tough loss, no question about it," said Dykstra, who tied a World Series record with four runs scored. "You don't have to be a baseball genius to figure out that we should have won that game."[23]

The 15–14 defeat was the highest-scoring game in World Series history, surpassing the old record of twenty-two runs set in 1936 by the New York Yankees and New York Giants.[24]

Facing elimination, the Phillies sent their young ace, Curt Schilling, to the mound for Game Five. "We had no choice," said John Kruk. "We had to win. We had to get nine innings from our starter. After all the running we did the night before, we needed a pitcher's game."[25]

Schilling responded with the Phils' first complete game in a World Series since Robin Roberts accomplished the feat in the second game of the 1950 Fall Classic. Before the game the right-hander stood up in the Phillies' clubhouse and told the team he intended to "give them everything I had."

"I was upset the night before after we'd given away the game," he explained. "So I wanted the ball. I wanted the responsibility. If you don't want the ball in those situations, why show up?"[26]

Schilling was good to his word. Not a single Blue Jay reached second base until the sixth inning. Even then Toronto's scoring threat was erased by the Phillies' third double play of the game.

The Phils got to Jays starter Juan Guzmán early, giving Schilling all the run support he needed in the first inning. Dykstra led off with a walk, scampered to third when catcher Pat Borders's throw skipped into center field, and scored on Kruk's ground out to second.[27] "I wanted to get on in the first and put up a run for Curt," Nails said. "That way, he'd relax out there and not have to worry. I told him before the game, 'Let's just play baseball like we did when we were eight years old. It's the same game, so let's have some fun.'"[28]

The Phillies scored their only other run in the second inning. Daulton led off with a double to right-center and advanced to third on Eisenreich's ground out to first. Stocker followed with

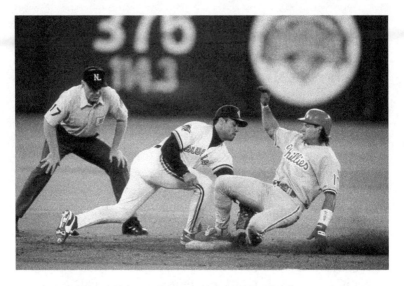

Fig. 40. Roberto Alomar of the Blue Jays applies the late tag to Daulton, who doubled in the fourth inning of Game Six. Photo by Al Tielemans.

a double down the right-field line to score Dutch, and the Phils enjoyed a 2–0 lead.

The Jays' greatest threat came in the eighth after Schilling surrendered back-to-back hits. But with runners on first and third, Rickey Henderson hit a hard smash back to the mound. Schilling fielded the ball and caught pinch runner Will Canate in a rundown between third and home. After Daulton recorded the out, Schilling retired the next five Blue Jays in order.[29]

"I started to run out of gas in the seventh," he admitted after his 2–0 victory, which was the first World Series shutout ever thrown by a Phillie pitcher. "In the eighth I looked in the bullpen and there was nobody up. That pumped me up because I knew it was up to me. So if I had to point to one inning in my career where I gave everything I had, that was the inning."[30]

"Schil showed us all tonight," Daulton said after the game. "He's turned into a big-time, big-game pitcher."[31]

While Schilling was pitching his masterpiece, the Phillies' received a phone call from a deranged fan, threatening Williams's life. Distraught because Wild Thing had given up the final three runs in the Jays' improbable 15–14 win in Game 4, the caller was determined to prevent Williams from appearing in Game Five and choking up another Phillies lead.

Police informed Williams of the death threat when he arrived at his Moorestown, New Jersey, home at two in the morning. "I was scared," he admitted. "I stayed up until 8:00 a.m., holding my gun." When asked if he would turn over the closer's role to another member of the bullpen, Wild Thing bristled at the thought. "No one's going to scare me that much," he snapped. "No one will make me hide."[32]

Schilling's gutsy five-hit shutout in Game Five sent the Series back to Canada and rejuvenated the Phillies, who resolved to bring a second world championship trophy back to Philadelphia. Even the naysayers were hard-pressed to bet against them. Time and again, the Phils had defied the odds to win. Surely they would do it again on baseball's most glamorous stage.

Game Six was played on Saturday, October 23, in Toronto's palatial SkyDome before 52,195 fans. The Phillies were due to face Dave Stewart, the Jays' ace and one of baseball's toughest pitchers. Still, they were loose and confident that they would win. "I think our chances are pretty good," mused John Kruk. "We're going against a guy that's 90-0 in the World Series and playoffs, so it shouldn't be that tough. He's due for a loss."[33]

Terry Mulholland started the game for the Phillies. Next to Schilling, he was the best big-game pitcher the team had, though he didn't have his best stuff on this night. The Blue Jays scored three times in the first inning, but Mulholland survived the next two without surrendering another run.

The Phillies got on the scoreboard in the fourth when Daulton doubled down the left-field line and scored on a single by outfielder Jim Eisenreich. Toronto padded their lead with two more runs in the fifth inning, sending Mulholland to the showers.

With the Jays holding a commanding 5–1 lead in the seventh, the Phillies launched a five-run assault to chase Stewart from the game. Shortstop Kevin Stocker opened the inning with a walk, and second baseman Mickey Morandini followed with a single, bringing Dykstra to the plate.[34]

"Man, it's the seventh inning," Nails told himself. "I better do something before it's too late."[35] Spitting a stream of tobacco juice from his mouth, Dykstra adjusted his batting helmet, stepped into the batter's box, and hit a towering drive into the right-field seats for his fourth home run of the Series.

"When Lenny hit that three-run homer, I said to myself, 'We just won the Series,' confessed Phillies president Bill Giles. "The momentum had shifted, and we were all convinced that the championship was ours."[36]

The dramatic three-run shot gave the Phillies momentum. Designated hitter Mariano Duncan singled, stole second base, and scored on another single by Hollins. Kruk struck out, but the Phils still had two outs to work with and put them to good use.

Daulton walked and Eisenreich singled to load the bases. Pinch hitter Pete Incaviglia slapped a high fly ball to right-center, scoring Hollins for the second out. Stocker ended the inning with a strikeout, but the Phillies now held a 6–5 lead.

Meanwhile, Roger Mason, a journeyman reliever with a 1.17 earned run average in the Series, shut down the powerful Toronto offense. Entering the eighth inning he had retired six Blue Jays in a row.[37] "I felt great," said Mason, a born-again Christian. "I felt as if God had promised me success if I took the mound. I just *knew* the Blue Jays weren't going to get a hit off me."[38]

Despite Mason's strong performance, Fregosi lifted him with one out and a runner on base in the eighth and went with left-hander David West. If things went according to Fregosi's plan, West would retire left-handed-hitting John Olerud and remain in the game to face switch-hitting Roberto Alomar, who batted only .245 against lefties. Then closer Mitch Williams would have to face only the light-hitting bottom of Toronto's order in the ninth.

But the best-laid plans don't always work out. West walked Olerud on five pitches, forcing Fregosi to go to right-handed setup man Larry Andersen. Andersen got Alomar to ground out, but pinch runner Alfredo Griffin advanced to second on the play. He hit the next batter, Tony Fernández, and walked Ed Sprague to load the bases before getting Pat Borders to pop up for the final out. But the damage was done. Williams would have to face the hot-hitting top of the Blue Jays' order in the ninth.

True to his name, Wild Thing walked the lead-off hitter, Rickey Henderson. Pitching coach Johnny Podres ambled to the mound and suggested that Williams go to the slide step in order to prevent the speedy Henderson from stealing second. After retiring White on a fly ball to left, Williams served up a single to Molitor. Now the Jays had runners on first and third with Joe Carter, Toronto's dangerous cleanup hitter, coming to the plate.

With the Phillies clinging to a slim 6–5 lead, the Phillies' closer chose to stay with the slide step. Williams worked the count to 2-2, getting the second strike on a slider.[39]

"In my mind, he had to come back with that same pitch," recalled Carter years later.

Daulton was thinking the same way and called for the slider. But Wild Thing shook him off. He wanted to throw a fastball, believing that he could get Carter to strike out or at most hit a lazy fly ball into the outfield. "If the pitch is up in the zone and away from Joe, he can't hit it out of the park," Williams reasoned. "He was a low ball hitter whose greatest damage came on pitches that were low and inside."

When Carter saw Williams shake off his catcher's sign, he thought the closer was "just messing with me" and continued to look for the breaking ball. No one was more surprised than Carter when he saw a fastball heading directly into his power-hitting zone. "The only reason I hit that ball fair was because I was looking for a breaking ball the whole time," Carter admitted. "I wasn't way out in front of the ball. I guarantee you, if I was looking fastball, I would've swung and missed, or hit a foul ball."[40]

The Jays' cleanup hitter buried Williams's fastball deep into the left-field stands for a game-winning walk-off home run. It also gave Toronto their second straight world championship with an 8–6 victory.[41]

Williams knew it was a home run as soon as the ball left his hand. He also realized that the slide step had altered his delivery, which resulted in the Series-clinching blow. "I knew I made a mis-

FIG. 41. Toronto's Joe Carter rounds the bases, celebrating
his World Series–clinching home run off Mitch Williams
in Game Six. Photo by Al Tielemans.

take," he admitted afterward. "That fastball was down and in, right
in Carter's nitro zone. I wanted to throw it up and away, which I
could've done if I'd gone with my full leg kick. But the slide step
altered my delivered and I ended up rushing the pitch."[42]

Dykstra headed in from center field as Carter rounded the bases
with his arms splayed aloft in victory. Passing Williams on his way
to the visitors' dugout, Nails muttered sarcastically, "Guess there
won't be a Game 7, will there?"[43]

The Series

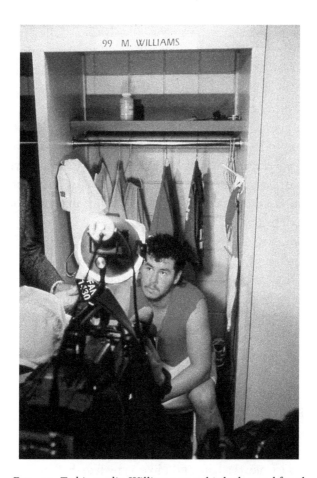

99 M. WILLIAMS

FIG. 42. To his credit, Williams sat at his locker and faced
the press after surrendering the Series-clinching home run
to Toronto's Joe Carter. "Ain't nobody walking this earth that
feels worse than I do," he told the sportswriters. "There are
no excuses. I just didn't get the job done."
Photo by Al Tielemans.

Dykstra was stunned, if not resentful. "It was a weird feeling
watching that ball go out," he remarked. "'Helpless,' I can't really
describe it. I didn't want to watch it. I really thought this was meant
to be our year. We battled and battled. But we had two heartbreak-
ing losses. Now it's over. Toronto's the better ball club. That's it."[44]
While the Blue Jays celebrated on the field, the Phillies retreated

to the visitors' clubhouse, which was eerily silent. Giles went looking for Daulton, whom he eventually found in the training room, icing his knees. "We almost did it for you, Uncle Bill," said the battle-hardened catcher. Unable to find the words to express his appreciation, Giles wrapped his arms around Dutch and began to cry.[45]

To his credit, Williams didn't hide from the media. Instead, he sat in front of his locker, patiently answering their questions. Nor did he make alibis. "Ain't nobody on the face of this earth who feels worse than I do about what happened," he said. "But there are no excuses. I just didn't get the job done. I threw a fastball down and in. It was a bad pitch. I'll have to deal with it."[46]

Publicly, Williams' teammates defended him. "We wouldn't have been here if it wasn't for Mitch," said Kruk.

Roger Mason, the reliever who pitched so effectively but was still lifted, echoed the Phillies' first baseman. "Mitch was the closer who got us to the Series," he insisted. "What if Fregosi kept me in the game and winning run scored?

"The writers are going to ask, 'You had a closer with 44 saves in the bullpen, why didn't you go to him?'"[47]

Even Lenny Dykstra later defended Williams. Three days after the Series ended, Nails made a guest appearance on *Late Night with Letterman* and told the host, "We wouldn't have been where we were without Mitch." "People don't realize that," he added. "He's not afraid to take the ball, and I like a guy like that on my team."[48]

The Phillies remained in the visitors' clubhouse well into the early-morning hours. Some yielded to their emotions and had a good cry. Others simply huddled around the lockers and rehashed what had been the most remarkable—and enjoyable—season of their careers. In the end, manager Jim Fregosi provided the most fitting epitaph. "This has been some fuckin' ride these guys have given us," he told bench coach John Vukovich. "We'll never have anything like this team again. God, how they fought. They fought and fought. But God, I'm proud of these guys."[49]

FIFTEEN

Inspiring Moneyball

How could the 1993 Phillies, a team without an easily recognizable starting pitcher or a star power hitter, run away with the National League East, defeat the heavily favored Atlanta Braves to win the pennant, and take the defending world champion Toronto Blue Jays to six games in the Fall Classic?

According to Billy Beane, general manager of the Oakland A's, the Phillies' remarkable success was due to their hitters, who "were taking tons of pitches, walking a lot and, therefore, creating a ton of runs." Beane, who was in Philadelphia watching the World Series that year, pointed out that "the Phillies led the National League by walking in 10.2 percent of their plate appearances" and that the "team's aggregate .351 on-base percentage also led the NL." In other words, the Phillies exchanged traditional power statistics like home runs and RBI for on-base percentage because their general manager, Lee Thomas, did not have the payroll to secure those superstars who could put up big numbers. It was an epiphany for Beane, who suddenly realized that "everything the Phillies were doing was exactly what sabermetrician Bill James and his disciples were writing about."[1] Instead of building an offense around one or two power hitters who could lead the league in home runs and RBI, Thomas built one around disciplined hitters who generated runs by simply getting on base and moving runners. Instead of building a team around a starting rotation with a bona fide twenty-game winner and two or three other starters who could record double-digit wins, Thomas built one around innings eaters with stingy earned run averages and a strong defense. Unwittingly, the 1993 Phillies redefined the way the game was played in the 1990s as well as the blueprint a front office used to build a winning team. It was the same strategy that became known as "Moneyball" and was adapted by Beane after watching the Phillies' sudden and remarkable success.

Moneyball is based on the belief that the collective wisdom of baseball insiders—players, managers, coaches, scouts, and the front office—over the past century is subjective and often flawed. Traditional statistics such as stolen bases, runs batted in, and batting average typically used to gauge players are no longer the best indicators of offensive success in the modern game, especially for small-market clubs that do not have the payroll to compete for expensive free agents. Instead, many small-market teams place a higher value on "sabermetrics," an empirical analysis of baseball that measures in-game activity.[2] Those teams that value sabermetrics are often said to be playing Moneyball.

Bill James, one of the earliest sabermetricians, defines the new statistics as "the search for objective knowledge about baseball."[3] Accordingly, sabermetrics attempts to answer objective questions about baseball, such as "Which player on the 1993 Phillies contributed the most to the team's offense?" It cannot deal with the subjective judgments such as "Who is your favorite player on the '93 Phillies?" In addition, sabermetricians often question traditional measures of baseball skill. For instance, they doubt that batting average is as useful as conventional wisdom claims because team batting average provides a relatively poor fit for team runs scored. Sabermetric reasoning would hold that runs win ball games and that a good measure of a player's worth is his ability to help his team score more runs than the opposing team. Although this kind of reasoning may suggest that the traditional RBI is an effective metric, sabermetricians also reject RBI. Instead, sabermetric measures are usually phrased in terms of either runs or team wins. For example, a player might be described as being worth fifty-four offensive runs more than a replacement-level player at the same position over the course of a full season, as indicated by the sabermetric statistic VORP, which refers to "value over replacement player."[4]

"If you're going to make decisions based on data," Beane explains, "you need a lot of it. And really it's all about getting as much information as possible to make a decision. That's what scouting is about, too." In both cases, "you're trying to get as much information as you can to make the most educated decision you can."[5]

When considering the remarkable offensive success of the 1993 Phillies, the key metrics are on-base percentage and slugging percentage. The Phillies finished first in the National League in OBP (.351) and second in SLG (.426) to finish first in the NL with a .777 OPS (OBP + SLG). OBP is calculated by the following equation:

hits + walks + hit by pitch + sacrifice flies
divided by
at bats + walks + hit by pitch + sacrifice flies

John Kruk's 1993 statistics illustrate the OBP calculation:

Hits: 169	At bats: 535
Walks: 111	Walks: 111
Hit by pitch: 0	Hit by pitch: 0
	Sacrifice flies: 5
Total: 280	Total: 651
280 divided by 651 = .430 OBP	

Source: Baseballreference.com.

Any player who compiles an OBP of .400 or more has had an excellent season in that category. Of the eleven Phillies to compile 300 or more plate appearances in '93, three had an OBP over .400: Kruk (.430), Lenny Dykstra (.420), and Kevin Stocker (.409). Three others had an OBP of .360 or higher: Darren Daulton (.392), Dave Hollins (.372), and Jim Eisenreich (.363).

One of the most underrated offensive statistics by traditional baseball insiders is the base on balls. But walks are a major component when calculating OBP. The 1993 Phillies led the National

League in walks with 665, which was 77 more than the St. Louis Cardinals, who came in second with 588 walks. The Phillies also had three players with 100 or more walks: Dykstra, who led the National League with 129; Daulton (117); and Kruk (111). No National League team had ever before had three players do that.[6] "Free passes are the key," replied Dykstra when asked why the Phillies were able to capture the NL East title. "Walks are such an underrated stat. They can drive the other team crazy. Sometimes they're even more effective than a hit.

"If I go up there and hit a line drive to right field for a single, that's just one pitch," he explained. "But if I go up there and foul off a lot of balls and make the pitcher work that much harder, make him throw seven or eight pitches, that's very frustrating for him. And not just for the pitcher, but for his manager and for the players in the field behind him." Dugout coach John Vukovich echoed Dykstra's philosophy. "We are very patient," said Vukovich. "Our hitters understand that a walk is just as good as a hit, sometimes even better. It's also why there haven't been many one-two-three innings this season. There are always people on base, and when there are people on base, anything can happen."[7]

While the number of walks increases a player's on-base percentage, OBP correlates better with scoring runs, something the 1993 Phillies did extremely well. The Phillies had three regulars who scored 100 or more runs: Dykstra, who led the NL with 143 runs; Hollins (104); and Kruk (100). Dykstra was the catalyst for scoring runs, though. In games where he scored 1 run, the Phillies were 35-27; when he scored 2 runs, the Phils were 25-2; and in games where Nails scored 3 or more runs, the Fightins were 9-0. In other words, the Phillies went 69-29 whenever Dykstra scored at least one run and 28-35 when he didn't score any.[8] In fact, Nails accounted for 16.3 percent of the total number of runs the '93 Phillies scored. That means he scored 1 run every ten innings. Here is a breakdown of the 1993 Phillies scoring percentage by player:[9]

Lenny Dykstra	16%
Dave Hollins	11.8%
John Kruk	11.4%
Darren Daulton	10.3%
Mariano Duncan	7.7%
Pete Incaviglia	6.8%
Mickey Morandini	6.5%
Jim Eisenreich	5.8%
Kevin Stocker	5.2%
Milt Thompson	4.8%
Wes Chamberlain	3.9%
Ricky Jordan	2.4%
Kim Batiste	1.6%
Todd Pratt	0.9%
Ruben Amaro	0.8%
Juan Bell	0.6%
Joe Millette	0.3%
Tony Longmire	0.1%
Doug Lindsay	0%
Jeff Manto	0%

Source: Baseballreference.com

Slugging percentage is the other key statistic when interpreting the remarkable success of the 1993 Phillies. SLG attempts to measure the power of a hitter by comparing the total number of bases a player gains divided by the total number of at bats. Players who hit with power (gain additional bases) will have a higher amount of total bases for each at bat, which is reflected in a higher slugging percentage. Pete Incaviglia's 1993 statistics illustrate the SLG calculation:

Total hits		Total bases
58	Singles	58
16	Doubles (x 2)	32
3	Triples (x 3)	9
24	Home runs (x 4)	96
101		195

195 total bases divided by 368 at-bats = .530 SLG

Source: Baseballreference.com

Any player who compiles an SLG of .475 or more has had a successful season in that category. Of the eleven Phillies to compile 300 or more plate appearances in '93, four had an SLG of .475 or higher: Incaviglia (.530), Daulton (.482), Dykstra (.482), and Kruk (.475).

Finally, the ability of a player both to get on base and to hit for power is represented when OBP and SLG are added. The resulting "on-base plus slugging" offers a very good measure of a player's overall offensive production and correlates quite well with team run scoring. Any player who compiles an 800 OPS or more has had a very successful season. Of the eleven Phillies with 300 or more at bats, six reached that benchmark or higher: Kruk (905), Dykstra (902), Daulton (874), Incaviglia (848), Hollins (814), and Jim Eisenreich (808). In addition, the Phillies led all NL teams in OPS with a 777 rating.

Because the 1993 Phillies led the National League in OBP (.351) and OPS (777) and were second in SLG (.426), it's not surprising that they also led the league in runs scored (877). What that means is that the '93 Phillies were not only the best team in the National League at getting on base, but also extremely successful in moving and scoring runners. Predictably, there are some important similarities between the 1993 Phillies and the 2002 Oakland A's, the team depicted in Michael Lewis's book *Moneyball* and later in Bennett Miller's film of the same name.

Both Lee Thomas and Billy Beane were forced to work with small-market clubs that could not afford to pay the huge salaries that star free agents were making. Both general managers had to make sure that when they invested in a player, they would have the highest probability in return.[10] Instead of investing in star free agents like Kirby Puckett and David Cone, Thomas divided his financial resources among proven veterans with much less star power, like John Kruk, Pete Incaviglia, Danny Jackson, Jim Eisenreich, and David West, or players that other organizations had given up on, like Dykstra and Williams. Similarly, Beane, unable to attract expensive free agents, signed relatively unknown players such as Scott Hatteberg, Mark Ellis, Jeremy Giambi, and Olmedo Sáenz, who had high on-base percentages. In addition, both Thomas and Beane spent little relative to the rest of their leagues. The 1993 pennant-winning Phillies had the seventh-lowest payroll of any nonexpansion team. Similarly, the 2002 A's, who won 103 games, had the lowest payroll in the MLB at $44 million, yet they proved to be competitive with larger-market teams such as the New York Yankees, who spent more than $125 million in payroll that same season. Because of Oakland's smaller revenues, Beane was forced to find players undervalued by the market, and his system for finding value in undervalued players took the A's to the American League playoffs in 2002 and 2003.[11]

Where Beane differed from Thomas, however, was in the use of metrics rather than team chemistry to gauge success. While Thomas hoped to secure the right mix of veterans, believing that chemistry would lead to winning, Beane rejected chemistry as the primary indicator for success because, as he said, "you can't measure it, and if you can't measure chemistry, you can't invest in it." Instead, Beane "invested in players who win." To determine who those players were, he studied their metrics, especially their on-base percentage. If you invest in those kinds of players, Beane believed, "chemistry" would follow. After all, he explained, "they're all going to get paid at the end of the year, and it's just like a business."[12]

Operating on this philosophy, Beane and the Oakland A's front office took advantage of more analytical gauges of player performance to field a team that could better compete against richer competitors in Major League Baseball. Because rigorous statistical analysis had demonstrated that on-base percentage and slugging percentage are better indicators of offensive success, Beane was convinced that these qualities were cheaper to obtain on the open market than more historically valued qualities such as speed and contact. Acting on this belief, the A's general manager built the 2002 Athletics around four players who recorded on-base percentages near .360 or better: Jeremy Giambi (.390), David Justice (.376), Scott Hatteberg (.374), and Mark Ellis (.359). Oakland's .345 team mark that year was six points lower than the OBP of the 1993 Phillies.

Since then Moneyball has changed the way most Major League front offices do business. In its wake teams such as the New York Mets, New York Yankees, San Diego Padres, St. Louis Cardinals, Boston Red Sox, Washington Nationals, Arizona Diamondbacks, Cleveland Indians, and Toronto Blue Jays have hired full-time sabermetric analysts. Ironically, the Phillies, who inspired Beane, were among the very last clubs in the MLB to adopt the philosophy, and it has prevented their organization from achieving sustained success.

SIXTEEN
Breaking the Code

Darren Daulton, Lenny Dykstra, John Kruk, Dave Hollins, and Pete Incaviglia all returned to the Phillies in 1994. Some even extended their playing careers into the latter part of the decade and beyond, though they did so with other organizations. But never again would any of them experience the special camaraderie of Macho Row or the magic of the 1993 season. Never again would they play on a team that lived by the Code and ultimately died by violating the unconditional loyalty that defined it.

Dykstra and Curt Schilling, the most prominent nonmember of Macho Row, violated the Code shortly after the Phillies lost the World Series. Both players went to the media, expressing a concern that Mitch Williams not return to the Phillies after surrendering the Series-clinching home run to Toronto's Joe Carter. Initially supportive of Williams, Dykstra reversed himself during the offseason. "I love the guy," said Dykstra in the wake of the painful loss. "He's a great competitor and I'm sure he wants to pitch here again, but for his sake I hope he doesn't have to."

Citing the death threats and the egging of Williams's South Jersey home by an unruly mob of teenagers, Nails predicted that "he'll probably never be able to pitch in Philly again." "Can you imagine what could happen on opening day?" he asked. "Suppose there are 60,000 screaming at the Vet and we've got a one-run lead and

Mitch comes in to start the ninth. Suppose he walks the first hitter? It would be brutal. Those fans would be all over him."

Schilling was more candid. He was adamant that trading Williams would be "a positive move for everybody involved." "What if we win and go to the postseason again next year?" he speculated. "We'd still be going in with the mentality of 'Can he do it?' Mitch was tired at the end of the season. It was a question of whether he was able to. Mitch gave his all every time out there, but, in the big leagues, it's not a matter of giving everything and wanting the ball. It's a matter of success."[1]

Dykstra and Schilling insisted that their comments should not be taken "personally" by Williams, and they were careful to acknowledge the important contribution Wild Thing made to the Phillies' success. But that became a moot point on December 2, when Lee Thomas traded the closer to the Houston Astros for pitchers Doug Jones and Jeff Juden.[2]

Insulted by Schilling's remarks, in particular, Williams attacked the ace pitcher in the Philadelphia newspapers. "I'll always have fond memories of Philly," he told the city's sportswriters, "with the exception of one guy—Curt Schilling, who went out of his way to make a mockery of me." He cited the right-hander's penchant not only for placing a towel over his head to spare himself from watching Williams pitch, but also for "blaming me for losing the World Series." "I have no respect for anybody who'll say something to the media and not to my face."

When Schilling learned of the remark, he admitted that "Mitch and I didn't get along from the first day." "He didn't show me any respect," he added, "and that's why I didn't show him any respect."[3]

No matter how they tried to present their cases, all three players—Dykstra, Schilling, and Williams—had broken the omertà of the Code by taking their remarks to the press. Over the years the resentment between the three players festered, occasionally spilling over into the media. On November 27, 2008, for example, Dykstra, in an interview with WIP Sports Radio host Howard Eskin, criticized Williams as a "barrel finder": "We did go to the big dance [World Series], but Mitch Williams kept hitting barrel after barrel [of the

Breaking the Code

Toronto Blue Jays' bats]. Mitch Williams is a joke. Why do you want to talk about him? It's painful dude. He kept me from getting another [world championship] ring."[4]

Speaking with WIP host Angelo Cataldi the next morning, Williams responded by calling Dykstra the "most common sense–void person I've ever met in my life." "Lenny makes no sense whatsoever," he added. "He's a savant with a bat in his hand. You could have a better conversation with a tree." Then Williams took aim at Dykstra's most recent business venture—Players Club, a high-end jet charter company and magazine to give advice on financial investments to professional athletes. Predicting that Nails would "fail miserably" in the venture, Williams said that his former teammate "won't have two nickels to rub together in three years" and that he "wouldn't give Lenny a single dollar to walk across the street and put it in the bank for me."[5]

Dykstra sought revenge a few years later when Williams became a baseball analyst for the MLB Network as well as for Philadelphia's WIP Sports Radio. "I know Mitch Williams is popular in Philly these days, and he'll bury me for this, but I don't give a damn," said Nails, prefacing his remarks in an interview with John Clark of NBC-10 TV on March 8, 2011. "I don't talk to Mitch after what he put me through," he said. "The guy hit barrel after barrel. He lost the World Series for us, and now he's actually popular with Philly fans. It's bullshit. I mean can you see Bill Buckner going back to Boston after blowing the '86 World Series for the Red Sox, and doing what Mitch Williams is doing in Philadelphia? Whatever, it's a fucking joke."[6]

About the same time, Williams resumed his attack against Curt Schilling. "If our team went 20-142, but Schilling had the 20 wins, that would be all he cared about," he wrote in *Straight Talk from Wild Thing*, an autobiographical baseball account he authored in 2010. "But he blamed me for blowing games. You know how many of his potential wins I blew? Zero. He won 16 games in 1993 and I saved 12 of them. He completed the other four wins himself.

"So when we were in the World Series and he put a towel over his head when I came in to pitch, well, that kind of stuff is just unforgivable as far as I'm concerned. Other guys on the team understood his selfishness, and kept him in check so it wouldn't affect our success."[7]

But the most damaging confrontation came between Dykstra and Williams on April 23, 2015, at a comedy roast hosted by WIP Sports Radio. The animosity seemed to rise to a whole new level as the former teammates exchanged expletive-filled barbs. Dykstra, who spent time behind bars for bankruptcy fraud, delivered one of the few jokes in the awkward exchange when he told Williams, "Prison was like a fuckin' fantasy camp compared to playing behind you."

Williams shot back by suggesting that Dykstra was a selfish player, angered by the walk-off home run to Joe Carter "only because it meant Lenny wouldn't win the 1993 World Series MVP." When Nails took exception to the remark, Williams stood up as if he was going to fight him.[8] Although the "comedy" roast didn't deteriorate into blows, the ugly remarks indicated just how severe their estrangement had become as well as the bitterness each ballplayer harbored over their playing careers.

Dykstra, Williams, and Schilling probably never imagined how their lives would turn out when they were teammates. Since 1993 each of the ballplayers has ridden a roller coaster of remarkable success and equally painful hardship. Dykstra's fall from grace has been especially tragic.

After an outstanding 1993 season in which he finished second in the National League's MVP balloting, the Phillies rewarded Nails with a $25 million contract, making him the highest-paid lead-off hitter in Major League Baseball.[9] But his career went into a sharp decline. In the strike-shortened 1994 season, Dykstra played in just eighty-four games due to back soreness. The following season he missed one hundred games due to ongoing back problems and an arthritic right knee. And in 1996 Nails' season ended in May after appearing in just forty games. Suffering from numbness in his legs and spinal stenosis—a congenital condition that causes severe pressure on the spinal cord—Dykstra had back surgery to relieve the pain. The procedure was unsuccessful, and he missed the entire 1997 season. A failed comeback attempt in the spring

Breaking the Code

of 1998 convinced Nails that his playing career was over, and he retired at age thirty-five.[10]

Dykstra appeared to reinvent himself as a successful financial entrepreneur. "Before I take a dirt nap [die], I'm going to build myself a financial empire," he told Ian Thompsen of *Sports Illustrated* in December 1993. Parlaying his considerable baseball earnings into a car-wash venture in Southern California, Nails partnered with longtime friend and businessman Lindsay Jones. His kid brother, Kevin, ran the day-to-day operations while Dykstra was still playing.[11] In 1998 after retiring from baseball, Lenny expanded the business to suburban Simi Valley.[12] About the same time he began investing his money in the stock market and learned as much as he could about Wall Street.

In 2005 Dykstra established an option-trading investment strategy called "Deep in the Money Calls." While not a registered financial adviser or stockbroker, Dykstra claimed that 95 percent of his stock-option tips made money. The claim seemed to have validity when Nails, in August 2007, bought the Southern California estate of hockey star Wayne Gretzky for a reported $18.5 million. He also spent lavishly on cars, vacations, clothing, and fine wines. The appearance—if not the reality—of success caught the attention of many professional investors, including Jim Cramer, a former hedge-fund manager and cofounder and chairman of TheStreet.com, an investment-counseling website. Cramer was so impressed by Dykstra that he hired him to write a regular column for his website. The exposure allowed Dykstra, in September 2008, to launch another venture called the *Players Club*, an investment-counseling magazine targeting professional athletes.[13] But red flags began to surface.

Dykstra's employees claimed that he failed to pay rent on the Players Club offices and that he bounced checks and refused to pay printing costs. By May 2009 the former ballplayer's businesses were in financial ruin, Cramer stopped running his column on TheStreet.com, and he was facing more than twenty lawsuits tied to his investment activities.[14] Although Dykstra's net worth was an estimated $58 million the year before, he filed for Chapter 11 bankruptcy, listing less than $50,000 in assets against $10 million to $50 million in liabilities. He claimed to be a victim of mortgage fraud after having lost his multimillion-dollar estate in Thousand Oaks, California, to foreclosure.[15] His personal life was also in disarray.

As early as 2005 Dykstra was dogged by allegations of steroid abuse. The initial charges arose from a lawsuit filed that year by former business partner Lindsay Jones. The lawsuit alleged that Dykstra used steroids and told Jones to place bets on Phillies games in 1993, when he was on the pennant-winning team.[16] Although Dykstra denied the allegations, the PED issue continued to dog him. On December 13, 2007, Senator George S. Mitchell, appointed by commissioner of baseball Bud Selig to investigate the use of performance-enhancing drugs in Major League Baseball, released an explosive 409-page report that identified Dykstra as one of eighty-nine Major League players who allegedly used steroids or other performance-enhancing drugs.[17] The Mitchell Report confirmed suspicions that the former Phillies center fielder had been doping during his playing career. The report cast doubt not only on Dykstra's personal integrity—suggesting that he cheated—but also on the integrity of his statistical achievements in the game. Together with his financial problems, the charges of PED use caused further damage to a marriage that was already severely strained. Finally, on April 23, 2009, Dykstra's wife, Terri, filed for divorce.[18] At that point his life spiraled out of control.

Nails' behavior became increasingly erratic. He used offensive terms when speaking about blacks, women, and homosexuals.[19] He was accused of vandalizing his foreclosed properties in Thousand Oaks and not maintaining home owners' insurance on them. Security officers were instructed to deny him access, and the court assigned a trustee to manage the properties.[20] There was also a series of charges arising from promiscuous behavior.

In December 2010 Dykstra was accused of hiring a female escort and then writing her a bad $1,000 check.[21] The following month he was accused of sexual assault by his housekeeper, who alleged that he would force her to give him oral sex. The woman told investigators that "she needed the job and the money, so she went along with his requests rather than lose her job."[22] When she quit,

Dykstra, according to the Los Angeles District Attorney's Office, placed ads on Craigslist, requesting a personal assistant or house-keeping services. Those who responded to the ad alleged that when they arrived, they were informed that the job also required massage service. Dykstra would then disrobe and expose himself. The ploy resulted in the former ballplayer being charged, on August 25, 2011, with indecent exposure.[23] By that time Dykstra's financial problems had also caught up with him.

On April 14, 2011, Nails, who was living out of his car and in hotel lobbies, was arrested and charged with bankruptcy fraud.[24] Federal prosecutors contended that after filing for bankruptcy, Dykstra hid, sold, or destroyed more than $400,000 worth of items from the $18.5 million mansion in question without permission of a bankruptcy trustee. The items allegedly ranged from sports memorabilia to a $50,000 sink. About the same time, the Los Angeles Police Department Commercial Crimes Division arrested Dykstra on separate grand-theft charges related to the purchase of vehicles.[25]

On June 6, 2011, Dykstra was arrested again and charged with twenty-five misdemeanor and felony counts of grand-theft auto, identity theft, filing false financial statements, and possession of cocaine, ecstasy, and human growth hormone. He first pleaded not guilty to the charges, but later changed his plea to no contest to grand-theft auto and providing false financial statements in exchange for dropping the drug charges.[26] On March 5, 2012, after unsuccessfully trying to withdraw his *nolo contendere* plea, he was sentenced to three years in state prison, receiving nearly a year's credit for time already served.[27] Dykstra was released from the federal penitentiary in Victorville, California, in July 2013 after serving six and one-half months of his sentence.[28]

The publication of Randall Lane's *The Zeroes: My Misadventures in the Decade Wall Street Went Insane* (2010) and Christopher Frankie's *Nailed! The Improbable Rise and Spectacular Fall of Lenny Dykstra* (2013) exposed Dykstra's dishonest business dealings, steroid use, and lavish spending habits as well as his exploitation of former employees and friends. Written by individuals who were once colleagues as well as personal confidants, the two accounts portray the former Phillie as a selfish opportunist who sought to increase his wealth at the expense of others.[29]

Dykstra further destroyed his credibility as a player on October 27, 2015, when he appeared on a national radio show and admitted that he spent $500,000 to hire private investigators to pry into the personal lives of umpires. Nails wanted to blackmail the umps into shrinking the strike zone so he could get more walks. "Their blood is just as red as ours," he explained. "Some of them like women, some of them like men, some of them gamble, some of them do whatever."

Dykstra, who led the National League in walks, runs, and at bats in 1993, claimed that he made the decision when he was trying to secure a huge contract from the Phillies. "It wasn't a coincidence that I led the league in walks the next few years," he said. "If the ump called a strike on me, all I'd have to do is remind him, 'Did you cover the spread last night?' and they'd shrink the zone."[30]

Finally, in 2016, Dykstra published an autobiography in order to tell his side of the story. Titled *House of Nails: A Memoir of Life on the Edge*, the book is a tragicomic tale of the intensity and hard work leading to Nails' fame and fortune as well as the excesses and poor decision making that resulted in his downfall and incarceration.

Among the most startling revelations is that Dykstra, while incarcerated at the Federal Correctional Institution in Victorville, was savagely—and illegally—beaten by sheriff's deputies, who threatened his life if he reported the incident. The beating was so severe that Nails lost consciousness and possibly suffered "some brain damage." But he also admitted that his time in prison forced him to "contemplate his existence." "While at times [my] brash, arrogant style served me well in the game of life, it was eventually instrumental in my undoing," Dykstra wrote in the final pages of his autobiography. "I know I have many flaws, and I have made many mistakes over the years. I know, too, that I will make more mistakes as I continue to work on regaining a life built with happiness and contentment; a life I can be proud of again."[31]

Schilling's story is not as tragic, though he is also responsible for some of the hardship he's experienced. After 1993 he became one of the most dominant pitchers in baseball while toiling for terrible Phillies teams.[32] In 2000 he lobbied the front office to be traded to a contender, and they complied, sending him to the Arizona Diamondbacks. Schilling pitched brilliantly for Arizona in 2001 and 2002, becoming a twenty-game winner in each season. He helped to lead the Diamondbacks to a world championship in 2002, being named a co-MVP of the World Series with fellow starter Randy Johnson, and finished second to Johnson in the Cy Young voting. After the 2003 season the Diamondbacks traded Schilling to Boston, where he helped to lead the Red Sox to their first world championship since 1918. He retired after the BoSox clinched a second world championship in 2007 with career statistics that are worthy of Hall of Fame consideration.[33]

Although he continued to stir controversy with his candid political opinions, Schilling was also known as a generous philanthropist and a dedicated family man. Throughout his Major League career, he dedicated considerable time and money to finding a cure for amyotrophic lateral sclerosis, or Lou Gehrig's disease, a rare—and fatal—neurological disorder that affects the spinal cord and lower brain stem. Schilling, along with his wife, Shonda, established Curt's Pitch for ALS, a charity program that donated money to the ALS Foundation for every strikeout he recorded. In addition, the former Phillie served as a spokesman for the foundation, raising more than $9 million for the cause, a commitment he continues in his retirement.[34] Sadly, Schilling's seven-year-old son, Grant, was diagnosed in 2007 with another neurological disorder called Asperger's syndrome. While the disorder is not fatal, it does affect the quality of the sufferer's life by impeding his perception of the world and, often, his ability to communicate, establish friendships, and demonstrate affection. It was a difficult and humbling experience for the pitcher and his wife and one they continue to struggle with today.[35]

Schilling himself also wrestled with health issues. In 2011 the forty-four-year-old suffered a heart attack. Three years later, in February 2014, he was diagnosed with mouth cancer, the result of years of tobacco chewing. But after seven weeks of chemotherapy and radiation treatment, Schilling went into remission.[36] He was less successful in business.

Like Dykstra, Schilling, in 2008, tried to trade on his baseball notoriety in the business world by establishing 38 Studios, a video game company. The pitcher, who earned an estimated total of $114 million during his baseball career, invested "north of 50 million" in the company, in addition to a $75 million loan. But in June 2012 Schilling announced that the venture had failed and that "all the money I earned and saved during my baseball career is gone." Accepting the blame for bankruptcy, he admitted that "it was my decision to do this and I failed. "Life will change for our family," he added. "It will be very different for us in the future."[37] Having to support his four children, Schilling took a job as a baseball analyst with ESPN, joining former teammate John Kruk.[38] But in April 2016, Schilling was dismissed from ESPN after posting an insensitive message on social media regarding transgender bathroom laws.[39]

Mitch Williams has also ridden a roller coaster of highs and lows since 1993. Wild Thing never really accepted the Phillies' reasons for trading him to the Houston Astros. "I believe in my heart to this day," he wrote in his 2010 baseball autobiography, *Straight Talk from Wild Thing*, "that I got traded because the [Phillies'] owners thought the fans would crucify me the next year. But they underestimated me. They didn't understand that the fans appreciated that I didn't run and hide after the World Series or during the offseason. The fans knew I was a guy who fit into their city. They knew that every day I walked out there I gave everything I had."[40] Williams was correct.

When the Astros came to Philadelphia to play the Phillies in May 1994, the fans gave Wild Thing a standing ovation, confirming their respect for the way he handled himself after surrendering the Series-clinching home run to Joe Carter and the Blue Jays. Predictably, Williams, after his playing career ended in 1997, returned to the Philadelphia area, first as a pitching coach for the Atlantic City (New Jersey) Surf of the Independent League and later as a pre- and postgame analyst for Comcast's *Daily News Live*. Even when he took a job with MLB Network in 2008, Williams commuted to New York from his Medford, New Jersey, home.[41]

Williams remarried in 1993 after his seven-year marriage to Dee Ann Grammer ended in divorce. He and his second wife have five children. The former closer is a dedicated parent, actively involved in the lives of his kids, something that led to his most recent misfortune.

On May 10, 2014, Williams was coaching his ten-year-old son's baseball team, the Jersey Wild, at a tournament in Aberdeen, Maryland. Mitch and an umpire got into a heated exchange, and he was ejected. The next day, in the title game, coaches and parents of the opposing team accused Williams of ordering his pitcher to intentionally hit a batter. *Deadspin*, a sports news and gossip website, reported the incidents in two separate stories, claiming that the former Phil also called a child on the other team a "pussy" and the umpire who ejected him a "motherfucker." After the news went viral, MLB Network, Mitch's employer, announced that he was taking a leave of absence. According to Williams, MLB Network told him he would be fired unless he signed a contract that barred him from his children's games. When he refused, the network terminated his contract. Since then Williams has filed lawsuits against Gawker Media, which owns *Deadspin*, and MLB Network, claiming that he "has suffered an enormous personal loss of reputation, has been humiliated publicly and permanently, and has had to endure severe stress."[42] Those suits are still pending at this writing.

Perhaps the event that has done the greatest damage to the reputation of Macho Row was the release of the Mitchell Report on December 13, 2007. The 409-page report authored by former U.S. senator George J. Mitchell identified former and current Major League players who used or were connected to performance-enhancing drugs. Of the eighty-nine players connected to steroids, the Mitchell Report identified Lenny Dykstra and reserve catcher Todd Pratt as the only members of the 1993 Phillies.[43] Since then, Dykstra has defended his doping, insisting that he "could not have led the Phillies to a World Series or made millions of dollars without using steroids."[44]

Seven days after the release of the Mitchell Report, on December 20, 2007, Pete Incaviglia was named in an unsealed affidavit as an alleged user of amphetamines by Jason Grimsley, who pitched for the Phillies from 1989 to 1991.[45] Not long after, ESPN sportswriters Shaun Assael and Peter Keating linked Dave Hollins to the Androstenedione derivative—a prohormone—allegedly supplied by bodybuilder Jeff Scott.[46] Despite Hollins's objections, the power-hitting statistics of both players appear to reinforce the allegations.

In 1993 Incaviglia set a career high in batting average (.274) and RBI (89) while leading the Phillies in slugging percentage (.530) and tying Darren Daulton for the team lead in home runs (24). All of this was done in only 368 at bats, which put him at the top of the league in RBI per at bat. Not since his early years with the Texas Rangers did Incaviglia produce similar numbers. In 1986, his rookie year, Incaviglia hit 30 home runs and 88 RBI and had a .463 slugging percentage. The following season he hit 27 homers and 88 RBI for a .497 slugging percentage. But he also had 154 additional at bats in 1986 and 141 additional at bats in 1987 than he did in 1993. In the five seasons between those two periods, Incaviglia averaged 17.8 home runs, 60 RBI, and .424 slugging percentage in an average of 417 at bats. Nor did Incaviglia ever enjoy the prodigious slugging statistics he compiled in 1993 again. Although he played four more seasons in the Majors, the muscle-bound outfielder never hit more than 16 homers or 42 RBI again, and that was in 1996, his final season with the Phillies.[47] After he retired Incaviglia managed the Grand Prairie AirHogs, an independent-league club, and later became the hitting coach for the Erie Seawolves, the Detroit Tigers' Class AA affiliate in the Eastern League.[48]

Hollins's decline is more difficult to gauge and might just as easily be attributed to his diabetes as to alleged steroid use. In 1993 the Phillie third baseman hit 18 home runs and 93 RBI and had a .442 slugging percentage in 543 plate appearances. Hollins would play eight more seasons in the Majors, but injuries limited his playing time, dramatically reducing his power numbers. When he returned to full strength in 1996 with the Minnesota Twins, Hollins hit 16 homers and 78 RBI with a .396 slugging percentage in

516 at bats. The following year he posted similar numbers (16 HR, 85 RBI, .430 SLG) in 572 plate appearances. After that Hollins's power hitting went into a sharp decline as he became a journeyman infielder, ending his career with the Phillies in 2002.[49] After his playing career ended, Hollins became a professional scout for the Baltimore Orioles and later for the Phillies.[50]

Dykstra's pioneering role with steroids, the extensive use of PEDS in professional baseball in the 1990s, and the sudden—if not remarkable—success of the 1993 pennant-winning Phillies also led some sportswriters to speculate that Darren Daulton was juicing.[51] While Daulton's chiseled physique, which resembled that of a bodybuilder's, and his close relationship to Dykstra suggested a steroid connection, the catcher's sudden offensive explosion in 1992 and 1993 appeared to reinforce the allegations.

During those two seasons Daulton averaged 25 home runs and 107 RBI with a .503 slugging percentage. Never before or after that two-year span did he hit more than 15 homers or collect more than 57 RBI in a season.[52] When asked, in 2009, if he ever used PEDS, Dutch replied:

> Look, I'm not going to apologize for the things I've done in my life. We've all done stuff that society perceives as "bad." That's life. That's how you learn.
>
> I've taken more drugs in rehab than steroids. There's probably no one in any sport that has taken more drugs than I have after all the injuries and operations I've had. But I don't feel that you or anyone else needs to know those details to respect me.
>
> It's not what goes in, it's what comes out of a person that is worth respecting. I just don't care to give the steroids issue any more energy because people will take it and run with it.[53]

Daulton neither admitted nor denied the allegations of PED use, but there were signs that the many drugs he admitted to taking during his career as well as the carefree lifestyle he led had a destructive influence on his personal life.

During the baseball season Daulton lived in Media, a Philadelphia suburb, while his wife, Lynne Austin, remained in Clearwater with their infant son, Zach. The physical separation allowed the strikingly handsome catcher to lead the carefree life of a bachelor, which placed great strain on his marriage. Lynne was "jealous of baseball" because she "never saw [her] husband." When asked if she worried about Darren being unfaithful to her, Austin admitted that she would be a "fool to say, 'Oh, my husband would never do that to me.' "I hope he would figure one night is not worth twenty years," she added. "But what can I do about it, really?" Shortly after the 1993 season ended, the couple separated.[54] After they divorced in 1994, Austin, who resumed her career as a spokesperson for Hooters Restaurants and a Tampa radio talk show host, spoke candidly about the pressures of being married to a Major League Baseball player:

> I'd never dated or been with a professional athlete before. I was really unprepared for that world. It was fun . . . but behind the fun is the stress. Baseball players have a very short lead time. They're in spring training and they're going to go for six months. Well, they're not going to leave you hanging for six months. They're going to marry your ass and take you. I had no idea that moving every six months would be as stressful as it was . . . and I had no idea that every girl would want my husband.[55]

Daulton continued to play for the Phillies until 1997, when he was traded to the Florida Marlins. His repeated knee injuries forced him to play first base and pinch-hit, but he still hit .263 with 14 home runs and 63 RBI in 395 plate appearances. Dutch also brought his remarkable leadership abilities to a young team that desperately needed veteran leadership. In fact, Florida manager Jim Leyland credited Daulton with creating a winning chemistry that allowed the Marlins to capture the World Series that season. But when the organization declined to exercise its $5 million option for the next year, Dutch decided to retire. "My knees are not where they need to be for me to continue to play," he admitted. "If I can't play at the level I'm used to, it's time to move on."[56]

Initially, Daulton appeared to make a smooth adjustment to life outside the game. He and his second wife, Nicole, gave birth to

FIG. 43. Daulton and his second wife, Nicole, wave to the
fans at Veterans Stadium before a July 21, 1997, game against
the Pittsburgh Pirates. Daulton had been traded to the Florida
Marlins earlier in the day. He would go on that season to
lead the expansion Marlins to their first World Series title.
Photo by Al Tielemans.

two children. Dutch also embraced Christianity. "I wouldn't say I'm
a new person," he said. "The difference now is I have a relationship with Jesus Christ, and I feel like I have a job to do for Him."
Although his fundamentalist religious beliefs distanced him from
some of his former teammates, he insisted that the estrangement

would not "stop me from believing in the good Lord." It also forced him to take stock of his previous behavior. Dutch seemed embarrassed by his earlier association with Macho Row. "I was as bad as it used to get," he admitted. "There are things I did back then that I don't necessarily agree with now."[57] But the serenity was short-lived. Without baseball, Daulton's life soon began to spiral out of control.

Dutch struggled with alcohol, being arrested and jailed for drunk driving on at least two occasions.[58] In 2003 the former Phillies catcher was arrested on a domestic violence charge after a dispute with his second wife, who later filed for divorce. A year later Daulton spent two months in jail for failing to comply with a court order issued in the divorce settlement.[59] "I've been thrown in jail five or six times," he explained. "Nicole thinks I'm crazy. She blames everything on drinking and drugs. But I don't take drugs and I'm not a drunk."[60]

When he wasn't getting into legal trouble, Daulton was stirring controversy with remarks about metaphysics, quantum physics, and the fifth dimension. He even compiled a 2008 book about his beliefs titled *If They Only Knew*. Among the revelations were that "the ancient pyramids are strategically placed across the planets; the universe is made of vibrating energy that becomes invisible when it reaches a certain speed; and that on December 21, 2012— the date the Mayans believed the world will end—those humans ready to ascend will vanish from this plane of existence on earth."[61] When former teammates ridiculed him for his beliefs in the supernatural, Daulton simply dismissed their criticism, saying that they were "limited to the five senses."[62]

Dutch's life improved when the Phillies became pennant contenders again in 2007. Comcast Sports Network asked him to return to Philadelphia as an analyst on their pre- and postgame shows. He accepted the offer and proved to be extremely popular with the viewers. In 2010 Daulton became a pitchman for Yuengling Beer and, later, a pregame baseball analyst on ESPN's satellite radio station in Philadelphia, 97.5 FM THE FAN.[63] Then, on July 9, 2013, Dutch hit rock bottom when doctors, after removing two cancerous brain tumors, discovered an aggressive form of brain cancer called "glioblastoma." The prognosis was not good. The survival rate can be anywhere from fourteen months to three years with chemotherapy and radiation treatment.[64]

Daulton's domestic problems and strange behavior suggest the possibility of PED use. Since the early 1990s various studies have established that anabolic steroid use can result in "hypomanic or manic symptoms," such as "aggressiveness, delusions and psychotic symptoms" as well as "impaired judgement stemming from feelings of invincibility and depressive symptoms during withdrawal."[65]

Regardless, either documented or circumstantial evidence exists supporting allegations of PED use among at least four of the six members of Macho Row and reserve catcher Todd Pratt. In addition, Phillies trainer Jeff Cooper claimed that Dykstra was not the only one on the team juicing. When Cooper approached another Phillies player whose use was "obvious," he was told to "mind his own business," and "the matter went no further."[66]

Curt Schilling, one of the most outspoken critics of PEDs in Major League Baseball, also admitted that "steroids were all over" when he played with the Phillies. When asked, in 2011, if he ever suspected any of his teammates as users, Schilling said, "Oh, absolutely!" "I had my ideas whenever guys showed up at spring training with twenty-five extra pounds on them," he explained. "Performance-enhancing drugs allowed them to be April fresh in September, and that helped their offensive numbers. PEDs weren't something you talked about, though."[67]

Macho Row member John Kruk kept his silence even longer, in deference to the Code. For years Kruk, who fought a successful battle against testicular cancer, denied any connection between the Phillies and steroids. In April 2005, when the Los Angeles Times reported allegations of steroid use and baseball-related gambling activity by former teammate Lenny Dykstra, Kruk was adamant that he "never heard it spoken about or saw it." "If someone was using steroids on that team they were awfully quiet about it," he insisted. "And we talked about everything on that club. That's how close we were. If someone had been doing it, they'd have no reason to lie to me, and I wouldn't lie about it now. What's it, 12 years ago? It's not like it's going to ruin someone's career."[68]

Kruk did not need to use the twelve-year disclaimer, though. Steroid use would not have jeopardized anyone's baseball career before 2002 because the drug was not banned by the MLB, and even if it were, the sport had no drug-testing policy.[69] Active players could juice without any fear of suspension, let alone banishment from the game. Nevertheless, Kruk continued to plead ignorance, even after the release of the Mitchell Report on December 13, 2007. By that time the former Phillie was a respected baseball analyst for ESPN Sports. When asked on air if he knew Dykstra was doing steroids, Kruk replied: "One year Lenny weighed next to nothing and the next he was all bulked up. I heard reporters wondering what he was on, so I asked him. I said, 'What did you do?' He said, 'I was working out hard.' I believed him. I had no reason not to. He'd never lied to me before, and I knew he was big into weightlifting. So many guys were getting big at that time from weights. To me, Lenny was no different."

When it was pointed out that anabolic steroids provided bodybuilders with the additional muscle mass and endurance to engage in excessive weight training, Kruk became testy. "Why do you gotta name the names?" he snapped. "Why drag them all through the mud? Let them go. You don't have to get out in public with this."[70]

Over the next few years as revelations broke of steroid abuse by such stars as Roger Clemens and Alex Rodriguez, Kruk engaged in doublespeak. On the one hand, he accused the fallen stars of "cheating" by using steroids. On the other, he exonerated the suspects because "everyone in Baseball, turned their backs on the issue, not only the clean players, but the front offices, managers, the commissioner, even the union."[71] Still, Kruk refused to implicate his former teammates. Ironically, the Code places a higher priority on loyalty to a crooked teammate than on cheating itself.[72] And PED use by professional ballplayers *is* cheating.

Historically, baseball players were notorious for doing whatever they could to gain a physical or mental edge in order to win. The hidden-ball trick, spitballs, and corking the bat are just some of the examples of pushing the rules to an extreme to achieve that edge. But they are also examples of *deception*, not cheating per se. That is, they are illegal only if you get caught. In other words, there is a fine line between deception and cheating.[73] Those players who used performance-enhancing drugs to gain a competitive advantage were cheating, and the Code prohibits cheating because it destroys the fundamental integrity of the game.[74] Like gambling, juicing, especially when done by several team members, altered the competitive balance of the game by giving the offending team an unfair advantage. Even if one player was doping, he was still cheating in the sense that his performance had the potential not only to alter the outcome of a game, but also to threaten the records of those past players who did not enjoy the same advantage.

Lenny Dykstra and any other member of Macho Row who might have used PEDs achieved an unfair advantage over opponents, one that allowed them to alter the competitive balance of a game. That is something that goes well beyond deception; it's cheating.[75] While they may not have broken some of the game's most cherished records, those Phillies who used PEDs threatened the integrity of the game by making victims of the majority of players who did not enjoy the same advantage, including their own teammates.

What's more, had even one of those teammates acted on their knowledge in 1993, Major League Baseball might never have been tainted by a "steroids era." Instead, PED use grew among some of the game's best players. At the same time, the '93 Phillies, who caught lightning in a bottle, descended in the standings almost as rapidly as they had risen.

AFTERWORD

The City of Brotherly Love can boast of respected universities, nationally recognized museums, and an ever-diminishing coterie of blue bloods. But Philadelphia's genuine spirit can be found in the clock punchers and blue collars, especially when it comes to sports. For better and worse, Macho Row embodied the city's hardscrabble personality.

Like the fans, Darren "Dutch" Daulton, Lenny "Nails" Dykstra, John "Krukker" Kruk, Mitch "Wild Thing" Williams, Dave "Mikey" Hollins, and Pete "Inky" Incaviglia were diehards who functioned in the same black-and-white world of heroes and bums. They showed their humanness—warts and all—and were admired because they were throwbacks to the days when baseball was played for little more than the love of the game.

Most of all, Macho Row endeared themselves to the city's blue-collar fans because they went from worst to first, returning the Phillies to the World Series for the first time in a decade and in a season when there were absolutely no expectations to succeed. Rooting for those wild, wacky, woefully wonderful Phillies during that enchanted season of dreams was, for many of us, like cheering for ourselves. But they were not the best role models.

Macho Row comprised grown men blessed with a God-given gift to play a child's game for a living, and they made millions of dollars doing it. Not surprisingly, they engaged in the very same narcissistic behavior of players from a bygone era when promiscuity, alcoholism, and gambling were even more rampant than today. In the final analysis, we really didn't know the members of Macho Row. They kept their most unattractive behaviors hidden, leaving the sportswriters and fans to speculate on exactly how they went from worst to first in the span of just one season. We all knew they partied, leading the lives of protracted adolescents. But we excused their narcissistic behavior because Macho Row was entertaining and, more important, they won. In fact, the only accountability those players knew was to the Code, and some of them even violated that by turning on teammates publicly after their careers ended.

Daulton, Dykstra, Kruk, Williams, Hollins, and Incaviglia have struggled since 1993, and some of the difficulty came because they never had to deal with the hard realities of life earlier. Only later were they forced to confront many of the same hardships that so many of their fans experience in life, including cancer, addiction, bankruptcy, incarceration, and divorce. Some learned the true meaning of humility, like Daulton, whose ongoing battle with brain cancer recently compelled him to admit, "Anything I did in the past is my fault. Not my ex-wives' fault, not any of my kids' faults, not baseball, not the media—me, my fault—I did the damage."[1] Others are still learning.

But I certainly would not want my sons to pattern their lives after any one of them. Nor do I believe that they ever wanted to be role models for the young fans. Kruk even admitted as much. "I know kids look up to athletes, so to a certain extent, we are role models, but for all the wrong reasons," he wrote in his 1994 book, "I Ain't an Athlete, Lady . . ." "A role model is someone you pattern your life after, right? Well, how can you pattern your life after someone you don't know? It's impossible."[2]

If we, the fans, want proper role models for our children, we should encourage them to emulate parents, teachers, and coaches. These are the figures who interact with youngsters on a daily basis, responsible adults who have a strong personal commitment to the lives of young people. While they may not earn much money or enjoy the public adulation of a Major League Baseball star, they are selfless in their devotion to the youngsters they care about. They also exercise a more profound influence on them and over a longer period of time.

Having said that, I am still very grateful to Macho Row for the thrilling entertainment they provided in 1993, for their accessibility to the fans, and for making Major League Baseball relevant again in my hometown after so many years of losing. Each player also demonstrated qualities I admire: Daulton was the epitome of a leader on the baseball field and minimized the factions and jealousies that often crop up off of it. Dykstra played the game with a fire that burned white-hot, especially in the postseason. Williams displayed moral courage, refusing to make excuses when he performed poorly. Kruk was the consummate entertainer with his quirky sense of humor. Hollins and Incaviglia played hurt, placing the team before their own health. Finally, Macho Row was an important benchmark in my own life, a point in early adulthood when I was embarking on a career as a historian and baseball writer. For all those reasons, I still care about them and sympathize with their personal struggles. Nor am I alone.

An entire generation of Phillies fans fell in love with Daulton, Dykstra, Kruk, Williams, Hollins, and Incaviglia. In the process, Macho Row made the 1993 Phillies the most beloved team in Philadelphia's baseball history.

APPENDIX A

Major League Career Statistics for Members of Macho Row

Key

G	games played
AB	at bats
R	runs scored
H	hits
2B	doubles
3B	triples
HR	home runs
RBI	runs batted in
BB	walks
SB	stolen bases
SO	strikeouts
HBP	hit by pitch
AVG	batting average
OBP	on base percentage
SLG	slugging percentage
FA	fielding average
DL	days on disabled list
*	selected to All-Star Game
+	participated in postseason
bold number	league leader

Darren Daulton

Born: January 3, 1962, Arkansas City, Kansas / 6'2", 190 pounds / Batted: Left / Threw: Right

Year	Team	G	AB	R	H	2B	3B	HR	RBI	BB	SB	SO	HBP	AVG	OBP	SLG	FA	DL
1983	Phillies (NL)	2	3	1	1	0	0	0	0	1	0	1	0	.333	.500	.333	1.000	
1985	Phillies (NL)	36	103	14	21	3	1	4	11	16	3	37	0	.204	.311	.369	.994	84
1986	Phillies (NL)	49	138	18	31	4	0	8	21	38	2	41	1	.225	.391	.428	.985	106
1987	Phillies (NL)	53	129	10	25	6	0	3	13	16	0	37	0	.194	.281	.310	.991	10
1988	Phillies (NL)	58	144	13	30	6	0	1	12	17	2	26	0	.208	.288	.271	.977	36
1989	Phillies (NL)	131	366	29	74	12	2	8	44	52	2	58	2	.201	.303	.310	.984	
1990	Phillies (NL)	143	459	62	123	30	1	12	57	72	7	72	2	.268	.367	.416	.989	
1991	Phillies (NL)	89	285	36	56	12	0	12	42	41	5	66	2	.196	.297	.365	.985	66
1992	Phillies (NL)*	145	485	80	131	32	5	27	**109**	88	11	03	6	.270	.385	.524	.987	

Year	Team	G	AB	R	H	2B	3B	HR	RBI	BB	SB	SO	HBP	AVG	OBP	SLG	FA	
1993	Phillies (NL)+*	147	510	90	131	35	4	24	105	117	5	111	2	.257	.392	.482	.991	
1994	Phillies (NL)	69	257	43	77	17	1	15	56	33	4	43	1	.300	.380	.549	.994	44
1995	Phillies (NL)*	98	342	44	85	19	3	9	55	55	3	52	5	.249	.359	.401	.994	37
1996	Phillies (NL)	5	12	3	2	0	0	0	0	7	0	5	1	.167	.500	.167	1.000	176
1997	Phillies (NL)	84	269	46	71	13	6	11	42	54	4	57	1	.264	.381	.480	.979	
	Marlins (NL)+	52	126	22	33	8	2	3	21	22	2	17	1	.262	.371	.429	.984	
Year		136	395	68	104	21	8	14	63	76	6	74	2	.263	.378	.463	.979	
Career Totals	14	1161	3630	511	891	197	25	137	588	629	50	726	24	.245	.357	.427	.989	559

1993 postseason	G	AB	R	H	2B	3B	HR	RBI	BB	SB	SO	HBP	AVG	OBP	SLG	FA
NL Championship Series	6	19	2	5	1	0	1	3	6	0	3	0	.263	.440	.474	1.000
World Series	6	23	4	5	2	0	1	4	4	0	5	1	.217	.357	.435	1.000
Totals	12	42	6	10	3	0	2	7	10	0	8	1	.240	.400	.455	1.000

Lenny Dykstra

Born: February 10, 1963, Santa Ana, California / 5'10", 167 pounds / Batted: Left / Threw: Left

Year	Team	G	AB	R	H	2B	3B	HR	RBI	BB	SB	SO	HBP	AVG	OBP	SLG	FA	DL
1985	Mets (NL)	83	286	40	60	9	3	1	19	30	15	24	1	.254	.338	.331	.994	
1986	Mets (NL)+	147	431	77	127	27	7	8	45	58	31	55	0	.295	.377	.445	.990	
1987	Mets (NL)	132	431	86	123	37	3	10	43	40	27	67	4	.285	.352	.455	.988	
1988	Mets (NL)	126	429	57	116	19	3	8	33	30	30	43	3	.270	.321	.385	.996 CF112	
1989	Mets (NL)	56	159	27	43	12	1	3	13	23	13	15	2	.270	.362	.41	.984	
	Phillies (NL)	90	352	39	78	20	3	4	19	37	17	38	1	.222	.297	.330	.991	
	Year	146	511	66	121	32	4	7	32	60	30	53	3	.237	.318	.356	.988	
1990	Phillies (NL)*	149	590	106	**192**	35	3	9	60	89	33	48	7	.325	**.418**	.441	.987	
1991	Phillies (NL)	63	246	48	73	13	5	3	12	37	24	20	1	.297	.391	.427	.977	111
1992	Phillies (NL)	85	345	53	104	18	0	6	39	40	30	32	3	.301	.375	.406	.989	83

1993	Phillies (NL)+	161	637	143	194	44	6	19	66	129	37	64	2	.305	.420	.482	.979	
1994	Phillies (NL)*	84	315	68	86	26	5	5	24	68	15	44	2	.273	.404	.436	.984	35
1995	Phillies (NL)*	62	254	37	67	15	1	2	18	33	10	28	3	.264	.353	.354	.987	86
1996	Phillies (NL)	40	134	21	35	6	3	3	13	26	3	25	2	.261	.387	.418	1.000	134
1997	Phillies (NL)	DID NOT PLAY																181
1998	Phillies (NL)	DID NOT PLAY																181
Career Totals:	12 years	1278	4559	802	1298	281	43	81	404	640	285	503	31	.285	.375	.419	.987	811

1993 postseason	G	R	H	2B	3B	HR	RBI	BB	SB	SO	HBP	AVG	OBP	SLG	FA
National League Championship Series	6	5	7	1	0	2	2	5	0	8	0	.280	.400	.560	1.000
World Series	6	9	8	1	0	4	8	7	4	4	0	.348	.500	.913	1.000
Totals	12	14	15	2	0	6	10	12	4	12	0	.314	.450	.737	1.000

Dave Hollins

Born: May 25, 1966, Buffalo, New York / 6'1", 195 pounds / Batted: Both / Threw: Right

Year	Team	G	AB	R	H	2B	3B	HR	RBI	BB	SB	SO	HBP	AVG	OBP	SLG	FA	DL
1990	Phillies (NL)	72	114	14	21	0	0	5	15	13	0	28	1	.184	.252	.316	.932	
1991	Phillies (NL)	56	151	18	45	10	2	6	21	17	1	26	3	.298	.378	.510	.922	21
1992	Phillies (NL)	156	586	104	158	28	4	27	93	76	9	110	**19**	.270	.369	.469	.954	
1993	Phillies (NL)+*	143	543	104	148	30	4	18	93	85	2	109	5	.273	.372	.442	.914	17
1994	Phillies (NL)	44	162	28	36	7	1	4	26	23	1	32	4	.222	.328	.352	.887	79
1995	Phillies (NL)	65	205	46	47	12	2	7	25	53	1	38	5	.229	.393	.410	.988	15
	Red Sox (AL)	5	13	2	0	0	0	0	1	4	0	7	0	.154	.363	.154	1.000	54
	Year	70	218	48	47	12	2	7	26	57	1	45	5	.225	.391	.394	.980	69
1996	Twins (AL)	121	422	71	102	26	0	13	53	71	6	102	10	.242	.364	.396	.953	

Year		G	AB	R	H	2B	3B	HR	RBI	BB	SB	SO	HBP	AVG	OBP	SLG	FA	
	Mariners (AL)	28	94	17	33	3	0	3	25	13	0	15	3	.351	.438	.479	.961	
Year		149	516	88	135	29	0	16	78	84	6	117	13	.262	.377	.411	.955	
1997	Angels (AL)	149	572	101	165	29	2	16	85	62	16	124	8	.288	.363	.430	.922	49
1998	Angels (AL)	101	363	60	88	16	2	11	39	44	11	69	7	.242	.334	.388	.929	33
1999	Blue Jays (AL)	27	99	12	22	5	0	2	6	5	0	22	0	.222	.260	.333	—	
2001	Indians (AL)	2	5	0	1	0	0	0	0	1	0	2	0	.200	.333	.200	—	
2002	Phillies (NL)	14	17	1	2	0	0	0	0	0	0	3	1	.118	.167	.118	1.000	142
Career Totals	12 years	983	3346	578	870	166	17	112	482	464	47	687	66	.260	.358	.420	.933	410

1993 postseason	G	AB	R	H	2B	3B	HR	RBI	BB	SB	SO	HBP	AVG	OBP	SLG	FA
NL Championship Series	6	20	2	4	1	0	2	4	5	1	4	0	.200	.360	.550	1.000
World Series	6	23	5	6	1	0	0	2	6	0	5	0	.261	.414	.304	1.000
Totals	12	43	7	10	2	0	2	6	11	1	9	0	.233	.389	.419	1.000

Pete Incaviglia

Born: April 2, 1964, Pebble Beach, California / 6'1", 230 pounds / Batted: Right / Threw: Right

Year	Team	G	AB	R	H	2B	3B	HR	RBI	BB	SB	SO	HBP	AVG	OBP	SLG	FA	DL
1986	Rangers (AL)	153	540	82	135	21	2	30	88	55	3	185	4	.250	.320	.463	.921	
1987	Rangers (AL)	139	509	85	138	26	4	27	80	48	9	168	1	.271	.332	.497	.945	
1988	Rangers (AL)	116	418	59	104	19	3	22	54	39	6	153	7	.24	.321	.467	.989	
1989	Rangers (AL)	133	453	48	107	27	4	21	81	32	5	136	6	.236	.293	.453	.973	15
1990	Rangers (AL)	153	529	59	123	27	0	24	85	45	3	146	9	.233	.302	.420	.974	
1991	Tigers (AL)	97	337	38	72	12	1	11	38	36	1	92	1	.214	.290	.353	.973	45
1992	Houston Astros	113	349	31	93	22	1	11	44	25	2	99	3	.266	.319	.430	.970	
1993	Phillies (NL)+	116	368	60	101	16	3	24	89	21	1	82	6	.274	.318	.530	.971	
1994	Phillies (NL)	80	244	28	56	10	1	13	32	16	1	71	1	.230	.278	.439	.979	

1996	Phillies (NL)	99	269	33	63	7	2	16	42	30	2	82	3	.234	.318	.454	.969
	Orioles (AL)+	12	33	4	10	2	0	2	8	0	0	7	1	.303	.314	.545	1.000
	Year	111	302	37	73	9	2	18	50	30	2	89	4	.242	.318	.464	.975
1997	Orioles (AL)	48	138	18	34	4	0	5	12	11	0	43	3	.246	.314	.384	.952
	Yankees (AL)	5	16	1	4	0	0	0	0	0	0	3	0	.250	.250	.250	—
	Year	53	154	19	38	4	0	5	12	11	0	46	3	.247	.308	.370	.952
1998	Tigers (AL)	7	14	0	1	0	0	0	0	1	0	6	0	.071	.133	.071	—
	Astros (NL)+	13	16	0	2	1	0	0	1	1	0	4	0	.125	.178	.188	1.000
	Year	20	30	0	3	1	0	0	2	2	0	10	0	.100	.156	.133	.973
Career Totals	12 years	1284	4233	546	1043	192	21	206	655	360	33	1277	45	.246	.310	.448	.966

1993 postseason	G	AB	R	H	2B	3B	HR	RBI	BB	SB	SO	HBP	AVG	OBP	SLG	FA
NL Championship Series	3	12	2	2	0	0	1	1	0	0	3	0	.167	.167	.417	1.000
World Series	4	8	0	1	0	0	0	1	0	0	4	0	.143	.125	.143	1.000
Totals	7	20	2	3	0	0	1	2	0	0	7	0	.155	.146	.280	1.000

John Kruk

Born: February 9, 1961, Charlestown, West Virginia / 5'10", 204 pounds / Batted: Left / Threw: Left

Year	Team	G	AB	R	H	2B	3B	HR	RBI	BB	SB	SO	HBP	AVG	OBP	SLG	FA	DL
1986	Padres (NL)	122	278	33	86	16	2	4	38	45	2	58	0	.309	.403	.424	.981	
1987	Padres (NL)	138	447	72	140	14	2	20	91	73	18	93	0	.313	.406	.488	.996	
1988	Padres (NL)	120	378	54	91	17	1	9	44	80	5	68	0	.241	.369	.362	.995	
1989	Padres (NL)	31	76	7	14	0	0	3	6	17	0	14	0	.184	.333	.303	.962	16
	Phillies (NL)	81	281	46	93	13	6	5	38	27	3	39	0	.331	.386	.473	.983	25
	Year	112	357	53	107	13	6	8	44	44	3	53	0	.300	.374	.437	.977	41
1990	Phillies (NL)	142	443	52	129	25	8	7	67	69	10	70	0	.291	.386	.431	.986	
1991	Phillies (NL)*	152	538	84	158	27	6	21	92	67	7	100	1	.294	.367	.483	.997	
1992	Phillies (NL)*	144	507	86	164	30	4	10	70	92	3	88	1	.323	.423	.458	.993	

Year	Team	G	AB	R	H	2B	3B	HR	RBI	BB	SB	SO	HBP	AVG	OBP	SLG	FA	
1993	+Phillies (NL)*	150	535	100	169	33	5	14	85	111	6	87	0	.316	.430	.475	.993	
1994	Phillies (NL)	75	255	35	77	17	0	5	38	42	4	51	0	.302	.395	.427	.995	28
1995	White Sox (AL)	45	159	13	49	7	0	2	23	26	0	33	0	.308	.399	.390	.909	16
Career Totals:	10 years	1200	3897	582	1170	199	34	100	592	649	58	701	2	.300	.397	.446	.995	85

1993 postseason	G	AB	R	H	2B	3B	HR	RBI	BB	SB	SO	HBP	AVG	OBP	SLG	FA
NL Championship Series	6	24	4	6	2	1	1	5	4	0	5	0	.250	.357	.542	1.000
World Series	6	23	4	8	1	0	0	4	7	0	7	0	.348	.500	.391	1.000
Totals	12	47	8	14	3	1	1	9	11	0	12	0	.299	.431	.468	1.000

Mitch Williams

Born: November 17, 1964, Santa Ana, California / 6'3", 205 pounds / Batted: Left / Threw: Left

Year	Team	W	L	PCT	G	GS	CG-SHO	SV-BS	IP	H	R	HR	HB	BB-IB	SO	ERA	DL
1986	Rangers (AL)	8	6	.571	80	0	0	8–7	98	69	39	8	11	79–8	90	3.58	
1987	Rangers (AL)	8	6	.571	85	1	0	6–1	108.2	63	47	9	7	94–7	129	3.23	
1988	Rangers (AL)	2	7	.222	67	0	0	18–8	68	48	38	4	6	47–3	61	4.63	
1989	Cubs (NL) +*	4	4	.500	76	0	0	36–11	81.2	71	27	6	8	52–4	67	2.76	
1990	Cubs (NL)	1	8	.111	59	2	0	16–4	66.1	60	38	4	1	50–6	55	3.93	30
1991	Phillies (NL)	12	5	.706	69	0	0	30–9	88.1	56	24	4	8	62–5	84	2.34	
1992	Phillies (NL)	5	8	.385	66	0	0	29–7	81	69	39	4	6	64–2	74	3.78	
1993	Phillies (NL) +	3	7	.300	65	0	0	43–6	62	56	30	3	2	44–1	60	3.34	
1994	Astros (NL)	1	4	.200	25	0	0	6–2	20	21	17	4	1	24–2	21	7.65	
1995	Angels (AL)	1	2	.333	20	0	0	0–1	10.2	13	10	1	2	21–0	9	6.75	
1997	Royals (AL)	0	1	.000	7	0	0	0–0	6.2	11	8	2	0	7–1	10	10.80	
Career Totals:	11 years	45	58	.437	619	3	0	192–56	691.1	537	317	49	52	544–39	660	3.65	30

1993 postseason	W	L	PCT	G	GS	CG-SHO	SV-BS	IP	H	R	HR	HB	BB-IB	SO	ERA
National League Championship Series	2	0	1.000	4	0	0	2-	5.1	6	2	0	0	2–0	5	1.69
World Series	0	2	.000	3	0	0	1-	2.2	5	6	1	0	4-	1	20.25
Totals	2	2	.500	7	0	0	3-	8	11	8	1	0	6-	6	

All player statistics taken from Palmer and Gillette, *ESPN Baseball Encyclopedia*, 163, 194, 313, 326–27, 373, 1263.

APPENDIX B

Individual Hitting & Pitching Statistics for the 1993 Phillies

Key

W	wins
L	losses
PCT	winning percentage
G	games appeared in
GS	games started
CG	complete games
SHO	shutouts
SV	saves
IP	innings pitched
H	hits surrendered
R	runs surrendered
HR	home runs surrendered
HB	hit batsmen
BB	walks
IB	intentional walks
SO	strikeouts
ERA	earned run average
*	selected to All-Star Game
+	participated in postseason
bold number	league leader

Individual Pitching Statistics for the 1993 Phillies (Regular Season)

Pitchers	Age	Throws	W	L	PCT	G	GS	CG	SHO	SV	IP	H	R	ER	BB	SO	ERA
Andersen, Larry	40	Right	3	2	.600	64	0	0	0	0	62	54	22	20	21	67	2.92
Ayrault, Bob	27	Right	2	0	1.000	10	0	0	0	0	10	18	11	11	10	8	9.58
Brink, Brad	28	Right	0	0	—	2	0	0	0	0	6	3	2	2	3	8	3.00
Davis, Mark	33	Left	1	2	.333	25	0	0	0	0	31	35	22	18	24	28	5.17
DeLeón, José	33	Right	3	0	1.000	24	3	0	0	0	47	39	25	17	27	34	3.26
Fletcher, Paul	26	Right	0	0	—	1	0	0	0	0	$^1/_3$	0	0	0	0	0	0.00
Foster, Kevin	24	Right	0	1	.000	2	1	0	0	0	7	13	11	11	7	6	14.85
Green, Tyler	23	Right	0	0	—	3	2	0	0	0	7	16	9	6	5	7	7.36
Greene, Tommy	26	Right	16	4	.800	31	30	7	2	0	200	175	84	76	62	167	3.42
Jackson, Danny	31	Left	12	11	.522	32	32	2	1	0	210	214	105	88	80	120	3.77
Mason, Roger	35	Right	5	5	.500	34	0	0	0	0	50	47	28	27	16	32	4.89
Mauser, Tim	27	Right	0	0	—	8	0	0	0	0	16	15	9	9	7	14	4.96
Mulholland, Terry	30	Left	12	9	.571	29	28	7	2	0	191	177	80	69	40	116	3.25
Pall, Donn	31	Right	1	0	1.000	8	0	0	0	0	18	15	7	5	3	11	2.55
Rivera, Ben	25	Right	13	9	.591	30	28	1	1	0	163	175	99	91	85	123	5.02
Schilling, Curt	27	Right	16	7	.696	34	34	7	2	0	235	234	114	105	57	186	4.02
Thigpen, Bobby	30	Right	3	1	.750	17	0	0	0	0	19	23	13	13	9	10	6.05

Name	Age	Hand	W	L	PCT	G	GS	CG	SHO	SV	IP	H	R	ER	BB	SO	ERA
West, David	29	Left	6	4	.600	76	0	0	0	3	86	60	37	28	51	87	2.92
Williams, Mike	25	Right	1	3	.250	17	4	0	0	0	51	50	32	30	22	33	5.29
Williams, Mitch	29	Left	3	7	.300	65	0	0	0	43	62	56	30	23	44	60	3.34
Phillies			**97**	**65**	**.670**	**162**	**162**	**(24)**	**8**	**46**	**1,473**	**1,419**	**740**	**649**	**573**	**(1,117)**	**3.95**
Opponents			65	97	.330	162	162	2	2	42	1,456	1,555	877	775	665	1,049	4.79

Key

W	Wins
L	Losses
PCT	Winning percentage
G	Games appeared
GS	Games started
CG	Complete Games
SHO	Shut outs
SV	Saves
IP	Innings pitched
H	Hits surrendered
R	Runs surrendered
ER	Earned runs
BB	Walks
SO	Strikeouts
ERA	Earned Run Average
( )	National League leader

Individual Hitting Statistics for the 1993 Phillies (Regular Season)

	Age	G	AB	R	H	2B	3B	HR	RBI	BB	SB	SO	HB	AVG	OBP	SLG
Amaro, Ruben, Jr.	28	25	48	7	16	2	2	1	6	6	0	5	0	.333	.400	.521
Andersen, Larry	40	64	1	0	1	0	0	0	0	0	0	0	0	1.000	1.000	1.000
Ayrault, Bob	27	10	2	0	0	0	0	0	0	0	0	2	0	.000	.000	.000
Batiste, Kim	25	79	156	17	44	7	1	5	29	3	0	29	1	.282	.298	.436
Bell, Juan	25	24	65	5	13	6	1	0	7	5	0	12	1	.200	.268	.323
Brink, Brad	28	2	1	0	0	0	0	0	0	0	0	0	0	.000	.000	.000
Chamberlain, Wes	27	96	284	34	80	20	2	12	45	17	2	51	1	.282	.320	.493
Daulton, Darren	31	147	510	90	131	35	4	24	105	117	5	111	2	.257	.392	.482
Davis, Mark	33	25	3	1	1	0	0	0	0	0	0	0	0	.333	.333	.333
DeLeón, José	33	24	6	0	0	0	0	0	0	0	0	5	0	.000	.000	.000
Duncan, Mariano	30	124	496	68	140	26	4	11	73	12	6	88	4	.282	.304	.417
Dykstra, Lenny	30	161	637	143	194	44	6	19	66	129	37	64	2	.305	.420	.482
Eisenreich, Jim	34	153	362	51	115	17	4	7	54	26	5	36	1	.318	.363	.445

Fletcher, Paul	26	1	0	0	0	0	0	0	0	0	0	0	0	.000	.000	.000
Foster, Kevin	24	2	2	0	0	0	0	0	0	0	0	0	0	.000	.000	.000
Green, Tyler	23	3	2	0	0	0	0	0	0	0	0	2	0	.000	.000	.000
Greene, Tommy	26	32	72	9	16	2	0	2	10	5	0	20	0	.222	.269	.333
Hollins, Dave	27	143	543	104	148	30	4	18	93	85	2	109	5	.273	.372	.442
Incaviglia, Pete	29	116	368	60	101	16	3	24	89	21	1	82	6	.274	.318	.530
Jackson, Danny	31	32	65	3	5	2	0	0	2	3	0	37	1	.077	.130	.108
Jordan, Ricky	28	90	159	21	46	4	1	5	18	8	0	32	1	.289	.324	.421
Kruk, John	32	150	535	100	169	33	5	14	85	111	6	87	0	.316	.430	.475
Lindsey, Doug	26	2	2	0	1	0	0	0	0	0	0	1	0	.500	.500	.500
Longmire, Tony	25	11	13	1	3	0	0	0	1	0	0	1	0	.231	.231	.231
Manto, Jeff	29	8	18	0	1	0	0	0	0	0	0	3	1	.056	.105	.056
Mason, Roger	35	34	3	0	1	0	0	0	0	0	0	1	0	.333	.333	.333
Mauser, Tim	27	8	4	0	0	0	0	0	0	1	0	2	0	.000	.200	.000
Millette, Joe	27	10	10	3	2	0	0	2	2	1	0	2	0	.200	.273	.200
Morandini, Mickey	27	120	425	57	105	19	9	3	33	34	13	73	5	.247	.309	.355

Mulholland, Terry	30	29	62	3	4	0	0	0	0	1	0	27	0	.065	.079	.065
Pall, Donn	31	8	0	0	0	0	0	0	0	0	0	0	0	.000	.000	.000
Pratt, Todd	26	33	87	8	25	6	0	5	13	5	0	19	1	.287	.330	.529
Rivera, Ben	25	30	51	3	5	0	0	0	0	3	0	24	0	.098	.148	.098
Schilling, Curt	27	34	75	3	11	1	0	0	2	2	0	19	0	.147	.169	.160
Stocker, Kevin	23	70	259	46	84	12	3	2	31	30	5	43	8	.324	.409	.417
Thigpen, Bobby	30	17	1	0	0	0	0	0	0	0	0	0	0	.000	.000	.000
Thompson, Milt	34	129	340	42	89	14	2	4	44	40	9	57	2	.262	.341	.350
West, David	29	76	5	0	2	1	0	0	2	0	0	2	0	.400	.400	.600
Williams, Mike	25	17	12	1	1	0	0	0	0	0	0	3	0	.083	.083	.083
Williams, Mitch	29	65	1	0	1	0	0	0	1	0	0	0	0	1.000	1.000	1.000
Phillies		162	5685	(877)	(1,555)	(297)	51	156	811	(665)	91	1,049	42	.274	(.351)	.426
Opponents		162	5642	740	1,419	247	39	129	673	573	101	1,117	37	.252	.322	.378

Pitching and hitting statistics taken from Westcott and Bilovsky, *The Phillies Encyclopedia*, 107.

1993 National League Championship Series Box Scores

Game One at Philadelphia / October 6 / Phillies 4, Braves 3
(10 innings)

Atlanta	AB	R	H	RBI	PHILLIES	AB	R	H	RBI
Nixon, CF	4	0	2	2	Dykstra, CF	4	1	1	0
Blauser, SS	4	0	0	0	Duncan, 2B	5	0	1	0
Gant, LF	4	1	1	0	Kruk, 1B	4	2	1	1
McMichael, P	0	0	0	0	Hollins, 3B	4	0	1	0
McGriff, 1B	5	0	1	0	Batiste, 3B	1	0	1	1
Justice, RF	4	0	0	1	Daulton, C	3	0	0	0
Pendleton, 3B	5	0	1	0	Incaviglia, LF	4	1	2	1
Berryhill, C	3	0	0	0	Thompson, LF	0	0	0	0
Pecota, PH	0	1	0	0	Chamberlain, RF	3	0	2	0
Olson, C	1	0	1	0	Williams, P	0	0	0	0
Lemke, 2B	4	0	1	0	Stocker, SS	3	0	0	0
Tarasco, PR, LF	1	0	0	0	Schilling, P	3	0	0	0
Avery, P	2	1	2	0	Eisenreich, RF	1	0	0	0
Sanders, PH	1	0	0	0					
Mercker, P	0	0	0	0					
Belliard, PH, 2B	0	0	0	0					
Totals	38	3	9	3	Totals	35	4	9	3

| Atlanta | 001 | 100 | 001 | 0–3 |
| Philadelphia | 100 | 101 | 000 | 1–4 |

One out when winning run scored. E—Batiste (1). DP—Atlanta 1. LOB—Atlanta 11, PHILLIES 8. 2B—Nixon (1), Olson (1), Avery (1), Dykstra (1), Kruk (1), Hollins (1), Chamberlain 2 (2). HR—Incaviglia (1). S—Belliard. SF—Justice.

Atlanta	IP	H	R	ER	BB	SO
Avery	6	5	3	3	4	5
Mercker	2	2	0	0	1	2
McMichael (L, 0-1)	$1^1/_3$	2	1	1	0	0

PHILLIES	IP	H	R	ER	BB	SO
Schilling	8	7	2	2	2	10
Williams (W, 1-0)	2	2	1	0	2	2

WP—Avery. Time—3:33. Attendance—62,012.

Game Two at Philadelphia / October 7 / Braves 14, Phillies 3

Atlanta	AB	R	H	RBI
Nixon, CF	4	2	3	2
Wohlers, P	0	0	0	0
Blauser, SS	5	1	2	1
Belliard, SS	1	1	0	0
Gant, LF	5	1	2	3
McGriff, 1B	5	2	3	2
Stanton, P	0	0	0	0
Tarasco, RF	0	0	0	0
Justice, RF	3	1	0	0
Sanders, CF	0	0	0	0
Pendleton, 3B	5	2	3	3
Berryhill, C	5	1	1	3
Lemke, 2B	5	1	0	0
Maddux, P	4	1	1	0
Bream, 1B	1	1	1	0
Totals	**43**	**14**	**16**	**14**

PHILLIES	AB	R	H	RBI
Dykstra, CF	4	1	1	1
Morandini, 2B	5	0	1	0
Kruk, 1B	3	1	2	0
Hollins, 3B	3	1	1	2
Daulton, C	4	0	1	0
Andersen, P	0	0	0	0
Eisenreich, RF	4	0	0	0
Thompson, LF	4	0	0	0
Stocker, SS	4	0	1	0
Greene, P	0	0	0	0
Thigpen, P	0	0	0	0
Longmire, PH	1	0	0	0
Rivera, P	0	0	0	0
Chamberlain, PH	1	0	0	0
Mason, P	0	0	0	0
Jordan, PH	0	0	0	0
West, P	0	0	0	0
Pratt, C	1	0	0	0
Totals	**34**	**3**	**7**	**3**

Atlanta	206	010	041	-14
PHILLIES	000	200	001	-3

3—Morandini (1), Stocker (1). LOB—Atlanta 6, PHILLIES 8. 2B—Nixon (2), Gant 2 (2). HR—Blauser (1), McGriff (1), Pendleton (1), Berryhill (1), Dykstra (1), Hollins (1). SB—Morandini (1). CS—Nixon (1).

Atlanta	IP	H	R	ER	BB	SO
Maddux (W, 1-0)	7	5	2	2	3	8
Stanton	1	1	0	0	1	0
Wohlers	1	1	1	1	0	3

PHILLIES	IP	H	R	ER	BB	SO
Greene (L, 0-1)	2$^1/_3$	7	7	7	2	2
Thigpen	$^2/_3$	1	1	1	0	1
Rivera	2	1	1	1	1	2
Mason	2	1	0	0	0	1
West	1	4	4	3	1	2
Andersen	1	2	1	1	0	1

PB—Daulton. Time—3:14. Attendance—62,436.

Game Three at Atlanta / October 9 / Braves 9, Phillies 4

PHILLIES	AB	R	H	RBI
Dykstra, CF	5	0	1	0
Duncan, 2B	5	2	2	0
Kruk, 1B	4	1	2	3
Hollins, 3B	3	0	0	0
Daulton, C	4	0	0	0
Incaviglia, LF	4	0	0	0
Chamberlain, RF	4	1	1	0
Stocker, SS	4	0	3	0
Mulholland, P	2	0	0	0
Mason, P	0	0	0	0
Thompson, PH	1	0	0	0
Andersen, P	0	0	0	0
West, P	0	0	0	0
Thigpen, P	0	0	0	0
Eisenreich, PH	1	0	1	1
Totals	37	4	10	4

Atlanta	AB	R	H	RBI
Nixon, CF	5	0	1	0
Blauser, SS	4	2	2	0
Gant, LF	4	1	1	0
McGriff, 1B	4	2	2	1
Pendleton, 3B	4	2	2	1
Justice, RF	4	1	1	2
Berryhill, C	3	1	1	0
Lemke, 2B	4	0	2	3
Glavine, P	3	0	0	0
Cabrera, PH	1	0	0	0
Mercker, P	0	0	0	0
Totals	36	9	12	8

PHILLIES	000	101	011	-4
Atlanta	000	005	40x	-9

E—Duncan (1). LOB—PHILLIES 7, Atlanta 7. 2B—Chamberlain (3), Stocker (1), Eisenreich (1), Blauser (1), Gant (3), McGriff (1), Justice (1), Lemke (1). 3B—Duncan 2 (2), Kruk (1). HR—Kruk (1). SB—Hollins (1). CS—Nixon (2)

PHILLIES	IP	H	R	ER	BB	SO
Mulholland (L, 0-1)	5	9	5	4	1	2
Mason	1	0	0	0	0	1
Andersen	1/3	2	3	3	1	0
West	2/3	1	1	1	1	2
Thigpen	1	0	0	0	1	2

Atlanta	IP	H	R	ER	BB	SO
Glavine (W, 1-0)	7	6	2	2	0	5
Mercker	1	1	1	1	1	0
McMichael	1	3	1	1	0	1

Mulholland pitched to five batters in the sixth. Time—2:44. Attendance—52,032.

Appendix C

Game Four at Atlanta / October 10 / Phillies 2, Braves 1

PHILLIES	AB	R	H	RBI	Atlanta	AB	R	H	RBI
Dykstra, CF	3	0	2	0	Nixon, CF	3	0	1	0
Morandini, 2B	5	0	2	0	Blauser, SS	4	0	0	0
Kruk, 1B	5	0	0	0	Gant, LF	5	0	0	0
Hollins, 3B	4	0	1	0	McGriff, 1B	4	1	2	0
Batiste, 3B	0	0	0	0	Pendleton, 3B	4	0	1	0
Daulton, C	1	1	0	0	Justice, RF	4	0	2	0
Eisenreich, RF	5	0	1	0	Olson, C	2	0	0	0
Thompson, LF	4	1	1	0	Berryhill, C	1	0	1	0
Stocker, SS	4	0	0	1	Lemke, 2B	4	0	1	1
Jackson, P	4	0	1	1	Smoltz, P	1	0	0	0
Williams, P	0	0	0	0	Mercker, P	0	0	0	0
					Cabrera, PH	1	0	1	0
					Sanders, PR	0	0	0	0
					Wohlers, P	0	0	0	0
					Pecota, PH	1	0	1	0
Totals	35	2	8	2	Totals	34	1	10	1

PHILLIES	000	200	000	- 2
Atlanta	010	000	000	- 1

E—Williams (1). Lemke (1), DP—PHILLIES 1. LOB—PHILLIES 15, Atlanta 11. 2B—Thompson (1), McGriff (2), Pendleton (1) Lemke (2). CS—Gant (1). S—Nixon 2. SF—Stocker.

PHILLIES	IP	H	R	ER	BB	SO
Jackson (W, 1-0)	$7^2/_3$	9	1	1	2	6
Williams (S, 1)	$1^1/_3$	1	0	0	0	0

Atlanta	IP	H	R	ER	BB	SO
Smoltz (L, 0-1)	$6^1/_3$	8	2	0	5	10
Mercker	$^2/_3$	0	0	0	0	0
Wohlers	2	0	0	0	3	5

HBP—Olson by Jackson. WP—Wohlers. Time—3:33. Attendance—52,032.

Game Five at Atlanta / October 11 / Phillies 4, Braves 3
(10 innings)

PHILLIES	AB	R	H	RBI	Atlanta	AB	R	H	RBI
Dykstra, CF	5	1	1	1	Nixon, CF	4	0	0	0
Duncan, 2B	5	1	1	0	Blauser, SS	4	1	1	0
Andersen, P	0	0	0	0	Gant, LF	5	1	1	0
Kruk, 1B	4	0	1	1	McGriff, 1B	4	1	2	1
Hollins, 3B	4	0	0	0	Justice, RF	2	0	0	1
Batiste, 3B	0	0	0	0	Pendleton, 3B	4	0	1	0
Daulton, C	3	1	2	1	Berryhill, C	3	0	1	0
Incaviglia, LF	4	1	0	0	Cabrera, PH, C	1	0	1	1
Thompson, LF	0	0	0	0	Lemke, 2B	4	0	0	0
Chamberlain, RF	3	0	1	1	Avery, P	2	0	0	0
Eisenreich, RF	0	0	0	0	Mercker, P	0	0	0	0
Stocker, SS	4	0	0	0	Sanders, PH	1	0	0	0
Schilling, P	2	0	0	0	McMichael, P	0	0	0	0
Williams, P	0	0	0	0	Pecota, PH	1	0	0	0
Morandini, 2B	1	0	0	0	Wohlers, P	0	0	0	0
Totals	35	4	6	4	Totals	35	3	7	3

PHILLIES	100	100	001	1–4
Atlanta	000	000	003	0–3

E—Batiste (2), Gant (1). LOB—PHILLIES 5. Atlanta 6. 2B—Kruk (2). HR—Dykstra (2), Daulton (1). S—Schilling. SF—Chamberlain, Justice.

PHILLIES	IP	H	R	ER	BB	SO
Schilling	8	4	2	1	3	9
Williams (W, 2-0)	1	3	1	1	0	1
Andersen (S, 1)	1	0	0	0	0	2

Atlanta	IP	H	R	ER	BB	SO
Avery	7	4	2	1	2	5
Mercker	1	0	0	0	0	2
McMichael	1	1	1	1	0	0
Wohlers (L, 0-1)	1	1	1	1	0	1

Schilling pitched to 2 batters in the 9th. WP—Avery. Time—3:21. Attendance—52,032.

Game Six at Philadelphia / October 13 / Phillies 6, Braves 3

Atlanta	AB	R	H	RBI
Nixon, CF	3	1	1	0
Blauser, SS	4	1	2	3
Gant, LF	4	0	0	0
McGriff, 1B	1	0	0	0
Justice, RF	4	0	0	0
Pendleton, 3B	4	0	1	0
Berryhill, C	4	0	0	0
Lemke, 2B	3	1	1	0
Maddux, P	0	0	0	0
Mercker, P	0	0	0	0
Sanders, PH	1	0	0	0
McMichael, P	0	0	0	0
Wohlers, P	0	0	0	0
Pecota, PH	1	0	0	0
Totals	29	3	5	3

PHILLIES	AB	R	H	RBI
Dykstra, CF	4	2	1	0
Morandini, 2B	5	1	1	2
Kruk, 1B	4	0	0	0
Hollins, 3B	2	1	1	2
Batiste, 3B	0	0	0	0
Daulton, C	4	0	2	2
Eisenreich, RF	4	0	0	0
Thompson, LF	4	1	2	0
Stocker, SS	3	0	0	0
Greene, P	0	1	0	0
Jordan, PH	1	0	0	0
West, P	0	0	0	0
Williams, P	0	0	0	0
Totals	31	6	7	6

Atlanta	000	010	200	-3
PHILLIES	002	022	00x	-6

E—Justice (1), Lemke (2), Maddux (1), Thompson (1). DP—PHILLIES 1. LOB—Atlanta 6, PHILLIES 9. 2B—Daulton (1). 3B—Morandini (1). HR—Hollins (2), Blauser (2). S—Maddux 2, Greene 2.

Atlanta	IP	H	R	ER	BB	SO
Maddux (L, 1-1)	5²/₃	6	6	5	4	3
Mercker	¹/₃	0	0	0	0	0
McMichael	²/₃	1	0	0	2	0
Wohlers	1¹/₃	0	0	0	0	1

PHILLIES	IP	H	R	ER	BB	SO
Greene (W, 1-1)	7	5	3	3	5	5
West	1	0	0	0	0	1
Williams (S, 2)	1	0	0	0	0	2

PB—Daulton. Time—3:04. Attendance—62,502.

NLCS Box Scores from Westcott and Bilovsky, *The Phillies Encyclopedia*, 510–11.

APPENDIX D

1993 World Series Box Scores

Game One at Toronto / October 16 / Blue Jays 8, Phillies 5

PHILLIES	AB	R	H	RBI	Toronto	AB	R	H	RBI
Dykstra, CF	4	1	1	0	Henderson, LF	3	1	1	0
Duncan, 2B	5	2	3	0	White, CF	4	3	2	2
Kruk, 1B	4	2	3	2	Alomar, 2B	4	0	1	2
Hollins, 3B	4	0	0	0	Carter, RF	3	1	1	1
Daulton, C	4	0	1	1	Olerud, 1B	3	2	2	1
Eisenreich, RF	5	0	1	1	Molitor, DH	4	0	1	1
Jordan, DH	5	0	1	0	Fernández, SS	3	0	0	1
Thompson, LF	3	0	0	0	Sprague, 3B	4	0	1	0
Incaviglia, LF	1	0	0	0	Borders, C	4	1	1	0
Stocker, SS	3	0	1	0					
Totals	38	5	11	4	Totals	32	8	10	8

| PHILLIES | 201 | 010 | 001 | -5 |
| Toronto | 021 | 011 | 30x | -8 |

E—Thompson (1), Alomar (1), Carter (1), Sprague (1) DP—PHILLIES 1, Toronto 1. LOB—PHILLIES 11, Toronto 4. 2B—White (1), Alomar (1). 3B—Duncan (1). HR—White (1), Olerud (1). SB—Dykstra (1), Duncan (1), Alomar (1). CS—Fernández (1). SF—Carter (1).

PHILLIES	IP	H	R	ER	BB	SO
Schilling (L, 0-1)	$6^1/_3$	8	7	6	2	3
West	0	2	1	1	0	0
Andersen	$^2/_3$	0	0	0	1	1
Mason	1	0	0	0	0	1

Toronto	IP	H	R	ER	BB	SO
Guzmán	5	5	4	4	4	6
Leiter (W, 1-0)	$2^2/_3$	4	0	0	1	2
Ward (S, 1)	$1^1/_3$	2	1	0	0	3

West pitched to 2 batters in the 7th. WP—Guzmán. PB—Daulton. Time—3:27. Attendance—52,011.

Game Two at Toronto / October 17 / Phillies 6 Blue Jays 4

PHILLIES	AB	R	H	RBI	Toronto	AB	R	H	RBI
Dykstra, CF	4	2	2	1	Henderson, LF	3	0	0	0
Duncan, 2B	4	1	1	0	White, CF	4	0	1	0
Kruk, 1B	5	1	2	1	Molitor, DH	3	2	2	0
Hollins, 3B	4	1	2	1	Carter, RF	4	1	1	2
Daulton, C	5	0	1	0	Olerud, 1B	3	0	0	1
Eisenreich, RF	4	1	1	3	Alomar, 2B	3	1	1	0
Incaviglia, LF	4	0	1	0	Fernández, SS	3	0	2	1
Thompson, LF	0	0	0	0	Sprague, 3B	4	0	0	0
Jordan, DH	4	0	1	0	Griffin, PR	0	0	0	0
Stocker, SS	3	0	1	0	Borders, C	4	0	1	0
Totals	37	6	12	6	Totals	31	4	8	4

PHILLIES	005	000	100	-6
Toronto	000	201	010	-4

DP—PHILLIES 1, Toronto 1. LOB—PHILLIES 9, Toronto 5. 2B—White (2), Molitor (1), Fernández (1). HR—Carter (1), Dykstra (1), Eisenreich (1). SB—Molitor (1), Alomar (2). CS—Stocker (1), Henderson (1), Alomar (1). SF—Olerud.

PHILLIES	IP	H	R	ER	BB	SO
Mulholland (W, 1-0)	$5^2/_3$	7	3	3	2	4
Mason	$1^2/_3$	1	1	1	0	2
Williams (S, 1)	$1^2/_3$	0	0	0	2	0

Toronto	IP	H	R	ER	BB	SO
Stewart (L, 0-1)	6	6	5	5	4	6
Castillo	1	3	1	1	0	0
Eichhorn	$^1/_3$	1	9	9	1	0
Timlin	$1^2/_3$	2	0	0	0	2

WP—Stewart. BK—Stewart. Time—3:35. Attendance—52,062.

Game Three at Philadelphia / October 19 /
Blue Jays 10 Phillies 3

Toronto	AB	R	H	RBI
Henderson, LF	4	2	2	0
White, CF	4	2	1	1
Molitor, 1B	4	3	3	3
Carter, RF	4	1	1	1
Alomar, 2B	5	2	4	2
Fernández, SS	3	0	2	2
Sprague, 3B	4	0	0	1
Borders, C	4	0	0	0
Hentgen, P	3	0	0	0
Cox, P	1	0	0	0
Ward, P	0	0	0	0
Totals	36	10	13	10

PHILLIES	AB	R	H	RBI
Dykstra, CF	5	0	1	0
Duncan, 2B	5	0	2	1
Kruk, 1B	3	1	2	0
Hollins, 3B	3	0	0	0
Daulton, C	3	0	0	0
Eisenreich, RF	4	0	1	1
Incaviglia, LF	3	0	0	0
Thigpen, P	0	0	0	0
Morandini, PH	0	0	0	0
Andersen, P	0	0	0	0
Stocker, SS	4	0	1	0
Jackson, P	1	0	0	0
Chamberlain, PH	1	0	0	0
Rivera, P	0	0	0	0
Thompson, LF	2	2	2	1
Totals	34	3	9	3

Toronto	301	001	302	-10
PHILLIES	000	001	101	-3

DP—Toronto 2. LOB—Toronto 7, PHILLIES 9. 2B—Henderson (1), Kruk (1). 3B—White (1), Molitor (1), Alomar (1). HR—Thompson (1), Molitor (1). SB—Alomar 2 (4). SF—Carter, Fernández, Sprague.

Toronto	IP	H	R	ER	BB	SO
Hentgen (W, 1-0)	6	5	1	1	3	6
Cox	2	3	1	1	2	2
Ward	1	1	1	1	0	2

PHILLIES	IP	H	R	ER	BB	SO
Jackson (L, 0-1)	5	6	4	4	1	1
Rivera	1⅓	4	4	4	2	3
Thigpen	1⅔	0	0	0	1	0
Andersen	1	3	2	2	0	0

HBP—Henderson by Thigpen. Time—3:16. Attendance—62,689.

Game Four at Philadelphia / October 20 / Blue Jays 15, Phillies 14

Toronto	AB	R	H	RBI	PHILLIES	AB	R	H	RBI
Henderson, LF	5	2	2	2	Dykstra, CF	5	4	3	4
White, CF	5	2	3	4	Duncan, 2B	6	1	3	1
Alomar, 2B	6	1	2	1	Kruk, 1B	5	0	0	0
Carter, RF	6	2	3	0	Hollins, 3B	4	3	2	0
Olerud, 1B	4	2	1	0	Daulton, C	3	2	1	3
Molitor, 3B	4	2	1	1	Eisenreich, RF	4	2	1	1
Griffin, 3B	0	0	0	0	Thompson, LF	5	1	3	5
Fernández, SS	6	2	3	5	Stocker, SS	4	0	0	0
Borders, C	4	1	1	1	Greene, P	1	1	1	0
Stottlemyre, P	0	0	0	0	Mason, P	1	0	0	0
Butler, PH	1	1	0	0	Jordan, PH	1	0	0	0
Leiter, P	1	0	1	0	West, P	0	0	0	0
Castillo, P	1	0	0	0	Chamberlain, PH	1	0	0	0
Sprague, PH	1	0	0	0	Andersen, P	0	0	0	0
Timlin, P	0	0	0	0	Williams, P	0	0	0	0
Ward, P	0	0	0	0	Morandini, PH	1	0	0	0
					Thigpen, P	0	0	0	0
Totals	44	15	17	14	Totals	41	14	14	14

Toronto	304	002	060	-15
PHILLIES	420	151	100	-14

E—Hollins (1). LOB—Toronto 10, PHILLIES 8. 2B—Henderson (2), White (3), Carter (1). Leiter (1), Dykstra (1), Hollins (1), Thompson (1). 3B—White (2), Thompson (1). HR—Dykstra 2 (3), Daulton (1). SB—Henderson (1), White (1), Dykstra (2), Duncan (2).

Toronto	IP	H	R	ER	BB	SO
Stottlemyre	2	3	6	6	4	1
Leiter	$2^2/_3$	8	6	6	0	1
Castillo (W, 1-0)	$2^2/_3$	3	2	2	3	1
Timlin	$^2/_3$	0	0	0	0	2
Ward (S, 2)	$1^1/_3$	0	0	0	0	2

PHILLIES	IP	H	R	ER	BB	SO
Greene	$2^1/_3$	7	7	7	4	1
Mason	$2^2/_3$	2	0	0	1	2
Andersen	$1^1/_3$	1	3	1	1	2
Williams (L, 0-1)	$^2/_3$	3	3	3	1	1
Thigpen	1	1	0	0	0	0

HBP—Daulton by Castillo, Molitor by West. Time—4:14. Attendance—62,731.

Game Five at Philadelphia / October 21 / Phillies 2, Blue Jays 0

Toronto	AB	R	H	RBI
Henderson, LF	3	0	0	0
White, CF	3	0	0	0
Alomar, 2B	3	0	1	0
Carter, RF	4	0	0	0
Olerud, 1B	4	0	0	0
Molitor, 3B	4	0	1	0
Fernández, SS	3	0	0	0
Borders, C	3	0	2	0
Canate, PR	0	0	0	0
Knorr, C	0	0	0	0
Guzmán, P	2	0	0	0
Butler, PH	1	0	1	0
Cox, P	0	0	0	0
Totals	30	0	5	0

PHILLIES	AB	R	H	RBI
Dykstra, CF	2	1	0	0
Duncan, 2B	4	0	0	0
Kruk, 1B	3	0	1	1
Hollins, 3B	3	0	1	0
Batiste, 3B	0	0	0	0
Daulton, C	4	1	1	0
Eisenreich, RF	4	0	0	0
Thompson, LF	3	0	0	0
Stocker, SS	2	0	1	1
Schilling, P	2	0	1	0
Totals	27	2	5	2

Toronto	000	000	000	-0	
PHILLIES	110	000	00x	-2	

E—Borders (1), Duncan (1). DP—Toronto 1, PHILLIES 3. LOB—Toronto 6, PHILLIES 8.
2B—Daulton (1), Stocker (1). CS—Alomar (2). S—Schilling.

Toronto	IP	H	R	ER	BB	SO
Guzmán (L, 0-1)	7	5	2	1	4	6
Cox	1	0	0	0	2	3

PHILLIES	IP	H	R	ER	BB	SO
Schilling (W, 1-1)	9	5	0	0	3	6

Time—2:53. Attendance—62,706.

Game Six at Toronto / October 23 / Blue Jays 8, Phillies 6

PHILLIES	AB	R	H	RBI	Toronto	AB	R	H	RBI
Dykstra, CF	3	1	1	3	Henderson, LF	4	1	0	0
Duncan, 2B	5	1	1	0	White, CF	4	1	0	0
Kruk, 1B	3	0	0	0	Molitor, DH	5	3	3	2
Hollins, 3B	5	1	1	1	Carter, RF	4	1	1	4
Batiste, 3B	0	0	0	0	Olerud, 1B	3	1	1	0
Daulton, C	4	1	1	0	Griffin, PR, 3B	0	0	0	0
Eisenreich, RF	5	0	2	1	Alomar, 2B	4	1	3	1
Thompson, LF	3	0	0	0	Fernández, SS	3	0	0	0
Incaviglia, ph, LF	0	0	0	0	Sprague, 3B, 1B	2	0	0	1
Stocker, SS	3	1	0	0	Borders, C	4	0	2	0
Morandini, 2B	4	1	1	0					
Totals	35	6	7	6	Totals	33	8	10	8

PHILLIES	000	100	500	-6
Toronto	300	110	003	-8

E—Alomar (2), Sprague (2). LOB—PHILLIES 9, Toronto 7. 2B—Daulton (2), Olerud (1), Alomar (2). 3B—Molitor (2). HR—Molitor (2), Carter (2), Dykstra (4). SB—Dykstra (4), Duncan (3). SF—Incaviglia, Carter, Sprague.

PHILLIES	IP	H	R	ER	BB	SO
Mulholland	5	7	5	1	1	1
Mason	$2^1/_3$	1	0	0	0	2
West	0	0	0	0	1	0
Andersen	$^2/_3$	0	0	0	1	0
Williams (L, 0-2)	$^1/_3$	2	3	3	1	0

Toronto	IP	H	R	ER	BB	SO
Stewart	6	4	4	4	4	2
Cox	$^1/_3$	3	2	2	1	1
Leiter	$1^2/_3$	0	0	0	1	2
Ward (W, 1-0)	1	0	0	0	0	0

Stewart pitched to 3 batters in the 7th. West pitched to 1 batter in the 8th. HBP—Fernández by Andersen. Time—3:26. Attendance—52,195.

World Series Box Scores from Westcott and Bilovsky, *The Phillies Encyclopedia*, 517–19.

NOTES

Introduction

1. Rich Westcott and Frank Bilovsky, *The Phillies Encyclopedia*, 3rd ed. (Philadelphia: Temple University Press, 2004), 104, 106.

2. Sam Carchidi, "Second-Guessing Is Second Nature at the World Series," *Philadelphia Inquirer*, October 25, 1993; Darren Daulton, interview, Bensalem PA, October 4, 2009.

3. John Kruk quoted in Les Bowen, "Kruk's Message to Williams Now Just a Haunting Reminder," *Philadelphia Daily News*, October 25, 1993.

4. Mitch Williams with Darrell Berger, *Straight Talk from Wild Thing* (Chicago: Triumph Books, 2010), x–xi; Marc Narducci, "Bittersweet Memories: Mitch Williams and Joe Carter Recall the Fateful Pitch of the '93 Series," *Philadelphia Inquirer*, February 5, 2011. Some sportswriters believed that Williams's 2-2 pitch to Carter was another slider, instead of a fastball, but after the game the Phillies' closer explained, "I jerked it so bad that it looked like a slider."

5. Lenny Dykstra quoted in Paul Hagen, "For Phillies, the End Hits Hard," *Philadelphia Daily News*, October 25, 1993.

6. Mitch Williams quoted in Michael Bamberger, "Williams Eyes Truth without Blinking," *Philadelphia Inquirer*, October 24, 1993.

7. Ted Silary, "Agony of Defeat: Sights, Sounds from Phillies' Locker Room," *Philadelphia Daily News*, October 25, 1993.

8. Robert Gordon and Tom Burgoyne, *More than Beards, Bellies and Biceps: The Story of the 1993 Phillies* (Champaign IL: Sports Publishing, 2002), 249–56.

9. Baseball Almanac, "1993 Phillies Salaries," www.baseball-almanac.com; Gordon and Burgoyne, *Beards, Bellies and Biceps*, 48. The Phillies' 1993 team payroll was $28.8 million. The Cincinnati Reds, with an overall payroll of 44.3 million, had the most expensive payroll, and the expansion Colorado Rockies, at $9.1 million, were at the bottom. The highest-paid Phillie was Mitch Williams, who was paid $3.5 million.

10. Jim Fregosi quoted in Rod Beaton, "Phillies' Roster Made Up of Some Special Characters," *Baseball Digest* (August 1993): 20–22.

11. See Ross Bernstein, *The Code: Baseball's Unwritten Rules and Its Ignore-at-Your-Own-Risk Code of Conduct* (Chicago: Triumph Books, 2008); Paul Dickson, *The Unwritten Rules*

of Baseball (New York: HarperCollins, 2009); and Jason Turbow, *The Baseball Codes: Bean-balls, Sign Stealing and Bench-Clearing Brawls; The Unwritten Rules of America's Pastime* (New York: Anchor Books, 2010).

12. Leigh Montville, "Leading Man," *Sports Illustrated*, October 11, 1993, 46; Rich Westcott, *Tales from the Phillies' Dugout* (New York: Sports Publishing, 2003), 161; Gordon and Burgoyne, *Beards, Bellies and Biceps*, 103–6; Westcott and Bilovsky, *The Phillies Encyclopedia*, 106.

13. John Kruk quoted in Gordon and Burgoyne, *Beards, Bellies and Biceps*, 106.

14. Rich Westcott, *Phillies '93: An Incredible Season* (Philadelphia: Temple University Press, 1994), 160, 206.

15. Steve Wulf, "Off and Running: Lenny Dykstra's .400-Plus Batting Spree Has the Surprising Phillies in the Chase," *Sports Illustrated*, June 14, 1990, 28–30, 33.

16. "Lenny Dykstra Compares Himself to Gandhi," interview with John Clark, NBC 10 Philadelphia, March 8, 2011.

17. George J. Mitchell, *Report to the Commissioner of Baseball of an Independent Investigation into the Illegal Use of Steroids and Other Performance Enhancing Substances by Players in Major League Baseball* (New York: Office of the Commissioner of Baseball, 2007), 149–50.

18. Westcott, *Phillies '93*, 206.

19. Dykstra quoted in Christopher Frankie, *Nailed! The Improbable Rise and Spectacular Fall of Lenny Dykstra* (Philadelphia: Running Press, 2013), 27.

20. Howard Bryant, *Juicing the Game: Drugs, Power, and the Fight for the Soul of Major League Baseball* (New York: Viking, 2005), 282; "Inflated Stats in Contract Years during Baseball's Steroid Era," *Baseball's Steroid Era*, September 28, 2006, www.thesteroid era.blog.com; Frank Fitzpatrick, "What Fueled the Wild Ride? Steroids Report Puts the '93 Phillies in a New Light," *Philadelphia Inquirer*, December 15, 2007; Duff Wilson and Michael S. Schmidt, "Missing from Mitchell Report, Sosa, Incaviglia Are Included in Grimsley Affidavit," *New York Times*, December 21, 2007; "Ex-Phillie Darren Daulton Is the Self-Proclaimed Drug-Lord of Sports," *Total Sports*, June 30, 2009, www.total sports.com; Mitchell, *Report to the Commissioner of Baseball*, 149–50, 195; Jon Pessah, *The Game: Inside the Secret World of Major League Baseball's Power Brokers* (Boston: Little, Brown, 2015), 75–76.

Kirk Radomski, who had been charged with distribution of a controlled substance and money laundering and faced up to thirty years in prison, provided most of the names in the Mitchell Report. Among those he identified as clients were Lenny Dykstra and Todd Pratt, both of whom played for the 1993 Phillies. Radomski reached a plea bargain that was conditioned upon his cooperation with the Mitchell investigation. See Kirk Radomski with David Fisher, *Bases Loaded: The Inside Story of the Steroid Era in Baseball by the Central Figure in the Mitchell Report* (New York: Hudson Street Press, 2009).

21. Bernstein, *The Code*, 223.

22. John Kruk with Paul Hagen, *"I Ain't an Athlete, Lady . . .": My Well-Rounded Life and Times* (New York: Simon & Schuster, 1994), 99.

23. Westcott and Bilovsky, *The Phillies Encyclopedia*, 204.

24. Kruk quoted in Wulf, "Off and Running," 33.

25. Kruk, *"I Ain't an Athlete,"* 57.

26. Kruk quoted in Steve Wulf, "John Kruk and John Olerud," *Sports Illustrated*, October 25, 1993, 29.

27. Westcott, *Phillies '93*, 162, 206.

28. Kruk quoted in Westcott and Bilovsky, *The Phillies Encyclopedia*, 278.

29. Mitch Williams quoted in Gordon and Burgoyne, *Beards, Bellies and Biceps*, 246.

30. Westcott, *Phillies '93*, 165, 207.

31. Gordon and Burgoyne, *Beards, Bellies and Biceps*, 245.

32. Roger Mason, interview, Bellaire MI, August 18, 2013; Gordon and Burgoyne, *Beards, Bellies and Biceps*, 245.

33. Mark Carfagno, interview, Philadelphia, July 6, 2007.

34. Westcott and Bilovsky, *The Phillies' Encyclopedia*, 192–93; Bowa quoted in Tim O'Shei, "Dave Hollins: He Should Be Called 'Mr. Intensity,'" *Baseball Digest* (May 1994): 42; Michael Schwager, "Dave Hollins: Works Hard, Plays Hard and Hits Hard," *Phillies Report*, December 19, 1991; Pete Williams, "Hollins' Intensity Both Feared and Revered," *USA Today's Baseball Weekly*, May 4, 1993.

35. Dana Heiss, "Pete Incaviglia, College Baseball's Home Run Champion, Retires," *USA Today Baseball Weekly*, May 1, 1999; Westcott, *Phillies '93*, 206; Gordon and Burgoyne, *Beards, Bellies and Biceps*, 126; Pete Palmer and Gary Gillette, eds., *ESPN Baseball Encyclopedia* (New York: Sterling, 2005), 326.

36. Earlier accounts of the 1993 Phillies include Nancy Cooney et al., *Worst to First: The Story of the 1993 Phillies* (Philadelphia: Philadelphia Inquirer, 1993); Kruk with Hagen, "*I Ain't an Athlete*"; Westcott, *Phillies '93*; and Gordon and Burgoyne, *Beards, Bellies and Biceps*.

37. Existing accounts on the Code include Bernstein, *The Code*; Dickson, *Unwritten Rules of Baseball*; and Turbow, *Baseball Codes*. Existing accounts on Major League Baseball's steroid era include Bryant, *Juicing the Game*; José Canseco, *Juiced: Wild Times, Rampant 'Roids, Smash Hits, and How Baseball Got Big* (New York: HarperCollins, 2005); Mark Fainaru-Wada and Lance Williams, *Game of Shadows: Barry Bonds, BALCO, and the Steroid Scandal That Rocked Professional Sports* (New York: Gotham Books, 2006); and Kirk Radamski with David Fisher, *Bases Loaded: The Inside Story of the Steroid Era in Baseball by the Central Figure in the Mitchell Report* (New York: Hudson Street Press, 2009).

1. Dutch

1. Michael Geffner, "From Anti-hero to Superhero," *USA Today Weekend*, September 24–26, 1993.

2. Darren Daulton interview, October 4, 2009.

3. Montville, "Leading Man." The Phillies selected Daulton in the twenty-fifth round (628th pick overall) of the 1980 amateur draft. The organization's first-round selection was another catcher, Henry Powell, from Pine Forest High School in Pensacola, Florida. Powell never made it higher than Single A and was out of baseball by 1983. See "1980 Philadelphia Phillies Picks in the MLB June Amateur Draft," www.baseballreference.com.

4. Darren Daulton interview, October 4, 2009.

5. Carol Daulton, interview, Arkansas City KS, December 18, 2014.

6. Darren Daulton interview, October 4, 2009.

7. Bill Giles, interview, Gladwynne PA, November 20, 2009.

8. Darren Daulton interview, October 4, 2009.

9. Giles interview, November 20, 2009.

10. For Lance Parrish's statistics, see Palmer and Gillette, *ESPN Baseball Encyclopedia*, 520.

11. Westcott and Bilovsky, *The Phillies Encyclopedia*, 159–60.

12. Darren Daulton interview, October 4, 2009.

13. David Daulton Sr., interview, Arkansas City KS, December 18, 2014.

14. Darren Daulton, interview, Jenkintown PA, June 3, 2013.

15. Carol Daulton interview.

16. Darren Daulton interview, June 3, 2013.

17. Dave Daulton Sr. interview.

18. Ron Hill, interview, Topeka KS, December 19, 2014.

19. Hill interview.

20. Mike Dobson, interview, Arkansas City KS, December 19, 2014.

21. David Daulton Sr. interview.

22. Interview of Mike West, Colusa CA, January 12, 2015.

23. Dobson interview.

24. Carol Daulton interview.

25. Larry Shenk, *If These Walls Could Talk: Stories from the Philadelphia Phillies Dugout, Locker Room, and Press Box* (Chicago: Triumph Books, 2014), 9. Powell, Maggio, and Kovar all signed professionally, but never advanced further than Class A ball. The only other player selected by the Phillies in the June 1980 amateur draft who had a substantial Major League career was shortstop Steve Jeltz. See "1980 Philadelphia Phillies Picks in the MLB June Amateur Draft," www.baseballreference.com.

26. "Daulton—Minor League Career Statistics," in *Phillies 1993 Yearbook* (Philadelphia: Phillies, 1993), 50.

27. Bill Dancy quoted in "Catching Prospects," in *Phillies 1984 Yearbook* (Philadelphia: Phillies, 1984), 39.

28. For Daulton's Major League batting statistics, see Palmer and Gillette, *ESPN Baseball Encyclopedia*, 163.

29. Richie Ashburn quoted in Bob Brookover, "Flaws and All, Daulton a Standup Guy," *Philadelphia Inquirer*, June 30, 2013.

30. Darren Daulton interview, June 3, 2013.

31. John Helyar, *Lords of the Realm: The Real History of Baseball*, 340–41, 347. Ueberroth would later deny that he had ever encouraged collusion among the owners.

32. The 1976 Major League Baseball Collective Bargaining Agreement stipulates that "Players shall not act in concert with other Players, and Clubs shall not act in concert with other Clubs." See MLB, *Collective Bargaining Agreement*, Article 18, Section H, mlb cba101.com/past-cbas-2/.

33. Barry Rona and Lou Haynes quoted in Helyar, *Lords of the Realm*, 354–55.

34. Helyar, *Lords of the Realm*, 354–55.

35. John B. Lord, *Bill Giles and Baseball* (Philadelphia: Temple University Press, 2014), 50–51. The $750,000 fine levied by the commissioner's office against the Phillies for signing free agent Lance Parrish was paid in the form of withheld central-fund money.

36. Westcott and Bilovsky, *The Phillies Encyclopedia*, 99–100.

37. Dan Stephenson, interview, Philadelphia, August 1, 2013.

38. Jayson Stark, "Elia Considering Moving Schmidt to First Base," *Philadelphia Inquirer*, July 10, 1988.

39. Westcott and Bilovsky, *The Phillies Encyclopedia*, 100–101; Frank Dolson, "A Sign That One Phillie Still Cares," *Philadelphia Inquirer*, August 24, 1988. Daulton punched his right fist against a wall in the Phillies' video room after being called out on strikes by umpire John Kibler in the ninth inning of a Phillies loss to the Los Angeles Dodgers. After watching the called third strike again on video, he got mad, punched the wall, and broke his right hand. "I want to apologize to my teammates," said Daulton afterward. "I feel like I let them down. I feel like a real jerk for embarrassing the club."

40. Darren Daulton interview, June 3, 2013.

41. Westcott and Bilovsky, *The Phillies Encyclopedia*, 157–58, 495–96.

42. Westcott and Bilovsky, *The Phillies Encyclopedia*, 188–89, 247, 576. Juan Samuel was traded to the New York Mets for outfielder Lenny Dykstra and relief pitcher Roger McDowell on June 18, 1989. Von Hayes was traded to the California Angels for pitcher Kyle Abbott and outfielder Ruben Amaro Jr. on December 8, 1991.

43. William C. Kashatus, *Almost a Dynasty: The Rise and Fall of the 1980 Phillies* (Philadelphia: University of Pennsylvania Press, 2008), 291–93.

2. Gang of Six

1. Warren Giles became the Cincinnati Reds' general manager and president on November 1, 1936, succeeding Larry MacPhail. While the 1937 Reds won only fifty-six games and slid into the basement of the National League, the 1938 team improved by twenty-six games to finish in the first division, earning Giles the 1938 Major League Executive of the Year Award from *The Sporting News*. Giles's success was largely due to one of the most successful trades in Cincinnati history, a deal that sent catcher Spud Davis, pitcher Al Hollingsworth, and cash to the Philadelphia Phillies for starting pitcher Bucky Walters. Walters helped lead the 1939–40 Reds to back-to-back National League Championships. In 1940 the Reds went on to defeat the Detroit Tigers in a seven-game World Series paced by Walters's two complete-game victories. It was Cincinnati's first world championship since the tainted 1919 title against the Chicago White Sox. See Leo H. Bradley, *Underrated Reds: The Story of the 1939–1940 Cincinnati Reds* (Owensville OH: Fried, 2009).

2. Bill Giles with Doug Myers, *Pouring Six Beers at a Time, and Other Stories from a Lifetime in Baseball* (Chicago: Triumph Books, 2007), ix.

3. Kashatus, *Almost a Dynasty*, 253–73. The name "Wheeze Kids" was also a popular takeoff on the "Whiz Kids," the Phillies' 1950 pennant winners, who fielded the youngest starting lineup in the Majors at the time.

4. Giles with Myers, *Pouring Six Beers*, 1–24.

5. Bill Giles, interview, Philadelphia, July 15, 2005.

6. Giles with Myers, *Pouring Six Beers*, 25–78.

7. Giles interview, July 15, 2005.

8. Rich Westcott, *Veterans Stadium: Field of Memories* (Philadelphia: Temple University Press, 2005), 85–102.

9. Giles with Myers, *Pouring Six Beers*, 309–11.

10. For accounts of the 1980 World Champion Phillies, see Kashatus, *Almost a Dynasty*; Hal Bodley, *The Team That Wouldn't Die: Philadelphia Phillies, 1980 World Champions* (Wilmington DE: Serendipity Press, 1981); and Frank Fitzpatrick, *You Can't Lose 'Em All! The Year the Phillies Finally Won the World Series* (Dallas: Taylor, 2001).

11. Giles interview, July 15, 2005; Giles with Myers, *Pouring Six Beers*, 132–33; Pete Rose and Roger Kahn, *Pete Rose: My Story*, 206–7.

12. Kashatus, *Almost a Dynasty*, 246–47.

13. Chuck Newman, "Bidding Ended Early for Some; Persistence Helped Giles Win the Battle," *Philadelphia Inquirer*, October 30, 1981; Larry Shenk, "President Bill Giles and the New Ownership," in *Phillies 1982 Yearbook* (Philadelphia: Phillies, 1982), 2.

14. Giles interview, July 15, 2005.

15. Larry Bowa with Barry Bloom, *Bleep! Larry Bowa Manages* (Chicago: Bonus Books, 1988), 74–77; Westcott and Bilovsky, *The Phillies Encyclopedia*, 95–97, 574.

16. Westcott and Bilovsky, *The Phillies Encyclopedia*, 188–89, 380, 574.

17. Westcott and Bilovsky, *The Phillies Encyclopedia*, 380.

18. Westcott and Bilovsky, *The Phillies Encyclopedia*, 379; Michael Y. Sokolove, *Hustle: The Myth, Life, and Lies of Pete Rose* (New York: Simon & Schuster, 1990), 213.

19. Peter Pascarelli quoted in *A Baseball Winter: The Off-Season Life of the Summer Game*, edited by Terry Pluto and Jeffrey Newman (New York: Macmillan, 1986), 15–16.

20. Westcott and Bilovsky, *The Phillies Encyclopedia*, 279, 318, 575.

21. Westcott and Bilovsky, *The Phillies Encyclopedia*, 215–16, 575.

22. Westcott and Bilovsky, *The Phillies Encyclopedia*, 575.

23. Westcott and Bilovsky, *The Phillies Encyclopedia*, 575.

24. Westcott and Bilovsky, *The Phillies Encyclopedia*, 263, 301, 316.

25. Westcott and Bilovsky, *The Phillies Encyclopedia*, 301, 575.

26. Westcott and Bilovsky, *The Phillies Encyclopedia*, 315.

27. Mark Winegardener, *Prophet of the Sandlots: Journeys with a Major League Scout* (New York: Atlantic Monthly Press, 1990), 279.

28. Interview of Bill Conlin, Turnersville NJ, June 16, 2005. Kevin Kerrane supports Conlin's assertion that Giles and the Gang of Six were not very respected among other baseball executives, especially the general managers. See Kerrane, *Dollar Sign on the Muscle: The World of Baseball Scouting* (New York: Simon & Schuster, 1984), 334.

29. Giles interview, July 15, 2005. Giles repeated the same views in another interview, four years later. See Giles interview, November 20, 2009.

30. Tug McGraw, interview, West Chester PA, August 11, 2000.

31. Giles quoted in Frank Dolson, "Decision Was Long Overdue," *Philadelphia Inquirer*, June 26, 1986.

32. Helyar, *Lords of the Realm*, 353.

33. Steve Carlton quoted in Paul Domowitch, "Carlton Proving He's Not the Retiring Type," *Philadelphia Daily News*, July 8, 1988.

34. Larry Shenk, "Community Relations," in *Phillies 1985 Yearbook* (Philadelphia: Phillies, 1985), 58, 70.

35. Westcott and Bilovsky, *The Phillies Encyclopedia*, 386–87. Six weeks after Woodward was fired by the Phillies, the Seattle Mariners hired him as vice president of baseball operations, a position he held until his retirement in 1989.

36. Giles interview, November 20, 2009.

37. Westcott and Bilovsky, *The Phillies Encyclopedia*, 387–88.

3. Nails

1. Lee Thomas, interview, Langhorne PA, November 5, 2011.

2. Westcott and Bilovsky, *The Phillies Encyclopedia*, 575–576.

3. Thomas interview.

4. According to Kirk Radomski, a Mets clubhouse attendant, Dykstra earned the nickname "Nails" because "no one played the game harder." "In the dugout Lenny was unbelievably intense," said Radomski. "He couldn't wait to get up, couldn't wait to get out into the field, couldn't wait to be better." See Radomski with Fisher, *Bases Loaded*, 53.

5. Peter Golenbock, *Amazin: An Oral History of the New York Mets* (New York: St. Martins' Press, 2002), 459–512; Jeff Pearlman, *The Bad Guys Won! A Season of Brawling, Boozing, Bimbo Chasing, and Championship Baseball with Straw, Doc, Mookie, Nails, the Kid, and the Rest of the 1986 Mets, the Rowdiest Team Ever to Put on a New York Uniform—and Maybe the Best* (New York: HarperCollins, 2011).

6. Frankie, *Nailed!*, 33; Lenny Dykstra and Marty Noble, *Nails: The Inside Story of an Amazin' Season* (New York: Doubleday, 1987).

7. Gary Carter, interview, West Palm Beach FL, July 20, 2005.

8. Dykstra quoted in Michael Martinez, "New Met Casualty: Dykstra's Morale," *New York Times*, July 8, 1987.

9. Lenny Dykstra, *House of Nails: A Memoir of Life on the Edge* (New York: William Morrow, 2016), 14–15.

10. Brian Dykstra quoted in Jeff Pearlman, "The Fall of Lenny Dykstra," *Maxim*, October 14, 2011, www.maxim.com/sports/fall-lenny-dykstra.

11. Frankie, *Nailed!*, 16–18. According to Dykstra, he never "stalked" Carew. Instead, when Carew learned of his hero worship, the Angels' infielder phoned Lenny to encourage his baseball ambitions. See Dykstra, *House of Nails*, 21.

12. Frankie, *Nailed!*, 16.

13. Dykstra, *House of Nails*, 17–18.

14. Pearlman, "Fall of Lenny Dykstra."

15. Dan Drake quoted in Frankie, *Nailed!*, 19–20.

16. Dykstra quoted in Frankie, *Nailed!*, 21.

17. Lenny Dykstra, interview, Simi Valley CA, September 9, 2001.

18. Brian Dykstra quoted in Pearlman, "Fall of Lenny Dykstra."

19. Pearlman, "Fall of Lenny Dykstra." According to Dykstra, the Mets' initial offer was just $7,000. See Dykstra, *House of Nails*, 31.

20. Frankie, *Nailed!*, 22–24.

21. Anonymous Minor League teammate and Marlin McPhail quoted in Pearlman, "Fall of Lenny Dykstra."

22. Lenny Dykstra, "Minor League Career Statistics," www.baseballreference.com.

23. Michael Lewis, *Moneyball* (New York: W. W. Norton, 2003), 45–47.

24. Lenny Dykstra, "Major League Career Statistics," in *ESPN Baseball Encyclopedia*, edited by Palmer and Gillette, 194. When Mookie Wilson came off the disabled list, the Mets released veteran left fielder George Foster and moved Wilson to left.

25. Pearlman, *Bad Guys Won!*; Rich English, "Boozing in the Big Leagues. How the '86 Mets Drank Their Way into the World Series," *Modern Drunkard Magazine*, www.drunkard .com/issues/07_05/0705_big_leagues.htm; Jeff Passan, "The Wild Bunch Returns," *Yahoo Sports*, August 18, 2006, www.sports.yahoo.com/mlb/news-86mets081806.

26. Doug Sisk quoted in Pearlman, "Fall of Lenny Dykstra."

27. Westcott and Bilovsky, *The Phillies Encyclopedia*, 169.

28. Dykstra, "Major League Career Statistics."

29. Dykstra quoted in Joseph Durso, "Dykstra Displays New Look," *New York Times*, February 25, 1988.

30. As early as 776 BC, the Olympic athletes of ancient Greece experimented with herbal substances and strychnine to gain a competitive edge over their opponents. Similarly, Roman gladiators used hallucinogens and consumed animal hearts or testicles in order to increase their strength and endurance in competition. See Sally Jenkins, "Winning, Cheating Have Ancient Roots," *Washington Post*, August 3, 2007; and E. R. Freeman, D. A. Bloom, and E. J. McGuire, "A Brief History of Testosterone," *Journal of Urology* 165, no. 2 (2001): 371–73.

At the turn of the nineteenth century, sports, drugs, and science became more closely linked as exercise physiologists began experimenting with various hallucinogens and ergogenic substances. In the public's mind, their academic credentials made the use of such substances "innovative" or "experimental" rather than controversial. Accordingly, in 1889 Dr. Charles-Édouard Brown-Séquard, a seventy-two-year-old French physiologist, injected himself and others with the extract of dog and guinea pig testicles. He assumed that the organs had "internal secretions that acted as physiologic regulators" that could eliminate pain in the human body. See C. E. Brown-Séquard, "The Effects Produced on Man by Subcutaneous Injection of a Liquid Obtained from the Testicles of Animals," *Lancet* 137 (1889): 105–7. One of Brown-Séquard's guinea pigs was James "Pud" Galvin, a star pitcher for the Pittsburgh Pirates. See Bernstein, *The Code*, 219–30. These and other experiments led to the discovery of hormones, in 1905, and the subsequent isolation of testosterone in 1935. See Michael J. Aminoff, "Brown-Séquard: Selected Contributions of a Nineteenth-Century Neuroscientist," *Neuroscientist* 6 (2000): 60–65.

Other performance-enhancing drugs originated during World War II when amphetamines were used by American soldiers to keep them alert on the battlefield. The German military went even further, using anabolic steroids to increase the aggressive behavior of its soldiers. See Michael Bamberger and Don Yeagar, "Over the Edge: Special Report," *Sports Illustrated*, April 14, 1997, 64.

While these practices provided the impetus for the increased use of drugs, they also resulted in a new framework of ethics, one that defined doping as "cheating" in order to gain a competitive edge. Olympic athletes were the first to test the boundaries of the new code.

31. Justin Peters, "The Man behind the Juice," February 2005, www.slate.com/articles /sports/sports_nut/2005/02/the_man_behind_the_juice.html.

32. Gerald Thorne, *Anabolic Primer: Ergogenic Enhancement for the Hardcore Bodybuilder* (Mississauga ON: 2009), 19. PED use among American bodybuilders boomed after 1976 when a young Arnold Schwarzenegger captured the "Mr. Olympia" title. Schwarzenegger, more than any other figure, was responsible for the popularity of bodybuilding in the United States. While he never admitted to using steroids when he was competing, the seven-time Mr. Olympia, in 2005, admitted to doping, insisting that he had "no regrets about it" because it was done "under doctors' supervision." In fact, the use of anabolic steroids was openly discussed among bodybuilders, in part because using them was legal. Schwarzenegger quoted in Chris Hawke, "Arnold: No Regrets about Steroids," CBS News, February 26, 2005, www.cbsnews.com.

33. Thomas M. Hunt, *Drug Games: The International Olympic Committee and the Politics of Doping, 1960–2008* (Austin: University of Texas Press, 2011). Not until 1986 did the International Federation of Bodybuilders (IFBB) introduce doping tests for steroids and other banned substances. This was done in hopes of joining the International Olympic Committee. See IFBB, *IFBB's Anti-doping Rules* (Madrid: IFBB, 2009), 7.

34. For a concise history of doping in sports, see Charles Yesalis and Michael Bahrke, "History of Doping in Sport," *International Sports Studies* 24, no. 1 (2002): 42–76.

35. Lyle Alzado as told to Shelley Smith, "'I'm Sick and I'm Scared,'" *Sports Illustrated*, July 8, 1991, 21, 23. Alzado also believed that his steroid use was "mentally addicting" and that it led to the brain tumor that eventually claimed his life at the age of forty-three.

36. Jim Haslett quoted in Sam Farmer, "Steroid Use Rampant in Old NFL," *Los Angeles Times,* March 23, 2005.

37. Canseco, *Juiced*, 3.

38. Bryant, *Juicing the Game*, 183–84. Methamphetamine or human growth hormone and erythropoietin were also used by athletes for the same purpose as anabolic steroids. Canseco, *Juiced*, 4–6.

39. Canseco, *Juiced*, 6–8.

40. Canseco, *Juiced*, 7–8, 133.

41. In 1990 the U.S. Congress declared anabolic steroids a Schedule III classification of the Controlled Substance Act. According to the law, steroids, like other Schedule III substances, are defined by a potential for abuse, a currently accepted medical use in treatment, and the possibility of moderate or low physical dependence or high psychological dependence. See U.S. Department of Health and Human Services, "Title 21, USC-812— Schedules of Controlled Substances," Controlled Substances Act (1990).

The next year baseball commissioner Fay Vincent issued a memo "strictly prohibiting the possession, sale or use of any illegal drug or controlled substance by Major League players." Any offender would be "subject to discipline by the Commissioner and risk permanent expulsion from the game." Some general managers at that time do not remember the circulation of such a memo. Nor was it emphasized or enforced. See Commissioner Fay Vincent's June 7, 1991, Memorandum, quoted in David Epstein, "The Rules, the Law, the Reality: A Primer on Baseball's Steroid Policy through the Years," *Sports Illustrated*, February 16, 2009, 18.

42. Bryant, *Juicing the Game*, 184.

43. Bernstein, *The Code*, 211–18.

44. Paul Hagen, "Dykstra Brags of Steroid Use in New Book," *Philadelphia Daily News*, June 30, 2010.

45. Frankie, *Nailed!*, 39.

46. Radomski with Fisher, *Bases Loaded*, 53. Radomski began working for the Mets as a batboy in the early 1980s. By 1985 when he met Dykstra, he was a clubhouse attendant who supplied players with "dietary supplements" and eventually became the point man for players who wanted anabolic steroids and human growth hormone. After being identified by several players as a supplier of steroids, Radomski was threatened by the government with jail time. Instead, he cooperated with the Mitchell investigation, providing many of the names and dates in the Mitchell Report. In the report Radomski claimed that Dykstra was "the first person I supplied with substances." See Mitchell, *Report to the Commissioner of Baseball*, 149–50.

47. Radomski with Fisher, *Bases Loaded*, 53–54.

48. Dykstra, *House of Nails*, 98–100, 110.

49. Harrison Pope, Katharine Phillips, and Roberto Olivardia, *The Adonis Complex: How to Identify, Treat and Prevent Body Obsession in Men and Boys* (New York: Free Press, 2000), 105–8; Thorne, *Anabolic Primer*, 64–65; "Different Types of Steroids on the Market," www.isteroids.com; "Types of Steroids," www.buysteroids.com. The most common anabolic-androgenic steroids are Nandrolone (Durabolin, Deca-Durabolin), Oxandrolene (Anavar/Var), Stanazol (Winstrol/Winny), Oxymetandrolone (Anadrol/droll/Abombs), and Methandrostenolone (Dianabol/Dbol). Each one of these drugs has a specific purpose and function, though there is some overlay in properties and effects with certain ones.

50. See Harrison G. Pope's research on steroids: "Adverse Health Consequences of Performance-Enhancing Drugs: An Endocrine Society's Scientific Statement," *Endocrine Reviews*, early release, December 17, 2013, doi:10.1210/er.2013–1058; "Risk Factors for Illicit Anabolic-Androgenic Steroid Use in Male Weightlifters: A Cross-sectional Cohort Study," *Journal of Biological Psychiatry* 71, no. 3 (2012): 254–61; "Illicit Anabolic-Androgenic Steroid Use," *Hormones and Behavior* 58, no. 1 (2010): 111–21; "Anabolic-Androgenic Steroid Abuse," in *Comprehensive Textbook of Psychiatry*, edited by Benjamin J. Sadock and Virginia A. Sadock, 8th ed. (Philadelphia: Lippincott, Williams, and Wilkins, 2004), 1318–28; "Psychiatric Effects of Exogenous Anabolic-Androgenic Steroids," in *Psychoneuroendocrinology: The Scientific Basis of Clinical Practice*, edited by O. M. Wolkowitz and A. J. Rothschild (Washington DC: American Psychiatric Press, 2003), 331–58; and "Past Anabolic-Androgenic Steroid Use among Men Admitted for Substance Abuse Treatment: Unrecognized Problem?," *Journal of Clinical Psychiatry* 64 (2003): 156–60.

51. Radomski with Fisher, *Bases Loaded*, 54.

52. Radomski with Fisher, *Bases Loaded*, 54–55.

53. Frankie, *Nailed!*, 35.

54. Palmer and Gillette, ESPN *Baseball Encyclopedia*, 194.

55. Dykstra to Romano quoted in Frankie, *Nailed!*, 35.

56. Frankie, *Nailed!*, 36.

57. Frankie, *Nailed!*, 37.

58. Westcott and Bilovsky, *The Phillies Encyclopedia*, 247.

59. Giles interview, November 20, 2009. Thomas, as it turned out, was correct about Samuel being on the "downside" of his career. In 1988, the year before the Phillies dealt him to New York, Samuel's average dipped from .272 to .243. His power numbers also dropped, from twenty-eight homers the previous year to just twelve and his RBI from one hundred to sixty-seven. He was still having trouble mastering the footwork at second base, so the Phillies moved him to center field. The move was a bust. Samuel's performance continued to decline with the Mets, who eventually dealt him to the Los Angeles Dodgers. Samuel ended his MLB career with the Kansas City Royals in 1992. See Westcott and Bilovsky, *The Phillies Encyclopedia*, 247.

60. Palmer and Gillette, ESPN *Baseball Encyclopedia*, 194.

61. Thomas interview.

62. Frankie, *Nailed!*, 38.

63. Thomas interview.

64. "Dykstra and Phillies Agree on 1990 Pact," *New York Times*, November 15, 1989; Baseball Almanac, "Lenny Dykstra's MLB Salary, 1985–1996," www.baseball-almanac.com /players/player.php?p=dykstle01.

4. Boo Birds

1. "Philadelphia Phillies: Franchise History," www.baseball-reference.com/teams/PHI/; Westcott and Bilovsky, *The Phillies Encyclopedia*, 595–97; Jere Longman, "Milestone Marks What Phillies Fans Already Knew," *New York Times*, June 12, 2007.

2. Westcott and Bilovsky, *The Phillies Encyclopedia*, 77, 600.

3. See William C. Kashatus, *September Swoon: Richie Allen, the '64 Phillies, and Racial Integration* (University Park: Pennsylvania State University Press, 2004).

4. Frank Fitzpatrick, "Heartbreak in '64: Phillies Collapse of 1964 Still Felt by Fans," *Philadelphia Inquirer*, September 29, 2014.

5. Joe Queenan, *True Believers: The Tragic Inner Life of Sports Fans* (New York: Picador/Holt, 2003), 11.

6. Queenan, *True Believers*, 125.

7. John Sexton, president of New York University and author of *Baseball as a Road to God*, believes that there is a great deal of common ground between religion and baseball. Both institutions, he argues, emphasize sacred places and times, faith and doubt, blessings and curses. The argument is a convincing one, with the exception of Sexton's interpretation of Phillies fans as "never buying into the notion of a curse" despite the club's long history of losing. "Instead," he writes, "they just chalk it up, loss after loss, year after year, to bad baseball." See Sexton, *Baseball as a Road to God* (New York: Gotham, 2013), 142. Having been a Phillies fan since 1964, I can confirm that those hometown fans who are deeply religious view all the losing as a curse. In fact, the Catholic fans are convinced that the Phils were given papal dispensation in 1980 and 2008 when the team won their only two World Series.

8. In his *New York Times* best seller, *Assholes*: A Theory*, Aaron James, a philosophy professor at the University of California, Irvine, defines an asshole as a person who "allows himself to enjoy special advantages" because of "an entrenched sense of entitlement," which "immunizes him against the complaints of others." See James, *Assholes*: A Theory* (New York: Doubleday, 2012), 5. Having witnessed the behavior of an inordinate number of assholes during my lifetime, especially at Phillies games, I believe James is spot-on in his definition.

9. Kruk, "*I Ain't an Athlete*," 147.

10. Larry Bowa, interview, Radnor PA, August 12, 2003.

11. Bowa quoted in Kruk, "*I Ain't an Athlete*," 34–35.

12. Kruk, "*I Ain't an Athlete*," 35.

13. Westcott and Bilovsky, *The Phillies Encyclopedia*, 204–5.

14. John Kruk, interview, Los Angeles, September 3, 2001.

15. Kruk, "*I Ain't an Athlete*," 44–45.

16. Leyvva quoted in Westcott and Bilovsky, *The Phillies Encyclopedia*, 359.

17. Kruk, "*I Ain't an Athlete*," 36; Darren Daulton interview, June 3, 2013. When Thomas was reminded of the clubhouse talk years later, he smiled and said, "Yeah, I guess I went overboard a little bit. But I basically reminded them that they should try to act like gentleman around the fans and that they would expect the same thing if they were parents taking their kids to a ballgame." See Thomas interview.

18. Michael Bamberger, "Phillies Are Out to Gain Some Respect; Leyva and Thomas Want a Team That's Accustomed to Winning," *Philadelphia Inquirer*, April 9, 1990.

19. Westcott and Bilovsky, *The Phillies Encyclopedia*, 102.

20. Westcott and Bilovsky, *The Phillies Encyclopedia*, 359.

21. Leigh McDonald, "A Taste of History," in *1991 Phillies Yearbook* (Philadelphia: Phillies, 1991), 61.

22. Mulholland quoted in McDonald, "A Taste of History."

23. Westcott and Bilovsky, *The Phillies Encyclopedia*, 102.

24. Chris Wheeler, "Coming into His Own," in *Phillies Today Magazine Scorecard* (Philadelphia: Phillies, 1991), 60.

25. Montville, "Leading Man," 48–49.

26. See Montville, "Leading Man," 48. Born on April 15, 1961, at Plant City, Florida, Lynne Austin captured the attention of Hooters Restaurant owners at a bikini contest in the mid-1980s. From there Austin's career took off. Selected as *Playboy*'s "Playmate of the Month" for July 1986, she appeared in several *Playboy* videos. A year later she was selected as the 1987 "Playmate of the Year" for the Dutch edition of the popular men's magazine. As the official spokeswoman for Hooters, Austin's likeness appeared on billboards across the nation. See Pat Cooper, "Lynne Austin: The Original Hooters Girl," *Hooters* (February–March 2008): 86–88.

27. "Dale Murphy," in *Phillies Today Magazine Scorecard*, 48.

28. "Dale Murphy," in *Phillies Today Magazine Scorecard*; Westcott and Bilovsky, *The Phillies Encyclopedia*, 103.

29. Leigh McDonald, "Meet Dale Murphy," in *1991 Phillies Yearbook*, 69.

30. Kruk, *"I Ain't an Athlete,"* 37.

31. Curt Schilling, interview, Medfield MA, November 17, 2015.

32. Kruk quoted in "John Kruk," in *Phillies Today Magazine Scorecard*, 60.

33. Westcott and Bilovsky, *The Phillies Encyclopedia*, 102.

34. Dykstra, "Major League Career Statistics."

5. Krukker

1. See Claire Smith, "Free Spirited Dykstra Belly Flops to Earth," *New York Times*, May 23, 1991; Dykstra, *House of Nails*, 118–19. A breathalyzer test administered by the Radnor Township, Pennsylvania, police indicated that Dykstra's blood-alcohol level was .179. It was the equivalent of drinking eight beers in one hour for someone of his physical stature. Dykstra was charged with a DUI. See Westcott and Bilovsky, *The Phillies Encyclopedia*, 168.

2. Geffner, "From Anti-hero to Superhero."

3. Monteville, "Leading Man," 48.

4. Geffner, "From Anti-hero to Superhero."

5. Westcott and Bilovsky, *The Phillies Encyclopedia*, 103.

6. Kruk, *"I Ain't an Athlete,"* 166–67.

7. "Obituary, Francis J. 'Moe' Kruk, Sr., Keyser, W.Va.," *Cumberland (WV) Times-News*, August 10, 2013.

8. Lena Kruk, interview, Keyser WV, March 22, 2015.

9. Kruk, *"I Ain't an Athlete,"* 58–60.

10. Lena Kruk interview.

11. Larry Kruk, interview, Keyser WV, March 22, 2015.

12. Kruk, *"I Ain't an Athlete,"* 60–61; Lena Kruk interview; Larry Kruk interview.

13. Larry Kruk interview.

14. Rick Rotruck quoted in Patrick Reusse, "Kruk's W. Virginia Roots Still Run Deep," *Minneapolis Star Tribune*, October 24, 1993.

15. Larry Kruk interview.

16. Kruk, "I Ain't an Athlete," 62–63.

17. Rotruck quoted in Reusse, "Kruk's W. Virginia Roots."

18. Kruk, "I Ain't an Athlete," 62–63.

19. Jack Reynolds, interview, Keyser WV, March 31, 2015.

20. Steve Bazarnic, interview, Cumberland MD, February 22, 2015.

21. Kruk, "I Ain't an Athlete," 65–66.

22. Kruk, "I Ain't an Athlete," 94–95. For Kruk's Minor League statistics, see "John Kruk's Minor League Statistics," www.baseball-reference.com/minors/player.cgi?id=kruk—001joh.

23. See "Kruk's Major League Statistics," in ESPN Baseball Encyclopedia, edited by Palmer and Gillette, 373.

24. Kruk, "I Ain't an Athlete," 107–8.

25. See John Kruk's 1988 Topps baseball card, no. 596.

26. Gary Harki, "Baseball Star John Kruk One of Many Fooled by Bank Robber," Charleston (WV) Gazette, August 5, 2008.

27. Westcott and Bilovsky, The Phillies Encyclopedia, 576.

28. Kruk, "I Ain't an Athlete," 145.

29. Westcott and Bilovsky, The Phillies Encyclopedia, 205.

30. "John Kruk."

31. John Kruk interview, Los Angeles, September 3, 2001.

32. Unnamed Bryn Mawr Hospital supervisor quoted in Mike Jensen, "Dykstra Makes yet Another Error," Philadelphia Inquirer, April 19, 2011.

33. Frankie, Nailed!, 43.

34. Herr quoted in Smith, "Free Spirited Dykstra Belly Flops."

35. Bill Conlin, "Phils Keep Chins Clear for Top Doc," Philadelphia Daily News, March 11, 1993.

36. Giles interview, November 20, 2009.

37. Radomski quoted in Frankie, Nailed!, 41.

38. Whenever the baseball commissioner meets with a ballplayer to discuss a disciplinary issue, the players' union sends an attorney to represent their and the player's interests.

39. Fay Vincent, The Last Commissioner (New York: Simon & Schuster, 2002), 174–75; Frankie, Nailed!, 41–42.

40. Radomski with Fisher, Bases Loaded, 56.

41. Radomski with Fisher, Bases Loaded, 56–57

42. Radomski with Fisher, Bases Loaded, 57–58.

43. Tim Elfrick and Gus Garcia-Roberts, Alex Rodriguez, Biogenesis, and the Quest to End Baseball's Steroids Era (New York: Dutton, 2014), 102; Brian Costello, "Dykstra Gambled on Phils and Used 'Roids," New York Post, April 25, 2005.

44. Lenny Dykstra quoted in Randall Lane, The Zeroes: My Misadventures in the Decade Wall Street Went Insane (New York: Portfolio, 2010), chap. 9. Dykstra admitted his steroid use to Lane during a late-night conversation in February 2008 in New York City. It came just a few days after the Mitchell Report identified him as a user of performance-enhancing substances. "You know," Dykstra told Lane, "I was like a pioneer for that stuff— the juice. I was like the very first to do that. Me and Canseco." See Hagen, "Dykstra Brags of Steroid Use."

45. Harrison G. Pope Jr., MD, director of the biological psychiatry laboratory at McLean Hospital–Harvard Medical School, is widely considered to be the leading authority on anabolic steroids, the most common PED used by professional baseball players. Pope's research was just beginning in the late 1980s and did not attain widespread interest until the twenty-first century. For Pope's research, see the sources listed in chap. 3, n. 48, as

well as "Effects of Supraphysiologic Doses of Testosterone on Mood and Aggression in Normal Men," *Archives of General Psychiatry* 57 (2000): 133–40; and "Affective and Psychotic Symptoms Associated with Anabolic Steroid Use," *American Journal of Psychiatry* 145 (1988): 487–90.

46. Bryant, *Juicing the Game*, 135, 185, 198; Todd Zolecki, "Mitchell Report: Phillies Mostly Clean, Except for Dykstra and Bell," *Philadelphia Inquirer*, December 14, 2007; Bernstein, *The Code*, 224. Androstenedione, or "andro," and creatine were legal over-the-counter substances used by power hitters to build "twitch muscles." It gave them more "impulse power" to swing the bat quicker and harder. These supplements also provided quick bursts of energy, increased muscle mass, and faster recovery time from an injury. See Bernstein, *The Code*, 220. Mark McGwire was using "andro" in 1998 when he was involved in the quest to break Roger Maris's single-season home run record. See Bryant, *Juicing the Game*, 134.

47. Westcott and Bilovsky, *The Phillies' Encyclopedia*, 103–4.

48. Westcott and Bilovsky, *The Phillies' Encyclopedia*, 182–83; Leigh Tobin, "Tommy Greene: Enjoying the Game," in *Phillies Souvenir Scorebook* (Philadelphia: Phillies, 1993), 58.

49. Westcott and Bilovsky, *The Phillies' Encyclopedia*, 103–4.

50. John Kruk quoted in Westcott and Bilovsky, *The Phillies' Encyclopedia*, 205.

51. See "Philadelphia Phillies' Player Salaries, 1991, 1992," usa *Today Sports*, www .experience.usatoday.com/sports/mlb/phillies/salaries/1992/player/if/. usa *Today's* baseball salaries database contains year-by-year listings of salaries for Major League Baseball players on opening-day rosters and disabled lists, 1988 through the current season. Figures, compiled by usa *Today*, are based on documents obtained from the mlb Players Association and club officials and filed with Major League Baseball's central office. Deferred payments and incentive clauses are not included. Team payrolls do not include money paid or received in trades or for players who have been released.

52. Rotruck quoted in Reusse, "Kruk's W. Virginia Roots."

53. Reynolds interview.

6. Fourth Estate

1. Westcott and Bilovsky, *The Phillies' Encyclopedia*, 95–103.

2. The Fourth Estate most commonly refers to the news media, especially print journalism. Scottish philosopher and satirical writer Thomas Carlyle attributed the origin of the term to Edmund Burke, who used it in a parliamentary debate in 1787 on the opening up of press reporting of the House of Commons of Great Britain. On that occasion Burke was referring to the press as an additional body to the traditional three estates of Parliament: the Lords Spiritual, the Lords Temporal, and the Commons. Earlier writers applied the term to lawyers, to the British queen (acting as a free agent, independent of the king), and to the proletariat. In these earlier cases, the term was a reference to the three Estates of the Realm.

3. Dickson, *Unwritten Rules of Baseball*, 26–29, 137.

4. Frank Fitzpatrick, interview, West Chester pa, March 15, 2015.

5. Fitzpatrick interview.

6. "Stories from the Press Box," History Channel documentary, aired on May 10, 2001; Kevin Kerrane, "Clean-up Hitter," in *Batting Cleanup, Bill Conlin*, by Conlin (Philadelphia: Temple University Press, 1997), xi–xii. Sportswriters Dick Young of the *New York Post* and Stan Isaacs of *Newsday* set the precedent for the new breed of sportswriter. Young once observed that a chipmunk "had to tell people they're full of shit and then go out and face them the next day." Isaacs is widely credited with popularizing the intrusive line of questioning. After New York Yankees pitcher Ralph Terry defeated the San Francisco Giants

in Game Five of the 1962 World Series, Terry excused himself from a group of sportswriters to take a telephone call from his wife. When he returned Terry mentioned that his wife was feeding their baby. From the back of the room, Isaacs asked, "Breast or bottle?" It was the kind of intrusive personal question that became a trademark of the chipmunks. These writers were dubbed the "chipmunks" allegedly because they went after the nuts.

7. Kerrane, "Cleanup Hitter," xi–xii, xvii.

8. Rathet quoted in Kerrane, "Cleanup Hitter," xvii.

9. Dick Schaap, foreword to *Batting Cleanup*, by Conlin, ix.

10. See "Bill Colin Wins Spink Award for Baseball Writing," *The Sporting News*, December 7, 2010; and Rich Hofmann, "The Bill of Writes: Conlin, the Choice Voice of Philadelphia Baseball, to Be Honored," *Philadelphia Daily News*, July 21, 2011. The Spink Award is the equivalent of a ballplayer's induction into the National Baseball Hall of Fame. The prestigious award marked a final bit of glory for Conlin who, in December 2011 resigned from the *Daily News* amid charges of pedophilia. See Nancy Phillips, "Four Say *Philly Daily News* Writer Bill Conlin Sexually Abused Them as Children," *Philadelphia Inquirer*, December 20, 2011; Nancy Phillips, "Another Woman Comes Forward over Abuse by Bill Conlin," *Philadelphia Inquirer*, December 21, 2011; and United Press International, "6th Person Alleges Sportswriter Abused Her," www.upi.com/Sports_News/2011/12/22/.

11. Daniel E. Slotnik, "Bill Conlin, Sportswriter Who Quit after Molestation Claims, Dies at 79," *New York Times*, January 10, 2014.

12. Paul Hagen, interview, Clearwater FL, March 4, 2015.

13. Paul Hagen, "Wife Delivers, He Hasn't. Now Daulton Can Focus on Hitting," *Philadelphia Daily News*, May 24, 1990. Lynne Austin gave birth to a seven-pound, fifteen-ounce boy, Zachary. It was the couple's first and only child.

14. Hagen interview.

15. Douglas Pils, "WIP, Philadelphia: The Station with the Big Mouth and Even Bigger Heart" in *Sports-Talk Radio in America: Its Context and Culture*, edited by Jack M. Dempsey (New York: Routledge, 2006), 112–13, 115. WIP first aired on March 17, 1922. The radio station was owned by Gimbel Brothers Department Store. In the spring of 1987, WIP was sold to Spectacor, which also owned the National Hockey League's Philadelphia Flyers and their venue, the Spectrum. In November of that year, WIP became an all-sports radio talk show and was virtually alone as a Sportstalk station on the radio airwaves for more than two decades.

16. Stephen Rosenfeld quoted in Jim Nolan, "The Amazing Eskin: Why Won't Howard Disappear?," *Philadelphia Daily News*, June 3, 1996.

17. Pils, "WIP, Philadelphia," 112–13, 120.

18. Pils, "WIP, Philadelphia," 112; Fitzpatrick interview.

19. Bob Brookover, "Frego Had an Ego, and a Command That Inspired," *Philadelphia Inquirer*, February 15, 2014; Matt Gelb, "Jim Fregosi Led the '93 Phillies to an NL title," *Philadelphia Inquirer*, February 15, 2014.

20. Fregosi quoted in *Phillies Souvenir Scorebook* (Philadelphia: Phillies, 1992), 7.

21. Dykstra interview.

22. Brookover, "Frego Had Ego."

23. "Phillies v. Cubs: Tuesday, April 7, 1992," www.baseball-reference.com/boxes/PHI /PHI199204070.shtml. Between the 1991 ad 1992 seasons, Dykstra played in just 145 games out of a possible 324.

24. Brookover, "Frego Had Ego"; Fitzpatrick interview.

25. Westcott and Bilovsky, *The Phillies' Encyclopedia*, 104. Roy Campanella of the Brooklyn Dodgers hit 142 RBI in 1953, Johnny Bench of the Cincinnati Reds hit 148 RBI in 1970, and Gary Carter of the Montreal Expos collected 106 RBI in 1984.

26. Darren Daulton quoted in Chris Wheeler, "Darren Daulton . . . Coming into His Own," in *Phillies Souvenir Scorebook*, no. 13 (Philadelphia: Phillies, 1992), 60. Daulton's numerous injuries included right shoulder (1985), torn cruciate ligament in left knee that required multiple surgeries (1986), right hand (1988), and right eye (1991).

27. Bryant, *Juicing the Game*, 282; Pessah, *The Game*, 75–76.

28. "Daulton's Major League Statistics."

29. Shenk, *If These Walls Could Talk*, 10.

30. "Daulton's Major League Statistics."

31. Pope et al., "Adverse Health Consequences," 1–2.

32. Darren Daulton interview, October 4, 2009; Shenk, *If These Walls Could Talk*, 9–10.

33. Lee Thomas quoted in Larry Shenk, "Healthy Numbers," in *Phillies' Souvenir Scorebook*, no. 25 (Philadelphia: Phillies, 1992), 60.

34. "Daulton, Gets $18.5 Million," *New York Times*, March 31, 1993. Daulton made $2.25 million in 1993, the final season of a three-year deal that was worth $6.75 million guaranteed. The new four-year contract gave the Phillies a 1998 option at $5 million with a $500,000 buyout.

35. Gene Dias, "Wes Chamberlain: Ready to Make a Name for Himself," in *Phillies Souvenir Scorebook* (Philadelphia: Phillies, June 1993), 54.

36. Morandini caught a line drive off the bat of Jeff King, touched second base to put out Andy Van Slyke, and tagged out Barry Bonds coming from first base. It was the first unassisted triple play since 1968 and the first in the National League since 1927. Although second baseman Bill Wambsganss turned an unassisted triple play in the 1920 World Series, Morandini became the first second baseman in National League history, and the first in the regular season, to achieve the feat.

37. Westcott and Bilovsky, *The Phillies' Encyclopedia*, 249–50.

38. Curt Schilling, interview, Boston, October 14, 2009.

39. Williams with Berger, *Straight Talk from Wild Thing*, 89.

40. Kruk, *"I Ain't an Athlete,"* 54.

41. Westcott and Bilovsky, *The Phillies Encyclopedia*, 576–77; Leigh Tobin, "David West: A Big Surprise," in *Phillies Souvenir Scorebook* (Philadelphia: Phillies, 1993), 58. For salaries, see "Philadelphia Phillies' Player Salaries, 1993," *USA Today Sports*, www.experience.usatoday.com/sports/mlb/phillies/salaries/1993/player/if/.

7. Spring Training

1. Westcott and Bilovsky, *The Phillies' Encyclopedia*, 169–70.

2. Darren Daulton interview, June 3, 2013.

3. Kruk, *"I Ain't an Athlete,"* 46–47.

4. Jim Eisenreich, interview, Philadelphia, August 1, 2013.

5. Daulton quoted in Westcott, *Phillies '93*, 22.

6. "Coaching Staff," in *Phillies Souvenir Scorebook* (Philadelphia: Phillies, 1993), 18.

7. Westcott, *Phillies '93*, 22–23.

8. Lee Thomas quoted in Westcott, *Phillies '93*, 24.

9. Westcott, *Phillies '93*, 25–26.

10. Giles with Myers, *Pouring Six Beers*, 186.

11. Eric Gregg with Marty Appel, *Working the Plate: The Eric Gregg Story* (New York: William Morrow, 1990); Dan Gelston, "Former Umpire Eric Gregg Dies after Stroke," *USA Today*, June 5, 2005.

12. Dykstra, *House of Nails*, 101; Thomas quoted in Zolecki, "Mitchell Report."

13. Vincent, "Memorandum" quoted in Epstein, "The Rules, the Law, the Reality."

14. John Kruk quoted in Jim Salisbury, "Kruk Never Saw Steroids on '93 Phils," *Philadelphia Inquirer*, April 26, 2005.

15. Bernstein, *The Code*, 211–13.

16. Dykstra, *House of Nails*, 101.

17. Westcott and Bilovsky, *The Phillies Encyclopedia*, 168.

18. Shaun Assael and Peter Keating, "Who Knew? Part II: The Tipping Point, 1994–1998, the Bodybuilder," ESPN *Magazine's Special Report on Steroids in Baseball*, ESPN.com, November 9, 2005; "Ex-Biz Partner Alleges Dykstra Took Steroids and HGH," ESPN.com, April 24, 2005.

19. Bruce Buschel, "Lips Gets Smacked," *Philadelphia Magazine*, January 1993, 36–37; Associated Press, "Magazine Says Dykstra a Sore Gambling Loser," *Los Angeles Times*, December 29, 1992. In spring training of 1991, Dykstra went to Mississippi to testify about his involvement in poker games in which he was reported to have lost $78,000. Fay Vincent, then baseball commissioner, placed him on probation for a year.

20. "Ex-Biz Partner Alleges Dykstra Took Steroids and HGH."

21. Frankie, *Nailed!*, 40–41; Conlin, *Batting Cleanup*, 202.

22. Giles with Myers, *Pouring Six Beers*, 310–11; Randy Miller, *Harry the K: The Remarkable Life of Harry Kalas* (Philadelphia: Running Press, 2010).

23. "Bringing You the Action . . . ," in *Phillies Souvenir Scorebook* (Philadelphia: Phillies, 1993), 12.

24. Giles with Myers, *Pouring Six Beers*, 185.

25. Larry Andersen, interview, Philadelphia, August 1, 2013.

26. Morandini quoted in Rich Wolfe, *Remembering Harry Kalas* (Chicago: Lone Wolf Press, 2009), 93.

27. Kalas quoted in Giles with Myers, *Pouring Six Beers*, 185.

28. Dave Hollins, interview, Fairless Hills PA, August 11, 2010.

29. Westcott, *Phillies '93*, 25; Cooney, *Worst to First*, 6–7.

30. Bernstein, *The Code*, 43.

31. Dykstra quoted in Cooney, *Worst to First*, 6–7.

32. Westcott, *Phillies '93*, 26.

33. Kruk quoted in Cooney, *Worst to First*, 5.

34. Bill Giles quoted in Frank Fitzpatrick, "Phillies Sign Daulton for 4 More Years; He's Guaranteed $18 Million," *Philadelphia Inquirer*, March 31, 1993.

35. Rich Westcott, *Tales from the Phillies Dugout* (New York: Sports Publishing, 2003), 165.

8. Wild Thing

1. Larry Shenk, "Road to Victory: The Enchanted Season," in *1993 National League Championship Series Program and Scorecard* (Philadelphia: Phillies, 1993), 74; Westcott, *Phillies '93*, 32.

2. Schilling quoted in Cooney, *Worst to First*, 7.

3. Westcott, *Phillies '93*, 33.

4. Westcott, *Phillies '93*, 33. Wes Chamberlain overslept and arrived more than two hours after Phillies players were required to report to the Vet for the game. The incident seemed to reinforce concerns about the young outfielder's flamboyant behavior. But Chamberlain apologized to his teammates and redeemed himself by playing problem-free baseball for the remainder of the season.

5. Shenk, "Road to Victory," 74.

6. Paul Hagen, "That Championship Season: Looking Back at the 1993 Phillies' Memorable Ride," in *Phillies 2013 Yearbook* (Philadelphia: Phillies, 2013), 90.

7. Gordon and Burgoyne, *Beards, Bellies and Biceps*, 57.

8. Mitch Williams, interview, Camden NJ, August 29, 2001.

9. Williams quoted in Greg Couch, "A Wiser 'Wild Thing': Mitch Williams Returns to the Game as a Pitching Coach," *Baseball Digest* (July 2001): 73.

10. Kruk quoted in Westcott and Bilovsky, *The Phillies' Encyclopedia*, 278.

11. Linda Kay, "Cubs Reliever Mitch Williams Is Known as a Wild Man, but Off the Field He's Just Wild about His Family," *Chicago Tribune*, June 4, 1989.

12. Williams with Berger, *Straight Talk from Wild Thing*, 1–2.

13. Kay, "Cubs Reliever Mitch Williams"; Matt Sherman, "West Linn High School Set to Induct New Class into Athletic Hall of Fame," *West Linn (OR) Tidings*, September 26, 2012.

14. "Mitch Williams' Minor League Statistics," www.baseball-reference.com/minors /player.cgi?id=willia001mit. The Rule Five draft aims to prevent teams from stockpiling too many young players on their Minor League affiliate teams when other clubs would be willing to have them play in the Majors. If chosen in the Rule Five draft, a player must be kept on the selecting team's twenty-five-man Major League roster for the entire season after the draft; he may not be optioned or designated to the Minors. The selecting team may, at any time, waive the Rule Five draftee. If a Rule Five draftee clears waivers by not signing with a new MLB team, he must be offered back to the original team, effectively canceling the Rule Five draft choice. Once a Rule Five draftee spends an entire season on his new team's twenty-five-man roster, his status reverts to normal, and he may be optioned or designated for assignment.

In Williams's case, he went to spring training with the Texas Rangers, the team that selected him. When the Rangers cut him on the final day of spring training, Williams went back to the Padres. The same night the Rangers traded one of their Minor League infielders, Randy Asadoor, for Williams. See Williams with Berger, *Straight Talk from Wild Thing*, 4.

15. John Kruk quoted in Williams with Berger, *Straight Talk from Wild Thing*, vi.

16. Williams with Berger, *Straight Talk from Wild Thing*, 7.

17. "Mitch Williams Major League Career Statistics," in *ESPN Baseball Encyclopedia*, edited by Palmer and Gillette, 1263.

18. Kay, "Cubs Reliever Mitch Williams."

19. Murray Chass, "Cubs Trade Palmiero for Williams of Rangers," *New York Times*, December 6, 1988. Joining Williams in the trade to Chicago were Paul Kilgus, a left-handed starter; Steve Wilson, a Minor League left-handed pitcher; and Curtis Wilkerson, an infielder.

20. "Mitch Williams Major League Career Statistics."

21. Pole quoted in Kay, "Cubs Reliever Mitch Williams."

22. Williams interview, August 29, 2001.

23. Westcott and Bilovsky, *The Phillies' Encyclopedia*, 278.

24. Richard Goldstein, "Johnny Podres, Series Star, Dies at 75," *New York Tines*, January 14, 2008.

25. Williams with Berger, *Straight Talk from Wild Thing*, 62, 101.

26. Cooney, *Worst to First*, 16.

27. Fregosi quoted in Westcott, *Phillies '93*, 35.

28. Dykstra quoted in Cooney, *Worst to First*, 14.

29. Cooney, *Worst to First*, 5, 59.

30. Shenk, "Road to Victory," 74.

31. Cooney, *Worst to First*, 66–68; Westcott, *Phillies '93*, 35; Gordon and Burgoyne, *Beards, Bellies and Biceps*, 83–84.

32. Cooney, *Worst to First*, 68–69; Westcott, *Phillies '93*, 37; Gordon and Burgoyne, *Beards, Bellies and Biceps*, 86.

33. Cooney, *Worst to First*, 69–70; Westcott, *Phillies '93*, 37; Gordon and Burgoyne, *Beards, Bellies and Biceps*, 86–87.

34. Cooney, *Worst to First*, 184.

35. Larry Andersen quoted in Hagen, "That Championship Season," 91.

9. Lightning in a Bottle

1. Cooney, *Worst to First*, 184.
2. Westcott, *Phillies '93*, 39; Giles with Myers, *Pouring Six Beers*, 186–87.
3. Darren Daulton quoted in Cooney, *First to Worst*, 65.
4. Fitzpatrick interview.
5. Dykstra and Kruk quoted in J. Edwin Smith, "Crazy about Winning," *The Sporting News*, May 24, 1993, 9–10.
6. Williams with Berger, *Straight Talk from Wild Thing*, 90.
7. Gordon and Burgoyne, *Beards, Bellies and Biceps*, 103–6; Beaton, "Phillies' Roster," 20–22. Mitch Williams had a sign above his locker that read "The Ghetto." But WIP Sports Radio host Mike Missanelli is credited with naming this section of the Phillies' clubhouse "Macho Row." See Hagen and Fitzpatrick interviews.
8. Tom Mahon, "Hollis Thomas: Eagles, Phils Shared Porn at Vet," *Philadelphia Daily News*, August 23, 2013.
9. Montville, "Leading Man," 46.
10. John Kruk interview.
11. Andersen quoted in Westcott, *Tales from Phillies' Dugout*, 163.
12. Mike Ryan quoted in Geffner, "From Anti-hero to Superhero."
13. Williams quoted in Geffner, "From Anti-hero to Superhero."
14. Lynne Daulton quoted in Geffner, "From Anti-hero to Superhero."
15. Fregosi quoted in Montville, "Leading Man," 47.
16. John Vukovich, interview, Scranton PA, May 11, 2006.
17. Kruk quoted in Giles with Myers, *Pouring Six Beers*, 182.
18. Montville, "Leading Man," 46.
19. Brookover, "Flaws and All."
20. Hagen interview.
21. Brookover, "Flaws and All."
22. Fitzpatrick interview.
23. Shenk, *If These Walls Could Talk*, 192.
24. Darren Daulton interview, September 6, 2001.
25. Frank Fitzpatrick, "Phils Outhit Giants for Win No. 19; Hollins Gets Game-Winning Home Run," *Philadelphia Inquirer*, May 5, 1993; Andersen interview; Kruk, "*I Ain't an Athlete*," 53–54.
26. Westcott, *Phillies '93*, 37–38.
27. Cooney, *Worst to First*, 73–74.
28. Duncan quoted in Gordon and Burgoyne, *Beards, Bellies and Biceps*, 89.
29. Bowa quoted in Cooney, *Worst to First*, 74.
30. Cox and Pendleton quoted in Smith, "Crazy about Winning," 10–11.
31. Cooney, *Worst to First*, 76–77.
32. John Kruk quoted in Gordon and Burgoyne, *Beards, Bellies and Biceps*, 90.
33. Westcott, *Phillies '93*, 41; Cooney, *Worst to First*, 18–19.
34. Westcott, *Phillies '93*, 41; Giles with Myers, *Pouring Six Beers*, 186–87.
35. Westcott, *Tales from the Phillies Dugout*, 170.
36. Mark Carfagno, interview, Philadelphia, July 6, 2007.
37. Kruk, "*I Ain't an Athlete*," 99.
38. Bill Conlin, "John Kruk's Top 10 List," *Philadelphia Daily News*, May 20, 1993.
39. Incaviglia quoted in Gene Dias, "Pete Incaviglia: A Fast Fan Favorite," *Phillies Souvenir Scorecard* (July 1993): 38.
40. Shenk, "Road to Victory," 76.
41. Gordon and Burgoyne, *Beards, Bellies and Biceps*, 91.

42. Shenk, "Road to Victory," 76.

43. Westcott and Bilovsky, *The Phillies Encyclopedia*, 229.

44. John Kruk quoted in Westcott, *Phillies '93*, 42.

45. Gordon and Burgoyne, *Beards, Bellies and Biceps*, 91.

46. Podres interview.

47. Schilling quoted in Paul Hagen, "Daulton Fined $400 for Flap with Ump," *Philadelphia Daily News*, June 9, 1993.

48. Darren Daulton interview, October 4, 2009; Fregosi interview.

49. Bernstein, *The Code*, 133, 137.

50. Daulton quoted in Hagen, "Daulton Fined $400."

51. Frank Fitzpatrick, "Umpire's Vacation Coincided with Series," *Philadelphia Inquirer*, July 7, 1993; Hagen, "Daulton Fined $400."

52. Hagen, "That Championship Season!," 91.

53. Shenk, "Road to Victory," 76.

54. Tom Pagnotti quoted in Gordon and Burgoyne, *Beards, Bellies and Biceps*, 115.

55. Westcott, *Tales from the Phillies Dugout*, 177.

56. Schilling and Daulton quoted in Cooney, *Worst to First*, 97–98.

57. Dickson, *Unwritten Rules of Baseball*, 30–33.

58. Daulton quoted in Frank Fitzpatrick, "Daulton Rails at Phils after Cards' Rout," *Philadelphia Inquirer*, July 2, 1993.

59. Schilling interview, October 14, 2009.

60. Darren Daulton interview, October 4, 2009.

61. Kruk, *"I Ain't an Athlete,"* 51–52.

62. Daulton quoted in Dave Caldwell, "Daulton, Phils Tight-Lipped after Closed-Door Regrouping," *Philadelphia Inquirer*, July 3, 1993.

10. Mikey

1. Sam Carchidi, "Tough Times over for Dave Hollins: Phillies Third Baseman Has Worked through Problems from Hand Surgery," *Philadelphia Inquirer*, August 12, 1993.

2. Glen Macnow, "One Tough Player with Two Personas Dave Hollins Can Be Congenial. He Can Also Be the Guy the Other Phils Call 'Mikey,'" *Philadelphia Inquirer*, May 16, 1993; O'Shei, "Dave Hollins," 42. John Kruk came up with the "Mikey" alter-ego reference after observing that Hollins prepared for games by becoming sullen and staring into his locker.

3. Michael Schwager, "Dave Hollins: Works Hard, Plays Hard and Hits Hard," *Phillies Report*, December 19, 1991; O'Shei, "Dave Hollins, 42–43."

4. Kruk interview; Hollins interview; Gordon and Burgoyne, *Beards, Bellies and Biceps*, 181.

5. Hollins interview.

6. Bernstein, *The Code*, 29–30.

7. Kruk, *"I Ain't an Athlete,"* 42–44. For a less profane version, see Frank Fitzpatrick, "Spring Turmoil Troubling Hollins," *Philadelphia Inquirer*, March 18, 1992.

8. Bowa quoted in Williams, "Hollins' Intensity Both Feared and Revered"; Westcott, *Tales from the Phillies' Dugout*, 174.

9. Hollins interview; Darren Daulton interview, October 4, 2009.

10. Hollins interview.

11. Paul Hagen, "Heightened Intensity Hollins Was Bred to Go Hard," *Philadelphia Daily News*, April 5, 1993; O'Shei, "Dave Hollins," 46.

12. "Western NY Baseball Legend Bob Barrows Dies," New York Sportswriters Association, July 17, 2013. See also Milt Northrop, "Bob Barrows, Orchard Park's Mr. Baseball, Dies at 79," *Buffalo (NY) News*, July 17, 2013.

13. Hollins quoted in Northrop, "Bob Barrows."

14. Mary Jo Monnin, "Orchard Park's Hollins Earned Top Baseball Honor," *Buffalo (NY) News*, July 3, 2014.

15. Hollins interview.

16. "Steven J. Hollins, Minor League Statistics," www.baseballreference.com.

17. Hollins quoted in Hagen, "Heightened Intensity Hollins Bred to Go Hard."

18. "Dave Hollins Minor League Statistics," www.baseballreference.com.

19. Westcott and Bilovsky, *The Phillies Encyclopedia*, 192; Frank Fitzpatrick, "Hollins Plans to Be Fan-Friendly," *Philadelphia Inquirer*, April 3, 1995; O'Shei, "Dave Hollins," 42.

20. Hollins quoted in Hagen, "Heightened Intensity Hollins Bred to Go Hard."

21. Westcott and Bilovsky, *The Phillies Encyclopedia*, 192.

22. Frank Fitzpatrick, "Phillies Sign Hollins to a $2.5 Million Contract," *Philadelphia Inquirer*, March 3, 1993.

23. Assael and Keating, "Who Knew? Part II."

24. Bryant, *Juicing the Game*, 282; Pessah, *The Game*, 76–77; "Inflated Stats in Contract Years during Baseball's Steroid Era," *Baseball's Steroid Era*, September 28, 2006, www .thesteroidera.blog.com; and Mitchell, *Report to the Commissioner of Baseball*, 195.What is unclear is if Pratt had been using PEDs during his time with the 1993 Phillies or only later, after he joined the New York Mets.

25. Jeff Cooper quoted in Zolecki, "Mitchell Report"; Bob Ford, "Mitchell's Report, in the End, Has No Juice," *Philadelphia Inquirer*, December 14, 2007. Cooper's charge is reported in the Mitchell Report as well. See Mitchell, *Report to the Commissioner of Baseball*, 67.

26. Hollins and Fregosi quoted in Carchidi, "Tough Times over for Hollins."

27. Gordon and Burgoyne, *Beards, Bellies and Biceps*, 134–35.

28. Cooney, *Worst to First*, 101.

29. Rich Ashburn quoted in Gordon and Burgoyne, *Beards, Bellies and, Biceps*, 134–35.

30. Westcott, *Phillies '93*, 49; Cooney, *Worst to First*, 101–2.

31. Jayson Stark, "A Long Night's Journey into the Record Books," *Philadelphia Inquirer*, July 4, 1993. According to Seymour Siwoff of the Elias Sports Bureau, the record for the latest starting time isn't actually known for sure. But Siwoff was virtually certain no game had ever started at 1:28 a.m. before, "because, until the last 20–25 years, you couldn't do that. We had laws. You couldn't begin an inning after 1 o'clock in the morning, let alone a game. So we have to think this is probably an all-time record."

32. Incaviglia quoted in Gordon and Burgoyne, *Beards, Bellies and Biceps*, 136.

33. Stark, "Long Night's Journey." When Game Two of the July 2 (and 3) twilight doubleheader ended at 4:40 a.m., the Phillies had set a new record for the latest finish by any game in MLB history, too. The old record was 3:55 a.m., set by the Braves and Mets on July 4 (and 5), 1985.

34. Eisenreich quoted in Gordon and Burgoyne, *Beards, Bellies and Biceps*, 135.

35. Darren Daulton quoted in Franz Lidz, "Beam Us Up, Dutchie. Darren Daulton Explains His Surreal Life," www.sportsillustrated.com.

36. Darren Daulton interview, June 3, 2013.

37. Lenny Dykstra, interview by Josh Innes, WIP Sports Radio, Philadelphia, June 28, 2016.

38. Lenny Dykstra interview, Simi Valley CA, September 9, 2001.

39. Pete Incaviglia, interview, Oaks PA, October 3, 2009.

40. John Kruk interview.

41. Andersen interview.

42. Shenk, "Road to Victory," 80.

43. Lenny Dykstra to Howard Eskin on *The Dan Patrick Show*, February 23, 2011, www .danpatrick.com.

44. Pessah, *The Game*, 76–77.

45. Paul Hagen, "We Interrupt This Free Fall . . . ," *Philadelphia Daily News*, July 12, 1993; Frank Fitzpatrick, "Phillies End First Half on a Sour Note," *Philadelphia Inquirer*, July 12, 1993.

46. Cooney, *Worst to First*, 184.

47. Paul Hagen, "The American Way Nationals Trip on Kirb," *Philadelphia Daily News*, July 14, 1993.

48. Sam Donnellon, "Kruk Just Tried to Stay Alive," *Philadelphia Daily News*, July 14, 1993; Kruk, *"I Ain't an Athlete,"* 217–18; Westcott and Bilovsky, *The Phillies' Encyclopedia*, 205.

49. Hagen, "American Way Nationals Trip on Kirb." Although the American League won the 1993 All-Star Game, the National League still led the overall series, 37-26-1.

11. Dog Days

1. Shenk, "Road to Victory," 80.

2. Jackson interview.

3. Shenk, "Road to Victory," 80.

4. Daulton quoted in Gordon and Burgoyne, *Beards, Bellies and Biceps*, 160.

5. Gordon and Burgoyne, *Beards, Bellies and Biceps*, 60–63.

6. Coppenbarger quoted in Gordon and Burgoyne, *Beards, Bellies and Biceps*, 60–63; Carfagno, Kruk, and Andersen interviews.

7. Bowa quoted in Westcott, *Phillies '93*, 54, 165.

8. Incaviglia quoted in Cooney, *Worst to First*, 107.

9. Hollins quoted in Carchidi, "Tough Times over for Hollins."

10. Jackson interview.

11. Gordon and Burgoyne, *Beards, Bellies and Biceps*, 165; Westcott and Bilovsky, *The Phillies Encyclopedia*, 107, 577; West quoted in Leigh Tobin, "David West: A Big Surprise," in *Phillies' Souvenir Scorebook* (Philadelphia: Phillies, 1993), 58.

12. Mitch Williams interview, Philadelphia, August 1, 2013.

13. Mason interview.

14. Westcott and Bilovsky, *The Phillies Encyclopedia*, 249–50.

15. Kruk, *"I Ain't an Athlete,"* 50–51.

16. Williams interview, August 1, 2013.

17. Darren Daulton interview, October 4, 2009.

18. Curt Schilling, interview, Medfield MA, October 21, 2015.

19. Schilling quoted in Westcott, *Phillies '93*, 62.

20. "Curt Schilling's Major League Baseball Statistics," in ESPN *Baseball Encyclopedia*, edited by Palmer and Gillette, 1174.

21. Michael Bamberger, "Schilling Filled the Most Important Seat in the Stadium for His Late Father and Mentor, Cliff," *Philadelphia Inquirer*, October 7, 1993.

22. Schilling quoted in Cooney, *Worst to First*, 35.

23. Schilling interviews, October 21, 2015, and October 14, 2009.

24. Cooney, *Worst to First*, 122–23, 124–25.

25. Gordon and Burgoyne, *Beards, Bellies and Biceps*, 164; Shenk, "Road to Victory," 82.

26. Cooney, *Worst to First*, 125–27; Shenk, "Road to Victory," 82.

27. Bernstein, *The Code*, 159, 162.

28. "Phillies Family: A Community-Caring Team," in *Phillies Souvenir Scorebook* (Philadelphia: Phillies, 1993), 70, 78, 80.

29. Cooney, *Worst to First*, 184–85.

30. Shenk, "Road to Victory," 82.

12. Inky

1. Frank Fitzpatrick, "Phils Grind Out 5–3 Win," *Philadelphia Inquirer*, September 7, 1993.

2. Incaviglia quoted in Sam Carchidi, "Phillies Defeat Astros; Curt Schilling Pitched 8¹⁄₃ Innings," *Philadelphia Inquirer*, September 11, 1993.

3. Bernstein, *The Code*, 155.

4. Kruk, *"I Ain't an Athlete,"* 244.

5. Incaviglia interview.

6. Steve Campbell, "Mending Fences," *Fort Worth (TX) Star-Telegram*, January 18, 1990; Jerry Crasnick, "Incaviglia Longs for Philadelphia's Magic of 1993," *Baseball America*, July 8–21, 1996.

7. Incaviglia interview.

8. Ken Rosenthal, "Incaviglia Saga Breath of Fresh Air," *Baltimore Sun*, February 25, 1997.

9. Dana Heis, "Pete Incaviglia, College Baseball's Home Run Champion, Retires," *USA Today Baseball Weekly*, May 1, 1999.

10. Tracy Ringolsby, "Big Leagues Quickly Learn about Incaviglia's Swagger," *Dallas Morning News*, July 29, 1989.

11. Williams with Berger, *Straight Talk from Wild Thing*, 17–20.

12. Campbell, "Mending Fences."

13. "Pete Incaviglia's Major League Career Statistics," in *ESPN Baseball Encyclopedia*, edited by Palmer and Gillette, 326–27.

14. Incaviglia interview.

15. "Incaviglia Rediscovers Success in Houston," *Syracuse (NY) Herald American*, April 26, 1992.

16. Asher B. Chancey, "The Bagwell Conspiracy," www.baseballevolution.com.

17. "Affidavit: Grimsley Named Players," CNN, December 20, 2007, www.cnn.com/2007/SPORT/12/20/drugs.grimsley; Associated Press, "Dykstra, Incaviglia among Those Named on Grimsley Document," *Philadelphia Daily News*, December 21, 2007. Although Incaviglia was not identified as a steroid user in the Mitchell Report, Grimsley, a former Phillies pitcher, claimed in his affidavit that the burly outfielder used amphetamines according to Internal Revenue Service special agent Jeff Noviytzky's sworn statement.

18. Chancey, "Bagwell Conspiracy." Sportswriters Steven Petrella and Howard Bryant also allege that Incaviglia used steroids. See Petrella, "Five for Friday: The Most Mediocre Baseball Players of the 1990s," *Baltimore Sun*, July 20, 2012; and Bryant, *Juicing the Game*, 282.

19. Gene Dias, "Pete Incaviglia: A Fast Fan Favorite," in *Phillies Souvenir Scorecard and Scorebook* (Philadelphia: Phillies, 1993), 38.

20. "Incaviglia's Major League Statistics."

21. Incaviglia interview.

22. Incaviglia interview.

23. Williams with Berger, *Straight Talk from Wild Thing*, 69–70.

24. Cooney, *Worst to First*, 186–87.

25. Frank Fitzpatrick, "Phils Loss Evokes Ghosts of '64 and More," *Philadelphia Inquirer*, September 10, 1993.

26. Jeff Blair, "Expos-Phillies Series Isn't Baseball, It's War," *Montreal Gazette*, September 18, 1993.

27. Gordon and Burgoyne, *Beards, Bellies and Biceps*, 168–69; Cooney, *Worst to First*, 131–34.

28. Bill Conlin, "Watching Mitch Is Sheer Torture," *Philadelphia Daily News*, September 20, 1993.

29. Don Bostrom, "Schilling Seven-Hitter Gives Phils Just What They Needed," *Allentown (PA) Morning Call*, September 21, 1993.

30. Gordon and Burgoyne, *Beards, Bellies and Biceps*, 170; Cooney, *Worst to First*, 134–35.

31. Kruk, *"I Ain't an Athlete,"* 172–73. For the video, see "John Kruk on David Letterman's Show, 1992," www.bigfool.com/kruk/92dl.htm.

32. Kruk, *"I Ain't an Athlete,"* 174–75. For the video, see "Kruk on Letterman's Show."

33. Gordon and Burgoyne, *Beards, Bellies and Biceps*, 170; Cooney, *Worst to First*, 137–38.

34. Paul Hagen, "Duncan's 'Biggest Hit' Is a Grand One," *Philadelphia Daily News*, September 29, 1993; Timothy Dwyer, "Phillies Make It from Worst to First," *Philadelphia Inquirer*, September 29, 1993; Frank Fitzpatrick, "Duncan Slam Sparks Victory," *Philadelphia Inquirer*, September 29, 1993.

35. Gordon and Burgoyne, *Beards, Bellies and Biceps*, 171–72.

36. Paul Hagen, "Send in the Crown," *Philadelphia Daily News*, September 29, 1993.

37. Chamberlain quoted in Westcott, *Phillies '93*, 73.

38. Kruk quoted in *Beards, Bellies and Biceps*, 171–72.

39. Thompson quoted in Westcott, *Phillies '93*, 73.

40. Giles quoted in Paul Hagen, "Dressed for Success: Giles Wore Old Clothes to Party for Champs," *Philadelphia Daily News*, September 29, 1993.

41. Gordon and Burgoyne, *Beards, Bellies and Biceps*, 172.

42. Kalas quoted in Andersen interview.

43. Morandini quoted in Wolfe, *Remembering Harry Kalas*, 93.

44. Westcott and Bilovsky, *The Phillies' Encyclopedia*. 106.

45. Giles with Myers, *Pouring Six Beers*, 181–82. During the 1993 season, the Phillies attracted more than fifty thousand fans sixteen times and enjoyed eight sellout crowds at Veterans Stadium, which seated seventy thousand. Day-of-game walk-up sales averaged fifteen thousand.

13. Hide the Women and Children!

1. The 1993 Atlanta Braves were the first National League team to win three straight division titles since the 1976–78 Phillies. The year 1993 was also the last that the Braves competed in the National League West. With the addition of two new teams—the Florida Marlins and the Colorado Rockies—the NL expanded to three divisions. In the realignment, the Braves shifted to the National League's Eastern Division for 1994.

2. "Greg Maddux's Major League Pitching Statistics," in *ESPN Baseball Encyclopedia*, edited by Palmer and Gillette, 1037.

3. "Tom Glavine's Pitching Statistics," in *ESPN Baseball Encyclopedia*, edited by Palmer and Gillette, 918. In 1991 Glavine posted a win-loss record of 20-11 with 192 strikeouts and a 2.55 ERA and led the National League in wins and complete games (9). Seven years later, in 1998, he went 20-6 with 157 strikeouts and a 2.47 ERA.

4. Palmer and Gillette, *ESPN Baseball Encyclopedia*, 761, 1062, 1197, 1590.

5. Palmer and Gillette, *ESPN Baseball Encyclopedia*, 63, 235, 348, 443.

6. Westcott, *Phillies '93*, 76–77. Twenty-two of the Atlanta Braves had postseason experience compared to just seven Phillies: Larry Andersen, Mariano Duncan, Lenny Dykstra, Danny Jackson, Roger Mason, David West, and Mitch Williams. While the Braves led the National League with 169 home runs, the Phillies were not far behind, with 156.

7. Westcott and Bilovsky, *The Phillies Encyclopedia*, 507.

8. For William Penn's actual "Prayer for Philadelphia" (1684), see Richard S. Dunn and Mary Maples Dunn, *The Papers of William Penn*, 5 vols. (Philadelphia: University of Pennsylvania Press, 1982), 2:590–91. Marjorie "Midge" Rendell, wife of then Philadelphia mayor Ed Rendell, made the suggestion to place the cap atop Billy Penn's head. Team president Bill Giles thought it was great idea and asked Dave Buck, the Phillies' marketing executive, to find someone to do it. Buck hired Dave Moscinski, a sheet-metal worker

who made costumes for the Mummers. Moscinski scaled the statue, took measurements, and then went to work producing the hat from cold-rolled steel, chicken wire, foam, and bright-red cloth. See Gordon and Burgoyne, *Beards, Bellies and Biceps*, 189–90.

9. Bamberger, "Schilling Filled the Most Important Seat." During the regular season, Schilling would sign a sheet before each of his starts, leaving his father's name on a list for a courtesy pass. But during the 1993 playoffs, that courtesy was not extended to the players. Each player was allotted twelve tickets for home games, and the tickets must be purchased. Accordingly, Schilling purchased a ticket for his father.

10. Batiste quoted in Frank Fitzpatrick, "Phillies Seize the Series Opener; Batiste's Clutch Hit in 10th Polishes Off Schilling Gem, 4–3," *Philadelphia Inquirer*, October 7, 1993.

11. Timothy Dwyer, "Game 1: A Slugfest That Wasn't, Spiced by Some Sloppiness," *Philadelphia Inquirer*, October 7, 1993.

12. Thompson quoted in Jayson Stark, "Batiste's Night: Comeback of the Year, and in One Game," *Philadelphia Inquirer*, October 9, 1993.

13. Fregosi quoted in Timothy Dwyer, "McGriff's Homer Was a Death Knell at the Beginning," *Philadelphia Inquirer*, October 8, 1993.

14. Williams and Kruk quoted in Gordon and Burgoyne, *Beards, Bellies and Biceps*, 174–77.

15. Schilling interview.

16. Cataldi quoted in Gordon and Burgoyne, *Beards, Bellies and Biceps*, 175.

17. Jayson Stark, "Greene Must Move on beyond the Nightmare," *Philadelphia Inquirer*, October 8, 1993.

18. Daulton quoted in Westcott, *Phillies '93*, 82.

19. Babe quoted in Michael Vitez, "Braves Fans Offer Lessons in Manners," *Philadelphia Inquirer*, October 10, 1993.

20. "HIDE THE WOMEN AND CHILDREN ATLANTA: AMERICA'S OTHER TEAM IS COMING TO TOWN!," *Atlanta Journal-Constitution*, October 9, 1992.

21. Incaviglia quoted in Westcott, *Tales from the Phillies' Dugout*, 161–62.

22. Fregosi and Mulholland quoted in Frank Fitzpatrick, "Phils Trail in Series after Braves Win, 9–4," *Philadelphia Inquirer*, October 10, 1993.

23. Fans quoted in Vitez, "Braves Fans Offer Lessons in Manners."

24. Glavine quoted in Michael Bamberger, "Glavine Solves a Team That Has Given Him Fits," *Philadelphia Inquirer*, October 10, 1993.

25. Michael Bamberger, "Phillies Are Blown Out, Trail 2–1," *Philadelphia Inquirer*, October 10, 1993.

26. Kruk quoted in Fitzpatrick, "Phils Trail in Series."

27. Jackson interview.

28. Jackson interview.

29. Jayson Stark, "Jackson's Work Brings a Sigh of Relief," *Philadelphia Inquirer*, October 11, 1993; Ted Silary, "For Mitch, Game Hard to Stomach," *Philadelphia Daily News*, October 11, 1993.

30. Frank Fitzpatrick, "Phils Hang Tough to Tie Series," *Philadelphia Inquirer*, October 11, 1993.

31. Jackson quoted in Westcott and Bilovsky, *The Phillies Encyclopedia*, 509.

32. Timothy Dwyer, "Pitching, Defense and Dykstra's Sense of Drama Stun Braves," *Philadelphia Inquirer*, October 12, 1993.

33. Rich Hofmann, "Play-Makers Wes, Inky Come Up Strong on Defense," *Philadelphia Daily News*, October 12, 1993.

34. Schilling quoted in Jayson Stark, "Schilling Close, yet So Far from Completing Shutout," *Philadelphia Inquirer*, October 12, 1993.

35. Dwyer, "Pitching, Defense and Dykstra's Sense of Drama."

36. Dykstra quoted in Jayson Stark, "In Dramatic Moments, Dykstra's Most Dandy," *Philadelphia Inquirer*, October 12, 1993.

37. Stark, "Schilling Close, yet So Far."

38. Frank Fitzpatrick, "Phillies Grab 1st Title in a Decade," *Philadelphia Inquirer*, October 14, 1993; Paul Hagen, "Phillies Show the World," *Philadelphia Daily News*, October 14, 1993.

39. Ted Silary, "Mitch's Finish as Easy as 1-2-3," *Philadelphia Daily News*, October 14, 1993.

40. McCarver quoted in Gordon and Burgoyne, *Beards, Bellies and Biceps*, 205.

41. Ron Goldwyn, "Bring on the Jays!," *Philadelphia Daily News*, October 14, 1993; Son Russell, Leon Taylor, and Ziva Branstetter, "Celebrations Wild, but Safe," *Philadelphia Daily News*, October 14, 1993.

42. Daulton quoted in Jayson Stark, "A Win Sweet for All, Sweetest for Daulton," *Philadelphia Inquirer*, October 14, 1993.

43. Williams quoted in Les Bowen, "MVP Winner Schilling, of Course," *Philadelphia Daily News*, October 14, 1993.

44. Schilling quoted in Jack Carney, "Schilling Wins MVP Award after Two Sparkling Games," *Phillies Report*, November 11, 1993, 4.

45. Kruk quoted in Westcott, *Tales from Phillies Dugout*, 172.

46. Dykstra quoted in Westcott, *Phillies '93*, 96.

14. The Series

1. Westcott and Bilovsky, *The Phillies Encyclopedia*, 511; Gordon and Burgoyne, *Beards, Bellies and Biceps*, 216. There was an interesting historical note to the Philadelphia-Toronto matchup. In 1944 Bob Carpenter, the new Phillies president, held a contest to find a new name for his team. When the winning entry turned out to be "Blue Jays," Carpenter added the bird to the team's uniforms. But the fans never embraced the name, probably because the team never completely dropped their former identification as the "Phillies." As a result, the name "Blue Jays" lingered on until it was finally abandoned in 1949.

2. Jayson Stark, "Phils vs. Blue Jays: The Matchups," *Philadelphia Inquirer World Series Guide*, October 15, 1993.

3. Rosie DiManno, "'I'm Not a Slob,' Kruk Protests," *Toronto Star*, October 16, 1993.

4. Gordon and Burgoyne, *Beards, Bellies and Biceps*, 213, 223.

5. Gordon and Burgoyne, *Beards, Bellies and Biceps*, 213.

6. Frank Fitzpatrick, "Jays Down Phils in Opener, 8–5," *Philadelphia Inquirer*, October 17, 1993.

7. Fregosi quoted in Michael Bamberger, "Fregosi Didn't Say Much after Game," *Philadelphia Inquirer*, October 17, 1993.

8. Bill Conlin, "Stewart on Long List of Mistakes Made by the Phils," *Philadelphia Daily News*, World Series Preview, October 15, 1993.

9. Jayson Stark, "Forgotten Ace Emerges to Put Mark on Game 2," *Philadelphia Inquirer*, October 18, 1993.

10. Molitor quoted on *Late Night with David Letterman*, season 1, episode 42, October 26, 1993, www.tv.com/shows/late-show-with-david-letterman/show.

11. Paul Hagen, "Surprise-enreich Another Mitchadventure," *Philadelphia Daily News*, October 18, 1993.

12. Gaston and Fregosi quoted in Joe Juliano, "Alomar Admits That He Made a Mistake Stealing Second Base Uncontested in the Eighth," *Philadelphia Inquirer*, October 18, 1993.

13. Frank Fitzpatrick, "Dykstra Shines as Phils Win," *Philadelphia Inquirer*, October 18, 1993.

14. Williams quoted in Mark Newman, "The Wild Series," *The Sporting News*, October 25, 1993, 13.

15. Williams with Berger, *Straight Talk from Wild Thing*, 93.

16. Jackson quoted in Les Bowen, "Jackson Says Eight-Day Layoff Did Him In," *Philadelphia Daily News*, October 20, 1993. In a 2013 interview, however, Jackson did not discount the adverse effect of the rain delay. "I'm out there ready to go," he recalled. "I'd already gone through my pre-game regimen, and then I'm told they're going to delay it for another hour. As intense as I was, I started yelling at the guy, 'Shit, you should've made this decision two hours ago.'"

17. Hentgen quoted in Frank Fitzpatrick, "Phils Never Really Get Started," *Philadelphia Inquirer*, October 20, 1993.

18. Michael Sokolove, "Phillies Lose Game 3," *Philadelphia Inquirer*, October 20, 1993.

19. Daulton quoted in Fitzpatrick, "Phils Never Really Get Started."

20. Rendell and Stottlemyre quoted in Gordon and Burgoyne, *Beards, Bellies and Biceps*, 226–27.

21. Timothy Dwyer, "Two Teams Played a Shameless Game on an Ugly Night," *Philadelphia Inquirer*, October 21, 1993; Frank Fitzpatrick, "Jays Make It a Wild Slugfest, Take a 3–1 Lead on Phils," *Philadelphia Inquirer*, October 21, 1993.

22. Williams quoted in Timothy Dwyer, "Williams Doesn't Try to Deflect Blame," *Philadelphia Inquirer*, October 21, 1993.

23. Dykstra quoted in Paul Hagen, "Nightmare on Broad Street: Blue Jays Win on Late Touchdown," *Philadelphia Daily News*, October 21, 1993.

24. Westcott and Bilovsky, *The Phillies Encyclopedia*, 514–15.

25. John Kruk interview.

26. Schilling quoted in Jayson Stark, "Schilling Comes on Strong. He Knew What He Had to Do. And He Did It," *Philadelphia Inquirer*, October 22, 1993.

27. Frank Fitzpatrick, "Phillies Win a Trip to Toronto; Schilling Rescues the Season," *Philadelphia Inquirer*, October 22, 1993.

28. Dykstra quoted in Paul Hagen, "Save: Schilling Back at You, Toronto," *Philadelphia Daily News*, October 22, 1993.

29. Hagen, "Save: Schilling Back at You, Toronto."

30. Schilling quoted in Stark, "Schilling Comes on Strong."

31. Darren Daulton quoted in Fitzpatrick, "Phillies Win a Trip to Toronto."

32. Williams quoted in Tim Kurkjian, "A Walk on the Wild Side," *Sports Illustrated*, November 1, 1993, 22–23.

33. John Kruk quoted in Frank Dolson, "Phils Have Moves and Decisions to Make," *Philadelphia Inquirer*, October 25, 1993.

34. Hagen, "For Phillies, the End Hits Hard."

35. Dykstra interview.

36. Giles interview; Giles quoted in Jennifer Frey, "If Only Dykstra Could Pitch in Relief," *New York Times*, October 24, 1993.

37. Hagen, "For Phillies, the End Hits Hard."

38. Mason interview.

39. Frank Fitzpatrick, "Carter Homers to Win the Series," *Philadelphia Inquirer*, October 24, 1993.

40. Carter and Williams quoted in Narducci, "Bittersweet Memories."

41. Steve Rushin, "Home Sweet Home," *Sports Illustrated*, November 1, 1993, 20. Carter's Series-clinching blast was just the second time a walk-off homer decided the outcome of a World Series. The first time came in 1960 when Bill Mazeroski's homer gave the Pittsburgh Pirates the clincher over the New York Yankees.

42. Williams with Berger, *Straight Talk from Wild Thing*, x.

43. Dykstra quoted in Thomas Zambito, "Ex-Met Lenny Dykstra Settles Bill with Accountants, Then Runs Mouth," *New York Daily News*, November 28, 2008.

44. Dykstra quoted in Jayson Stark, "Dykstra Delivered Magic, but Magic Wasn't Enough," *Philadelphia Inquirer*, October 24, 1993.

45. Giles interview.

46. Williams quoted in Bamberger, "Williams Eyes Truth without Blinking."

47. Kruk and Mason quoted in Hagen, "For Phillies, the End Hits Hard."

48. Dykstra quoted on *Late Night with Letterman*, October 26, 1993.

49. Fregosi quoted in Bill Conlin, "A Crying Shame for Vanquished," *Philadelphia Daily News*, October 25, 1993.

15. Inspiring Moneyball

1. Beane quoted in Jeffrey S. Moorad et al., "Moneyball's Impact on Business and Sports," *Jeffrey S. Moorad Sports Law Journal* 19, no. 2 (2012): 425.

2. David J. Grabiner, "The Sabermetric Manifesto," SeanLahman.com (1994). The term is derived from the acronym SABR, which stands for the Society for American Baseball Research. It was coined by Bill James, who is one of its pioneers and is often considered its most prominent advocate and public face.

3. "Bill James, beyond Baseball," *Think Tank with Ben Wattenberg*, PBS, June 28, 2005.

4. Benjamin Baumer and Andrew Zimbalist, *The Sabermetric Revolution: Assessing the Growth of Analytics in Baseball Paperback* (Philadelphia: University of Pennsylvania Press, 2015); Gabriel B. Costa, *Understanding Sabermetrics: An Introduction to the Science of Baseball Statistics* (Jefferson NC: McFarland, 2007).

5. Beane quoted in Moorad et al., "Moneyball's Impact on Business and Sports," 445–46.

6. Michael Knisley, "By Walking, the Phillies Are Off and Running," *The Sporting News*, October 25, 1993, 14.

7. Dykstra and Vukovich quoted in Cooney, *Worst to First*, 128.

8. Cooney, *Worst to First*, 16.

9. Cooney, *Worst to First*, 190. Barry Bonds, who won the 1993 National League's MVP Award, was second to Dykstra in runs scored. Bonds scored a run every 11.2 innings.

10. Lewis, *Moneyball*. Several themes Lewis explored in the book include insiders versus outsiders (established traditionalists versus upstart proponents of sabermetrics), the democratization of information causing a flattening of hierarchies, and "the ruthless drive for efficiency that capitalism demands." The book also touches on Oakland's underlying economic need to stay ahead of the curve: as other teams begin mirroring Beane's strategies to evaluate offensive talent, diminishing the Athletics' advantage, Oakland begins looking for other undervalued baseball skills, such as defensive capabilities.

11. Beane quoted in Moorad et al., "Moneyball's Impact on Business and Sports," 447.

12. Beane quoted in Moorad et al., "Moneyball's Impact on Business and Sports," 448.

16. Breaking the Code

1. Dykstra and Schilling quoted in Frank Fitzpatrick, "Some Phillies Believe Williams Should Go," *Philadelphia Inquirer*, December 2, 1993. Williams earned the wrath of some deranged Boo Birds who sent death threats after the closer's blown save in Game Four. Then after Wild Thing surrendered the Series-clinching homer to Joe Carter in Game Six, a mob of some thirty teenagers descended on his Moorestown, New Jersey, home and pelted it with eggs while shouting obscenities. See Laurent Sacharoff, "Mitch Williams' Home Takes a Hit," *Philadelphia Inquirer*, October 26, 1993.

2. Paul Hagen, "Ex-Teammates Say Its Better Mitch Is Gone," *Philadelphia Daily News*, December 3, 1993. When asked why he traded the closer, Thomas, in a 2011 interview,

denied any pressure from Schilling or Dykstra. Instead, he insisted that "it would have been very difficult for Mitch to stay in Philly" because "there would have been a lot of [fan] pressure on him if he had come back here." See Thomas interview. Manager Jim Fregosi agreed, with Thomas, saying that "with short relievers like Mitch, it's sometimes best to move on after a couple years, and he had reached that point with the Phillies and the fans." Fregosi interview.

3. Williams and Schilling quoted in "'Wild Thing'; In a Wild Feud," *Chicago Tribune*, December 1993.

4. Dykstra quoted in Zambito, "Ex-Met Lenny Dykstra Settles Bill with Accountants, Then Runs Mouth."

5. Mitch Williams quoted in Rich Scarcella, "Williams Has Hard Words for Ex-Teammate Dykstra," *Reading (PA) Eagle*, January 16, 2009. A year later Williams would clarify his remarks in his book (with Berger), *Straight Talk from Wild Thing*. "Lenny was bar-none the smartest baseball player I ever played with—baseball smart," he explained. "But he's also the most devoid of common sense of anybody I've met. When he played baseball he was hyper-focused, but not so focused in any other aspect of life." Williams with Berger, *Straight Talk from Wild Thing*, 96.

6. Dykstra quoted in interview with John Clark, "Why Lenny Dykstra Hates Mitch Williams," NBC-10 TV Philadelphia, March 8, 2011, www.nbcphiladelphia.com.

7. Williams with Berger, *Straight Talk from Wild Thing*, 92–93.

8. Ron Dicker, "Feud between Former Phillies Lenny Dykstra and Mitch Williams Gets Ugly at Comedy Roast," *Huffington Post*, May, 7, 2015. Video of the comedy roast can be found at www.msn.com/en-us/video/sports/williams-vs-dykstra-roast/vp-BBjfL8V.

9. Ross Newhan, "Dykstra, Phillies Agree on Contract," *Los Angeles Times*, December 24, 1993. Dykstra, who finished second to Barry Bonds of the San Francisco Giants in NL MVP balloting in 1993, was guaranteed $24.9 million in the four-year contract extension and $30.4 million if he qualified for a fifth-year option. He would receive a $2 million signing bonus and salaries of $5.7 million in 1995 and '96 and $5.5 million in 1997 and '98. A $6 million salary in 1999 automatically vested if he had five hundred plate appearances in 1998. Otherwise, he would receive a $500,000 buyout. The $6.225 million average annual value of the guarantee put Dykstra among the five highest-paid players in MLB and dwarfed the $4.4 million average that Rickey Henderson, generally considered the greatest lead-off hitter ever, received in his return to the Oakland Athletics.

10. "Dykstra Out of '97 Picture," *Los Angeles Times*, February 16, 1997; "Dykstra: 'They Have No Confidence in Me,'" *Los Angeles Times*, March 10, 1998; "Dykstra Halts Comeback," *Los Angeles Times*, March 18, 1998; Frankie, *Nailed!*, 46–49, 168–69.

11. Lenny Dykstra quoted in Ian Thompsen, "Oo-La-La, Lenny: Fun-Loving, Free-Spending Phillie Lenny Dykstra Toured Europe as Baseball's Unlikely Ambassador," *Sports Illustrated*, December 6, 1993, 32.

12. Chris Jones, "The Game," *Esquire*, March 1, 2003, 51.

13. Paul Hagen, "Dykstra's Downfall: Bad Decisions, Bad Timing, Bad Behavior," *Philadelphia Daily News*, June 17, 2011; Frankie, *Nailed!*, 56–58, 139. For Dykstra's own account of his life after baseball, see *House of Nails*, 237–52, 263–300.

14. Hagen, "Dykstra's Downfall"; Frankie, *Nailed!*, 90, 126–31, 244.

15. "Dykstra Files for Chapter 11," ESPN.com, July 8, 2009.

16. Hagen, "Dykstra's Downfall."

17. Mitchell, *Report to the Commissioner of Baseball*, 66–67, 72, 149–50.

18. "Lenny Dykstra's Wife Files for Divorce," *Ventura County (CA) Star*, April 24, 2009.

19. "Lenny Dykstra, Formerly of the Mets, Is 'Nailed' as Racist in Mag," *New York Daily News*, March 17, 2009.

20. Stephanie Hoops, "Dykstra Shut Out of Lake Sherwood," *Ventura County (CA) Star*, September 17, 2009.

21. "Ex Baseball Player Lenny Dykstra 'Nails' Rips Off Escorts," www.blogspot.com, December 21, 2010; "EXCLUSIVE INTERVIEW: Scorned Hooker Says Baseball Legend Lenny Dykstra 'Thinks He Can Treat People Like Crap,'" www.radaronline.com, December 31, 2010. Adult film star and escort Monica Foster claimed he had hired her on December 13, 2010, and then wrote her a check that bounced. Foster later posted a copy of the bounced check on her blog.

22. "Lenny Dykstra Accused of Sexual Assault by Housekeeper; No Charges Filed," *Los Angeles Times*, January 11, 2011.

23. Stella Chan, "Baseball's Lenny Dykstra Charged with Indecent Exposure," CNN .com, August 25, 2011.

24. Jane Wells, "Lenny Dykstra: I Live in the Street," CNBC.

25. David Epstein, "How Lenny Dykstra Got Nailed," *Sports Illustrated*, March 12, 2012, 50–55.

26. "Former MLB Star Lenny Dykstra Admits to Financial Fraud," *CBS News*, July 13, 2012.

27. Greg Risling, "Lenny Dykstra Sentenced to Three Years in Prison in Grand Theft Auto Case," Toronto, Associated Press, March 5, 2012.

28. R. Sandomir, "Lenny Dykstra: Out of Prison, and Still Headstrong," *New York Times*, August 2, 2014.

29. Lane, *Zeroes*, chap. 9; Frankie, *Nailed!* Lane was the editor of *Trader Monthly*, a glossy magazine dedicated to chronicling the lives of spoiled Wall Street traders. His book chronicles his own downfall and his ugly dispute with Dykstra. Frankie, a financial journalist, worked side by side with Dykstra as editor of the *Players Club*.

30. Associated Press, "Dykstra Said He Benefitted by Getting Dirt on Umps," *Philadelphia Inquirer*, October 28, 2015; Dykstra, *House of Nails*, 125.

31. Dykstra, *House of Nails*, 298–99, 310–11.

32. Westcott and Bilovsky, *The Phillies' Encyclopedia*, 250. During his nine-year tenure with the Phillies, Schilling won 101 games, sixth most in team history. He is also the only pitcher in team history to record fifteen or more strikeouts in a single game three times and among the leaders in games started (sixth at 226), innings pitched (seventh at 1,659), and strikeouts (fourth at 1,554).

33. Westcott and Bilovsky, *The Phillies' Encyclopedia*, 250.

34. See "Phillies Charities, Inc.: ALS," *Phillies Yearbook* (Philadelphia: Phillies, 1999), 70; Mike Falcon, "Curt Schilling Pitches for ALS," *USA Today*, July 8, 2002; and "Curt's Pitch for ALS," www.curtspitchforals.org/default.asp.

35. Shonda Schilling, *The Best Kind of Different: Our Family's Journey with Asperger's Syndrome* (New York: William Morrow, 2010).

36. Stan Grossfeld, "Schilling Has New Lease on Life," *Boston Globe*, August 11, 2013; Matt Gelb, "Curt Schilling Diagnosed with Cancer," *Philadelphia Inquirer*, February 5, 2014; Steve Silva, "Curt Schilling Reveals He Was Diagnosed with Mouth Cancer," *Boston Globe*, August 20, 2014.

37. Kevin Kaduk, "Schilling Tapped Out Financially after Failure of Video Game Company," www.sports.yahoo.com, June 23, 2012.

38. Chad Finn, "Curt Schilling Returning to ESPN in Studio Role," *Boston Globe*, September 9, 2014.

39. "Analyst Curt Schilling Dismissed by ESPN for 'Unacceptable Conduct,'" ESPN. com, April 20, 2016. Schilling, who had worked as a studio analyst for ESPN since 2010, was suspended in August 2015 after comparing extremist Muslims to Nazis in a social media posting.

40. Williams with Berger, *Straight Talk from Wild Thing*, 176.

41. Greg Couch, "A Wiser 'Wild Thing': Mitch Williams Returns to the Game as a Pitching Coach," *Baseball Digest* (July 2001): 72–74; Richard Rys, "A Wild Tale: Mitch Williams's Career Is in Tatters over an Allegedly Ugly Incident at a Youth Baseball Tournament. But What Really Happened?," *Philadelphia Magazine*, April 2015, 56. After one season with the Houston Astros, Williams closed out his career with the California Angels in 1995 and the Kansas City Royals in 1997.

42. Michael Brown, "Former Phillies Pitcher Sues MLB Network," *Philadelphia Inquirer*, September 25, 2014; Rys, "Wild Tale," 56.

43. Mitchell, *Report to the Commissioner of Baseball*, 66–67, 72, 149–50, 195. According to Kirk Radomski, who distributed PEDs to players, Dykstra was his first regular customer, and he continued to provide the former Met with steroids after Dykstra was traded to the Phillies in 1989. Radomski also told Mitchell investigators that he "sold [Todd] Pratt anabolic steroids twice" sometime in 2000 or 2001 when he was playing for the New York Mets. But Radomski also added that Pratt told him he had "acquired the steroid Deca-Durabolin from another source previously."

44. Dykstra, *House of Nails*, 100.

45. Jason Grimsley, "Sworn Affidavit by Jeff Novitsky," *Internal Revenue Service* (May 2006); quoted in Associated Press, "Grimsley Testimony Included Former Phils," *Philadelphia Inquirer*, December 21, 2007.

46. See Assael and Keating, "Who Knew? Part II." Bodybuilder Jeff Scott alleged that Hollins, who'd lost 15 pounds after it was discovered he had diabetes in the winter of 1993, was struggling to get back to his 205-pound playing weight. On visits to Scott's apartment, Hollins asked about steroids. While Hollins denies ever being in Scott's apartment, a second source besides Scott insists he was there often.

47. "Incaviglia's Major League Statistics," 326–27.

48. Paul Vigna, "What Ever Happened to the 1993 Phillies?," *Philadelphia Daily News*, October 9, 2008.

49. "Hollins's Major League Statistics," in ESPN *Baseball Encyclopedia*, edited by Palmer and Gillette, 313.

50. Vigna, "What Ever Happened to the 1993 Phillies?"

51. Bryant, *Juicing the Game*, 282; Fitzpatrick, "What Fueled the Wild Ride?"; Pessah, *The Game*, 75–76.

52. "Daulton's Major League Statistics," 163.

53. Darren Daulton interview, October 4, 2009. Daulton gave a similar response about steroid use to Mike Missanelli on 97.5 FM THE FAN, the ESPN Radio station in Philadelphia, on June 29, 2009. See "Ex-Phillie Darren Daulton Is the Self-Proclaimed Drug Lord of Sports," online interview at www.totalprosports.com.

54. Ann Gerhart, "Sports Wife: Lynne Austin-Daulton, Phillies' Catcher's Wife, Has Career as 'Hooters Girl,'" *Boca Raton (FL) News*, November 2, 1993; W. Speers, "The Darren Daultons Are on the Outs at Home," *Philadelphia Daily News*, February 2, 1994.

55. Lynne Austin interviewed by Roxanne Wilder, "Lynne Austin: The Original Hooters Girl," Web Sports Channel, January 31, 2011, www.youtube.com/watch?v=06azvOszvbo.

56. Hal Bodley, "Phils Deal Daulton to Marlins," *USA Today*, July 22, 1997; Associated Press, "Retiring Daulton: Time to Move On," *New York Post*, January 30, 1998.

57. Daulton quoted in Jim Salisbury, "Daulton's Inspired Comeback," *Philadelphia Inquirer*, February 9, 1997.

58. Associated Press, "Daulton Is Charged with DUI, Driving with Suspended License," *Philadelphia Inquirer*, January 5, 2001; Associated Press, "Former Catcher Darren Daulton Arrested on DUI Charges," *Miami Herald*, January 4, 2003.

59. Bob Cooney, "Daulton Jailed 2 Days in Probation Matter," *Philadelphia Daily News*, October 4, 2003; Jim Salisbury, "Daulton Endures Tough Times Away from Game," *Philadelphia Inquirer*, February 7, 2004.

60. Daulton quoted in Lidz, "Bean Us Up, Dutchie."

61. Darren Daulton, *If They Only Knew* (Melbourne FL: Blue Note Books, 2008). See also Todd Zolecki, "Former Phil Daulton Insists Life Is Ducky, He's Not Daffy," *Philadelphia Inquirer*, March 4, 2006.

62. Daulton quoted in Lidz, "Bean Us Up, Dutchie."

63. Joel Mathis, "Darren Daulton Now Pitching for Yuengling," *Philadelphia Magazine*, June 25, 2014, www.phillymag.com/news/2014/06/25/darren-daulton-now-pitching -yuengling/#tZ1sXsgDtcV3MrPb.99; Matthew Veasey, "Philography: Darren Daulton," December 20, 2014, www.thatballsouttahere.com/2014/12/20/philography-darren-daulton/.

64. Chris Branch, "Former All-Star Daulton Has Brain Cancer," *USA Today*, July 10, 2013.

65. See P. Y. Choi, A. C. Parrott, and D. Cowan, "High-Dose Anabolic Steroids in Strength Athletes: Effects upon Hostility and Aggression," *Human Psychopharmacology* 5 (1990): 349–56; P. J. Fudala et al., "An Evaluation of Anabolic-Androgenic Steroid Abusers over a Period of 1 Year: Seven Case Studies," *Annals of Clinical Psychiatry* 15, no. 2 (2003): 121–30; T. A. Pagonis et al., "Psychiatric Side Effects Induced by Supraphysiological Doses of Combinations of Anabolic Steroids Correlate to the Severity of Abuse," *European Psychiatry* 21, no. 8 (2006): 551–62; T. A. Pagonis et al., "Psychiatric and Hostility Factors Related to Use of Anabolic Steroids in Monozygotic Twins," *European Psychiatry* 21, no. 8 (2006): 563–69; and C. Wilson-Fearon and A. C. Parrott, "Multiple Drug Use and Dietary Restraint in a Mr. Universe Competitor: Psychobiological Effects," *Perceptual and Motor Skills* 88, no. 2 (1999): 579–80.

66. Mitchell, *Report to the Commissioner of Baseball*, 67; Zolecki, "Mitchell Report"; Ford, "Mitchell's Report, in the End, Has No Juice."

67. Schilling interview with Mike Missanelli on ESPN Radio 97.5 FM THE FAN, July 7, 2011; "Curt Schilling: No Winning Team Was Steroid-Free, Not Even My Own," July 7, 2011, www .deadspin.com/5819068/curt-schilling-no-winning-team-was-steroid-free-not-even-my-own.

68. Kruk quoted in Salisbury, "Kruk: Never Saw Steroids on '93 Phils."

69. See MLB, "Joint Drug Prevention and Treatment Program," adopted 2002 Basic Agreement: Attachment 18, www.mlb.com/mlb/downloads/joint_drug_prevention _program. Prior to 2002 MLB had no drug-testing policy. Beginning in the spring of 2002, MLB conducted one unannounced mandatory test each year for every player and random tests for selective players during the season and the off-season. The tests examined players for steroids, steroid precursors, and designer steroids. If a player was caught, a suspension without pay occurred. The first positive tests resulted in a suspension for ten days, the second for thirty days, the third for sixty days, and the fourth positive test resulted in a one-year suspension.

Beginning in the spring of 2006, MLB adopted a new program that "prohibited all players from using, possessing, selling, facilitating the sale of, distributing, or facilitating the distribution of any Drug of Abuse and/or Steroid." Players requiring prescription medication can still use it with a "Therapeutic Use Exemption" granted by MLB. Initially, testing was administered only during the season and on the basis of "reasonable cause," that is, when a Health Policy Advisory Committee uncovered evidence that a player has used, possessed, or sold banned substances in the previous twelve months. On January 10, 2013, however, MLB and the players' union reached a new agreement that dramatically increased testing and punishments. Random in-season HGH testing and a new test to reveal the use of testosterone were added. A test is considered positive if any steroid is present in the urine. The new agreement also stipulates that unannounced tests will be taken twice a year for all players, and random testing will still occur for selected players. Testing is also done for seven different kinds of abusive drugs, forty-seven different kinds of steroids, and thirty different kinds of stimulants. One of the forty-seven different kinds of steroids is HGH, a once popular substance among Major Leaguers that was never tested for before the Mitchell Report.

Stiffer penalties were also instituted: a 50-game suspension for the first positive test, 100 games for the second, and a lifetime ban for the third. Despite the stiffer penalties, players continued to violate the policy. As a result, MLB and the Players Union, in March 2014, enacted even tougher penalties. First-time suspensions were increased from 50 to 80 games, second offenses from 100 games to a full 162-game season, and suspended players are ineligible for postseason play. See Associated Press, "MLB Toughens Drug Penalties," *Philadelphia Inquirer*, March 29, 2014.

70. Kruk quoted in Terri Thompson et al., *American Icon: The Fall of Roger Clemens and the Rise of Steroids in America's Pastime* (New York: Alfred A. Knopf, 2009), 188.

71. Kruk quoted in Brian Smith, "Kruk Minces No Words in Criticizing 'Cheaters,'" *Reading (PA) Eagle*: February 25, 2009.

72. Bernstein, *The Code*, 228–29.

73. Bernstein, *The Code*, 163–72.

74. Bernstein, *The Code*, 219–34.

75. The Mitchell Report declared that PED use was cheating in its most absolute form because it "poses practical threats to the integrity of the game" by "intentionally giving a player or players an advantage over other players," "shaking the faith of the fans in the integrity and fairness of the contest," "devaluing the competition," and "victimizing the majority of players who do not use those substances." See Mitchell, *Report to the Commissioner of Baseball*, 11–14.

Afterword

1. Daulton quoted in Brookover, "Flaws and All."

2. Kruk, *"I Ain't an Athlete,"* 157–58.

SELECTED BIBLIOGRAPHY

Baumer, Benjamin, and Andrew Zimbalist. *The Sabermetric Revolution: Assessing the Growth of Analytics in Baseball*. Philadelphia: University of Pennsylvania Press, 2015.

Bernstein, Ross. *The Code: Baseball's Unwritten Rules and Its Ignore-at-Your-Own-Risk Code of Conduct*. Chicago: Triumph Books, 2008.

Bryant, Howard. *Juicing the Game: Drugs, Power, and the Fight for the Soul of Major League Baseball*. New York: Viking, 2005.

Conlin, Bill. *Batting Cleanup, Bill Conlin*. Philadelphia: Temple University Press, 1997.

Cooney, Nancy, et al. *Worst to First: The Story of the 1993 Phillies*. Philadelphia: Philadelphia Inquirer, 1993.

Costa, Gabriel B. *Understanding Sabermetrics: An Introduction to the Science of Baseball Statistics*. Jefferson NC: McFarland, 2007.

Dickson, Paul. *The Unwritten Rules of Baseball*. New York: HarperCollins, 2009.

Dykstra, Lenny. *House of Nails: A Memoir of Life on the Edge*. New York: William Morrow, 2016.

Epstein, David. "How Lenny Dykstra Got Nailed." *Sports Illustrated*, March 12, 2012, 50–55.

Fish, Mike. "Dykstra's Business: A Bed of 'Nails.'" ESPN.com, April 22, 2009.

Frankie, Christopher. *Nailed! The Improbable Rise and Spectacular Fall of Lenny Dykstra*. Philadelphia: Running Press, 2013.

Giles, Bill, with Doug Myers. *Pouring Six Beers at a Time, and Other Stories from a Lifetime in Baseball*. Chicago: Triumph, 2007.

Gordon, Robert, and Tom Burgoyne. *More than Beards, Bellies and Biceps: The Story of the 1993 Phillies*. Champaign IL: Sports Publishing, 2002.

Helyar, John. *Lords of the Realm: The Real History of Baseball*. New York: Villard, 1994.

Kashatus, William C. *Almost a Dynasty: The Rise and Fall of the 1980 Phillies*. Philadelphia: University of Pennsylvania Press, 2008.

———. *September Swoon: Richie Allen, the '64 Phillies, and Racial Integration*. University Park: Pennsylvania State University Press, 2004.

Kindred, Dave. "Measuring Up in the Face of Heartbreak: In Phillies' Clubhouse, One Man Smiled, Another Stood Up to the Pain." *The Sporting News*, November 1, 1993, 7.

Kruk, John, with Paul Hagen. *"I Ain't an Athlete, Lady . . .": My Well-Rounded Life and Times*. New York: Simon & Schuster, 1994.

Lane, Randall. *The Zeroes: My Misadventures in the Decade Wall Street Went Insane*. New York: Portfolio, 2010.

Lewis, Michael. *Moneyball*. New York: W. W. Norton, 2003.

Lidz, Franz. "Beam Us Up, Dutchie: Darren Daulton Explains His Surreal Life." Sports Illustrated.com, February 16, 2006.

Lord, John B. *Bill Giles and Baseball*. Philadelphia: Temple University Press, 2014.

Mitchell, George J. *Report to the Commissioner of Baseball of an Independent Investigation into the Illegal Use of Steroids and Other Performance Enhancing Substances by Players in Major League Baseball*. New York: Office of the Commissioner of Baseball, 2007.

Montville, Leigh. "Leading Man." *Sports Illustrated*, October 11, 1993, 46–48.

Moorhad, Jeffrey S., Billy Beane, Omar Minaya, and Phil Griffin. "Moneyball's Impact on Business and Sports." *Jeffrey S. Moorhad Sports Law Journal* 19, no. 2 (2012): 425–61.

Newman, Mark. "The Wild Series." *The Sporting News*, October 25, 1993, 12–14.

Palmer, Pete, and Gary Gillette, eds. ESPN *Baseball Encyclopedia*. New York: Sterling, 2005.

Pessah, Jon. *The Game: Inside the Secret World of Major League Baseball's Power Brokers*. New York: Little, Brown, 2015.

Queenan, Joe. *True Believers: The Tragic Inner Life of Sports Fans*. New York: Picador/ Holt, 2003.

Radomski, Kirk, with David Fisher. *Bases Loaded: The Inside Story of the Steroid Era in Baseball by the Central Figure in the Mitchell Report*. New York: Hudson Street Press, 2009.

Rys, Richard. "A Wild Tale: Mitch Williams's Career Is in Tatters over an Allegedly Ugly Incident at a Youth Baseball Tournament. But What Really Happened?" *Philadelphia Magazine*, April 2015, 54–59.

Shenk, Larry. *If These Walls Could Talk: Stories from the Philadelphia Phillies Dugout, Locker Room and Press Box*. Chicago: Triumph Books, 2014.

Smith, J. Edwin. "Crazy about Winning: All the Zaniness in the World Can't Obscure the Bottom Line on the Phillies—They Can Play." *The Sporting News*, May 24, 1993, 9–11.

Turbow, Jason. *The Baseball Codes: Beanballs, Sign Stealing and Bench-Clearing Brawls; The Unwritten Rules of America's Pastime*. New York: Anchor Books, 2010.

Vincent, Fay. *The Last Commissioner*. New York: Simon & Schuster, 2002.

Westcott, Rich. *Phillies '93: An Incredible Season*. Philadelphia: Temple University Press, 1994.

———. *Veterans Stadium: Field of Memories*. Philadelphia: Temple University Press, 2005.

Westcott, Rich, and Frank Bilovsky. *The Phillies Encyclopedia*. 3rd ed. Philadelphia: Temple University Press, 2004.

Williams, Mitch, with Darrell Berger. *Straight Talk from Wild Thing*. Chicago: Triumph Books, 2010.

INDEX

Page numbers in italics indicate illustrations.

Conlin, Bill, 25–26, 74, 83–85; on Mitch Williams, 191–92
Cooper, Jeff, 158
Cox, Bobby, 139; and 1993 NLCS, 203

Daulton, Carol, 4–5, 8–9
Daulton, Darren, xv, xviii–xix, xxviii, 10, 54–55; and 1991 car accident, 63–64, 73; and 1993 NLCS, 202, 206, 208, 217; and 1993 World Series, xiv, 221, 224, 226, 229–30, 230, 233, 236; appearance of, xvii, 92, 257; arrests of, 260; boyhood of, 4–9; and the Code, xix, 142–44, 153–54; health problems of, 260- 261; injuries of, 1–2, 15, 63, 92; leadership of, xviii–xix, 5, 59, 91, 133–34, 134, 163–64; and Macho Row, xviii–xix, 131–37, 259–60, 265–67; Major League statistics of, 91, 105, 239–42, 257, 270–71; marital problems of, 257- 258, 259; Minor League career of, 9–10; philanthropy of, 179; post-Phillies career of, 258- 261; and relationship with Bill Giles, 1–4, 114, 236; and relationship with Kruk, 54, 64–65, 101, 115; and relationship with pitchers, 146–49, 163–64, 224; and relationship with press, 85, 101, 136–37; salary of, 59, 93, 114–15; and suspected steroid use, xx, 91–92, 257, 261; on winning, 131; work ethic of, 5, 92–93
Daulton, Dave, Sr. , 4–5, 7, 9
Daulton, Lynne Austin, 59–60, 60, 64, 85, 133–34, 257–58
Davidson, Bob, 142–44
Duncan, Mariano, xvi, 96, 104, 144; and 1993 NLCS, 202, 209, 211; and 1993 World Series, 222, 226, 227, 232; and division-clinching grand slam, 196, 196; and Mother's Day home run, 138; and relationship with press, 136
Dykstra, Lenny, xvi, xix–xx, 30, 41, 54–55, 86, 126; and 1991 car accident, 63–64, 73; and 1993 NLCS, 202, 206, 213, 213–14, 215, 218; and 1993 World Series, xv; awards won by, xix, 222, 223, 227–28, 229, 231–32, 234–36; bankruptcy of, 249–50; blackmails umpires, 252; boyhood of, 33–36; and the Code, xx, 245–46; crude behavior of, xix, 39–40, 73–76, 100–101, 106, 160–61, 250–51; entrepreneurial career of, 249; on fans, 161; and gambling addition, 40, 74–76, 109–10, 160; incarceration of,

251–52; injuries of, 90, 109, 248; on *Late Night with David Letterman*, 236; as lead-off hitter, 125–26; and Macho Row, xix–xx, 131–37, 265–67; Major League statistics of, 39, 61, 163, 239–42, 272–73; Minor League career of, 36–38; parents, 33–35; and relationship with Kirk Radomski, 43–44; and relationship with press, 86, 132, 135–36; and relationship with Williams, 245–46, 247–48; requests trade, 47, 48; salary of, 33, 47, 48, 248; siblings of, 34; steroid use and, xx, 43–46, 76–78, 106–9, 107, 162–63, 250, 255–56; style of play of, xix; superstitions of, 169

Eisenreich, Jim, xvi, 96; and 1993 NLCS, 209; and 1993 World Series, 223, 226, 229; and Tourette's, 99–102, 179
Eskin, Howard, 48, 86–88, 162–63, 246–47

Fernandez, Tony, 219; and 1993 World Series, 225, 228, 232
Fitzpatrick, Frank, 82–83, 88; compares 1993 and 1964 Phillies, 189; on Incaviglia, 181; on Macho Row, 131–32, 136
Fregosi, Jim, xvi, 78, 89, 102; and 1993 NLCS, 203–4, 208, 213–14; and 1993 World Series, xiii–xiv, 222, 223–24, 225, 232, 236; on Daulton, 134; defends Williams, 192; on Dykstra, 125; Major League playing career of, 88–89; management style of, 188–89; managerial career of, 89–90; and relationship with press, 83, 88; on Schilling, 203; on Stocker, 170; superstitions of, 169

Gang of Six, 23–29
Gant, Ron, 200; and 1993 NLCS, 202, 207–8, 211
Gaston, Cito, and 1993 World Series, 223, 225
Giles, Bill, 20; and 1993 World Series, 236, 232; and community service, 28, 74, 232; at division-clinching celebration, 198; on Dykstra, 47–48; and free agency, 12–14; and Gang of Six, 23–29; marketing ability of, 19–21; as Phillies president, 17–18, 22–29; and press, 83; purchases Phillies, 22; and relationship with Carpenter family, 21–22; and relationship with Daulton, 1–4, 114, 236; and relationship with father, 17–18, 20; superstitions of, 169

Shenk, Larry: and relationship with Macho Row, 136–37
Smoltz, John, 199; and 1993 NLCS, 209–11
spring training: in 1990, 55–57; in 1993, 99–115
Stephenson, Dan, 14–15, 202
steroids, xx; Anabolic Steroid Control Act (1990), 43; effects of, 42–43; and history of use in sports, 41–43; and Major League Baseball, 77–78, 107–8, 250, 255–56. *See also* Mitchell Report
Stewart, Dave, 219, 220; and 1993 World Series, 222–23, 231
St. Louis Cardinals, 112–13, 137–38, 145–46, 168
Stocker, Kevin, xv, 96, 144, 170; and 1993 NLCS, 209, 212; and 1993 World Series, 222, 225, 231
Stottlemyre, Todd: and 1993 World Series, 226–27

Texas Rangers, 121–22
Thigpen, Bobby, xvi, 172; and 1993 NLCS, 205–6
Thomas, Lee, xvi, 56, 238, 242–43; acquisitions made by, 31–32, 47–48, 96–97, 242–43; and hired by Phillies, 15–16, 29; personality of, 55–57, 95–96
Thompson, Milt, xvi, 96, 105, 128; and 1993 NLCS, 204, 209, 211; and 1993 World Series, 222, 227, on clinching division, 198; philanthropy of, 179
Toronto Blue Jays, 105; and 1993 World Series, xiii–xiv, 219–36
Toronto Globe and Mail, 221
Toronto SkyDome, 221, 231
Toronto Star, 221
Toronto Sun, 221

Ueberroth, Peter, 12–13

Veterans Stadium, 53; and 1993 NLCS, 202, 217–18; and 1993 World Series, 225–26; atmosphere of, 19–20; attendance at, 117, 195, 225
Vincent, Fay, 43; and Dykstra's gambling, 74–76; on steroids, 108
Vukovich, John, 102–3, 134, 236, 240

West, David, xvi, 97, 102; and 1993 NLCS, 209, 215; and 1993 World Series, 222, 228, 232; pitching performances of, 127–28, 172, 209, 215, 222, 228, 232
William Penn statue, 200–201, *201*
Williams, Mitch, xvi, xxi–xxii, 7, *116*, 123; and 1993 NLCS, 203–5, 210–11, 213–14, 215–18, *216*; and 1993 World Series, xiii–xv, 223–25, *224*, 228–29, 230–31, 232–34, 235, 236; boyhood of, 119–20; and the Code, xxii; competitiveness of, xxii, 123–24; death threats receive by, 230–31; dismissed from MLB Network, 255; generosity of, 172; and Macho Row, 131–37, 265–67; Major League statistics of, 93, 118, 121–22, 280–81; Minor League career of, 120–21; nickname of, 119; philanthropy of, 179; and pitching mechanics, 119, *192*; post-Phillies career of, 254–55; and relationship with Dykstra, 247–48; and relationship with father, 119; and relationship with Schilling, 174, 203–5, 213, 217–18, 224–25, 247; and save opportunities, 117, 128–29, 159–60, 177, 190–92, 203–5, 210–11, 213–14, 215–18; superstitions of, 169; traded by Phillies, 245–46; on winning, 132
Wilson, Mookie, 33, 37, 38
WIP Sports Radio, 48, 86–88, 205, 246–47
Wohlers, Mark: and 1993 NLCS, 206, 211, 214
World Series: in 1986, 32–33; in 1993, xiii–xv, 219–36

9 781496 214089